WORKING WITH
INSURANCE
AND
MANAGED
CARE
PLANS

A Guide for Getting Paid

Disclaimer

This book is intended as a guide and cannot address the specific requirements of all insurance and managed care plans. It is a basic core text of principles which allow medical office personnel to build knowledge when working with their individual healthcare delivery system insurance payers. The text stresses the environment of change within the healthcare industry and offers tools to adapt to changes affecting payment and reimbursement.

The examples were created by the authors and do not represent any actual patient, physician, physician practice, or other healthcare vendor. Except when insurance or managed care plans are specifically named, recommendations apply to the general operating principles of all insurance and managed care plans.

The HCPCS codes, descriptions, and modifiers are from the January 1, 1995, printing. The ICD-9-CM codes and descriptions are current from the October 1, 1994 printing. These printings are needed for the correct answers to the coding exercises. Please note that while the answers to the coding exercises in the book may be correct according to coding principles, they may not be acceptable to certain payers. The coding recommendations of the payer must in all cases be followed. This book is not a substitute for current coding books.

Working with Insurance and Managed Care Plans: A Guide to Getting Paid is designed to provide accurate and authoritative information on the subject matter covered. All information contained in this guide is based on the experiences of the authors, and the recommendations are to be considered the opinion of the authors. It is sold with the understanding that neither the publisher nor authors are engaged in rendering legal, medical, accounting, or other professional service in specific situations. Although prepared for professionals, this publication should not be utilized as a substitute for professional service in specific situations. If legal or medical advice is required, the services of a professional should be sought. Neither the authors nor the publisher may be held liable for any misuse or misinterpretation of the guidelines in this text. All information provided is believed and intended to be reliable, but accuracy cannot be guaranteed by the author or the publisher.

WORKING WITH INSURANCE AND MANAGED CARE PLANS

A Guide for Getting Paid

JAN DAVISON
MAXINE LEWIS

Practice Management Information Corporation
Los Angeles, California 90010

Working with Insurance and Managed Care Plans:
A Guide for Getting Paid

ISBN: 1-57066-081-6

Practice Management Information Corporation (PMIC)
4727 Wilshire Blvd.
Los Angeles, CA 90010

http://www.medicalbookstore.com

Printed in the United States of America

Table of Contents

Preface *xi*

CHAPTER 1

Introduction to the Claims Process *1*

THE PARTIES IN THE HEALTHCARE BUSINESS **1**

TYPES OF PAYERS **2**
  Government Plans *2* / Private Plans *3* / Managed Care Plans *4*

METHODS OF PAYMENT *6*
  Fee for Service *6* / Capitation *6* / Variations on the Basic Methods *6*

THE RESPONSIBILITIES OF A MEDICAL PRACTICE **6**
  Keeping Up with the Changes *9*

EXERCISING KNOWLEDGE **10**

CHAPTER 2

The Physician Payment Process *13*

THE CRITICAL PATHWAY OF A CLAIM **13**
  Registration *14* / The Encounter *20* / Exit *23* / Posting and
  Billing *25* / Monitoring Claims Reported to the Plan *25*

REPORTING HOSPITAL CHARGES **28**

EXERCISING KNOWLEDGE **29**

CHAPTER 3

Common Operations and Terminology *39*

ENROLLMENT **39**

CLAIMS PROCESSING **41**

MEDICAL RESOURCE MONITORING **43**
  Monitoring Claims: Computerized Checks *46* / Monitoring Physician
  Costs *47* / Capitation *51* / Utilization Management *51*

EXERCISING KNOWLEDGE **54**

CHAPTER 4   **Diagnosis Coding with ICD-9-CM** *61*

THE HISTORY OF DIAGNOSTIC CODING **61**

THE LANGUAGE OF ICD-9-CM **62**

HOW ICD-9-CM IS USED **62**

PREVENTING DENIAL OF CLAIMS **64**

ICD-9-CM AND MEDICARE **65**

SOME CODING BASICS **65**
   Sequencing Diagnosis Codes: Primary and Secondary Diagnoses 65 /
   Combination Codes 67

THE STRUCTURE OF ICD-9-CM **67**
   The Organization of Diseases: Tabular List 67 / The Organization of
   Diseases: Alphabetic Index 68

CONVENTIONS USED IN ICD-9-CM **76**
   Tabular List Conventions 76 / Use Additional Code if Desired 77 /
   Symbols 77 / Alphabetic Index Conventions 78 / Conventions Used in
   Both the Tabular List and the Alphabetic Index 78 / Other Conventions 80

V CODES **81**

DIAGNOSTIC CODING OF DISORDERS OF THE CIRCULATORY SYSTEM **83**

DIAGNOSTIC CODING OF NEOPLASMS **85**
   Sequencing Malignant Neoplasms 87

DIAGNOSTIC CODING FOR PREGNANCY, CHILDBIRTH, AND THE PUERPERIUM **87**

DIAGNOSTIC CODING FOR NEWBORNS AND CONDITIONS ORIGINATING IN THE
PERINATAL PERIOD **89**

DIAGNOSTIC CODING FOR INJURIES **89**
   Fractures 89 / Open Wounds and Superficial and Internal Injuries 90 /
   Burns 90 / Late Effects 91

CODING FOR COMPLICATIONS **91**

E CODES: EXTERNAL CAUSES OF INJURY AND POISONING **92**
   Guidelines for Using E Codes 92

A WORD ABOUT ICD-10 **94**

EXERCISING KNOWLEDGE **94**

CHAPTER 5   **Procedure Coding and HCPCS** *101*

INTRODUCTION TO CPT **102**

USES OF CPT CODES **103**

THE STRUCTURE OF CPT-4 **103**

The Index 104 / Subcategories and Ranges 104 / Format 104 /
Wording of Descriptions 105 / Notes 105 / Guidelines 106 /
Code Changes from Previous Editions 106 / Unlisted Procedures 107 /
Using Modifiers for Unlisted Procedures 107 / Some Frequently Used
CPT Modifiers 108

NINE BASIC CPT CODING PRINCIPLES **115**

EVALUATION AND MANAGEMENT **116**

Components of E&M Encounters 116 / Overview of the E&M
Subcategories 121 / E&M Codes Which Are Not Always Covered 126

MEDICINE **128**

Immunizations 129 / Therapeutic and Diagnostic Injections 129 /
Cardiovascular Services 130 / Special Services and Reports 131

RADIOLOGY **131**

PATHOLOGY AND LABORATORY **132**

SURGERY **134**

Listed Surgical Procedures 135 / Separate Procedure Guideline 136

INTEGUMENTARY SYSTEM **137**

MUSCULOSKELETAL SYSTEM **138**

THE HCPCS SYSTEM **138**

Three Levels in HCPCS Coding 139 / Steps for Using HCPCS When Billing
Medicare and Other Government Plans 139 / Steps for Using HCPCS Level
II Codes When Billing Nongovernment Plans 140 / Categories of HCPCS in
Level II 140 / Examples Using Level II Codes with CPT Codes 142 /
Temporary HCPCS Codes 142 / Level II 143 / Level III 143

EXERCISING KNOWLEDGE **144**

CHAPTER 6

Completing the Universal Claim Form 157

OPTIONS IN BILLING **157**

THE UNIVERSAL CLAIM FORM, HCFA 1500 (12-90) **159**

REQUIREMENTS FOR COMPLETING INFORMATIONAL ITEMS ON THE UNIVERSAL
CLAIM FORM **160**

Patient and Insured Information 160 / Physician or Supplier
Information 168

THE ROLE OF COMPUTERIZED SYSTEMS IN THE INSURANCE CLAIMS
PROCESS **177**

Optical Character Recognition 177 / Electronic Claims 178 /
Workgroup for Electronic Data Interchange (WEDI) 181

EXERCISING KNOWLEDGE **183**

CHAPTER 7   ***Backing Up the Codes with Documentation   195***

THE IMPORTANCE OF DOCUMENTATION **195**
Quality of Care and Utilization of Resources 196 / Fines for Inadequate
Documentation 196 / Principles of Medical Record Documentation 197 /
Development of Principles of Documentation 197

METHODS OF DOCUMENTATION **201**
Documenting Face-to-Face Encounters with the Physician-Caregiver 201 /
SOAP Format of Record Keeping 202 / Counseling 209 / Telephone
Calls 209 / Use of Templates 209 / Obtaining a Patient Release 210 /
Use of the Fax 210 / Length of Time Medical Records Are Kept 211 /
Termination of the Physician-Patient Relationship 211 / Consent for
Medical Treatment 212 / Conducting a Documentation Audit 212 /
Smart Card 212

EXERCISING KNOWLEDGE **212**

CHAPTER 8   ***Medicare: A Complicated Government Program   225***

ENROLLMENT **225**
Funding for Part A and Part B 227 / Medicare Trust Funds 227

MANAGEMENT AND RESPONSIBILITY OF THE MEDICARE PROGRAM **227**
Benefits for Part A 228 / Benefits for Part B 228 / Excluded Services
228 / Claims Denied as Not Reasonable and Necessary 230 / Conditional
Coverage 231 / Prepayment Screens 232 / Preventive Medicine
Benefits 232

THE ID CARD **232**

OUT-OF-POCKET COSTS **233**
Medigap Coverage 234 / One-Time Authorization for Medicare
Beneficiaries 235

CHANGES IN MEDICARE RULES AND REGULATIONS **236**
The Medicare Participation Program 236 / Nonparticipating Physicians
236 / Other Rules When a Claim is Not Assigned 238 / Physician
Payment for Purchased Diagnostic Services 238 / Payment for Ancillary
Professional Services 239 / Health Professional Shortage Areas 240 /
Assistants at Surgery 240 / Site of Service Differential 240

*MEDICARE'S FEE SCHEDULE: THE RESOURCE BASED RELATIVE VALUE SCALE
(RBRVS)* **240**
Relative Values Units for Procedure Codes 241 / Geographic Practice Cost
Indices 242 / The Conversion Factor 242 / Working with the Formula
244 / Phase-in Period 246 / Volume Performance Standard 247

MEDICARE CLAIM RULES **249**
Medicare as a Secondary Payer 249 / Automobile Liability and Work-
Related Injuries 251 / Regionalization of DMEPOS Claims Filing 251 /
Appeals 252 / Administrative Law Judge 253 / Appeals Council 253

FRAUD AND ABUSE **254**
Avoidance of Fraud and Abuse 255

EXERCISING KNOWLEDGE **256**

CHAPTER 9   **Other Government Plans** **273**

THE MEDICAID PROGRAM **273**
Physician Contract Requirements 274 / Administration of Medicaid 274 /
Eligibility 275

DIFFERENCES IN MEDICAID **277**
Restricted Benefits 277 / Spend-Down 277 / Payment for Services
279 / Claim Reporting 279

CHAMPUS **280**
Eligibility 280 / Identification Cards 281 / DEERS 281 /
Catastrophic Out-of-Pocket Limit 285 / Secondary Coverage 285 /
TriCare 285 / Payment 286 / Claims Reporting 286 / Appeals 288

CHAMPVA **289**
Eligibility 289 / Benefits 290 / Payment and Claims Reporting 290

WORKERS' COMPENSATION **290**
Benefits 291 / Payment for Coverage 291 / Compensation for
Employees 291 / Physician on Record 292 / Different Forms to
Complete 292 / Determination of Fault 293

CLAIMS AND REIMBURSEMENT **294**

EXERCISING KNOWLEDGE **295**

CHAPTER 10   **Private Insurance Plans and Self-Insured Organizations** **309**

THE HISTORY OF BLUE CROSS AND BLUE SHIELD **310**

TIMELINE FOR DEVELOPMENT **310**

DISTINCTIONS OF BLUE SHIELD **311**

BENEFIT OPTIONS **312**
    Blue Shield Payment for All Services Based on Medical Necessity *312* /
    Clinical Guideline for Preventive Care *313*

CERTIFICATE **313**
    Reciprocity Plan *313* / Central Certification *315* / Federal Employees
    Program *315*

COORDINATION OF BENEFITS **316**

METHODS OF PHYSICIAN PAYMENT **316**

RBRVS **317**

CLAIMS REPORTING **318**

LEAVING THE TRADITIONAL INDEMNITY ROLE **318**

SELF-INSURED PLANS **319**
    Benefits to Employers *320* / Claims Reporting to Self-Insured Employers
    320 / Denials of Claims or Coverage *320*

EXERCISING KNOWLEDGE **321**

CHAPTER 11   **Managed Care Plans 323**

HOW MANAGED CARE PLANS BECAME IMPORTANT **323**

METHODS FOR CONTROLLING HEALTHCARE COSTS **324**
    Definition of Managed Care *325*

THE ALPHABET SOUP OF MANAGED CARE **325**
    Types of HMOs *327*

MANAGED CARE CONTRACTS: AN OVERVIEW **331**
    Contract Evaluation *336* / Contract Breakers *337* / Give Points *338* /
    Thirty Administrative Issues *340*

EXERCISING KNOWLEDGE **346**

CHAPTER 12   **Quality Improvement Controls in a Medical Practice 365**

QUALITY IMPROVEMENT CONTROLS IN A MEDICAL PRACTICE **365**

QUALITY IMPROVEMENT IN THE MONITORING OF PAYMENT **366**
    Studying Slow Fee for Service Payers *370* / Studying Low Fee for Service
    Payers *371*

SENDING ANOTHER CLAIM BECAUSE OF SIMPLE ERRORS **372**

REGISTERING A FORMAL APPEAL **372**

COLLECTION RATES **376**

Gross Collection Ratio 376 / Net Collection Ratio 377 / Posting
Withholds and Extra Fees 377 / Monitoring the Capitation Rate 379

THE QUALITY IMPROVEMENT CONNECTION **382**

Defining and Measuring Clinical Quality with Guidelines 382 / Adopting
a Clinical CQI Program 384

THE FUTURE OF PRACTICE GUIDELINES **387**

EXERCISING KNOWLEDGE **387**

Information Sources 403

Glossary 405

Answer Section 423

Index 443

Preface

In the days when physicians provided medical services to patients and accepted cash or goods as payment, the patient-physician relationship was relatively simple. The doctor recommended a procedure which the patient authorized and paid for directly. Authorization and direct payment for the majority of services by the patient are now the exception rather than the rule. Insurance and managed care plans have inserted themselves as a third party, making the relationship one of provider–insurance plan–patient. This complex relationship, involving many types of plans, each with different claims-filing requirements and different methods of payment, has made the contemporary American healthcare delivery system one of the most complicated in the world for a physician practice to work with. No matter what their size, physician practices must have on staff people who can carry out the administrative and clerical tasks needed to work effectively with these plans while maintaining the business relationships that bind patients, plans, and doctors.

In some practices, office administrators or managers coordinate insurance-related tasks. In others, medical assistants specially trained in the insurance claims process have primary responsibility in this area. *Working with Insurance and Managed Care Plans: A Guide for Getting Paid* can be used by all medical office personnel—from the physician to thereceptionist—as a step-by-step guide through the maze of rules, regulations, and procedures that characterize the insurance claims process. All medical office personnel play a role in this process.

Chapter 1 provides an overview of the parties in the healthcare business and a general description of the types of plans that provide healthcare benefits. Chapter 2 outlines the insurance-related tasks in each step of the claims process, from patient registration to posting and billing. Chapter 3 covers the terminology and procedures common to all health benefit plans. Chapters 4 and 5 are devoted to a practical analysis of the two major coding systems used in the insurance claims process: the ICD-9-CM, or diagnostic codes, which convey the clinical condition of a patient, and the CPT-4 and HCPCS codes, which are codes for services provided. Both chapters make use of Coding Tips and Clinical Examples designed to give the user a hands-on grasp of current diagnostic and procedural codes.

Chapter 6 provides instructions for the placement of coding data and other information required by plans on a universal claim form, and Chapter 7 discusses the medical record and the documentation required to back up the codes reported on a claim. Chapters 8 through 11 provide more detail about the various government insurance plans and selected private plans, including self-insured plans and managed care plans. Chapter 12 discusses quality improvement controls in a medical practice.

At the end of each chapter there are practical tools consisting of instructional notes, listings, charts, and forms. These tools were designed to help all medical office personnel including the physician simplify the tasks involved in claims processing. Some of these tools can be photocopied and used as models for documentation; others are examples of document types one is likely to encounter in working with a variety of insurance and managed care plans. All the tools are designed to enhance the physician's ability to report accurate claims and receive entitled payment.

ACKNOWLEDGMENTS

This book is a compilation of our experiences in the healthcare industry as a physician practice manager, a managed care plan administrator, and as seminar instructors and consultants to physician practices—combined experiences spanning forty years. Throughout those years, we have seen many changes, but none so sweeping as the current changes in physician payment. We wrote this book at the request of physician office personnel, who face the difficult task of keeping up with these sweeping changes. Many requested one source of information in order to receive fair payment for their doctors. This book compiles all of the necessary information to keep up with claim processing and payment trends from the huge variety of insurance and managed care plans. We wrote this book for those hard working personnel who have the doctor's best interests at heart.

This book would not have been possible without the help and support of many people. We want to give special thanks to:

Lisa Hohler and Ruth Harris of Physician Strategies 2000, Franklin, Ohio, who helped us in research and groomed us as seminar instructors and consultants.

Barbara Durr, Carol Sprinkle, and Shirley Toepfert, our friends within the quality improvement departments of several large managed care plans in Cincinnati, Ohio.

Jim and Carolyn McIntosh and the late Dr. Donald Harrington of Shingle Springs, California, the original inventors of utilization management computer edits.

Elliott Blankendorf and Cheryl Van Tilburg of the legal department of the National office of Blue Cross and Blue Shield in Chicago, Illinois.

Jenny Kohler and Jeanie Clemmons of Blue Cross and Blue Shield in Louisville, Kentucky.

Dave Potts and Gary Whitaker of the national office of OCHAMPUS in Aurora, Colorado.

Judy Armstrong, Ohio Medicare Manager, Nationwide Mutual Insurance Company, Columbus, Ohio.

Our husbands and children, who took over many household responsibilities

Our clients, who had to wait until they fit into our schedule

Our students at Raymond Walters Branch, University of Cincinnati, and Virginia Wiley, department chair of Office Administration, who served as a sounding board for some of the chapters

Jan Davison, R.N., B.S.N., M.S.A.

Maxine Lewis, B.A.

Introduction to the Claims Process

CHAPTER OVERVIEW

The patient, the physician, and the insurance or managed care plan are the three parties in today's complex healthcare payment system.

The major types of insurance and managed care plans, also known as third-party payers, are government plans and private plans. Within the category of private plans, there are traditional indemnity benefit plans, self-insured plans, and managed care plans. Traditional indemnity benefit and self-insured plans are adopting the medical resource monitoring techniques used by managed care plans. All these plans are moving in the direction of managed care.

After reading the material in this chapter, doing the exercises, and using the end-of-chapter tools, you will be able to:

■ *Explain why insurance plans are regarded as third parties in today's healthcare system*

■ *Understand the similarities and differences between the major types of insurance plans*

■ *List the main clerical and administrative tasks that must be carried out if a practice is to receive the maximum payment for services*

■ *Discuss the opportunities for medical office personnel who want to take on more responsibility in solving operational problems that result from the complexity of the claims process*

THE PARTIES IN THE HEALTHCARE BUSINESS

When patients become eligible and enroll in insurance plans, the plans underwrite and accept the financial risks for the healthcare of their enrollees. Enrollees receive the assurance that they will not have to pay for catastrophic healthcare costs themselves. Insurance plans carry the *risks*, and that is why they are also known as *carriers*. When a plan receives a premium, it covers the services provided by a physician as long as those services meet the definition of the benefits included in the calculation of the premium rate. *Non-covered* services are listed in the *policy*—the written contract between the patient and the insurance mechanism of the plan—and are not paid for by the plan. As a medical practice provides healthcare services which are paid for by patients' third-party payers, it finds itself positioned between patient and payer. In some cases a doctor must hold a contract with a plan to receive any payment at all.

TYPES OF PAYERS

This section classifies insurance and managed care plans according to the payer. The two basic types of payers are government and private, and private payer plans can be further subdivided into traditional indemnity benefit plans, self-insured, and managed care plans.

Government Plans

Many government payer programs have been legislated by Congress. Congress makes laws determining things such as covered benefits and exclusions and expenditures. Congress delegates the administration of its programs to government agencies, and together they regulate those programs. The operational policies of government plans are available as public information. The policies by which these plans determine whether a service is payable can be obtained by a physician practice under the *freedom of information privilege.* The Freedom of Information Act of 1966 allows citizens to obtain information about government operations. A physician practice can write to governmental programs, such as Medicare, within its state to obtain copies of policies. Operational policies are also published in newsletters and physician administrative manuals. An explanation of how to obtain policies under the Freedom of Information Act appears in Chapter 8.

The rules of a government plan are known as regulations. When a practice does not follow the rules of a government plan, it breaks the law. There are standard fines and other strict penalties for this. Government plans include Medicare, Medicaid, CHAMPUS, and workers' compensation.

Medicare is a federal plan which is an entitlement program administered by HCFA (Health Care Financing Administration) for patients over age 65 years, certain disabled individuals, and those with end-stage renal disease.

Medicaid is a federal and state plan, operated by the states, which is an entitlement program under the Social Security Administration of the federal government for patients whose income and resources are insufficient to pay for health care.

CHAMPUS (Civilian Health and Medical Program of the Uniformed Services) is a cost-sharing program for military families, retirees and their families, some former spouses, and survivors of deceased military personnel.

Workers' compensation is a requirement of the federal government for employers of patients who are injured or become sick on the job. It is operated by various plans chosen by the employer or can be operated by state governments.

Government plans are discussed in detail in Chapters 8 and 9.

Private Plans

Private plans are operated by private companies which act as the payer. Examples of private plans include Blue Cross/Blue Shield and the Prudential Insurance Company. When private plans began, they did not monitor medical resources and offered only traditional indemnity benefits. *Traditional indemnity benefits* pay only when a patient is ill or injured. A diagnosis which implies that the patient has a pathologic condition or symptom must be reported on the claim for payment of benefits under these policies. There are still some traditional indemnity benefits sold by private plans, but most of these plans now offer other product options which cover preventive care. They had to do this to survive the tremendous competition among health plans today.

Private plans can be regulated by state insurance laws which mandate that certain benefits be covered at least up to a state's minimum requirements. Private plans cause a great deal of confusion within a physician practice, especially for the office staff. Since these plans are privately owned, their operational policies are not public information. Some of the medical policies they use to determine whether they will pay for a service may not be shared with a medical practice. Unlike goverment plans, when rules are not followed, the practice is not breaking the law unless false information is submitted. There are two subtypes of private plans.

Self-insured plans

A *self-insured plan* is one in which the payer is an employer or other group, such as a labor union. Examples include the Proctor and Gamble company and the Teamsters' Union. The employer or other group assumes full risk for the payment of healthcare services by taking the premium it would have paid to an insurance mechanism and establishing a fund to provide benefits for its employees or group members. When an employer group is self-insured, it is regulated by the federal government under the Employee Retirement Income Security Act of 1974 (ERISA). A self-insured plan provides healthcare benefits at the employer's or group's discretion without being subject to certain state insurance laws. A self-insured employer usually contracts with an administrator who acts on behalf of the self-insured plan to process the claims. Working with Blue Shield, a private plan, and self-insured plans will be discussed in Chapter 10.

Managed Care Plans

Managed care plans are operated by private companies which act as the payer. Examples include PruCare (an HMO) and USA HealthNet (a PPO). Physicians sign a contract with a managed care plan to accept the plan's fee schedule, which is usually lower than the prevailing market rate. Thus, these physicians are considered a part of the *managed care organization's (MCO's)* panel of providers. Rules and payment methods for a practice are outlined in a contractual agreement and a physician administrative manual. Managed care plans differ from other types of private plans in that they strictly monitor the necessity of healthcare payments. In certain instances the monitoring occurs on a case-by-case basis. The service data reported by a medical practice allow the practice patterns of physicians to be monitored as well. The two most common managed care plans are the health maintenance organization and the preferred provider organization.

Health Maintenance Organizations

A *health maintenance organization (HMO)* is regulated by state HMO laws. These laws require an HMO to cover benefits for preventive care, which includes routine physician examinations, and other services. Coordination of care by a primary care physician is required for patients to receive benefits. HMOs also do not provide any benefits for patients unless medical services are provided by contracted physicians, although HMOs today can and do offer variations of this basic product option. HMOs prepay the doctor for the care of a population assigned to the practice. HMOs also may pay the doctor under a fee for service method. Regardless of the method of payment, HMOs were the first plans to place the physician's payment at risk by either capitation or withhold. Capitation will be addressed later in this chapter. *Withhold* means that a certain proportion of the payment due to a physician will be withheld by the HMO (e.g., 10 to 40 percent) for a defined period, until the HMO has had time to pay all the claims for that period. If an HMO exceeds its budget for the payment of claims for a period, the withheld money is not paid to the doctor. If the HMO has a withhold clause in its contract, a medical practice uses an additional method to keep track of the payments owed to the doctor.

Preferred Provider Organizations

A *preferred provider organization (PPO)* may or may not be regulated by state insurance laws. PPOs can be regulated by state insurance laws if they are owned by a private insurance plan or the PPO operates within a state which has an insurance law that regulates PPOs. Not all states have regulations for PPOs. If PPOs are not state-regulated, they are not required to cover certain benefits required by state laws. Typically, PPOs do not cover preventive benefits unless they are regulated by a state which requires this. PPOs do not generally require coordination of care by a primary care physician. PPOs were the first plans to allow patients to freely seek services from physicians not contracted with a plan. However, if a patient seeks services outside the panel of contracted physicians, benefits are reduced and the patient must pay out-of-pocket expenses that usually range from 20 to 30 percent of the total costs. PPOs do not place physician payment at risk and pay physicians under the discounted fee for service method. Not all PPOs are owned by private insurance plans. If a PPO is not owned by a private insurer, it is not the payer of benefits; it is only a broker for the services of the contracted panel of physicians. As a broker, it contracts the services of the panel to private plans, such as a self-insured plan. In this example, claims are sent to the PPO only for repricing to the discounted fee and forwarding to the insurer for payment. The broker arrangement is outlined in the physician's PPO contract. Table 1-1 shows the distinguishing features of HMOs and PPOs. It describes features of HMOs and PPOs as they historically began. In today's healthcare benefits marketplace, there are now variations on these historical features. HMOs now have point of service products which make them act like PPOs, and PPOs now have exclusive provider options which make them act like HMOs. The options will be explained in Chapter 11.

TABLE 1-1

Distinguishing Features of HMOs and PPOs

Feature	HMO	PPO
Regulation	State HMO laws	Varies
Preventive care coverage	Required	Not required
Coordination of care by a primary care physician	Required	Not Required
Eligible providers	Services must be provided by contracted physicians or no benefits are paid	Services can be provided by noncontracted physicians, but benefits are reduced
Method of payment	Capitation and fee for service	Fee for service
At-risk status	Payment at risk	Payment not at risk

METHODS OF PAYMENT

Insurance and managed care plans pay physicians according to two basic methods: fee for service and capitation.

Fee for Service

Until relatively recently most physicians were paid according to the *fee for service* method, in which the practice charged a fee for the service provided. After the service was performed, either the doctor or the patient submitted a *claim* and then received a check for payment.

Capitation

Many managed care plans now pay physicians a *capitation* rate, a fixed pre-paid amount based on the number of patients assigned to a practice for a specified period of time. "Capitation" means "head count." Capitation payment includes the cost of certain services whether or not the patient receives care in the designated period.

Variations on the Basic Methods

The *episode of care* method is a hybrid of the fee for service and capitation methods. In this method, the physician is paid a flat payment per treatment, diagnosis, or episode of care. For example, the workup for a tumor, plus x-rays, is paid at one price. Still other methods are under consideration, and medical office personnel should know about any new payment methods mandated by healthcare reform.

THE RESPONSIBILITIES OF A MEDICAL PRACTICE

Figure 1-1 shows the complex flow of services, information, and payment in today's healthcare system from the perspective of a medical practice. As the figure suggests, medical office personnel who are responsible for facilitating or administering the physician and patient aspects of the insurance claims process work in a complicated environment that is in change. To function effectively within the healthcare system, they must be flexible enough to adapt to change and be willing to implement operational solutions within the practice to the problems caused by change. For example, the drive to contain healthcare costs has resulted in steadily increasing rules for the physician. Most plans now have rules for *Preauthorization*. Preauthorization also commonly known as *precertification* means contacting the plan prior to hospital-

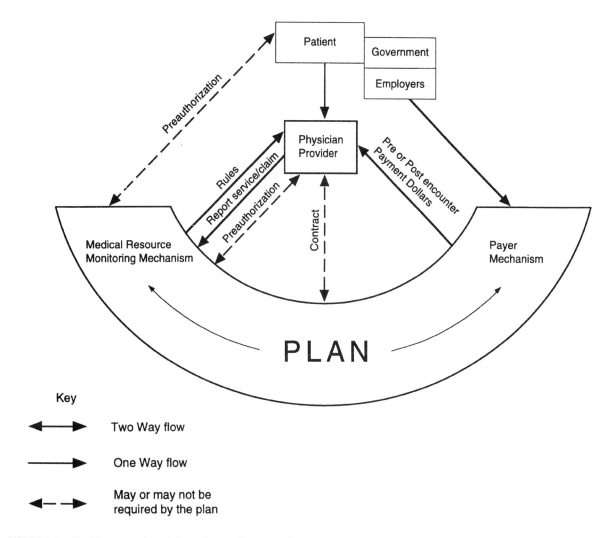

FIGURE 1-1 Healthcare services, information, and payment flow.

izing a patient or prior to providing certain outpatient services to explain the clinical reasons why the service is necessary for the patient's condition. Depending on the plan, either the patient or provider must seek preauthorization. Without required preauthorization, physicians may not be paid for certain services. If it is the patient's responsibility to preauthorize the service, full benefits may not be paid. There are over 1500 plans, and a physician must follow the rules of each patient's plan in the insurance claims process. These rules can range from relatively straightforward ones for reporting a medical service in an information format acceptable to the plan to exchanging highly clinical information before, during, and after the treatment of a patient.

Figure 1-2 gives an overall picture of the responsibilities of medical office personnel participating in the insurance claims process. The diagram breaks down the tasks into three categories: those related to (1) the physician/provider, (2) the patient, and (3) the plan. The result of not carrying

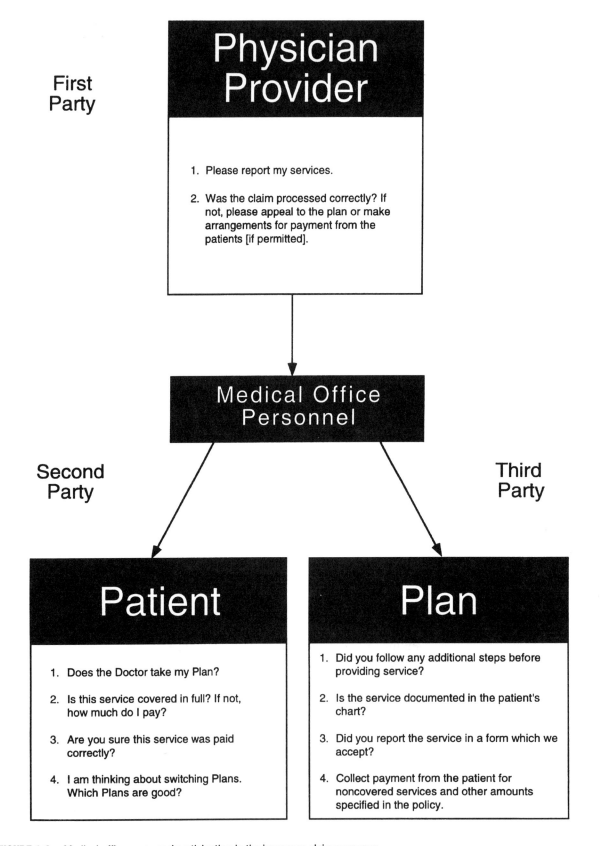

FIGURE 1-2   Medical office personnel participating in the insurance claims process.

out any one of these tasks can be an interruption in the flow of payments to the practice and even a reduction in revenue. Note that one important task involves giving guidance to patients who are confused about the varieties of plans and often do not understand their benefits or responsibilities when they seek medical services. Patients may ask direct questions about plans when they make appointments, when they get explanations of payments from their plans which they believe to be incorrect, and when they switch to other plans. In addition, plans have checkpoints to determine whether the physician has reported or filed the claim according to the proper rules, and the practice must be able to field direct questions from the plan representative when a service is reported.

The office personnel participating in the insurance claims process must do the following:

1. Understand and comply with the rules and regulations of each plan
2. Know the contractual relationships, if any, between the practice and each payer
3. Help the physician and other employees understand what needs to be done to comply with the rules
4. Assist in the design of forms for reporting services and/or use computer software in order to submit data quickly, accurately, and consistently
5. Make sure the practice is receiving the maximum payments to which it is entitled
6. Assist patients in understanding their benefits and what they need to do to receive full benefits

Keeping Up With the Changes

Carrying out the responsibilities listed in the last section requires a commitment to careerlong education. We are in the middle of the most dramatic changes in the history of healthcare delivery. The medical assistant, supervisor, or office manager responsible for claims processing should view these changes as challenges to his or her professionalism. Keeping up with changes is nothing new for medical office personnel. There have always been changes in state and federal laws with which physician practices have had to comply, changes in medical technology, changes in coding systems, and changes in the rules of insurance and managed care plans. The changes are more challenging at this time because of healthcare reform. To prepare for a more secure and rewarding career, do the following:

■ Keep abreast of events by talking to colleagues, representatives of hospitals, and state and local medical societies.
■ Make sure to be on the mailing lists of plan newsletters and ask questions of plan representatives when changes are unclear.

■ Attend educational meetings to stay current on the necessary data reported on encounter and claims forms.

■ Follow the implementation of state and federal healthcare reform laws.

■ Network with people to get information about the activities of hospitals, physician groups, and health plans which are changing their structures to deliver new healthcare benefit options in your community.

■ Be sure your office has the most recent edition of three books on coding systems:

—*Current Procedural Terminology,* 4th edition (CPT-4), published by the American Medical Association (AMA): describes services rendered by physicians and other providers

—*Health Care Financing Administration Common Procedural Coding System (HCPCS),* published by the Health Care Financing Administration: describes services rendered by other providers and some physician services

—*International Classification of Diseases—Clinical Modification,* 9th Revision (ICD-9-CM), published by the U.S. Department of Health and Human Services: describes diagnoses, symptoms, and conditions.

EXERCISING KNOWLEDGE

1. List the three parties involved in the business of healthcare.

2. What are the two types of payers?

3. Name the four major government plans.

4. Name the two original managed care plans.

5. Name six tasks of medical office personnel who handle insurance claims.

Explain These Terms or Abbreviations

6. Self-insured plan

7. Preauthorization

8. Fee for service

9. Capitation

Refer to the Tools Section

10. In what season is a new CPT book ordered?

11. In what season is a new ICD-9-CM book ordered?

12. When is the *Federal Register* ordered? Explain.

13. How is freedom of information received from a government plan?

14. Rules of a government plan are known as _____ .

15. HMOs are regulated by _____ laws.

The Physician Payment Process

CHAPTER OVERVIEW

Regardless of what happens outside a medical practice as a result of healthcare reform and despite all the recent changes in healthcare delivery, the basic tasks inside the practice will be the same. Patients will continue to get sick and receive services from the doctor, and charges will be posted to patient accounts. In capitated care and other types of risk-bearing arrangements, the doctor's payment and payment owed will also be posted to an account for the managed care plan. Regardless of the method of payment, the doctor's services will require coding and the practice will still report a claim either electronically or on a paper form. After reading the material in this chapter, doing the exercises, and using the end-of-chapter tools, you will be able to:

- *Diagram and explain the various stations in the critical pathway of a claim, including*
  - *Registration*
  - *Encounter (office, hospital, home, or other location)*
  - *Exit*
  - *Posting and billing*
- *Use the following tools to ensure accurate, effective claims processing:*
  - *registration form*
  - *financial policy*
  - *encounter form (superbill)*
  - *truth-in-lending form*
  - *explanation of benefits (EOB)*

THE CRITICAL PATHWAY OF A CLAIM

The tasks involved in every part of the physician payment process occur in a logical sequence. There is a pathway of information and data collection stations when a patient encounters a physician in a medical practice. Each station collects and processes information which leads to the reporting of a *claim*. A claim is the formal reporting of data about the patient and the services provided by the doctor to an insurance or managed care plan. The critical pathway of a claim begins when a patient arrives for an appointment and ends with payment (Figure 2-1). The information collection stations in the figure are shown as Registration, Medical Encounter, Exit, and Posting and Billing. Medical office personnel fill several roles at these stations, including entry and exit receptionist, overseer of the completion of the encounter form, credit counselor, claim reporter, and payment processor. Some practices refer to the tasks involved in the physician payment process as front office functions. In most practices such functions are carried out by more than one person. In others one person may fill several roles; for example, a medical assistant may perform both registration and exit functions. No matter how many people are involved, they all must work as a team to make the process successful.

Registration

Registration is the process of collecting patient information and orienting the patient to the policies of the medical practice. When a patient first requests an appointment, before the formal registration process begins, the practice should ask the patient for the name of his or her insurance company. For example, if a patient has an insurance plan that requires him or her to seek services only from a contracted physician and the practice does not include a contracted physician from that plan, the patient must be informed. If patients insist on an appointment, they are informed of their obligation to pay the doctor in full on the day of the appointment. If patients belong to a plan which requires a *referral* (an authorization from the patient's primary care physician), the correct referral information—the proper paper form or an authorization number—must be collected. Many potential insurance problems for the patient and the physician can be prevented if the office asks the right questions before an appointment is scheduled.

Once the appointment has been scheduled, the formal registration process begins. Many practices mail a prepackaged welcome packet containing information about policies and procedures to new patients on the day when the appointment is made.

The Welcome Packet

A *welcome packet* is a mailable collection of information that includes a practice brochure booklet, the office's financial policy, and a registration form. The *practice brochure booklet* acquaints patients with the practice and makes them feel welcome. It contains descriptions of the staff, the training of the physicians, and their medical specialties. It outlines policies on appointment times and cancellations, registration procedures, telephone calls and prescriptions, what to do in an emergency, charges, billing, and insurance procedures. It can be given to established patients whenever policies or procedures change. Tool 2-1 shows a typical practice brochure booklet.

The *financial policy* of a practice outlines the credit policy and states when payment is expected for services that are not covered by an insurance

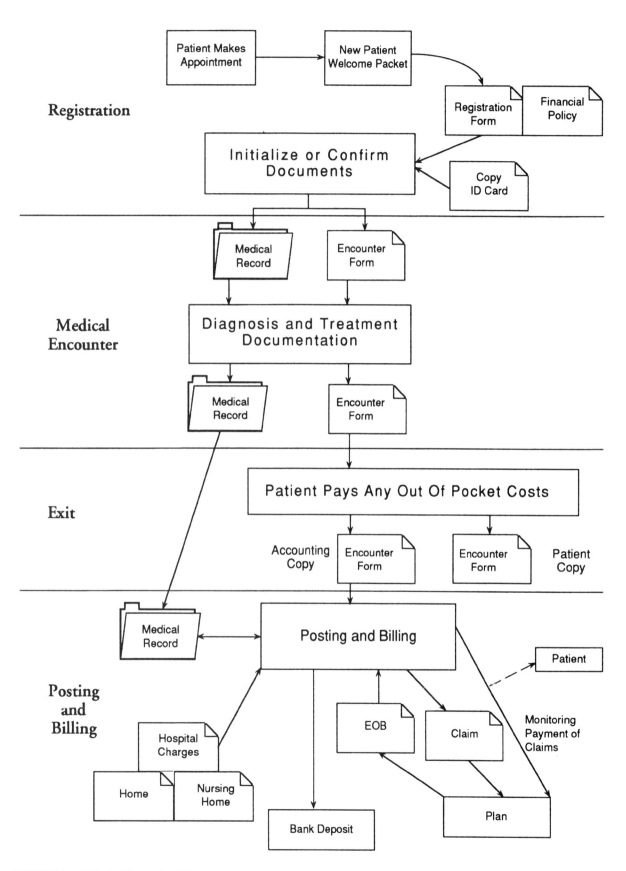

FIGURE 2-1 Critical pathway of a claim.

plan. A financial policy should state that the practice has no obligation to negotiate a claim if it does not have a contract with a particular plan. When there is no contract between the doctor and the plan, the only contract remaining is that between the patient and the plan. Tool 2-2 shows a typical financial policy statement that might be included in a welcome packet.

The Registration Form

The *registration form* is a document for collecting the information needed to set up patient accounts. It requests patient addresses, phone numbers, responsible parties, and names of insurance plans. It contains spaces for patients to list the *primary insurance plan* (the plan which pays first) and the *secondary insurance plan* (the plan which pays second if there are payments left after the primary plan has paid). On this form patients may sign their names to assign their medical benefit payments directly to the physician. Obtaining a patient's signature depends on the policy of the practice. However, a patient must sign his or her name, giving the office permission to release medical information to report a claim. The bottom of this form contains special phrases pertaining only to the signatures of Medicare and/or Medigap patients for the assignment and release of medical information (Figure 2-2).

Obtaining complete, accurate information on the registration form at the time of the initial encounter is vital, whereas seeking information after the patient has left the office is time-consuming. That is why mailing the form before an appointment is a good idea. It is also important to keep the information on the registration form current. Established patients are asked to complete a new form at least once a year if any of the information has changed, especially in regard to their insurance plans. Patients enroll in plans throughout the year. The months in which the greatest changes in enrollment occur for employer group medical insurance are January, April, July, and September. These are good months for medical office personnel to ask patients about changes in their plans. Some practices ask patients to update this information with each visit and routinely make copies of plan identification cards.

Plan Identification Card

A plan *identification card* provides proof of coverage issued by insurance or managed care plans to patients during the process of enrollment. It is valid as long as the patient maintains his or her eligibility and pays any applicable premiums. All practices should photocopy the plan identification card, front and back, at the time of registration. The photocopy is used for the following purposes:

1. To assure that the correct plan identification numbers or letters are recorded

PATIENT REGISTRATION FORM								

PLEASE PRINT Physician or person who sent you to us _____

PATIENT INFORMATION (TO BE COMPLETED BY PATIENT OR RESPONSIBLE PARTY)   DATE _____

NAME:	SEX:	AGE:	BIRTHDATE:			MARITAL STATUS (✓ ONE)	
ADDRESS:	☐ M ☐ F		Month	Day	Year	☐ Single	☐ Married
CITY: STATE: ZIP:	SSN:					☐ Divorced	☐ Widowed
HOME PHONE: ( )	EMPLOYER:						
WORK PHONE: ( )	ADDRESS:						
DRIVER'S LICENSE :	CITY: STATE: ZIP:						

TO BE COMPLETED BY RESPONSIBLE PARTY (IF OTHER THAN PATIENT)

NAME:	RELATIONSHIP TO PATIENT: ☐ Spouse ☐ Child ☐ Other
ADDRESS:	BIRTHDATE: SSN.:
CITY: STATE: ZIP:	EMPLOYER:
HOME PHONE: ( )	ADDRESS:
WORK PHONE: ( )	CITY: STATE: ZIP:

BLUE SHIELD	PRUDENTIAL	HMO/CARE	MEDICARE	MEDICAID	WORKERS' COMP..	PPO/CARE	OTHER
☐	☐	☐	☐	☐	☐	☐	☐

Please give us all information regarding your insurance plan(s). Please show all numbers on your card(s). IF YOUR BENEFITS DEPEND ON **PRE-AUTHORIZATION, IT IS YOUR RESPONSIBILITY TO INFORM US, UNLESS WE ARE A PROVIDER FOR YOUR PLAN(S).**

Primary Plan Name:	Secondary Plan Name:
Address:	Address:
Insured (Name on ID Card):	Insured (Name on ID Card):
Relationship to Patient: ☐ Self ☐ Spouse ☐ Child ☐ Other	Relationship to Patient: ☐ Self ☐ Spouse ☐ Child ☐ Other
Insured ID No.:	Insured ID No.:
Group No. or Company Name: Plan #	Group No. or Company Name: Plan No.
Effective Date:	Effective Date:

Signature of patient or authorized person
I hereby authorize release of medical information necessary to report a claim to my plans(s).
A copy of this signature is valid as the original.   SIGNATURE _____

Signature of insured or authorized person to ASSIGN BENEFITS OTHERWISE PAYABLE TO THE INSURED TO THE PHYSICIAN INDICATED ON THE CLAIM. I understand I am financially responsible for benefits not covered by my insurance plan.
A copy of this signature is valid as the original   SIGNATURE _____

TO BE COMPLETED BY PATIENTS COVERED BY MEDICARE and /or those with a Medigap
Name of Beneticiary _____ HI Claim Number _____
I request that payment of authorized Medicare benefits be made either to me or on my behalf to _____ for any services furnished me by that physician. I authorize any holder of medical information about me to release to the Health Care Financing Administration and its agents any information needed to determine these benefits or the benefits payable for related services. I hereby authorize Medicare to furnish to the above-named doctor any information regarding my Medicare claims under Title XVIII of the Social Security Act.   SIGNATURE _____
I request that payment of authorized Medigap benefits be made to me or on my behalf to _____ for any services furnished me by that physician/supplier. I authorize any holder of medical information about me to released to _____(name of Medigap insurer) any information needed to determine these benefits or the benefits payable for related services. Medigap Policy Number _____ SIGNATURE _____

FIGURE 2-2   Patient registration form.

2. To provide notice to the person handling the exit encounter about any out-of-pocket costs to be paid at exit
3. To maintain a permanent record of the type of plan, including any special regulations and/or restrictions

Some plans allow only contracted facilities to perform certain laboratory and diagnostic tests. The nurse, doctor, and medical assistant need a notice before they direct the patient or send a specimen to a laboratory or another facility. Some of the rules of managed care plans can be located on the back of the ID card. Preauthorization requirements for certain services are usually noted there. Many practices make it a policy to attach a sticker to individual patient records that gives the name of the managed care plan. This sticker helps alert all staff members to the patient's membership in a plan.

Figure 2-3 shows a plan identification card. In the plan ID card shown in the figure, the policy number 1234-567-89-0 is the patient's plan identification number, which is given on enrollment for the determination of eligibility. Out-of-pocket costs that must be paid by the patient at the time of service should be listed on the card. In this example, they are known as co-payments. Copayments apply to certain types of services, such as office visits and eye examinations. Some of the copayments listed on the card may not apply to the services of the practice if it does not function as a pharmacy or durable medical supplier. Other names for out-of-pocket costs that are seen on ID cards include "deductible" and "coinsurance."

Plans sell a variety of benefit products to patients. One plan may offer several different products, and a practice cannot assume that all enrollees of, say, the XYZ plan are responsible for the same out-of-pocket costs. The plan

XYZ PLAN NAME

P.O. Box 1234 City and State

Name JOHN Q. PATIENT

Policy Number 1234-567-89-0

Birthdate 10-01-xx   Plan Code 083   Effective Date 1-01-xx

Copayment(s) $10.00 per office visit $ 5.00 per prescription

                $15.00 per eye exam $25.00 per mental health visit

                20% of physical therapy services and durable medical goods

FIGURE 2-3 Plan identification card (front).

code on the ID card notes the benefit product. Plan codes may be listed as other names, such as benefit code and group number, depending on the plan. Plans like to invent their own names for their products, and this can be a source of confusion. Look for the ID number issued to the patient and then look for other numbers or letters that specify the benefit product. Some ID cards have three or more numbers which may be needed in reporting a claim so that the plan can identify the patient and the benefits to which the patient is entitled. Rather than rely on the patient to list all the numbers and letters correctly on the registration form and volunteer the specifics of his or her out-of-pocket responsibilities, the practice should photocopy all cards for each patient to provide a correct reference for this vital information.

Note the back of the patient's ID card in Figure 2-3. "Precertification" is the name the XYZ plan uses for its preauthorization program. Do not be misled by the name the plan has adopted. The actions of a practice in obtaining preauthorization when it is required are always the same. Note that in this example the address where claims are sent is different from the address of the plan. One plan can have multiple addresses for sending claims. If claims are sent to the wrong address, payment will be delayed.

If a patient forgets his or her ID card or states that he or she has not been issued one, the practice has several options:

- Call the plan to verify enrollment
- Check the roster of names sent by the plan to the practice if the plan issues a roster
- Request that the patient mail a photocopy or bring the ID card at a future date

---

ATTENTION PROVIDERS AND ENROLLEES

This patient is enrolled in the Precertification program. Precertification requires notificaton of all elective hospital admissions, outpatient surgery, and MRI scans. Notification for emergency and maternity admissions must take place within 24 hours or 1 working day.

To obtain Preauthorization or for questions regarding any of these procedures, call 1-800-009-0000 or (999)123-0000 between 9:00 a.m. and 4:30 p.m. (EST), Monday through Friday.

Claims for services are mailed to:
XYZ Benefit Administrators
P.O. Box 0000
Columbus, America 43216
Fax: (999) 777-0000

Plan identification card (back).

Depending on how expensive the services are, some practices use an insurance worksheet to verify benefits (Tool 2-3).

Photocopies of a patient's driver's licenses are also made during registration, at the time of the patient's first visit. This task has two purposes: to record a picture identifying the person presenting the plan ID card as the individual to whom the card belongs and to trace that person if he or she moves. The practice has a responsibility to the plan to report the invalid use of ID cards. The practice must also maintain the ability to obtain a current address for patients when they move. In some states a driver's license number can be used to trace a patient's forwarding address for billing purposes. Photocopying a license number may help if the patient moves and the practice is unable to locate the patient at a new address but knows the state in which the patient lives. When one is tracing a patient who has moved, it is worth calling the state's bureau of motor vehicles, using the license number on the photocopy, to see if that agency will provide a new address. Some states have laws prohibiting the release of new addresses, and others do not.

The Encounter

Once the initial patient documents have been initialized and confirmed, the pathway of information leads to an encounter. An *encounter* is the physical contact of a patient with a provider of medical services, either the doctor or other medical personnel at the practice. The services provided and the diagnosis or condition of the patient are noted on a paper known as the *encounter form*. Encounter forms are also known as superbills, service slips, or charge tickets. Some practices circle or check procedures and diagnoses on the form; in others, the diagnoses are handwritten on the form in a designated space. Not all encounter forms look alike, as medical practices design them to meet their specific needs (Figure 2-4).

Once the patient's name has been filled in on the encounter form (practices with computerized record-keeping systems can generate an encounter form with the patient's name preprinted), the form is attached to the medical record for the doctor and others who provide services. The encounter form is used by the doctor and others involved in patient care to communicate charges for their services. This form is a vital link in the pathway to the posting and billing personnel who report claims. The form contains code numbers of the CPT-4 and/or HCPCS systems for procedures and code numbers of the ICD-9-CM system for patient diagnoses and conditions. Insurance and managed care plans require both CPT and ICD-9-CM codes on claims.

An encounter form consists of one to three copies, depending on the needs of the practice. While this is primarily an internal communication tool, a copy is given to patients upon their exit to explain the charges. It is acceptable to give patients a copy even if they are enrollees of plans with which the doctor has a contract as long as the copy is marked "this is not a

UPIN A76709

Tax I.D.#31-0000978

Tracy Lewis, M.D.
Medical Healing Arts Practice
4915 Muirwoods Court
Green Ash, America 45299
Telephone: (593) 000-1230

BCBC 123-09-567

XYZ # LE34567

OFFICE VISIT - NEW PATIENT

Level 1	99201 _____
Level 2	99202 _____
Level 3	99203 _____
Level 4	99204 _____
Level 5	99205 _____

OFFICE VISIT -ESTABLISHED PATIENT

Level 1	99211 _____
Level 2	99212 _____
Level 3	99213 _____
Level 4	99214 _____
Level 5	99215 _____

Others

_____

_____

_____

Immunizations

DTaP	90700	_____
DPT	90701	_____
Influenza	90724	_____
Pneumoccal	90732	_____
Hepatitis B	90731	_____
Tetanus	90703	_____
Measles	90705	_____
Rubella	90706	_____
Polio	90712	_____
Varicella	90716	_____
Poliomyelitis	90712	_____

Injection	90782	_____
Unlisted Drug J3490	_____	
Vit.B-12	J3420	_____

Diagnostic Codes

382.00 Abcess, ear,no rupture
789.07 Abdominal Pain,generalized
790.6 Abnormal Bld Sugar
706.1 Acne Vulgaris
477.0 Allergic Rhinitis
281.0 Anemia, pernicious
441.4 Abdominal aneurysm
411.1 Angina, unstable
719.07 Ankle sprain
783.0 Anorexia
427.9 Arrhythmia, NOS
493.90 Asthma, Bronchial
466.0 Bronchitis, acute
786.50 Chest Pain
372.00 Conjunctivitis,acute
564.0 Constipation
496 COPD

Procedures

EKG 93000	_____
Sigmoid.45330	_____
Spirometry 94010	_____
TB 86580	_____
Cerumen 69210	_____
I & D 10060	_____
Complicated 10061	_____
Skin tags (15).11200	_____
add. (10) 11201	_____

Others

_____

LABORATORY

Venipuncture	36415	_____
CBC	85022	_____
Chem 5	80006	_____
Chem 24	80019	_____
Glucose	82947	_____
Hematocrit	85014	_____
Platelet Count	85590	_____
Potassium	84132	_____
Prothrombin	85610	_____
Stool Occult	82270	_____
Urinalysis	81000	_____

_____

_____

Prolonged Services F-T-F

First Hour   99354 _____
Each add.30 min 99355 _____

Prolonged Service NF-T-F

First Hour   99358 _____
Each add.30 min 99359 _____

692.9 Dermatitis, contact
250.0_ Diabetes Mellitus, ID
250.0_ Diabetes Mellitus NID
558.9 Dirrhea, non-infectious
562.11 Diverticulitis
388.70 Ear pain
782.3 Edema
492.8 Emphysema
604.90 Epididymitis, non-veneral
V18.0 Family History Diabetes
780.6 Fever, unknown origin
578.9 G.I. Bleeding, unspecified
535.00 Gastritis, acute
784.0 Headache
455.6 Hemorrhoids
401.1 Hypertension, benign
380.4 Impacted cerumen

Doctor's Signature

_____

CPT Code	DX Code	Charge

_____ Total

Charges _____
Amount Paid _____
Previous Balance _____
Balance Due _____

Date of Service _____

X-Ray

Chest (PA & L)   71020 _____
Forearm (AP & L). 73090 _____
Wrist (AP & L).......73100 _____
Hand (2V)..............73120 _____
Finger (2V)............73140 _____

Other Services

_____

Dates of Disability

From _____
To _____
Restrictions _____

487.1 Influenza, respiratory
464.0 Laryngitis,acute
454.9 Leg Varicosities
715.09 Osteoarthritis, generalized
715.16 Osteoarthritis, knee
462   Pharyngitis, acute
486   Pneumonitis
625.4 Premenstrual Tension
782.1 Rash
569.3 Rectal Bleeding
398.90 Rheumatic Heart Disease
463   Tonsilitis, acute
474.0 Tonsilitis, chronic
465.9 U.R.I.
599.0 U.T.I.
Others _____

_____

_____

FIGURE 2-4   Encounter form.

bill" and when the copy contains balances which are the patient's responsibility in regard to payment. Copies of the encounter form must be given to patients who wish to complete their own insurance forms for plans with which the doctor does not have a contract. A few plans allow medical practices to bill them by attaching a copy of the encounter form to a paper claim form. The attachment of an encounter form to a claim submitted on paper is not recommended because of the possibility that the plan's claims processor will make an error in data entry. Not all encounter forms look alike, and some are printed in small type, making them difficult to read. As was stated above, encounter forms in today's medical practice are designed for internal communication.

Matching CPT and ICD-9-CM Codes on the Encounter Form

One criterion for the payment of benefits for procedures is that they be justified for the patient's diagnosis. When a medical service is reported with a CPT codes, the code must make sense medically in terms of the patient's diagnosis (ICD-9-CM code); that is, the diagnosis codes must *match* the CPT codes. For example, the performance of a urinalysis (CPT code 81000) would not be justified for a diagnosis of fibrocystic disease (ICD-9-CM code 610.1). Service and diagnosis are reported together in specific locations on a claim. Specific locations and the placement of these numbers are identified in Chapter 6. The matching process using both coding systems is easy as long as the patient has only one diagnosis, but the process can be confusing if the doctor provides more than one procedure and the patient has more than one diagnosis. Often it is difficult to select the diagnosis which matches each procedure for placement on a claim. Sometimes all the diagnoses must be used to justify the services of the doctor; at other times a single code is sufficient. Additionally, some plans enter only one diagnosis per procedure code; this is most often the case with electronic claims. This means that there is only one chance to be correct in the matching process. Medical practices use several methods to match multiple codes from one encounter. Most of the time, the personnel who review the encounter form for the procedures and diagnoses use their medical knowledge to determine the match. These persons have knowledge of medical practice or learn with time to make these selections. You should read plan newsletters for lists of ICD-9-CM diagnosis codes which justify payment for certain CPT codes. When faced with a difficult selection, ask the doctor and other medical personnel directly involved with patient care for help.

In an effort to monitor medical resources, plans are refining payment policies and claim edits regarding the *medical necessity* of a procedure for a certain set of diagnoses. Medical necessity in this instance means that the procedures must be appropriate for the diagnosis that is being reported. Increased monitoring results in claim denials when procedure and diagnosis codes are incorrectly matched. Medical practices must be on the lookout for increases in claim denials caused by incorrect matches and must implement corrections in office routines to rectify the problem.

One effective approach is to rank diagnoses in order of importance and then match them with the procedures. A practical way to rank-order diagnoses is to assign them letters, starting with the letter *a* for the primary diagnosis. Figure 2-5 shows an encounter form in which this system has been used.

On the encounter form the most important diagnosis, the primary diagnosis, was ranked as abdominal pain, generalized, code 789.07, with the letter *a* in the underlined space next to it. The most important procedure, the primary procedure, during the encounter was a Level 3 visit, code 99203. The letter *a* is placed next to the code 99203. The diagnosis of pernicious anemia, code 281.0, was the second most important diagnosis and was ranked with the letter *b*. One procedure, code J3420, was provided for code 281.0 (pernicious anemia), ranked as b. The doctor also had to consider the diagnosis of pernicious anemia in the medical decision-making process of assessing the abdominal pain. Therefore, the letter *b* has been placed next to *a* to justify the code 99203. Assessing multiple diagnoses in one visit increases the amount of work for the doctor during the encounter and justifies the reporting of a higher level of service.

Exit

After services have been provided and notations have been made on the encounter form, the patient is ready to be checked out. The doctor and medical personnel are responsible for documenting these services in the medical record and returning the record for filing. The tasks involved on patient exit include checking the encounter form for completeness, totaling the charges, giving the patient a copy of the encounter form, and requesting payment for the charges that are the patient's responsibility. The person handling the exit encounter must be direct with the patient regarding which charges are the patient's responsibility. The financial policy of the practice is followed in determining whether to collect these payments while the patient is in the office. Reasons for collecting payments at the time of service are as follows:

- Maintaining a steady cash flow
- Saving time in the production of a statement
- Saving the mailing expenses associated with statements

The mailing of statements is time-consuming and expensive for the practice, and payments are often hard to collect once a patient has left the office. In addition to cash and personal checks, many practices now accept credit cards. If the patient has no method of payment on the day of the encounter, have the patient sign a credit card charge slip and then make a note to call the patient to get the account number and expiration date later. If the

UPIN A76709
Tax I.D.#31-0000978

Tracy Lewis, M.D.
Medical Healing Arts Practice
4915 Muirwoods Court
Green Ash, America 45299
Telephone: (593) 000-1230

BCES 123-09-567
XYZ # LE34567

OFFICE VISIT - NEW PATIENT

Level 1	99201	_____
Level 2	99202	_____
Level 3	99203	__a,b__
Level 4	99204	_____
Level 5	99205	_____

OFFICE VISIT -ESTABLISHED PATIENT

Level 1	99211	_____
Level 2	99212	_____
Level 3	99213	_____
Level 4	99214	_____
Level 5	99215	_____

Others

_____
_____

Immunizations

DTaP	90700	_____
DPT	90701	_____
Influenza	90724	_____
Pneumoccal	90732	_____
Hepatitis B	90731	_____
Tetanus	90703	_____
Measles	90705	_____
Rubella	90706	_____
Polio	90712	_____
Varicella	90716	_____
Poliomyelitis	90712	_____

Injection   90782 _____

Unlisted Drug J3490 _____
Vit.B-12   J3420   **b**

Diagnostic Codes

Abcess, ear,no rupt.382.00 _____
Abdominal Pain, gen.789.07 __a__
Abnormal Bld Sugar 790.6 _____
Acne Vulgaris 706.1 _____
Allergic Rhinitis 477.0 _____
Anemia, pernicious 281.0 __b__
Abdominal aneurysm441.4 _____
Angina, unstable 411.1 _____
Ankle sprain 719.07 _____
Anorexia783.0 _____
Arrhythmia, NOS 427.9 _____
Asthma, Bronchial 493.90 _____
Bronchitis, acute 466.0 _____
Chest Pain 786.50 _____
Conjunctivitis,acute 372.00 _____
Constipation 564.00 _____
COPD 496   _____

Procedures

EKG 93000 _____
Sigmoid.45330 _____
Spirometry 94010 _____
TB   86580 _____
Cerumen 69210 _____
I & D   10060 _____
  Complicated 10061 _____
Skin tags (15).11200 _____
  add. (10)   11201 _____
Others

_____

LABORATORY

Venipuncture	36415	_____
CBC	85022	_____
Chem 5	80006	_____
Chem 24	80019	_____
Glucose	82947	_____
Hematocrit	85014	_____
Platelet Count	85590	_____
Potassium	84132	_____
Prothrombin	85610	_____
Stool Occult	82270	_____
Urinalysis	81000	_____

_____
_____

Prolonged Services F-T-F
First Hour   99354 _____
Each add. 30 min 99355 _____

Prolonged Service NF-T-F
First Hour   99358 _____
Each add. 30 min 99359 _____

Dermatitis, contact 692.9 _____
Diabetes, ID 250.0_   _____
Diabetes, NID 250.0_   _____
Dirrhea, non-infectious 558.9 _____
Diverticulitis 562.11   _____
Ear pain 388.70 _____
Edema 782.3 _____
Emphysema 492.8 _____
Epididymitis, non-ven. 604.90 _____
Family History DiabetesV18.0 _____
Fever, unknown origin780.6 _____
G.I. Bleeding, unspecified578.9 _____
Gastritis, acute 535.00 _____
Headache 784.0 _____
Hemorrhoids 455.6 _____
Hypertension, benign 401.1 _____
Impacted cerumen380.4 _____

Doctor's Signature

CPT Code	DX Code	Charge
_____	_____	_____
_____	_____	_____
_____	_____	_____
_____	_____	_____
_____	_____	_____

Total Charges _____
Amount Paid _____
Previous Balance _____
Balance Due _____

Date of Service _____

X-Ray
Chest (PA & L)   71020 _____
Forearm (AP & L).73090 _____
Wrist (AP & L).......73100 _____
Hand (2V)...............73120 _____
Finger (2V).............73140 _____

Other Services

_____
_____

Dates of Disability
From _____
To _____
Restrictions _____

Influenza, respiratory 487.1 _____
Laryngitis,acute 464.0 _____
Leg Varicosities.454.9 _____
Osteoarthritis,gen.715.09 _____
Osteoarthritis, knee 715.16 _____
Pharyngitis, acute 462 _____
Pneumonitis 486 _____
Premenstrual Tension 625.4 _____
Rash 782.1 _____
Rectal Bleeding 569.3 _____
Rheumatic Ht. Disease 398.90 _____
Tonsilitis, acute 463 _____
Tonsilitis, chronic 474.0 _____
U.R.I. 465.9 _____
U.T.I. 599.0 _____
Others _____

_____

FIGURE 2-5 Encounter form for matching.

patient has no credit card, a member of the office staff assumes the role of credit counselor and explains the financial policy of the practice. If the situation warrants, the patient should sign a truth-in-lending form. A *truth-in-lending form* is a formal agreement between the patient and the practice that is used if the patient owes an amount of money which will take more than four installments to pay. The credit counselor arranges a payment plan and helps the patient complete this form in compliance with the federal Truth in Lending Act. Tool 2-4 is a sample truth-in-lending form.

Posting and Billing

On the day of the encounter the person doing the billing and posting takes the office copy of the encounter form and posts the charges to the patient's account. If the practice has computerized billing, codes and charges may be scanned with a wand or scanning machine to enter data into the patient's account. Any payments made by the patient are credited to the account. If the patient belongs to a plan which pays on a fee for service basis, the claim is reported to the primary plan that day. All claims are reported as soon as possible. Although a heavy workload sometimes makes it impossible to report all claims on the day of service, reporting claims for encounters as they occur is the best way to achieve the steady cash flow that is vital to a successful practice.

The information needed for reporting encounters to almost all insurance and managed care plans, whether payment is made on a fee for service, capitation, or combination basis, is gathered according to the items listed on the HCFA 1500 form (Figure 2-6). The *HCFA 1500* items request information and data (codes) which can be filed on paper form or electronically. It provides a standard format for collecting and reporting all the necessary information needed by a plan to process a claim. HCFA stands for the Health Care Financing Administration of the federal government.

Monitoring Claims Reported to the Plan

Once a claim has been reported, the monitoring tasks begin. If the practice has not received a notice from the plan verifying the completion of the processing of a claim, the practice must monitor the status of outstanding claims until they have been processed by the insurance or managed care plan. At regular intervals, such as 30 days from the date of posting, again at 60 days, and then at 90 days, the practice takes action to expedite the claim during processing. The procedures for handling delinquent claims are explained in Chapter 12.

Once claims have been processed and it has been determined that benefits are payable, the plan will issue an *explanation of benefits (EOB)*, also known as remittance advice, to the practice for all patients who have assigned benefits to the doctor. Plans generally send the practice an EOB for

PLEASE
DO NOT
STAPLE
IN THIS
AREA

HEALTH INSURANCE CLAIM FORM

| | PICA | | | | | | | | PICA | | |

1. MEDICARE	MEDICAID	CHAMPUS	CHAMPVA	GROUP HEALTH PLAN	FECA BLK LUNG	OTHER	1a. INSURED'S I.D. NUMBER	(FOR PROGRAM IN ITEM 1)
(Medicare #)	(Medicaid #)	(Sponsor's SSN)	(VA File #)	(SSN or ID)	(SSN) X	(ID)	983475 SH	

2nd FOLD

2. PATIENT'S NAME (Last Name, First Name, Middle Initial)	3. PATIENT'S BIRTH DATE / SEX	4. INSURED'S NAME (Last Name, First Name, Middle Initial)
SHERMAN WILLIAM J	03 03 67 M F X	SHERMAN WILLIAM J

5. PATIENT'S ADDRESS (No., Street)	6. PATIENT RELATIONSHIP TO INSURED	7. INSURED'S ADDRESS (No., Street)
5262 MAIN STREET	Self X Spouse Child Other	5262 MAIN STREET

CITY	STATE	8. PATIENT STATUS	CITY	STATE
ANYTOWN	AM	Single X Married Other	ANYTOWN	AM

ZIP CODE	TELEPHONE (Include Area Code)		ZIP CODE	TELEPHONE (INCLUDE AREA CODE)
45000	(599) 000-0000	Employed X Full-Time Student Part-Time Student	45000	(599) 000-0000

9. OTHER INSURED'S NAME (Last Name, First Name, Middle Initial)	10. IS PATIENT'S CONDITION RELATED TO:	11. INSURED'S POLICY GROUP OR FECA NUMBER
		NONE

a. OTHER INSURED'S POLICY OR GROUP NUMBER	a. EMPLOYMENT? (CURRENT OR PREVIOUS) YES NO X	a. INSURED'S DATE OF BIRTH MM DD YY / SEX 03 03 67 M X F
b. OTHER INSURED'S DATE OF BIRTH MM DD YY SEX M F	b. AUTO ACCIDENT? PLACE (State) YES NO X	b. EMPLOYER'S NAME OR SCHOOL NAME ROAD TRUCKING
c. EMPLOYER'S NAME OR SCHOOL NAME	c. OTHER ACCIDENT? YES NO X	c. INSURANCE PLAN NAME OR PROGRAM NAME XYZ PLAN
d. INSURANCE PLAN NAME OR PROGRAM NAME	10d. RESERVED FOR LOCAL USE	d. IS THERE ANOTHER HEALTH BENEFIT PLAN? YES NO X If yes, return to and complete item 9 a-d.

READ BACK OF FORM BEFORE COMPLETING & SIGNING THIS FORM.

12. PATIENT'S OR AUTHORIZED PERSON'S SIGNATURE I authorize the release of any medical or other information necessary to process this claim. I also request payment of government benefits either to myself or to the party who accepts assignment below.

SIGNED SIGNATURE ON FILE   DATE 09-01-9X

13. INSURED'S OR AUTHORIZED PERSON'S SIGNATURE I authorize payment of medical benefits to the undersigned physician or supplier for services described below.

SIGNED SIGNATURE ON FILE

1st FOLD

14. DATE OF CURRENT: ILLNESS (First symptom) OR INJURY (Accident) OR PREGNANCY(LMP) MM DD YY 08 28 9X	15. IF PATIENT HAS HAD SAME OR SIMILAR ILLNESS. GIVE FIRST DATE MM DD YY 09 01 9X	16. DATES PATIENT UNABLE TO WORK IN CURRENT OCCUPATION FROM MM DD YY TO MM DD YY
17. NAME OF REFERRING PHYSICIAN OR OTHER SOURCE	17a. I.D. NUMBER OF REFERRING PHYSICIAN	18. HOSPITALIZATION DATES RELATED TO CURRENT SERVICES FROM MM DD YY TO MM DD YY
19. RESERVED FOR LOCAL USE		20. OUTSIDE LAB? YES NO $ CHARGES

21. DIAGNOSIS OR NATURE OF ILLNESS OR INJURY. (RELATE ITEMS 1,2,3 OR 4 TO ITEM 24E BY LINE)	22. MEDICAID RESUBMISSION CODE ORIGINAL REF. NO.
1. 729 5 3.	23. PRIOR AUTHORIZATION NUMBER
2. 4.	

24. A. DATE(S) OF SERVICE From To MM DD YY MM DD YY	B. Place of Service	C. Type of Service	D. PROCEDURES, SERVICES, OR SUPPLIES (Explain Unusual Circumstances) CPT/HCPCS MODIFIER	E. DIAGNOSIS CODE	F. $ CHARGES	G. DAYS OR UNITS	H. EPSDT Family Plan	I. EMG	J. COB	K. RESERVED FOR LOCAL USE
1	09 01 9X 09 01 9X	11	1	99203	1	75 00	1				
2	09 01 9X 09 01 9X	11	1	36415	1	5 00	1				
3											
4											
5											
6											

25. FEDERAL TAX I.D. NUMBER SSN EIN 310000978 X	26. PATIENT'S ACCOUNT NO. 736	27. ACCEPT ASSIGNMENT? (For govt. claims, see back) X YES NO	28. TOTAL CHARGE $ 80 00	29. AMOUNT PAID $ 10 00	30. BALANCE DUE $ 70 00

31. SIGNATURE OF PHYSICIAN OR SUPPLIER INCLUDING DEGREES OR CREDENTIALS (I certify that the statements on the reverse apply to this bill and are made a part thereof.) *Tracy Lewis, MD* SIGNED DATE 9/1/9X	32. NAME AND ADDRESS OF FACILITY WHERE SERVICES WERE RENDERED (If other than home or office)	33. PHYSICIAN'S, SUPPLIER'S BILLING NAME, ADDRESS, ZIP CODE & PHONE # TRACY LEWIS, M.D. 4915 MUIRWOODS COURT GREEN ASH, AM 45299 (593) 000-0000 PIN# 8974210 GRP#

(APPROVED BY AMA COUNCIL ON MEDICAL SERVICE 8/88)   **PLEASE PRINT OR TYPE**

APPROVED OMB-0938-0008 FORM HCFA-1500 (12-90). FORM RRB-1500.
APPROVED OMB-1215-0055 FORM OWCP-1500.   APPROVED OMB-0720-0001 (CHAMPUS)

ST11782 HCFA-1500 (1-PLY 12 90 OCR BC)

FIGURE 2-6 Health insurance claim form.

each reported claim which has been received and processed in their computer systems. The EOB is actually an explanation of how benefits were processed. Figure 2-7 shows a portion of a typical EOB.

EOBs contain amounts of money paid, paid under capitation, denied, or pending in process. The status of the claim is noted on the EOB, along with reason codes. *Reason codes* explain the actions of the plan. For example, if a claim is allowed at less than the billed rate, reason codes explain the justification for that action. Not all plans use the same set of notations for reason codes; most government and private plans create their own sets. There is no universal set of reason codes, although many medical office personnel wish there were. The plans try to be as specific as possible but sometimes are limited in the number of characters they can use for a reason code. In Figure 2-7, a reason code for Mary Jones is 160a, "The amount has been reduced by contractual agreement." Other reason code explanations are listed in the lower left quadrant of the form.

One EOB contains information about multiple claims for all claims processed within a plan's payment period. Multiple patient names may appear on one EOB for the practice. The EOB also may contain processing explanations for more than one physician in the practice. After the EOB has been received, individual payments are posted to each patient's account.

If the physician has a contract with the plan, writeoffs are deducted from the patient's account. In the example of Mary Jones, the write off amount for

ID number Patient's Name	Claim No.	Dates Of Service	Procedure Code	Provider Charges	Allowed Amount	Reason Codes	Enrollee Liability	Amt Paid	Benefit Code	Payment Type
I887642390784 Jones Mary	22695489562	03/04/9X	99213	40.00	31.60	160a	6.32	25.28	300	FFS
			36415	5.00	3.00	160a	0.00	3.00	300	FFS
							TOTAL	28.28		
I559782354967 Greer Betty	75922589752	03/25/9X	99211	20.00	0.00	720c	0.00	0.00	200	0
							TOTAL	0.00		
I652335908824 Smith Jerry	27752789546	03/12/9X	11300	50.00	0.00	150a	0.00	0.00	200	0
							TOTAL	0.00		
I55398654422 Jenkins Sam	22853447622	03/14/9X	99204	80.00	46.00	620b	5.00	0.00	100	CAP
			81000	10.00	5.00	620b	0.00	0.00	100	CAP
			93000	45.00	31.00	621b,160a	0.00	31.00	100	FFS
							TOTAL	31.00		
							TOTAL	59.28		

160a=The amount has been reduced by contractual agreement
720c=This is a duplicate service which has been paid
150a=Pending
620b=Included in capitation rate
621b=Excluded from capitation rate, paid FFS

FIGURE 2-7 Explanation of benefits (EOB).

code 99213 is $8.40, which is the difference between the provider charge and the allowed amount. This will close the account if Ms. Jones has paid the amount for which she is responsible at the time of service; this amount is $6.32, the enrollee liability. Typically, contracts between a doctor and a managed care plan state that the patient is responsible only for noncovered services, copayments, deductibles, and coinsurance amounts. In the figure Mary Jones has a liability of $6.32, which is a 20 percent coinsurance according to her benefit option. For Sam Jenkins's benefit option, he has a $5.00 flat co-payment fee for CPT code 99204. Both patients may ask the medical office to file a claim with a secondary insurance plan to recover any out-of-pocket costs.

EOBs are usually sent to a practice for capitated care. In addition to sending the practice a check for its capitated rate per patient per month, the plan explains how the noncapitated claims were processed. In Figure 2-7 the Sam Jenkins claim contains the reason code 621b, which explains which services were not paid under capitation but instead were paid on a fee for service basis. Reason code 620b explains that 99204 and 81000 are included in the capitation rate. If plans have multiple product options, such as an HMO, a PPO, and an indemnity benefit plan, all claim explanations can be put on one EOB. The tasks involved in posting from the EOB are similar regardless of the method of payment. Chapter 12 explains in detail how to handle EOBs.

The person who does the billing and posting totals the checks received by the plans and patient cash payments each day. A bank deposit should be made on every working day to improve cash flow.

REPORTING HOSPITAL CHARGES

Many services performed by physicians are not performed in the office but in other locations, such as a hospital, a nursing home, or a patient's home. No matter where a service has been performed, the same administrative procedures for information gathering and reporting must be followed.

When a patient has been admitted to a hospital, the practice is responsible for making sure that correct and complete information is gathered. To get the address, phone number, procedures, diagnoses, and insurance plan information for the patient, office staff must gather information from the hospital or doctor on paper copy or pick up the information from the hospital. Some hospitals fax this information to the practice. Others arrange for the practice to directly access that hospital databank by modem. Waiting for a patient to be discharged before reporting a claim often delays processing and payment. Timely arrival of information allows hospital services to be reported within several days after they have been provided. It is routine for hospitals to fax operative reports which can be used by the practice to code procedures from these reports as long as they arrive promptly at the practice and do not delay the submission of a claim.

For information regarding other specific services provided, the office staff must rely on data from the doctor or other personnel associated with the practice who accompany the doctor at the hospital. Several options exist for communicating this daily hospital information.

■ Written notations on hospital rounds cards beside the patient's name

■ Dictation of a note describing the services provided to each patient for each day

■ Completion of an encounter form.

The best option is the one which works best for the doctor and the office staff as long as the information is reported promptly and accurately. All information which is coded and reported must be documented in the hospital medical record. Tool 2-5 shows one option: a hospital encounter form listing the most common hospital procedures and their CPT codes.

EXERCISING KNOWLEDGE

1. Name the stations in the office for collecting information and data in the physician payment process.

2. The plan which pays first is the _____ .

3. The formal process of registration begins _____ .

4. Registration forms should be updated at least _____ per year.

5. Preauthorization requirements are generally found on the _____ .

6. Insurance and managed care plans want the _____ matched to the procedures.

7. The universal claim form is titled _____ .

Define These Terms or Abbreviations

8. encounter

9. encounter form

10. claim

11. EOB

12. referral

Applying Concepts

Use Figure 2-1 to answer the following questions about the critical pathway of a claim.

13. What is contained in a welcome packet?

14. What are the two reasons for obtaining patient signatures on the registration form?

15. Why does a medical practice make a photocopy of the plan ID card?

Use the EOB in Figure 2-7 to answer these questions.

16. Why were the doctor's charges not paid in full according to the allowed amount for Mary Jones? What will be done when posting these payments?

17. Is CPT code 81000 a capitated service?

18. Was the doctor already paid for code 81000 for this patient?

Use the encounter form in Figure 2-5 to fill in the code number for the following descriptions.

Procedure Codes

19. Level 2 office visit for a new patient _____

20. Level 2 office visit for an established patient _____

21. DPT immunization _____

22. EKG _____

23. Urinalysis _____

Diagnostic Codes

24. Abscess, ear _____

25. Chest pain _____

26. Edema _____

27. Headache _____

28. Impacted cerumen _____

Use Tool 2-5 to provide the code number for the following descriptions.

CPT Codes

29. Proctosigmoidoscopy _____

30. Needle bx., Liver _____

31. Hospital Discharge _____

32. Tube Thoracostomy _____

33. Colectomy with proctectomy & ileostomy _____

Use Tool 2-2 to answer the following question:

34. What are the three requirements for maintaining an account in good standing?

▼ TOOL 2-1
PRACTICE BROCHURE BOOKLET

WELCOME TO OUR PRACTICE

Medical Healing Arts Practice
4915 Muirwoods Lane
Green Ash, America 45299
Telephone: (595) 000-1230

Welcome to the Office of Medical Healing Arts Practice. Our health team is dedicated to providing you and your family with the best possible medical treatment.

Our medical staff is composed of two physicians, a receptionist, two medical transcriptionists, an administrative medical assistant, and two clinical medical assistants.

Please take a few minutes to read this brochure about our practice. It explains how we provide high-quality, comprehensive medical care 24 hours a day, 7 days a week. If you have additional questions or concerns, please feel free to ask us at any time. With your understanding, improved health care is a goal we can all achieve.

Physicians
Dr. Daniel Jones is a graduate of the University of Ohio School of Medicine. He completed his residency program at the University Hospital in Atlanta, Georgia. Then he completed a Fellowship in Internal Medicine and became Chairman of the Intensive Care Department at the University Hospital. He maintains active on the staff at The Georgetown Hospital and St. Anthony's Medical Center.

Dr. Tracy Lewis is a graduate of Jefferson Medical School in Philadelphia and completed his residency training at The Children's Hospital in Atlanta, Georgia. He maintains active staff privileges at the same hospitals as Dr. Jones.

Appointments
The office is open from 9:00 A.M. to 6:00 P.M. Monday through Friday. On Saturday it is open from 9:30 A.M. to 1:00 P.M. Patients are seen by appointment. This enables us to work as efficiently as possible. We will try to honor your appointment, for we value your time and want to avoid long waiting periods. Please understand that medical emergencies may occasionally cause delays and in these instances we ask for your consideration.

To schedule an appointment call 000-1230. The receptionist will ask a few routine questions before scheduling an appointment. If you are in pain or acute discomfort, please tell us at once and an examination will be scheduled as soon as possible.

Cancellations
If you cannot keep an appointment, we ask that at least 24 hours' notice be given to the office. This

▼ **TOOL 2-1 (CONTINUED)**

makes it possible to give that time to another patient who desires to be seen.

Registration

Please try to complete the PATIENT REGISTRATION form prior to your first visit to the office or you will be asked to fill out a registration form then. It is important the information you provide be accurate since we will rely on this data as you make future visits. Whenever there is a change of address, telephone number, or insurance coverage, please tell us.

Telephone/Prescriptions

We welcome telephone calls concerning medication or health concerns. However, it is not possible to practice good medicine consistently over the telephone without the benefit of patient observation and examination. When calling, PLEASE BE SPECIFIC. It is important to give the receptionist necessary information regarding your medical problem. If the problem is not an emergency, the call will be brought to the doctor's attention as soon as he or she is free. Routine calls will be returned at the end of the day. If you are calling to renew a prescription, it is important to do so during office hours when medical records are available. Calculate in advance when you need a refill on medicines. Please have the telephone number of the pharmacy as well as the prescription number.

Emergencies

In an emergency, call anytime. The physicians can be reached by calling the office telephone number (593) 000-1230.

Charges and Billing

An itemized statement covering your medical services will be mailed every 30 days. The administrative medical assistant will gladly answer any questions you may have about your statement. All accounts with a balance due will receive a monthly statement until the account is paid in full. A statement of Financial Policy outlining when other payments are due is included with this brochure.

Insurance

Dr. Jones and Dr. Lewis are participating physicians with Carechoice, The HMO, GHI, and Medicare as well as other private plans. If you are uncertain if we participate with your plan(s), please ask us.

It is the sincere goal of Dr. Jones, Dr. Lewis, and the staff of Medical Healing Arts to offer the best and most complete medical health care. We hope this brochure has been informative but most importantly, it has made you feel welcome at the office of Medical Healing Arts Practice.

▼ TOOL 2-2
FINANCIAL POLICY

Medical Healing Arts Practice
4915 Muirwoods Lane
Green Ash, America 45299
(593) 000-1230

FINANCIAL POLICY

It is our sincere desire to provide the best possible medical care. This involves mutual understanding between the patients, doctors, and staff. We encourage, you, our patient, to discuss any questions you may have regarding our payment policy.

Payment is expected at the time of your visit for services not covered by your insurance plan. We accept cash, check, MasterCard, and Visa.

Credit will be extended as necessary.

Credit Policy

Requirements for maintaining your account in good standing are:

1. All charges are due and payable within 30 days of the first billing.

2. For services not covered by your insurance plan, payment in advance is necessary.

3. If other circumstances warrant an extended payment plan our credit counselor will assist you in these special circumstances at your request.

We welcome early discussion of financial problems. Our credit counselor will assist you.

An itemized statement of all medical services will be mailed to you every 30 days. We will prepare and file your claim forms to the insurance plan. If further information is needed, we will provide an additional report. However, if more than two copies of the same service are requested, there will be an additional charge.

Insurance

Unless we have a contract directly with the insurance plan, we cannot accept the responsibility of negotiating claims. You, the patient, are responsible for payment of medical care regardless of the status of the medical claim. In situations where a claim is pending or when treatment will be over an extended period of time, we will recommend that a payment plan be initiated. Your insurance plan is a contract between you and your insurance company. We cannot guarantee the payment of your claim. If your insurance company pays only a portion of the bill or denies the claim, any contact or explanation should be made to you, their policy holder. Reduction or rejection of your claim by your insurance company does not relieve the financial obligation you have incurred.

▼ **TOOL 2-3**
INSURANCE WORKSHEET

This is _(your name)_ of Medical Healing Arts Practice, and I would like your help in verifying benefits for a patient being seen in this office.

Account Number _____

Patient Name _____

Enrollee Name _____

    ID Number _____

    Benefit Code _____

    Group Number _____

    Employer _____

Primary Plan (#1) _____	Secondary Plan (#2) _____
Address _____	Address _____
_____	_____
Phone Number _____	Phone Number _____
Contact Name _____	Contact Name _____
Date _____	Date _____

1) What is this patient's copayment amount? _____

2) Does this patient have a deductible amount? _____

3) Has the deductible been met for this year? No _____ Yes _____ Amt. _____

4) What is the coverage regarding office visits?_____

5) What is the coverage regarding surgery? _____

▼ **TOOL 2-4**
TRUTH-IN-LENDING STATEMENT

Medical Healing Arts Practice
4915 Muirwoods Lane
Green Ash, America 45299
(593) 000-1230

Truth-in-Lending Statement

Patient Name _____

Address _____

Telphone Number _____

Total Fee   _____

Less Initial Payment   _____

Balance of Fee (Unpaid Portion)   _____

Amount to Be Financed   _____

FINANCE CHARGE   NONE_____
ANNUAL PERCENTAGE RATE   NONE_____

Total Payments   _____

Patient hereby agrees to pay Medical Healing Arts Practice and (physician's name at the address above) the total of payments shown above in
_____ monthly installments of $_____ , first installment
due and payable _____ , 199X, and all such install-
ments on the same day of each consecutive month until the charges are
paid in full.

_____   _____
(date)   (signature of patient)

▼ TOOL 2-5
HOSPITAL ENCOUNTER FORM

HOSPITAL ENCOUNTER FORM

Name _____ Date _____ Hospital _____

Diagnosis: 1. _____ 2. _____ 3. _____ 4. _____

1. Hospital visits

DATE	SERVICE	CPT	FEE
	Init. Hosp.Care-Level 1	99221	
	Init. Hosp.Care- 2	99222	
	Init. Hosp.Care- 3	99223	
	F/U Hosp.Care- Level 1	99231	
	F/U Hosp.Care- Level 2	99232	
	F/u Hosp.Care- Level 3	99233	
	Hospital Discharge	99238	
	Init Hosp.Consult 1	99251	
	Init. Hosp.Consult 2	99252	
	Init. Hosp.Consult 3	99253	
	Init. Hosp.Consult 4	99254	
	Init. Hosp.Consult 5	99255	
	F/U Hosp.Consult 1	99261	
	F/U Hosp.Consult 2	99262	
	F/U Hosp.Consult 3	99263	
	ER consult(no admit)	99241	
	ER consult "	99242	
	ER consult "	99243	
	ER consult "	99244	
	ER consult "	99245	
	ER visit (estab. patient)	99281	
	ER visit no admit	99282	
	ER visit "	99283	
	ER visit "	99284	
	ER visit "	99285	
	Observation Status 1	99218	
	Observation Status 2	99219	
	Observation Status 3	99220	
	Observation Discharge	99217	
	Critical Care 30-74 min.	99291	
	Critical Care Ea. Add'l 15	99292	
	Prolonged Care 30-74 m.	99356	
	Prolonged C. Ea.Add'l 15	99357	

2. SURGERY

SERVICE	CPT
I&D Abscess- 10 FUD	10060*
Exc. Pilonidal Cyst Compl.	11772
Aspiration Breast cyst 0	19000*
Bx. Breast,needle core 0	19100
Bx. Breast, incisional 10	19101
Exc.Br.tumor,one or more	19120
Exc.Br. ", by marker, one	19125
Exc. Br. ", " Each add'l	19126
Mastectomy/gynecomastia	19140
" Compl-Simple-uni	19180
" ", Bil.	-50
" ", Mod Radical	19240
Preop needle wire 0	19290
" ",each add'l	19291
Tracheostomy, planned	31600*
Thoracentesis	32000*
Tube Thoracostomy	32020
Subclavian Cath	32491
Portacath,insert	36530
Portacath,removal	36532
Esophagogastric (Nissen)	43324
Partial Gastrectomy I	43631
Partial Gastrectomy II	43632
Vagotomy w 43631 or 32	43635
Vagotomy & Pyloroplasty	43640
Gastrostomy Temp.	43830
Gastrostomy Permanent	43832
Enterolyisis	44005
Enterotomy decompress.	44021
Enterectomy w anastom.	44120
Enterorrhaphy	44602
Colectomy-part. w anast.	44140
" ", skn level Cecostomy or Colostomy	44141
Colectomy Hartmann	44143
" ,Resect. w colostomy or Ileostomy&mucofistula	44144
Colectomy w. low pelv.anas.	44145
" " w Colostomy	44146
" ", Total w ileostomy w/o Proctectomy	44150
Colectomy w.proctectomy & Ileostomy	44155
Colectomy, rem.term Ileum & Ileocolostomy	44160
Enterostomy	44300
Colostomy	44320
Appendectomy, open	44950
Appendectomy, ruptured	44960
Append for a purpose	44955
Proctosigmoidoscopy	45300
" w dilation	45303
" w biopsies (s)	45305
" w removal FB	45307
" w rem.tumor hot bx.	45308
" w rem. snare	45309
"rem.multip. tumors	45315
"control bldg.	45317
" Ablation of tumor(s)	45320
" decompression of Volv.	45321
Sigmoidoscopy, flex., dx.	45330
" w bx.,single or multiple	45331
" rem. FB	45332
" rem. tumor(s) by hot bx.	45333
" w control of bleeding	45334
" w decompress volvulus	45337
" w remo. tumor(s) snare	45338
" w ablation tumor(s)	45339
Hemorrhoidectomy-Simple	
" Complex	46260
Anoscopy , dx.	46600
Needle Bx., Liver	47000
Liver bx. for a purpose	47001
Wedge bx. liver	47100
Choledochotomy w explor w/o cholecystotomy	47420
Cholecystectomy	47600
" w grams	47605
' w explor com. duct	47610
Choledochoscopy	47550
Whipple	48150
Pancreatectomy, total	48155
Laparotomy, explor	49000
Init. ing. hernia repair	49505
" bilateral	-50
Init. ing. "incar./strang.	49507
Rec. ing. hern. reducible	49520
" incar. or strangulated	49521
" Sliding	49525

CHAPTER 3

Common Operations and Terminology

CHAPTER OVERVIEW

Although internal operating policies vary among plans, certain external operations do not. All plans operating as a third party in the healthcare business enroll and attempt to provide cost-effective insurance coverage for consumers. All insurance plans issue identification cards which identify a benefit package to which the enrollees are entitled. When plans receive claims to pay benefits, they process the claims in accordance with the benefit package of the enrollee. This chapter introduces some operations and terminology common to insurance and managed care plans and discusses the mechanisms plans use to monitor and control healthcare costs and the quality of care. After reading the material in this chapter, doing the exercises, and using the end-of-chapter tools, you will be able to:

■ *Define terms used by most plans, such as "open enrollment," "effective date," "waiting period," and "preauthorization"*
■ *Identify the components of patient enrollment that are most relevant to successful claims processing, such as the proper use of a patient's plan identification card*
■ *Distinguish between the methods of physician payment used by plans*
■ *Describe the monitoring mechanisms, including computerized methods, used by plans to screen and deny claims that have coding errors or do not contain complete information*

ENROLLMENT

All types of medical insurance plans, including government and privately operated plans, offer benefits during open enrollment. *Open enrollment* is a specified period during which an individual can select an insurance or managed care plan. An enrollment form is completed by the individual and sent for processing. After enrolling, the enrollee cannot change this selection until another open enrollment period. The government or private plan selected by the patient becomes the insurer. The *insurer* is the insurance or managed care plan which has agreed to accept the risk of underwriting medical benefits for a cost—the *premium*—that is used to fund the medical benefits package. Premiums are usually paid by the insured in full or in part to maintain benefits. Some employers pay all of the premium for their employees. In some government plans, such as Medicaid, no premium is paid by the enrollee; instead, the benefit package is funded by the government. In a sense, the government pays the premium for each enrollee.

An individual who selects and enrolls in a plan is the insured. An *insured,* also known as a *policyholder,* is a person who was eligible to enroll on behalf of himself or herself and any dependents. An individual covered under the benefit package is an *enrollee.* Depending on the plan, policyholders may be known as subscribers, recipients, members, or beneficiaries. The terms used by specific plans are listed in Chapters 8, 9, and 10.

A *dependent* of the enrollee is a spouse, child, or person other than the policyholder who is eligible to be covered under the benefit package of the insured. In this manner, the policyholder has *family coverage,* which includes medical benefits for an individual and one or more dependents. What is covered is outlined in a policy which is usually given to the insured. If a written document is not provided, plans make benefit package information available before, during, or after enrollment. A *policy* outlines covered and noncovered benefits and any requirements of the insured and his or her dependents for obtaining care. A policy is a contract between the patient and the insurance mechanism. A policy is also called a certificate of coverage.

A policy begins on an *effective date,* which is the date when medical benefits begin for those carried by the plan. Before the benefits become effective, there is a waiting period. A *waiting period* is the length of time a policyholder and/or his or her dependents must wait between the time when they enroll, including the application processing period, until the time when benefits are effective.

Enrollees in a plan receive an *identification card* (*ID card*), a wallet-sized card issued by the plan that identifies the patient as a person who is insured by the plan. One card and one identification number may be issued to the insured and used by all the dependents under the policy. Managed care plans usually issue cards for each member of the family with the ID number of the enrollee and a suffix for each dependent. ID cards should be issued before the benefits are effective; thus, if a patient who does not have a new ID card with an effective date visits a physician, the practice must call the plan to verify enrollment before care is provided and to make certain that it is safe to send a claim to the new plan.

Benefit codes may appear on ID cards. *Benefit codes* identify the set of benefits for which the enrollee is eligible. Benefit codes are also known as plan or group numbers. A *benefit* is the amount payable by a plan, as stated in the policy, toward the cost of a medical service. Common covered benefits include inpatient hospital care, emergency room visits, outpatient surgical procedures, and physician services. No plan covers all services. Noncovered benefits are called exclusions. An *exclusion* is a medical service which is not payable by the plan because the service is not a benefit that is outlined in the policy. Common exclusions include work-related injuries covered by workers' compensation, fees for cosmetic surgery, personal convenience items, and services that are not medically necessary. The definition of medical necessity is given later in this chapter.

Another exclusion that is part of the package offered by private plans is the preexisting condition. Preexisting condition exclusions are commonly seen in policies sold to individuals who are not members of a group purchasing arrangement. A *preexisting condition (PEC)* is one which has been diagnosed and treated before the effective date. A plan will not cover preexisting conditions until the enrollee waits for a period of time, such as 60 or 90 days, during which no treatment is given for this condition. For example, a recently enrolled patient with active cancer who must see a doctor will not be covered for the cancer. Because of PEC, the sickest patients should not enroll in these plans. Often, however, they do not have a choice. The patient is billed for all services that are not covered because of an exclusion in the policy. There has been talk of eliminating PEC exclusions in healthcare reform legislation.

CLAIMS PROCESSING

When plans receive claims from physicians, they process or adjudicate claims in accordance with the benefit package of the enrollee. *Adjudication* is the operational process carried out by a plan from receipt of the claim through completion of the explanation of benefits (EOBs). If the claim is not properly completed, it will be denied. An EOB notifies the practice and/or enrollee of the status of a claim that is in the process of adjudication or of how the claim was adjudicated. Plans cannot adjudicate a claim unless the claim is clean. A *clean claim* is a claim that has been properly completed in accordance with the insurance or managed care plan's rules. A plan's definition of a clean claim can be obtained from plan representatives. Some representatives provide physician administrative manuals (Tool 3-1) and newsletters with specific instructions (Tool 3-2). Others make it clear that a properly filled out HCFA 1500 is sufficient. The proper completion of an HCFA 1500 is addressed in Chapter 6.

Even when a plan has followed all the rules for reporting, filing, and submitting a claim, the claim will not be adjudicated if it is received by a plan after the cutoff date. The *cutoff date* is a period of time, beginning with the actual date of service, after which a claim will not be paid. For example, insurance plans typically adjudicate claims for up to 1 year beyond the date of service, while some managed care plans deny a claim that is received beyond 60 or 90 days after the date of service.

When a plan adjudicates a claim, any cost-sharing arrangements in which the insured is responsible for paying are noted on the EOB. *Cost sharing* is an arrangement between the insured and the insurer that is outlined in the policy and allows patients to share the payments of medical services with the insurer. Cost-sharing arrangements are commonly used by plans to deter enrollees from using benefits unwisely. Plans believe that patients will not abuse benefits if they must pay some of the costs. Examples are copayments, deductibles, coinsurance, and annual limits, which are out-of-pocket costs for enrollees. *Out-of-pocket costs* are any payments made by the enrollee directly to the provider for services under a cost-sharing arrangement with the plan. *Copayments* are dollar amounts which the enrollee must pay toward certain services, such as office visits, mental health visits, and hospitalizations. Examples of amounts collected by medical offices at the time of service are $10 for an office visit and $20 for a mental health visit. Copayments for hospitalizations usually begin at $100 for patients. *Deductibles* are fixed dollar amounts which the enrollee must pay for covered services at the beginning of each calendar year, before medical benefits begin. Typical deductible amounts range from $100 to $1000. Excluded services do not count toward the payment of a deductible. Each January medical offices increase their efforts to collect out-of-pocket costs for patients with deductibles. When patients receive services from many physicians, they often do not know if the deductible has been met. In the months of January, February, and March the billing of patients with deductibles may be unavoidable.

Coinsurance is another term meaning "cost sharing" and is based on percentages or a ratio of allowed services. The enrollee must also pay coinsurance amounts directly to the provider. *Annual limits* are set for certain services. After the limits have been exceeded, the enrollee must pay for further services. Examples of typical limits are 20 outpatient mental health visits per calendar year and 30 physical therapy sessions a year. Coinsurance and annual limits may have dollar amount limits for out-of-pocket payments. Examples are $1500 per individual and $3000 per family policy per calendar year. After dollar amount limits have been exceeded by the enrollee, the plan pays for all the covered benefits. To learn when annual limits have been met, a medical office must continue to report claims and use the EOB as the only reliable source of this information.

The first plan to which a practice sends a claim is the primary insurer. The *primary insurer* is the plan which pays first when patients have more than one policy. The *secondary insurer* is the plan which pays after the primary insurance has paid. A copy of the EOB from the primary plan is sent with a claim to the secondary insurance plan. Secondary insurers may pay for copayments, deductibles, or other cost-sharing arrangements of the primary insurer. To make certain primary and secondary insurers do not overpay claims, all plans attempt to coordinate benefits with one another. *Coordination of benefits (COB)* involves the coordination of operations between two or more plans to assure that no plan issues payment for benefits in excess of 100 percent of a provider's services. If overpayments occur, the office staff should return excess amounts to the plan which issued the secondary payment. The extra payment should not be sent to the patient. Table 3-1 identifies the primary insurer in COB situations.

TABLE 3-1

Table of Primary Insurers in COB

The Primary Insurer Is	Examples
1. The plan in the patient's name unless the patient is retired and covered under the policy of an active employee	1. Mary has her own policy from the company and is retired. She is also covered under her husband, John's, policy, and John is actively working. John's plan is primary.
2. The plan in effect the longest when patients have multiple policies in their names	2. Jim has been enrolled in the XYZ plan for 10 years and in the QRX plan for 2 years. The XYZ plan is primary.
3. The plan without a COB clause in its policy	3. The QRX plan has no COB clause in its policy, but the XYZ plan does. The QRX plan is primary.
4. The plan of the custodial parent where there are divorced parents whose policies both carry the children	4. Mary and John are divorced. Both of their policies carry Tommy. Mary has custody, and her plan is primary.
5. The plan which covers the parent whose birthday falls first in a calendar year in situations where there are married parents whose policies both carry the children	5. When Mary and John were married, both policies carried Tommy. John's birthday is in January, and Mary's is in March. John's plan was primary before their divorce.

One aspect of COB involves subrogation. *Subrogation* is a process that is coordinated between plans. The plan which first receives a claim which has the potential to be the liability of another insurance company pends the claim and adds a reason code to the EOB. A patient's potential subrogation case usually results from an accident or an external cause. An example of potential subrogation is an individual falling and sustaining injuries at a neighbor's home. The plan may investigate the possibility of having the neighbor's homeowner insurance company pay the claim in full or in part. The office staff will see reason codes explaining that the claim has been suspended for subrogation and may be asked to resubmit claims to another insurance company.

MEDICAL RESOURCE MONITORING

Reviewing where, when, how, and by whom healthcare dollars are spent is the function of medical resource monitoring. Medical resource monitoring mechanisms invented by managed care plans have been adopted in whole or in part by government and private plans. As was emphasized in Chapters 1 and 2, physicians are expected to follow certain rules to obtain payment from insurance and managed care plans. Common operational rules allow plans to monitor medical services consistently. All plans have an obligation to monitor medical resources on behalf of the enrollees and other funders. Employers and the government demand responsible cost containment efforts from these plans, and funders question the plans as well as monitor their management capabilities. Some plans are stricter than others in regard to the scope and discipline of their rules for physicians. Rules "with teeth" are written in formal contracts between the physician and the plan; a physician that does not comply with written rules is in breach of contract.

Tool 3-3 can be used by medical office staff to record information that is pertinent to all the plans with which the practice has dealings. This form also may be used as a central sheet for organizing and complying with any unusual claims-filing requirements to get a claim processed the first time it is reported. Resubmitting claims creates extra work for the office staff if the claims are not reported accurately and correctly the first time.

Tracking a practice's compliance with the rules of a plan is one of the purposes of medical resource monitoring. Others are achieving cost containment, establishing standards of quality, and managing catastrophic care. When a plan adopts a medical resource monitoring mechanism, it resembles a managed care plan. Examples of areas in which monitoring mechanisms are likely to be used include preauthorization; proper use of CPT codes; the amount of reimbursement allowed; and quality control.

Preauthorization

Preauthorization, also known as precertification, preadmission certification, and prior authorization, refers to the requirement to notify a plan of certain planned services, and certainly all elective inpatient hospitalizations, before they occur. Depending on the plan, either the patient or the provider must seek preauthorization for these services. Without required preauthorization, the plan will not pay the full benefits.

Medical office personnel must keep abreast of which services require preauthorization. Plans may notify physicians of changes in preauthorization requirements by letter, contract amendment, newsletter, or revision of the physician administrative manual.

Another requirement of the preauthorization process may be to obtain a second opinion. A _second opinion_ is the requirement that the patient obtain the opinion of an impartial physician regarding the necessity of a planned procedure before the procedure is performed. The plan will not authorize the planned procedure for the attending physician unless the second opinion has been received.

When a plan's preauthorization agent authorizes a service, an _authorization number_ is given. The issuance of an authorization number does not guarantee payment for the physician's service. The patient must be a valid enrollee of the plan at the time of service, and the service must be _medically necessary_ under the plan's definition. A service is deemed medically necessary if it meets the following criteria:

1. It is appropriate for the diagnosis being reported.
2. It is provided in the appropriate location.
3. It is not provided for the patient's convenience or the convenience of the family.
4. It is not custodial care. (*Custodial care* is care that can be provided by people who are not trained medical professionals.)

A practice may have to include preauthorization numbers on claims that are to be adjudicated. If the doctor does not have a contract with a plan which requires preauthorization, the patient will not be reimbursed for the cost of the service. Practices can help patients avoid the potential hardship of paying noncontracted physicians by assuming the responsibility for preauthorization. Certainly the practice is better equipped than the patient to field questions asked by the authorizing agent that involve clinical knowledge. For example, if a procedure is usually performed in an outpatient facility, authorization will not be given for the same procedure performed in an inpatient facility unless the practice provides specific clinical reasons.

The office staff person doing preauthorization should have at least the following information on hand:

- Patient's name, identification number, and chart
- Physician name and provider number
- Planned procedure and planned date
- Planned place of service
- Diagnosis or symptoms
- History of current illness and results of diagnostic tests
- Physical findings

Depending on the plan, preauthorization can be performed by phone, fax, or mail. Tool 3-4 is a preauthorization form that can be used to document the preauthorization procedure. The date, time, and authorizing agent's name should be documented on the form in case the plan loses its records and tries to deny the claim. The form can also be copied for faxing and mailing. All plans cover services mentioned in the policy if those services are medically necessary. Plans with preauthorization, however, will not cover the service if preauthorization is not obtained even if the procedure is medically necessary.

Physician-Plan Contracts

When a physician contracts with a plan, that physician is a *participating physician* with the plan and must follow the rules outlined in the contract. Contracts give the plan control over the physician as part of the process of medical resource monitoring. If there is no contract, the physician is a *nonparticipating physician*.

At the discretion of each plan, participating physicians are issued provider identification numbers which must be placed on the claims they report to that plan. A *provider identification number* identifies for the plan the physician who provided the services.

Monitoring Claims: Computerized Checks

Plans check claims for the correct use of codes and to determine when benefits are covered. Today an increasing number of managed care plans are using computerized checks to catch claims to deny. One program, called here Edit-Audit (not its real name), screens claims for errors in 34 basic categories. Hypothetical examples from some of these categories follow.

Example 1

A claim is submitted with procedure codes 38760 for inguinofemoral lymphadenectomy ($908) and 56630 for vulvectomy, radical, partial ($2143).

Edit-Audit converts these codes to 56631, radical vulvectomy with femoral lymphadenectomy ($2566).

The savings to the plan is $485.

The error made by the practice submitting the claim is called *code fragmenting* or *unbundling.* Under the rules of the plan, only the bundled procedure, in which both services are covered by the same code, is allowable.

Example 2

A practice submits a claim with the code 56630 for vulvectomy, radical, partial, together with a diagnosis of 221.2 for benign neoplasm of the vulva.

Edit-Audit disallows the CPT code, suggesting a code number change to 56620 for vulvectomy, simple, partial, and throws the claim into the "denied pending further information" category.

The error identified by the program here is called *upcoding,* or using a code for a more complex procedure or greater service than is justified by the diagnosis. Edit-Audit has *downcoded* to a less expensive procedure.

Example 3

A practice submits a claim using the code 99385 for evaluation of a healthy individual age 18 to 39 years. Edit-Audit disallows the claim because 99385 is allowed under the rules only once every 3 years and the patient for whom the claim has been submitted had the same evaluation only 2 years earlier.

Example 4

A claim with code 74710 for pelvimetry with or without placental localization is submitted for a male patient. Edit-Audit disallows the claim because 74710 is a female procedure and cannot be performed on a male patient.

Another type of edit screens claims by the primary diagnosis to check the frequency of CPT codes submitted in a rolling month, quarter, or 12-

TABLE 3-2

Diagnosis Edit 250

Diabetes Mellitus and Related Conditions

CPT Code*	Description	Month	Quarter	Year
		Times Done per		
99201–99205	Office visit, initial			1/History
99211–99213	Office visit, established	2	2	6
99214 or 99215	Office visit, established			1
	Total established office visits	2	2	6
99221–99223	Hospital, initial			1/Admit
99231–99233	Per hospital days authorized			No. days
99238	Hospital discharge			1/Discharge

*CPT codes, descriptions, and two-digit numeric modifiers only are copyright 1993 American Medical Associaiton. All rights reserved.
Source: Model Treatment Program developed by Donald C. Harrington, M.D.

month period. A claim can be automatically denied, and the practice will have to file an appeal proving the medical necessity of the procedure. At times, claims are placed in a pending category and the reason code may read, "Submit a copy of the medical record for this date of service." Diagnosis edit 250 in Table 3-2 shows the diagnosis of diabetes mellitus and other related conditions by ICD-9-CM code. The first column lists CPT codes. The second column contains the narrative description of the code number. The last three columns show the rolling frequencies from the date of service per month, per quarter, and per year.

Monitoring Physician Costs

As was stated in Chapter 1, plans use different methods to pay physicians, including fee for service and capitation. In addition, plans use different ways to calculate the maximum amount they will allow for a given service. Since the basis for reporting a service on an insurance claim is the CPT code for that service, most methods of physician payment relate payment amounts to CPT codes.

Maximum Allowable Fee

Under a fee for service method of payment, it is extremely important for a practice to be aware of the different methods for calculating maximum allowable fees. Most plans establish a *maximum allowable fee* (MAF) for each service. When the practice submits a claim, payment for a CPT code–identified service is equal to either the billed charge or the MAF, whichever is lower. The MAF is also known as the *allowed fee* or *allowed amount*.

For example, if a practice reports a dilatation and curettage (D&C procedure, CPT code 58120), charging $550, and the plan's MAF is $500, the doctor will be paid $500. If the doctor has a contract with the plan to accept the allowed fee, the remaining $50 is credited to the patient's account. Under the terms of such contracts, patients cannot be billed for the difference between the doctor's charge and the MAF. Such credits are called *writeoffs*. If the physician does not have a contract with the plan, the patient can be billed for the difference.

Usual, Customary, and Reasonable   Plans that pay on a fee for service basis may use the *usual, customary, and reasonable (UCR)* method of calculating reimbursement. When a plan uses this method, it looks at the fees billed historically by physicians and bases the payment for a procedure on what other physicians have charged. With UCR, payment can be extremely low for a rarely performed but highly complex procedure because the plan has no history of billed charges from other physicians on which to base its payment. Plans are moving toward replacing the UCR method with the relative value unit to determine MAFs.

Relative Value Unit   The relative value unit (RVU) method of determining physician payment assigns an RVU number for each type of physician service that has a CPT code. The RVU numbers are called units of physician services and are mathematically related to one another under a system of weighting in which the skill, time, and other work of the physician doing the service are taken into account. The higher the RVU number, the greater the skill and time required to perform the service. To calculate the MAF for an individual CPT code, the RVUs must be multiplied by a dollar amount called the conversion factor (the payment per RVU), which is arbitrarily set by the plan according to its budget for physician services:

Maximum allowable fee (MAF) = RVU x conversion factor

For example, if CPT code 58120 is valued by an insurance or managed care plan at 4 units and the plan's conversion factor is $100, the plan will pay the doctor up to $400 for the procedure. When a plan wants to raise or lower an allowed fee, it simply modifies the conversion factor.

Table 3-3 is an excerpt from McGraw-Hill's *Relative Values for Physicians,* 1993, a system currently used by many medical practices to calculate their charges for each CPT code. When one uses McGraw-Hill's RVU method, up to six different conversion factors are necessary, depending on the type of CPT code.

To read the table, locate 58120 in the CPT column. Next, locate 4.0 in the units column. Notice the codes below it, which are "relatives" of 58120. Note the higher unit assignments to the codes below this code. In the table, 58140, which is more complex and involves more skill and time than does 58120, is assigned 12 RVUs.

TABLE 3-3
Relative Value Unit Table

CPT Code	Description of Services	Units	FUD	Anesthesiology Units
58120	Dilation and curettage, diagnostic and/or therapeutic (nonobstetric)	4.0	0	3
58140	Myomectomy, excision of fibroid tumor or uterus, single or multiple (separate procedure); abdominal approach	12.0	45	6
58145	Vaginal approach	9.0	45	4
58150	Total abdominal hysterectomy (corpus and cervix), with or without removal of tube(s), with or without removal of ovary(s)	17.0	45	6
58152	With colpo-urethrocystopexy (Marshall-Marchetti-Krantz type)	23.0	45	6
58200	Total abdominal hysterectomy, including partial vaginectomy, with para-aortic and pelvic lymph node sampling, with or without removal to tube(s), with or without removal of ovary(s)	20.0	120	6

Source: Relative Value Studies, Inc., *Relative Values for Physicians, 1994/1994,* New York, McGraw-Hill Healthcare Management Group, 1995, p. 295.

The fourth column, "FUD," lists the follow-up days. Follow-up days are a specific number of days after a procedure during which the payment includes routine follow-up encounters (visits) with the doctor. For example, 58120 has an FUD of 0, which means that the practice could bill the plan for all follow-up visits, no matter how soon they occurred after the initial procedure was performed. FUD can also include visits before and during the procedure, depending on the plan's rules. The fifth column lists the RVUs used to determine payment to anesthesiologists involved in the case who use the same procedure code number as did the attending surgeon. Note code 58140, below code 58120. This has a 45-day FUD. A follow-up visit could not be charged until the forty-sixth day after the surgery date.

Resource Based Relative Value Scale (RBRVS) Another method for determining fee for service physician payment, the RBRVS system, was put in place in 1992 by the Health Care Financing Administration as the method for determining physician payment for Medicare patients. It is now being used by many other plans in place of traditional methods. In this system, the unit value for a CPT code is calculated by the assignment of three separate unit values for (1) physician work, (2) practice expense, and (3) malpractice expenses. Table 3-4 shows representative RVUs for some gynecologic procedures; the table is an excerpt from the *Federal Register,* which is the source for RBRVS values pertaining to each year. These values change each calendar year. Refer back to Tool 1-1 for ordering information.

Find code 58120 in the table. The work RVU is 2.48, the practice expense RVU is 2.73, the malpractice RVU is 0.57, and the total of the three units is 5.78. The global period column in the table, like the FUD column in Table 3-3, refers to payment for services related to the main coded service. Global periods in an RBRVS include payments for preoperative, intraoperative, and postoperative care. In the system, 000 means zero, 010 means 10 days, and 090 means 90 days. The global period value column for 58120 is 010. This is different from the RVU method in Table 3-3. In Table 3-3, the FUD value is not 10 but 0. This means that plans using McGraw-Hill's *Relative Values for Physicians* would be billed for any follow-up office visits. Under the RBRVS system, Medicare would deny a claim for a visit during the first 10 postoperative days but would pay for a visit on postoperative day 11. Inconsistencies in postoperative visit payment rules used by the plans cause confusion in billing for care associated with surgical procedures. Most practices are establishing policies for when to bill for postoperative services. Many practices are adopting the rules of RBRVS.

When Medicare uses RBRVS, it takes into consideration the costs of practicing medicine in different geographic locations. After all, an urban practice in New York has higher practice costs than does a rural practice in Kentucky and should be compensated differently. (Other plans using RBRVS may or may not consider geographic costs.) Chapter 8 deals with the calculation of payments using Medicare's RBRVS system, including geographic costs.

TABLE 3-4

RBRVS Values

HCPCS[1]	MOD	Status	Description	Work RVUs	Practice expense RVUs[2]	Mal-practice RVUs	Total	Global period	Update
58100	....	A	Biopsy of uterus lining	0.72	0.67	0.14	1.53	000	S
58120	....	A	Dilation and curettage (d&c)	2.48	2.73	0.57	5.78	010	S
58140	....	A	Removal of uterus lesion	7.69	8.42	1.73	17.84	090	S
58145	....	A	Removal of uterus lesion	7.44	8.33	1.56	17.33	090	S
58150	....	A	Total hysterectomy	13.14	9.68	2.10	24.92	090	S
58152	....	A	Total hysterectomy	14.26	12.12	2.62	29.00	090	S
58180	....	A	Partial hysterectomy	9.16	9.87	2.13	21.16	090	S
58200	....	A	Extensive hysterectomy	20.57	13.12	2.83	36.52	090	S

[1]All numeric CPT HCPCS Copyright 1994 American Medical Association.
[2]*Indicates reduction of Practice Expense RVUs as a result of OBRA 1993.
Source: *Federal Register,* Vol. 58, No 230. Thursday, December 2, 1993. Rules and Regulations.

Capitation

While there are variations in how plans pay capitation rates, the most common method involves a fixed amount paid per month for each person assigned to the practice in that month. It may include payment for hospital care, and it almost always includes services for the CPT codes commonly used in a doctor's office. Capitation rates usually include certain CPT codes and exclude others, which may be negotiated with the plan. A practice must know which CPT codes are excluded, because the practice can be paid separately for those services. Each plan's contract states which codes are either excluded or included in capitation, and these lists of code numbers are different for each plan. All services provided to capitation patients must be reported through claims to the plan. The plan uses these data to analyze actual physician services for quality of care studies and to adjust capitation rates in new contract years.

Utilization Management

Another technique used by plans to control costs is the process of utilization management. *Utilization management* refers to the monitoring of care to assure that only medically necessary benefits are paid. Utilization management monitors services prospectively with preauthorization, concurrently with on-site review of hospital charts, or retrospectively with the review of claims and software programs for physician profiling.

Physician Peer Review Profiling

Physician peer review profiling uses claims data to determine which physicians are high-cost for the specialty compared with their peers. When physicians are identified as high-cost and as using more medical resources than do their peers, the plan may investigate to obtain an explanation of the reasons for the high cost or may cancel the doctor's contract. An example of a peer review profile for Tracy Lewis, M.D., a family practitioner, is shown in Figure 3-1. Do not expect to understand this profile fully. It is shown to make medical practices aware of the detailed physician information plans can obtain from claims data. If plans use physician profiles as a starting point for investigations, the office staff may be involved in helping the doctor confirm or dispute the data. The office staff may provide assistance in preparing the practice for an audit by the plan. Audits are explained in Chapter 7.

Medical Directors and Case Managers

Medical directors are physicians who are responsible for monitoring the clinical care provided by the practicing physicians caring for the plan's enrollees. Any time a practice has a problem with a plan, instruct the doctor to phone

Profiling period 1-01-XX through 12-31-XX based on claims processed.	Doctor	Doctor's Rank	Specialty Average
Number of patients treated or seen	39	19	52
Total cost/patient treated	$294.00	10	$290.00
Average number encounters per patient	1.4	23	1.8
Average number procedures per patient	1.8	26	2.6
Average total cost of prescriptions per patient	$9.00	11	$8.00
Number of inpatient admissions per 100 patients treated	13.00	4	8.0
Average length of stay	1.6	8	1.4
Hospital cost per inpatient	$986.00	18	$1,107.00

Explanation of categories in the physician peer review profile:

Term	*Definition*
Rank	The lowest number reflects the highest rank; e.g., the physician within a specialty with the highest costs is number 1.
# Patients Treated or Seen	The number of patients who have received any type of medical service ordered or rendered by the physician.
Total Cost/Patient Treated	The cost per patient, including all services ordered by this physician, e.g., office visits, lab, x-ray, pharmacy, hospital outpatient or emergency room, and any inpatient hospital bills. Total costs for all patients are divided by the number of patients treated to determine the average cost per patient.
Average # Encounters/Patient	The number of visits patients have received; e.g., 15 patients had 45 visits or three encounters each (45 divided by 15 = 3).
Average # Procedures/Patient	Any procedure for which a claim has been processed with the physician's ID number (using the AMA's Current Procedural Terminology) divided by the number of patients.
Average Total Cost of Prescriptions/ Patient	The total costs of prescriptions written by the physician is divided by the number of patients who received them.
# of Inpatient Admissions per 100	The number of actual admissions by the physician extrapolated to 100 patients.
Average Length of Stay	The average number of days in the hospital. For example, if 10 patients were admitted, 40 hospital days were used for an average length of stay of 4 days (40 divided by 10 = 4).
Hospital Cost/Inpatient Admission	The average cost of a hospitalization under the physician as attending physician.

FIGURE 3-1   Example of a physician peer review profile. There are 31 physicians within family practice in this profile.

or write to the medical director of that plan. The medical director is a peer of the doctor, and they should be able to exchange clinical information.

Medical directors appoint peer review committees of practicing physicians to assist them. *Peer review* is a process in which physicians review the care provided by other physicians on a retrospective basis to identify abnormal practice patterns. The office staff may be asked to copy a patient chart for mailing to a peer review committee. Other ways in which the staff may be involved include telephoning during a concurrent review. For example, a plan may call for additional information from the doctor about a hospitalized patient who is expected to be discharged or who may be a good candidate for case management.

Case management is a process in which a plan's case manager intervenes in cases in which extraordinary costs are involved. One of the tasks of case managers, who work under medical directors, is to arrange alternatives for catastrophic care. Case managers are usually very helpful and have the authority to provide benefits that are not usually covered in the policy in the hopes of decreasing the costs of care. For example, a case manager can purchase physical therapy equipment for use in a patient's home rather than have the patient make daily trips to the outpatient department of a hospital. The case manager also coordinates discharge planning whenever a catastrophic patient is hospitalized. *Discharge planning* is the early planning and arranging of services to be provided in the patient's home or another setting. Discharge planning is also performed on patients who are not case-managed if the plan employs a nursing staff to perform concurrent review in the hospital.

Quality Improvement

The medical director is also responsible for quality improvement. *Quality improvement (QI)* is a process for monitoring the quality of care being provided to enrollees. Quality improvement assures that patients are not being underserved by giving them access to care and is used to monitor the clinical care in such a way that it is always being improved. The quality improvement committee (or another name adopted by the plan) is composed of peers and is responsible for adopting standards of care which serve as clinical guidelines for certain illnesses and procedures. Employees of plans involved with quality improvement and audits may ask the office staff to prepare patient records for a QI study. Documentation in the patient record will be measured against the standards of care adopted by the plan's QI committee. The committee reviews the QI studies. Some committees publish the results of quality of care studies in plan newsletters. When data are published, physicians will take corrective action to improve care for patients.

The medical resource monitoring mechanism of quality improvement has been and will always be present in healthcare delivery. Some experts say that healthcare reform and the advent of capitation will increase QI but will ease the burden of preauthorization and utilization management. The burden of monitoring care will then rest with the physician practice that accepts a risk contract under capitation. Plans will then work with practices to monitor quality of care.

EXERCISING KNOWLEDGE

Fill in the blanks with the term that fits the definition given.

1. The cost of medical benefits and payment by the insured to keep healthcare benefits effective _____

2. A wallet-sized card issued to the insured by the plan that identifies a patient as being insured by the plan _____

3. The amount payable by a plan as covered under the policy _____

4. Payments made by the enrollee directly to the provider for services under cost-sharing arrangements with the plan _____

5. Dollar amounts which enrollees must pay toward certain services _____

6. Fixed dollar amounts which the enrollee must pay for covered services before benefits begin _____

7. A percentage or ratio of covered services which the enrollee must pay _____

8. The plan which pays first _____

9. Primary and secondary insurance pay benefit amounts assuring that the claim is not overpaid _____

10. A physician who has a contract with the plan _____

Applying Concepts

Use Figure 3-1 to answer these questions.

11. Was the physician in the example of physician profiling at the specialty average for the row "Total cost/patient treated"?

12. Was the physician at the specialty average for the row "Hospital cost per inpatient"?

Refer to Tables 3-3 and 3-4 to answer these questions about unit values in determining physician payment.

13. What is the unit value of 58200 for the surgeon according to McGraw-Hill's Relative Values for Physicians?

14. If the conversion factor is $150.00, what is the maximum allowable fee for 58200?

15. What is the unit value of 58200 for the anesthesiologist?

16. What are the follow up days (FUD) for 58200?

17. What are the followup days (global period) for 58200 according to RBRVS?

18. What are the total number of units for 58200 according to RBRVS?

19. Does 58200 have the same total unit value on Table 3-3 (RVU) that it does on Table 3-4 (RBRVS)?

20. Will 58200 have the same MAF under RVS and RBRVS? Explain.

Using Tools 3-1 and 3-2   21. Describe XYZ's process of precertification.

22. Will XYZ permit a physician to bill for the examination of a specimen if the physician did not examine the specimen?

23. Will XYZ accept 90749 under special review?

▼ TOOL 3-1
XYZ PHYSICIAN ADMINISTRATIVE MANUAL

Subject: Preadmission certification

Preadmission certification (PAC) is a process of XYZ Health Plan or its designee which assures that elective hospitalizations and other services are medically necessary and are provided in the most cost-efficient setting. Since preadmission certification may determine that an inpatient stay is not required, the location of service may be changed. Physician payment for that treatment or service is contingent on the authorizing agent's recommendation as to the medical necessity of the service.

Admissions requiring preadmission certification:

- All elective hospital admissions for medical, surgical, or psychiatric treatment

Treatment is considered elective if the services provided can be postponed for at least 48 hours without causing the patient physical impairment, bodily injury, or death.

Admissions not requiring preadmission certification:

- Emergency admissions with the exception of emergency psychiatric admissions
- Maternity admissions

Services and procedures requiring certification:

- Elective hospital outpatient surgery
- Magnetic Resonance Imaging (MRI)
- Physical Therapy sessions after the first ten sessions

Obtaining Preadmission Certification:

ProReview Company has been contracted to conduct the preadmission process. It is the authorizing agent which will issue a PAC authorization number. This seven-digit number is to be placed in item 23 of an HCFA 1500 claim form or field XC on an electronic claim. The claim will not be paid without the PAC number. The PAC number does not guarantee payment if the patient is not a valid member of XYZ at the time of the service due to nonpayment of the premium.

Participating Physicians must request preadmission certification by placing a telephone call to ProReview Company at 1-800-101-0000. It is the member's responsibility to obtain PAC when under the care of a nonparticipating physician. No written requests or fax will be accepted. Calls should be placed at least 5 working days prior to the admission of an XYZ member.

Appeals of cases not authorized:

Providers may not bill members for unpaid charges resulting from failure to authorize an elective admission. Appeals must be directed to ProReview Company within 30 days from the date of the admission. If the company does not change its original determination, a second appeal can be made to the Medical Director of XYZ. The Medical Director will respond within 30 days of the date of receipt of this appeal, which shall be considered final and binding.

▼ TOOL 3-2
XYZ PROVIDER NEWSLETTER

Announcing PROVIDER LINE!

As a special service to physicians, hospitals, and other providers, we are implementing PROVIDER LINE with a voice response. This line will allow our provider quick access to the status of any claim filed into our system or member eligibility. Hours are from 8:30 a.m. to 7 p.m., Monday through Friday. Just dial 1-800-PRO-LINE. Then listen to the menu, input 1 for claim status and 2 for member eligibility. To access a voice response, input the seven-digit provider number and eleven-digit member ID number, member birthdate, date of service, and provider charge. Listen for the voice response.

New client accounts

XYZ's marketing department has been successful in enrolling these employer groups effective January 1.

Tom Jones Advertising—300 new members
S&L Manufacturing—582 new members
Ed Smith Body Shop—28 new members

Physicians must bill only for their own services

The claims-processing department has reported physicians who are billing for pathology services which were not interpreted by them. The pathologist who examined the specimen should bill for these services using CPT codes 88300–88309. Physicians who excise the specimen are not permitted to bill for these services if the specimen is sent to a pathologist outside the practice.

Coding procedure for unlisted immunizations

XYZ's claims-processing department will now accept CPT code 90749, unlisted immunization procedures for the administration of vaccine not listed in the CPT book. These claims will undergo special review for a determination if the benefit will be covered. When reporting an unlisted immunization procedure, list the generic name for the drug, dosage and amount administered in Box 24 D of the HCFA 1500 claim form. Electronic billers, use the free form field.

▼ **TOOL 3-3**
CLAIM REPORTING RULES BY PLAN

Name of Plan	Type of Plan	Contract Yes? No?	Provider Number PIN	Claims Rules	Cutoff Date	Authorization No. Needed on Claim? Yes? No?	Claim Status Phone #

Instructions for using Tool 3-3:

This form can be used for all major types of plans you work with, or the data can be entered in a specially designed computer program.

Title of Column	*Instruction*
Name and Type of Plan	List names of the most frequent plans you work with. Then list the type of plan, e.g., HMO, PPO, Medicare, Medicaid.
Contract?	List yes if there is a formal contract for each of your doctors, such as "Yes, all doctors in the practice" or "Yes, with the exception of Dr. (name of your doctor which does not have a contract)." List no if none of your doctors has a contract.
Provider Number	List any issued provider numbers for your doctors. List any group numbers assigned to each practice location by the plan. Write none if you have no PIN or use Tax ID No.
Claims Rules	Note any plan-specific rules. Note if they do not accept the HCFA 1500 format and then list plan's specific format. Note if the plan accepts electronic claims; note the specific electronic claim format.
Cutoff Date	List how many days from the date of service you have to submit a claim.
Authorization Number Needed on Claim	List yes if authorization number is to be sent on the claim. List no when no number is required on the claim.
Claim Status Phone Number	List the phone number to call for each plan to determine if the claim is still in process.

▼ TOOL 3-4
PREAUTHORIZATION FORM

Admission ( )   Outpatient procedure ( )

Patient Name _____   ID # _____

Address _____

City, State, ZIP Code _____

Plan Name _____

Phone Number _____   Fax Number _____

Attending Physician _____   Provider Number _____

Hospital/Facility _____   Procedure Date _____

Diagnosis/Symptoms _____

Planned Treatment/Procedures _____

Other Circumstances _____

Estimated Stay at Facility _____

Second Opinion ( ) Yes   ( ) No   If yes, obtained from Dr. _____

Authorized   ( ) Yes, Authorization Number _____

Authorizing Agent Name _____   Date _____

( ) No.   Reason for Denial _____

Preauthorization completed by _____

CHAPTER 4

Diagnosis Coding with ICD-9-CM

CHAPTER OVERVIEW

ICD-9-CM (International Classification of Diseases 9th Revision—Clinical Modification) is one of two coding systems used in the claims process; the other is the CPT (HCPCS) system. Most books cover the CPT (HCPCS) codes before explaining the ICD-9-CM system, perhaps because physicians often perform procedural services before making a diagnosis. However, there are two reasons for reversing that order: (1) The primary diagnosis used on an insurance claim form often governs the procedures that a plan will reimburse, and (2) ICD-9-CM, unlike CPT (HCPCS), has an internal logic that makes it an easier system to learn.

The ICD-9-CM numbers and letters that classify thousands of diagnoses and conditions make up a coding language recognized around the world. Using these codes correctly is essential for speedy claims processing, allowing diagnoses and conditions to be translated by the computers of insurance and managed care plans.

After reading the material in this chapter, doing the exercises, and using the end-of-chapter tools, you will be able to:

- *Explain the reporting of a patient diagnosis or condition with ICD-9-CM*
- *Use the Tabular List and Alphabetic Index skillfully*
- *Apply the correct coding conventions*
- *Code to the highest degree of specificity*

THE HISTORY OF DIAGNOSTIC CODING

The language of diagnostic coding began as ICD, an international coding system developed by the World Health Organization to classify diseases. Its primary purpose is to track disease incidence (morbidity) and death rates (mortality). The clinical version of the International Classification of Diseases, 9th revision, Clinical Modification (ICD-9-CM), was developed as an extension of the World Health Organization's ICD-9. It was adopted for use in the United States in 1979, when the need arose for a more specific coding system for morbidity and mortality. It was never intended for use in the reporting of claims for physician payment, but since it is the most complete classification system, it has been adopted by most third-party payers. ICD-9-CM is the principal coding system for the prospective payment of hospitals that is used by Medicare in determining diagnosis related groups. *Diagnosis related groups (DRGs)* are fixed reimbursement rates for hospital admissions up to certain lengths of confinement. The ICD-9 codes that hospitals report are grouped into over 400 payment rates. Medicare began using DRGs as the basis for reimbursing hospitals in 1983. The principal diagnosis code—the first code reported—triggers hospital reimbursement. Not only Medicare and Medicaid but also some managed care plans contract with hospitals for payment by DRGs. Medicare has studied the possibility of using DRGs as a basis for reimbursement to physicians.

THE LANGUAGE OF ICD-9-CM

ICD-9-CM consists of three volumes, but medical practices use only the Tabular List (volume 1) and the Alphabetic Index (volume 2). Volume 3 is used by hospitals to report procedures for DRG reimbursement. The coding language of ICD-9-CM has its own conventions. These conventions convey special coding directions and consist of abbreviations, punctuation, symbols, and other notations. Instructional notations, cross-references, and conventions direct the user to the correct code.

The ICD-9-CM system allows for detailed specificity in its descriptions. It contains 999 three-digit categories for diseases, injuries, symptoms, and manifestations. Some of the categories are further divided with fourth- and/or fifth-digit subcategories, primarily to add clinical detail. The fourth and/or fifth digits are separated from the first three digits by a period (.).

In addition to the 999 categories for diseases and injuries, two supplementary coding sections are part of the language. The supplementary sections begin with the letters V and E followed by up to four digits. The V codes describe a patient's health status. E codes note the external cause of an episode of illness or injury. E codes are not widely used by physician practices.

HOW ICD-9-CM IS USED

Thousands of government organizations and private companies throughout the world use ICD-9-CM. The following types of oganizations use ICD-9-CM codes from physician claim forms:

Government agencies
Hospitals
Physicians

Insurance and managed care plans
Marketers of healthcare products
Healthcare planners
Drug companies

These organizations use diagnostic code data in the following ways:

- To collect healthcare statistics throughout the world
  - Track the frequency and type of disease
  - Alert countries of pending disease
- To facilitate provider payment
  - Pay healthcare providers by DRG
  - Explain the medical necessity of a procedure
- To direct health planning efforts
  - Identify major health problems by city, region, or country
  - Focus on research projects involving major diseases
- To determine marketing plans
  - Identify illness and injury growth areas which need services
- To determine patient insurability and benefit determination
  - Eligibility for certain services
  - Ability to receive coverage from workers' compensation, automobile insurance, and life insurance
- To measure quality improvement
  - Monitor patient outcomes from a process of medical treatment
- To enable insurance and managed care plans to review utilization profiles
  - Identify practitioners whose services exceed the average for a diagnostic category

An example of how insurance and managed care plans use ICD-9 codes to review utilization is shown in Figure 4-1. This figure compares the total costs of fees charged per patient by physicians for the treatment of a diagnosis.

Physician $ claimed per patient   Average total costs = $360.00

Dr. A _____ $268.00

Dr. B _____ $359.00

Dr. C _____ $582.00

FIGURE 4-1 Costs of care for ICD-9-CM 480.0—pneumonia due to adenovirus.

Figure 4-1 profiles the costs of care for all physicians who have filed a claim with the primary diagnosis of code 480.0, pneumonia due to adenovirus, within a 1-year period. The average total costs for services on claims with 480.0 as the primary diagnosis was $360. As the figure indicates, Physicians A and B are within the average amount for claims paid per patient per year. Physician C is beyond the average cost line, and that doctor's practice patterns may be questioned. The plan's utilization and quality improvement personnel may conduct an on-site audit of patient medical records pertaining to this diagnosis. If the audit fails to reveal a reasonable explanation for the physician's pattern of care, the physician may be put on probation or fined. That physician and every physician in the practice may be excluded from that managed care program.

PREVENTING DENIAL OF CLAIMS

The main reason for using ICD-9-CM codes correctly is, of course, to ensure that claims processing is not delayed or denied. As was indicated in Chapter 3, plans are increasingly using computerized monitoring systems to catch coding errors on claims and deny services due to lack of medical necessity and exclusions in the policy.

Table 4-1 is also an example of a report used by a managed care plan that tabulated the amount of savings generated by its diagnoses edit programs, which were designed to catch claims with inappropriate diagnosis codes in specific areas. As you can see from the table, a large amount of money was involved. All the diagnoses were grouped by diagnosis codes into

TABLE 4-1

HMO Monthly Edit Analysis under Fee for Service
Claim Payment
Top 11 Edits Ranked by Number of Claims with Total Dollars

Edit	Services	Dollars
01 Chronic Lung	4,047	76,289
02 Acute URI	4,020	24,808
03 Acute Lung	4,011	39,827
04 Diabetes	3,498	31,856
05 Ear Inflam	3,227	77,481
06 Chronic Ent	2,246	40,327
07 Bowel Habits	1,574	27,783
08 Gynecologic	1,936	46,577
09 Pregnancy	1,350	64,258
10 Arthritis	974	47,435
11 Special Edit	820	46,860

edits numbered 01–11. The column titled "Services" lists the number of services denied. The column titled "Dollars" lists the amount of charges denied. Edits 01–10 primarily denied services by downcoding. Edit 11, special edit, was used by the plan as a catchall category. In this example, some of the $46,860 denied by the plan was for claims submitted with code V70.3, "driver's license examination." The plan excludes coverage of examinations for other than medical reasons, and the edit program denied all claims with V70.3 listed as the diagnosis.

ICD-9-CM AND MEDICARE

The Medicare Catastrophic Coverage Act of 1988 (Public Law 100-330) requires physicians and other health professionals to place ICD-9-CM codes on all claims submitted to Medicare. Medicare said that as of April 1, 1989, any claim for physician services submitted on behalf of Medicare beneficiaries had to include an ICD-9-CM diagnosis code or the claim would be denied. This requirement includes both electronic media claims and paper claims. Included also in the requirement is the use of the V codes, V01.0 through V82.9, but not the E codes. Medicare will accept up to four ICD-9-CM codes per claim. Coexisting conditions also may be reported.

Penalties for failure to use the ICD-9-CM codes range from payment denial, to civil monetary penalties (not to exceed $2000), to exclusion from the Medicare program. The requirement to use ICD-9-CM codes on claims reflects Medicare's increased interest in using coding data for utilization profiling. Medicare has also requested the installation of outpatient code editors (OCEs) during claim adjudication to assure coding to the highest degree of specificity (using fouth and fifth digits when listed).

SOME CODING BASICS

The purpose of coding is to convey a clear picture of the diagnostic statements that describe patients' conditions for an insurance or managed care plan and of what the medical office did in response to those conditions.

Sequencing Diagnosis Codes: Primary and Secondary Diagnoses

The primary diagnosis is listed first on a claim when one is reporting multiple diagnoses. The *primary diagnosis* is the condition for which the primary procedure was performed. It is the chief condition assessed during the encounter with the physician to justify the medical services provided. The *primary procedure* is the chief procedure provided during the encounter. It is usually the most expensive and extensive procedure.

To assure payment of services with the original claim submittal and to create accurate physician utilization profiles, all diagnoses for which the physician is providing treatment and all diagnoses which are not treated directly but affect the doctor's treatment or decision making should be coded and reported. There are also conditions that are chronic and coexist at the time of the encounter—comorbidities—which the doctor must take into consideration even when treating other illnesses. These comorbid conditions sometimes are chronic conditions which increase the physician's work when he or she is treating another illness. The same rationale holds true for a patient who has developed a complication during the course of treatment for an illness. The doctor's work will be increased, and the frequency of the patient's visits may increase. Diagnoses that relate to an earlier episode of care but have no current effect on the doctor's work in the treatment of a current illness or do not affect the doctor's decision making for the current illness are not reported. It is best to ask the physician when one has doubts about reporting another diagnosis and never report a condition which the physician has not documented in the medical record.

There are four spaces in a standard claim-reporting format in which to list up to four diagnoses. Here is an example of how those four spaces can be used in reporting comorbid conditions and complications:

1. Primary diagnosis of treatment   Pneumonia
2. Secondary diagnosis of treatment   Urinary tract infection
3. Comorbid condition   Emphysema
4. Complication   Resistance to penicillin

There are codes for all these conditions. If the patient has an acute condition and a comorbid chronic condition to code (just two diagnoses), list the acute condition first as the primary diagnosis.

Do not code symptoms if a diagnosis is established, such as convulsions with the diagnosis of epilepsy or abdominal pain with the diagnosis of ectopic pregnancy. It is expected that patients with these diagnoses will have convulsions with epilepsy and abdominal pain with ectopic pregnancies. There is no need to report them as a second, third, or fourth diagnosis.

Proper sequencing and reporting of codes are also important in justifying a particular type (level) of office visit. It would be difficult to justify the medical necessity of a Level 5 office visit (the highest level of payment) with the diagnosis of a common cold alone. Although the primary diagnosis and primary procedure are listed first, the remainder of the coding sequence must be reported in a manner that makes the relationship between diagnoses and procedures clear and indicates sound medical necessity.

Combination Codes

A *combination* code is a single code which classifies two diagnoses or manifestations as one code. A combination code can also classify a disease associated with a secondary disease. Often a combination code is found with descriptions which contain the words "due to," "in," "with," and "associated with." For example,

> Combination code 648.20 is pregnancy with pernicious anemia.
>
> Two code numbers are not required to convey pregnancy and pernicious anemia.

THE STRUCTURE OF ICD-9-CM

The three volumes of ICD-9-CM are:

Volume 1   Diseases: *Tabular List* (a numeric list from categories 001 to 999 and codes beginning with the letters V and E)
Volume 2   Diseases: *Alphabetic Index* (from A to Z)
Volume 3   Procedures: Tabular List and Alphabetic Index

The Organization of Diseases: Tabular List

The classification of diseases and injuries includes 17 chapters that cover groupings by types of disorders and diseases of body systems. Table 4-2 shows the overall organization of the official government edition (which has a red and white cover) of the 9th Revision, 4th edition, published by the U.S. Department of Health and Human Services.

Physician practices do not use the Appendices. If it is not published by the government, your version may not include all the appendices. Look over all 17 chapters. These chapters are used heavily by physician practices. Approximately half of them are devoted to conditions that affect a specific body system, and the remainder classify conditions according to disorder. For example, Chapter 8 addresses diseases of the respiratory system only, while Chapter 2 lists the disorder of neoplasms for all body systems. Practices often do not use the codes from Chapter 16, "Symptoms, Signs and Ill-Defined Conditions," erroneously believing that these codes will constitute grounds for claims rejection. In fact, most plans recognize the Chapter 16 category codes, 780–799, as acceptable codes for claims processing.

TABLE 4-2
ICD-9-CM Tabular List Chapter Organization

Chapter	Categories
1. Infectious and Parasitic Diseases	001–139
2. Neoplasms	140–239
3. Endocrine, Nutritional, and Metabolic Diseases and Immunity Disorders	240–279
4. Diseases of the Blood and Blood-Forming Organs	280–289
5. Mental Disorders	290–319
6. Diseases of the Nervous System and Sense Organs	320–389
7. Diseases of the Circulatory System	390–459
8. Diseases of the Respiratory System	460–519
9. Diseases of the Digestive System	520–579
10. Diseases of the Genitourinary System	580–629
11. Complications of Pregnancy, Childbirth, and the Puerperium	630–677
12. Diseases of the Skin and Subcutaneous Tissue	680–709
13. Diseases of the Musculoskeletal System and Connective Tissue	710–739
14. Congenital Anomalies	740–759
15. Certain Conditions Originating in the Perinatal Period	760–779
16. Symptoms, Signs, and Ill-Defined Conditions	780–799
17. Injury and Poisoning	800–999
Supplementary Classification	
Classification of Factors Influencing Health Status and Contact with Health Service	V01–V82
Classification of External Causes of Injury and Poisoning	E800–E999
Appendices	

A. Morphology of Neoplasms
B. Glossary of Mental Disorders
C. Classification of Drugs by American Hospital Formulary Service List Number and Their ICD-9-CM Equivalents
D. Classification of Industrial Accidents According to Agency
E. List of Three-Digit Categories

The Organization of Diseases: Alphabetic Index

The *Alphabetic Index* lists medical conditions alphabetically in three sections:

Section 1   Index to Diseases and Injuries. This section also contains special tables for indexing the codes for hypertension and neoplasms.

Section 2   Table of Drugs and Chemicals

Section 3   Index to External Causes of Injuries and Poisonings

Beginning the Search for a Code

Physician practices use the entire index. Codes (numeric and alphanumeric) follow the main term or subterm entry in the Alphabetic Index (volume 2) for reference to that code in the Tabular List (volume 1). Begin a code search according to the first letter of the patient's disease, condition, or symptom in the Alphabetic Index. The *main term* is the first word indexed and appears in boldface type. Next, drop to the next line. This is a subterm which describes different anatomic body sites, type of patient condition, or cause. *Subterms* are two typed spaces under the main term. The person searching for a code should make sure to note the number of spaces the subterms appear under the main term. It is often helpful to line up the columns of main terms and subterms with a ruler. All the subterms under a main term must be read to avoid missing the most appropriate code. If you are having difficulty finding the right code, don't give up. ICD-9-CM provides cross-references and suggestions to search under other main terms.

Using the Tabular List to Verify Codes

After a selection is made in the Alphabetic Index, take the first three digits from the index and look up those three digits in the Tabular List. Never end the code search in the Alphabetic Index: Code selections must be verified in the Tabular List. This list contains important coding conventions for choice of the correct code. *Coding conventions* are the directions for the ICD-9-CM coding system and must be addressed before you arrive at the final code selection. The Tabular List contains the choices for the final selection of fourth and fifth digits.

Every disease process, injury, and patient condition has been assigned a three-digit category. Some categories contain only three digits, some contain fourth digits, and others contain up to five digits. Fourth and fifth digits describe patient conditions more specifically, identifying the cause, type, location, or manifestation of a disease or injury. It is the responsibility of a medical practice to code to the *highest degree of specificity*. That means that the selection of fourth and fifth digits, when they are listed in the ICD-9-CM book, is required.

Basic Steps in ICD-9-CM Coding

Most medical practices use encounter forms that contain the most recent ICD-9-CM codes (see Figure 2-4). Others use software programs to call up the current codes when they want to use them for submitting a claim. When encounter forms and software programs are used, the person submitting the claim will not have to routinely refer to the ICD-9-CM book, but that does not excuse medical office personnel from understanding the basic steps for the correct use of the ICD-9-CM coding system. Encounter forms and computer software programs need to be updated each year, and there will always be a certain patient with an unusual condition or diagnosis which is not available on an encounter form or within a computer system. You will then refer to the book to obtain the code. Some physicians prefer to write the patient's *diagnostic statement* (medical terms describing patient diagnoses and conditions) on the encounter form for the person who will report the claim. If you work in an office in which this is routine, you will be using the book.

Step 1 From the diagnostic statement indicated by the physician, use the Alphabetic Index to look up the patient's diagnosis or condition by name. For example, if the doctor indicates diabetes mellitus without complication, start in the index with the word **Diabetes**. Figure 4-2 shows a page from the index to diseases for the main term **Diabetes**. Specific types of diabetes appear in parentheses after the words **Diabetes, diabetic**. You are looking for diabetes mellitus without complication. It is the first number, 250.0.

Step 2   Read all the indented subterms to make certain the index does not contain a better code to describe the patient's condition.

Step 3   While in the index, look for any helpful notes to prepare you for the choices you will have to make when you confirm the final code selection in the Tabular List. Helpful notes are not always present in the Alphabetic Index. However, in the case of diabetes mellitus, a note in a box informs users that category 250.0 requires a fifth digit (see Figure 4-2). Be prepared to make a choice of a fifth digit when you refer to the Tabular List.

Step 4   Refer to the Tabular List to make your final code selection. Some categories in ICD-9-CM end with fourth digits. If so, pick a fourth digit and stop there. Some categories in ICD-9-CM end with three digits. If so, stop at three digits.

Selecting and Using Fourth Digits

In Figure 4-2 you learned diabetes mellitus has been assigned to category 250 in the Tabular List. A fourth-digit category has been added to provide specificity to this diagnosis regarding types of manifestations. Manifestations are other conditions that are evident as a result of diabetes. Since a fourth digit is listed, one must be selected from the choices provided.

As the figure shows, there are nine choices for a fourth digit in the diabetes mellitus category:

250	Diabetes mellitus	
	250.0	Diabetes without mention of complication
	250.1	Diabetes with ketoacidosis
	250.2	Diabetes with hyperosmolarity
	250.3	Diabetes with other coma
	250.4	Diabetes with renal manifestations
	250.5	Diabetes with ophthalmic manifestations
	250.6	Diabetes with neurological manifestations
	250.7	Diabetes with peripheral circulatory disorders
	250.8	Diabetes with other specified manifestations
	250.9	Diabetes with unspecified complications

In many categories there are entries in the fourth or even the fifth digit position numbered .8 for "other specified" and .9 for "unspecified." These are called *residual subcategories*. In our example, .8 and .9 are residual subcategories in the fourth-digit position. It is best for the treating physician and office staff to avoid the selection of a .8 or .9, which are vague subcate-

♦ **Diabetes, diabetic** (brittle) (congenital) (familial) (mellitus) (severe) (slight) (without complication) 250.0

> *Note — Use the following fifth–digit subclassification with category 250:*
>
> 0 *type II [non–insulin dependent type] [NIDDM type] [adult–onset type] or unspecified type, not stated as uncontrolled*
>
> 1 *type I [insulin dependent type] [IDDM] [juvenile type], not stated as uncontrolled*
>
> 2 *type II [non–insulin dependent type] [NIDDM type] [adult–onset type] or unspecified type, uncontrolled*
>
> 3 *type I [insulin dependent type] [IDDM] [juvenile type], uncontrolled*

with
  coma (with ketoacidosis) 250.3
    hyperosmolar (nonketotic) 250.2
  complication NEC 250.9
    specified NEC 250.8
  gangrene 250.7 *[785.4]*
  hyperosmolarity 250.2
  ketosis, ketoacidosis 250.1
  specified manifestations NEC 250.8
acetonemia 250.1
acidosis 250.1
amyotrophy 250.6 *[358.1]*
angiopathy, peripheral 250.7 *[443.81]*
asymptomatic 790.2
autonomic neuropathy (peripheral) 250.6 *[337.1]*
bone change 250.8 *[731.8]*
bronze, bronzed 275.0
cataract 250.5 *[366.41]*
chemical 790.2
  complicating pregnancy, childbirth, or puerperium 648.8
coma (with ketoacidosis) 250.3
  hyperglycemic 250.3
  hyperosmolar (nonketotic) 250.2
  hypoglycemic 250.3
  insulin 250.3
complicating pregnancy, childbirth, or puerperium (maternal) 648.0
  affecting fetus or newborn 775.0
complication NEC 250.9
  specified NEC 250.8
dorsal sclerosis 250.6 *[340]*
dwarfism–obesity syndrome 258.1
gangrene 250.7 *[785.4]*
gestational 648.8
  complicating pregnancy, childbirth, or puerperium 648.8
glaucoma 240.5 *[365.44]*
glomerulosclerosis (intercapillary) 250.4 *[581.81]*
glycogenosis, secondary 250.8 *[259.8]*
hemochromatosis 275.0
hyperosmolar coma 250.2
hyperosmolarity 250.2
hypertension–nephrosis syndrome 250.4 *[581.81]*
hypoglycemia 250.8
hypoglycemic shock 250.8
insipidus 253.5
  nephrogenic 588.1

pituitary 253.5
  vasopressin–resistant 588.1
intercapillary glomerulosclerosis 250.4 *[581.81]*
iritis 250.5 *[364.42]*
ketosis, ketoacidosis 250.1
Kimmelstiel (–Wilson) disease or syndrome (intercapillary glomerulosclerosis) 250.4 *[581.81]*
Lancereaux's (diabetes mellitus with marked emaciation) 250.8 *[261]*
latent (chemical) 790.2
  complicating pregnancy, childbirth, or puerperium 648.8
lipoidosis 250.8 *[272.7]*
♦ macular edema 250.5 *[362.83]*
maternal
  with manifest disease in the infant 775.1
  affecting fetus or newborn 775.0
microaneurysms, retinal 250.5 *[362.01]*
mononeuropathy 250.6 *[355.9]*
neonatal, transient 775.1
nephropathy 250.4 *[583.81]*
nephrosis (syndrome) 250.4 *[581.81]*
neuralgia 250.6 *[357.2]*
neuritis 250.6 *[357.2]*
neurogenic arthropathy 250.6 *[713.5]*
neuropathy 250.6 *[357.2]*
nonclinical 790.2
peripheral autonomic neuropathy 250.6 *[337.1]*
phosphate 275.3
polyneuropathy 250.6 *[357.2]*
renal (true) 271.4
retinal
  edema 250.5
  hemorrhage 250.5 *[362.01]*
  microaneurysms 250.5 *[362.01]*
retinitis 250.5 *[362.01]*
retinopathy 250.5 *[362.01]*
  background 250.5 *[362.01]*
  proliferative 250.5 *[362.02]*
steroid induced
  correct substance properly administered 251.8
  overdose or wrong substance given or taken 962.0
stress 790.2
subclinical 790.2
subliminal 790.2
sugar 250.0
ulcer (skin) 250.8 *[707.9]*
  lower extremity 250.8 *[707.1]*
  specified site NEC 250.8 *[707.8]*
xanthoma 250.8 *[272.2]*
Diacyclothrombopathia 287.1
Diagnosis deferred 799.9
Dialysis (intermittent) (treatment)
  anterior retinal (juvenile) (with detachment) 361.04
  extracorporeal V56.0
  peritoneal V56.8
  renal V56.0
    status only V45.1
  specified type NEC V56.8
Diamond–Blackfan anemia or syndrome (congenital hypoplastic anemia) 284.0
Diamond–Gardener syndrome (autoerythrocyte sensitization) 287.2
Diaper rash 691.0
Diaphoresis (excessive) NEC 780.8

Diaphragm — *see* condition
Diaphragmalgia 786.52
Diaphragmitis 519.4
Diaphyseal aclasis 756.4
Diaphysitis 733.99
Diarrhea, diarrheal (acute) (autumn) (bilious) (bloody) (catarrhal) (choleraic) (chronic) (gravis) (green) (infantile) (lienteric) (noninfectious) (presumed noninfectious) (putrefactive) (secondary) (sporadic) (summer) (symptomatic) (thermic) 558.9
achlorhydric 536.0
allergic 558.9
amebic (*see also* Amebiasis) 006.9
  with abscess — *see* Abscess, amebic
  acute 006.0
  chronic 006.1
  nondysenteric 006.2
bacillary — *see* Dysentery, bacillary
bacterial NEC 008.5
balantidial 007.0
bile salt–induced 579.8
cachectic NEC 558.9
chilomastix 007.8
choleriformis 001.1
chronic 558.9
♦ ulcerative (*see also* Colitis, ulcerative) 556.9
coccidial 007.2
Cochin–China 579.1
  anguilluliasis 127.2
  psilosis 579.1
Dientamoeba 007.8
dietetic 558.9
due to
  achylia gastrica 536.8
  Aerobacter aerogenes 008.2
  Bacillus coli — *see* Enteritis, E. coli
  bacteria NEC 008.5
  bile salts 579.8
  Capillaria
    hepatica 128.8
    philippinensis 127.5
  Clostridium perfringens (C) (F) 008.46
  enterococci 008.49
  Enterobacter aerogenes 008.2
  Escherichia coli — *see* Enteritis, E. coli
  Giardia lamblia 007.1
  Heterophyes heterophyes 121.6
  irritating foods 558.9
  Metagonimus yokogawai 121.5
  Necator americanus 126.1
  Paracolobactrum arizonae 008.1
  Paracolon bacillus NEC 008.47
    Arizona 008.1
  Proteus (bacillus) (mirabilis) (Morganii) 008.3
  Pseudomonas aeruginosa 008.42
  S. japonicum 120.2
  specified organism NEC 008.8
    bacterial 008.49
    viral NEC 008.69
  Staphylococcus 008.41
  Streptococcus 008.49
    anaerobic 008.46
  Strongyloides stercoralis 127.2
  Trichuris trichiuria 127.3
  virus NEC (*see also* Enteritis, viral) 008.69
dysenteric 009.2
  due to specified organism NEC 008.8
dyspeptic 558.9
endemic 009.3
  due to specified organism NEC 008.8

FIGURE 4-2 Alphabetic Index for diabetes mellitus. (Context Software Systems, *ICD-9-CM 1995,* vols. 1 and 2, New York, McGraw-Hill Healthcare Management Group, 1995, p. 467.)

DISEASES OF OTHER ENDOCRINE GLANDS (250–259)

250 Diabetes mellitus

> Excludes: gestational diabetes (648.8)
> hyperglycemia NOS (790.6)
> neonatal diabetes mellitus (775.1)
> nonclinical diabetes (790.2)
> that complicating pregnancy, childbirth, or the puerperium (648.0)

The following fifth–digit subclassification is for use with category 250:

0 type II [non–insulin dependent type] [NIDDM type] [adult–onset type] or unspecified type, not stated as uncontrolled

1 type I [insulin dependent type] [IDDM] [juvenile type], not stated as uncontrolled

2 type II [non–insulin dependent type] [NIDDM type] [adult–onset type] or unspecified type, uncontrolled

3 type I [insulin dependent type] [IDDM] [juvenile type], uncontrolled

250.0 Diabetes mellitus without mention of complication
Diabetes mellitus without mention of complication or manifestation classifiable to 250.1–250.9
Diabetes (mellitus) NOS

250.1 Diabetes with ketoacidosis
Diabetic:
acidosis
ketosis } without mention of coma

250.2 Diabetes with hyperosmolarity
Hyperosmolar (nonketotic) coma

250.3 Diabetes with other coma
Diabetic coma (with ketoacidosis)
Diabetic hypoglycemic coma
Insulin coma NOS

> Excludes: diabetes with hyperosmolar coma (250.2)

☐ 250.4 Diabetes with renal manifestations
Use additional code, if desired, to identify manifestation, as:

diabetic:
nephropathy NOS (583.81)
nephrosis (581.81)
intercapillary glomerulosclerosis (581.81)
Kimmelstiel–Wilson syndrome (581.81)

250.5 Diabetes with ophthalmic manifestations
Use additional code, if desired, to identify manifestation, as:

diabetic:
blindness (369.00–369.9)
cataract (366.41)
glaucoma (365.44)
retinal edema (362.83)
retinopathy (362.01–362.02)

☐ 250.6 Diabetes with neurological manifestations
Use additional code, if desired, to identify manifestation, as:

diabetic:
amyotrophy (358.1)
mononeuropathy (354.0–355.9)
neurogenic arthropathy (713.5)
peripheral autonomic neuropathy (337.1)
polyneuropathy (357.2)

☐ 250.7 Diabetes with peripheral circulatory disorders
Use additional code, if desired, to identify manifestation, as:

diabetic:
gangrene (785.4)
peripheral angiopathy (443.81)

250.8 Diabetes with other specified manifestations
Diabetic hypoglycemia
Hypoglycemic shock

Use additional code, if desired, to identify manifestation, as:

diabetic bone changes (731.8)

Use additional E code, if desired, to identify cause, if drug-induced

> Excludes: intercurrent infections in diabetic patients

250.9 Diabetes with unspecified complication

251 Other disorders of pancreatic internal secretion

251.0 Hypoglycemic coma
Iatrogenic hyperinsulinism   Non-diabetic insulin coma

Use additional E code, if desired, to identify cause, if drug–induced

> Excludes: hypoglycemic coma in diabetes mellitus (250.3)

251.1 Other specified hypoglycemia
Hyperinsulinism:
NOS
ectopic
functional
Hyperplasia of pancreatic islet beta cells NOS

Use additional E code, if desired, to identify cause, if drug-induced

> Excludes: hypoglycemic coma (251.0)
> hypoglycemia in diabetes mellitus (250.8)
> hypoglycemia in infant of diabetic mother (775.0)
> neonatal hypoglycemia (775.6)

251.2 Hypoglycemia, unspecified
Hypoglycemia:
NOS
reactive
spontaneous

> Excludes: hypoglycemia:
> with coma (251.0)
> in diabetes mellitus (250.8)
> leucine–induced (270.3)

251.3 Postsurgical hypoinsulinemia
Hypoinsulinemia following complete or partial pancreatectomy
Postpancreatectomy hyperglycemia

251.4 Abnormality of secretion of glucagon
Hyperplasia of pancreatic islet alpha cells with glucagon excess

FIGURE 4-2 (CONTINUED) Tabular List for diabetes mellitus. (Context Software Systems, *ICD-9-CM 1995,* vols. 1 and 2, New York, McGraw-Hill Healthcare Management Group, 1995, pp. 48–49.)

Code ?

Orbit Films to

check for metal

before MRI study.

gories which do not accurately describe a patient's condition. If the physician or another person in the practice has used a code with .8 or .9 in the fourth-digit position, show that person the other choices of digits within the category and ask him or her if another digit might be more appropriate in this patient's case. In some cases it may be impossible to avoid the use of a .8 or .9, but it is important to be as accurate as possible in describing a patient's condition to an insurance or managed care plan to avoid claim denials.

Selecting and Using Fifth Digits

Fifth-digit subcategories were added when the need for further classification and greater specificity of clinical details became apparent. In Figure 4-2, look at the section beginning with the words: "The following fifth-digit subclassification is for use with category 250." The fifth-digit possibilities shown are 0, 1, 2, and 3, which specify the type of diabetes mellitus—type I or type II—and whether it is controlled or uncontrolled.

Clinical Example

Betty Jones is 87 years old and has insulin-dependent diabetes which has caused cataracts. The examining physician finds that her blood sugar is slightly elevated but indicates in the office progress note that this condition is under control. The existence of the diabetes-caused cataracts is also noted.

This is coded with a fourth digit of 5 and a fifth digit of 1. The correct code is 250.51. The fourth digit of 5 is selected because cataracts are located in the eye and .5 pertains to ophthalmic (eye) problems.

In the example, if the physician had not documented the cataract complication, the fourth digit of .0 would have been selected. If the physician had documented a manifestation that is not listed as one of the choices, .8 would have been selected because the manifestation of the patient was *not* one of the choices available in the Tabular List. The selection of the fourth digit of .9 is not recommended for use by the treating physician. "Unspecified" means that the doctor has not documented or specified enough information to select a more specific subcategory from the choices in the book.

The fifth digit of 1 is selected because Betty is an insulin-dependent diabetic and the doctor documented it as under control. Office staff cannot rely on laboratory test results to select this fifth digit. It is a physician's decision to call this condition uncontrolled.

It is the responsibility of the person inputting codes on the claim form to inform physicians when codes require greater specificity. It is also an office staff responsibility to inform doctors when code changes necessitate more clinical details from year to year. Some practices have a system of internal codes that can be used by physicians to convey specific details on encounter forms, for example, the letter *U* for "diabetes, uncontrolled." Failure to develop methods of communication about diagnostic specificity between the physician and the person reporting the claim results in a multitude of coding errors.

Other errors occur as a result of the false labeling of a patient with a particular diagnosis. An example is labeling the patient as an insulin-dependent diabetic because the patient required insulin a few times. Patients may occasionally require insulin on a temporary basis, but this does not indicate that a patient should be coded as an insulin-dependent diabetic. Often pregnant women become diabetic, requiring insulin only for the duration of the pregnancy. Once the baby is delivered, they no longer require it. Recall who uses the codes from the claims submitted. If a patient is labeled with a false diagnosis, a life insurance company may review the claim and determine an insurance rate that is much higher than it should be or may not insure the patient at all. Review the medical record carefully and code accordingly. When in doubt, ask the physician.

Finding Fifth-Digit Descriptions

Fifth-digit descriptions appear in four places in the Tabular List:

1. Within a four-digit subcategory. Fifth-digit descriptions are listed within a fourth-digit subcategory. For example, the code 380.12 refers to acute swimmers' ear and is listed that way.
2. At the beginning of a three-digit category. Again look at the section in Figure 4-2 beginning with the words, "The following fifth-digit subclassification is for use with category 250."
3. At the beginning of a section within a chapter. See Figure 4-3, which shows the beginning of the subsection "Complications of the Puerperium." The note lists the three-digit categories to which the fifth digits apply.

Brackets [ ] under three-digit categories list limitations on the selection of fifth-digit description numbers. In Figure 4-3, for example, immediately below the number 670 is [0,2,4]. This means that only descriptor numbers 0, 2, and 4 should be used as fifth digits for category 670.

Coding Tip
There is no fourth-digit selection with 670. The coding rule is to use a 0 for the fourth digit when there are no fourth-digit descriptions.

4. At the beginning of a chapter. When fifth-digit subclassification rules apply to more than one three-digit main category, they appear in complete form at the beginning of the chapter and are repeated in abbreviated form for each relevant main category. See, for example, the beginning of Chapter 13, "Diseases of the Musculoskeletal System and Connective Tissue."

Since fifth-digit requirements and descriptors are difficult to locate, most physician practices purchase books with a color-coded identifier for fifth digits. Color-coded books are sold by several medical publishers. The AMA

COMPLICATIONS OF THE PUERPERIUM (670–676)

Note: Categories 671 and 673–676 include the listed conditions even if they occur during pregnancy or childbirth.

The following fifth–digit subclassification is for use with categories 670–676 to denote the current episode of care:

  0 unspecified as to episode of care or not applicable

  1 delivered, with or without mention of antepartum condition

  2 delivered, with mention of postpartum complication

  3 antepartum condition or complication

  4 postpartum condition or complication

§ 670 Major puerperal infection ♀ MAT
[0,2,4]

Use 0 as fourth–digit for this category

Puerperal: Puerperal:
  endometritis   peritonitis
  fever   pyemia
  pelvic: salpingitis
    cellulitis   septicemia
  sepsis

Excludes: infection following abortion (639.0)
          minor genital tract infection following delivery
            (646.6)
          urinary tract infection following delivery (646.6)

§ 671 Venous complications in pregnancy and the puerperium

671.0 Varicose veins of legs ♀ MAT
[0–4]
  Varicose veins NOS

671.1 Varicose veins of vulva and perineum ♀ MAT
[0–4]

671.2 Superficial thrombophlebitis ♀ MAT
[0–4]
  Thrombophlebitis (superficial)

671.3 Deep phlebothrombosis, antepartum ♀ MAT
[0,1,3]
  Deep–vein thrombosis, antepartum

671.4 Deep phlebothrombosis, postpartum ♀ MAT
[0,2,4]
  Deep–vein thrombosis, postpartum
  Pelvic thrombophlebitis, postpartum
  Phlegmasia alba dolens (puerperal)

671.5 Other phlebitis and thrombosis ♀ MAT
[0–4]
  Cerebral venous thrombosis
  Thrombosis of intracranial venous sinus

671.8 Other venous complications ♀ MAT
[0–4]
  Hemorrhoids

671.9 Unspecified venous complication ♀ MAT
[0–4]
  Phlebitis NOS
  Thrombosis NOS

§ 672 Pyrexia of unknown origin during the puerperium ♀ MAT
[0,2,4]

Use 0 as fourth–digit for this category

  Puerperal pyrexia NOS

§ 673 Obstetrical pulmonary embolism

Includes: pulmonary emboli in pregnancy, childbirth, or the
          puerperium, or specified as puerperal

Excludes: embolism following abortion (639.6)

673.0 Obstetrical air embolism ♀ MAT
[0–4]

673.1 Amniotic fluid embolism ♀ MAT
[0–4]

673.2 Obstetrical blood–clot embolism ♀ MAT
[0–4]
  Puerperal pulmonary embolism NOS

673.3 Obstetrical pyemic and septic embolism ♀ MAT
[0–4]

673.8 Other pulmonary embolism ♀ MAT
[0–4]
  Fat embolism

§ 674 Other and unspecified complications of the puerperium, not elsewhere classified

674.0 Cerebrovascular disorders in the puerperium ♀ MAT
[0–4]
  Any condition classifiable to 430–434, 436–437 occurring
    during pregnancy, childbirth, or the puerperium, or
    specified as puerperal

Excludes: intracranial venous sinus thrombosis (671.5)

674.1 Disruption of cesarean wound ♀ MAT
[0,2,4]
  Dehiscence or disruption of uterine wound

674.2 Disruption of perineal wound ♀ MAT
[0,2,4]
  Breakdown of perineum   Secondary perineal tear
  Disruption of wound of:
    episiotomy
    perineal laceration

674.3 Other complications of obstetrical surgical
[0,2,4] wounds ♀ MAT

  Hematoma
  Hemorrhage   } of cesarean section or perineal wound
  Infection

Excludes: damage from instruments in delivery
          (664.0–665.9)

674.4 Placental polyp ♀ MAT
[0,2,4]

674.8 Other ♀ MAT
[0,2,4]
  Hepatorenal syndrome, following delivery
  Postpartum:
    cardiomyopathy
    subinvolution of uterus
    uterine hypertrophy

§ Requires fifth–digit; valid digits are in [brackets] under each code. See above for definitions.

FIGURE 4-3 Complications of the puerperium (670–676). (Context Software Systems, *ICD-9-CM 1995,* vols. 1 and 2, New York, McGraw-Hill Healthcare Management Group, 1995, p. 165.)

catalog mentioned in Chapter 1 has several of these books for sale. The official version of ICD-9-CM published by the government is not color-coded.

CONVENTIONS USED IN ICD-9-CM

The conventions used in ICD-9-CM include abbreviations, punctuation marks, symbols, and instructional notations. Certain conventions apply to only the Tabular List, while others appear only in the Alphabetic Index. Still other conventions are contained in both parts. Some of these conventions are essential in selecting the correct code number; others are helpful time-savers but have no bearing on the final selection of a code. Once office personnel read and understand the directions for ICD-9-CM, they can apply them to diagnosis coding for any medical specialty.

Tabular List Conventions

Includes and Excludes

Includes is used to indicate that the terms that follow the colon apply to the entire category and are always boxed. *Excludes* is used after entries when the terms that follow are *excluded* from the entire category and is always boxed. For example,

910	**Superficial injury of face, neck, and scalp except eye**	
Includes:	cheek	lip
	ear	nose
	gum	throat

Excludes:	*eye and adnexa (918.0–918.9)*

In this example, the "includes" list means that injuries to the cheek, lip, ear, nose, gum, and throat are included in category 910.

Note that even if a specific condition noted by a physician does not appear in the "includes" list, this does not mean that the assignment of that condition to the category is incorrect.

The "excludes" listing means that injuries to the eye and adnexa are not included in category 910. Excludes entries signify to the user that if the patient has an injury that is related to the excluded term, a different three-digit main code must be used. The correct code or range of codes is given in parentheses after the excluded term or terms.

Clinical Example

A patient has superficial injuries to the forehead and eyelid. Codes 910.0 and 918.0 are correct, and both must be used.

Use Additional Code If Desired

This direction is a suggestion to use an additional code if it is needed to paint a clearer picture of the severity of a patient's illness or condition.

Clinical Example

A patient is diagnosed with an atonic bladder; this patient is also afflicted with urge incontinence. Under the main listing 596, Other disorders of bladder, which includes 596.4, Atony of bladder, is found the entry "Use additional code, if desired, to identify urinary incontinence (625.6, 788.30–788.39)." After checking the suggested codes given in parentheses, use codes 596.4 for atony of bladder and 788.31 for urge incontinence.

Symbols

Square Brackets [ ]

Square brackets enclose synonyms, alternative wordings, abbreviations, and explanations. They often serve as guides to medical abbreviations. For example, in the entry

421.0   **Acute and subacute bacterial endocarditis**
          Endocarditis (acute) (chronic) (subacute):
             septic
             ulcerative
             vegetative
          Infective aneurysm
          Subacute bacterial endocarditis [SBE]

the square brackets enclosing [SBE] show that it is the abbreviation for subacute bacterial endocarditis.

Colon :

At least one or more of the words listed to the right of a colon must be present in the patient's condition and in the medical record to select that category. For example,

471.0   **Polyp of the nasal cavity**
          Polyp:
             choanal
             nasopharyngeal

The polyp must be choanal or nasopharyngeal or both for category 471 to be selected as the final code choice.

Brace }

A single brace serves a purpose similar to that of the colon, but braces enclose a series of phrases, not just one-word terms. For example,

743.1 Microphthalmos

Dysplasia

Hypoplasia   } of eye

Rudimentary eye

One or more words to the left of the brace must be associated with one or more phrases to the right of the brace and must be present in the patient for the code to be chosen. In code 743.1, the patient must have either dysplasia or hypoplasia of the eye.

Section Symbol §

Section symbols appear only in the official government version of ICD-9-CM. This symbol indicates a fifth-digit requirement for the code category when it is seen to the left of the code number or in a footnote. If the U.S. Department of Health and Human Services official publication for ICD-9-CM is not used, the section symbol is not usually seen. The example below shows the use of this symbol as it occurs in category 653.

§653 Disproportion

Lozenge □

The lozenge appears to the left of a four-digit code. This symbol is unique to the CM version of ICD-9 and indicates that the code did not appear in previous versions of ICD-9. The lozenge is helpful to researchers but has no significance in a physician practice and can therefore be ignored.

Alphabetic Index Conventions

Cross-reference terms are listed with the italicized words *see, see category,* or *see also.* For example,

Saint

Anthony's fire (*see also* Erysipelas) 035

Guy's dance—*see* Chorea

Conventions Used in Both the Tabular List and the Alphabetic Index

Notes

Notes give important tips about codes; they can clarify medical terminology and are a valuable source of medical education. Notes may be located in any number of locations and may or may not be introduced by the word "note." A note found in the Tabular List above code 860 is a good example. The note is not formally introduced with the word "note," but the definition given in the note is very important. It defines the words "with open wound" when they are seen in the fourth digit. In this instance, this phrase refers to wounds with an infection or a foreign body.

Notes in the Alphabetic Index are enclosed in boxes and printed in italic type. For example,

Injury
    internal
        multiple 869.0

> *Note—Multiple internal injuries of sites classifiable to the same three- or four-digit category should be classified to that category.*
>
> *Multiple injuries classifiable to different fourth-digit subdivisions of 861.—(heart and lung injuries) should be dealt with according to coding rules.*

Code Also Underlying Condition

When reporting conventions require that at least two diagnoses be reported, with one being the underlying condition, *double coding* is required. In the Tabular List, the need for double coding is indicated by putting the direction in italic type as follows:

484.3 Pneumonia in whooping cough
    Code also underlying disease (033.0–033.9)

In the Alphabetic Index, the need for double coding is indicated by slanted brackets enclosing an italicized code, as follows:

Amyloidosis
    pulmonary 277.3 *[517.8]*

Parentheses

One use of parentheses is to enclose supplementary words or explanatory information that may be either present or absent in the patient's condition without affecting the coding. For example, in the Alphabetic Index, the entry Salivation is followed by the parenthetic term "(excessive)," which means that salivation need not be excessive for code 527.7 to be selected and that this may be the final code choice after it has been checked for coding conventions found in the Tabular List. Terms in parentheses do not modify the selection and are officially called *nonessential modifiers*.

Another use of parentheses is to enclose explanatory information that adds to the understanding of medical descriptions in the Tabular List. The words in parentheses also give the medical name of the disease. For example,

Syndrome
    Dyke-Young (acquired macrocytic hemolytic anemia) 283.9

NEC and NOS

NEC stands for "not elsewhere classified." It is used to indicate that there is no separate code in ICD-9-CM for the condition even though the doctor has indicated a very specific condition.

Example

To code isorhythmic heart conduction disorder, use the index to find the main term **Disorder**— and the subterms

conduction, heart 426.9
    specified NEC 426.89

Category 426 classifies a number of disorders of the heart, but there is no fourth digit for a diagnosis of isorhythmic heart conduction disorder. For any of the heart conduction disorders not listed in ICD-9-CM, code 426.89, Other conduction disorder, is assigned. It is correct to select 426.89 because isorhythmic heart disorder is not elsewhere classified.

NEC cannot be used as a shortcut in coding to avoid looking up more specific codes. An example of the incorrect use of NEC appears in code 459.0 when it is used by a treating physician. This code cannot be reported by the physician, because the treating physician should specify the anatomic location of a hemorrhage. If the doctor does not specify the location of a hemorrhage on a claim, the office staff should send a note to the doctor to specify the location. For example,

459.0 Hemorrhage, unspecified
    Rupture of blood vessel NOS
    Spontaneous hemorrhage NEC

NOS stands for "not otherwise specified." In the example above, NOS is the equivalent of "unspecified." The doctor did not give enough information to select other code numbers. Codes with NOS should be avoided. Ask the doctor and other medical personnel to help you select a more specific code.

Other Conventions

Italic type is used for all exclusion notes and to identify situations in which double coding is required.

Eponyms, or proper names that appear as the titles for diseases and conditions, can appear as main terms in the Alphabetic Index and appear throughout the Tabular List. When eponyms are used, the medical name is also given. For example,

716.0 Kaschin-Beck disease
[0–9] Endemic polyarthritis

V CODES

V codes are a frequent source of confusion in medical offices because not all plans cover benefits for preventive medicine and "well" care. If the office personnel use them exclusively for patients who have no preventive medicine benefits, the claim is denied and the patient must pay. To avoid nonpayment, it is best to convey at least one diagnosis, injury, or symptom code with every V code. However, there are patients who have no condition to convey. They are well.

In the absence of disease, injury, or symptoms and when the primary intent of the patient's visit is to receive therapy or treatment, it is still necessary to match an ICD-9-CM code to a CPT code. V codes describe the reason for the patient's visit in these situations. Tool 4-1 can be used to begin the search for V codes.

There are three situations in which it is appropriate to use V codes:

1. When patients are not sick but receive services for a purpose, such as patients receiving vaccinations and those donating organs.
2. When patients with a current or recovering disease receive treatment. The sole purpose of the encounter in this case is to receive radiation, chemotherapy, or another therapeutic treatment. These patients could also be refitted for a medical device or recasted.
3. When patients have a past condition which influences the status of their current health, such as those with a personal or family history of a life-threatening disease and those with donated or artificial organs and other conditions.

When one is sequencing code numbers, situations 1 and 2 can be the primary diagnosis, but situation 3 is always a secondary diagnosis that enhances the purpose for the encounter.

The eight V-code categories and their alphanumeric number ranges are as follows.

Code Ranges	Description
V01–V09	Persons with potential health hazards related to communicable diseases
V10–V19	Persons with potential health hazards related to personal and family history
V20–V28	Persons encountering health services in circumstances related to reproduction and development
V30–V39	Liveborn infants according to type of birth
V40–V49	Persons with a condition influencing their health status
V50–V59	Persons encountering health services for specific procedures and aftercare
V60–V68	Persons encountering health services in other circumstances
V70–V82	Persons without reported diagnosis encountered during examination and investigation of individuals and population

Certain V codes are known as *status post codes;* these codes identify events that occurred in the past which influence current care. Status post categories include the following:

Personal history (V10–V15)   Aftercare (V51–V58)
Postoperative surgery (V42–V45)   Follow-up examination (V67)

Categories V10–V15 (history of) are reported when the previous condition can influence current care. A history of previously treated carcinoma may be important in establishing the medical necessity of performing certain tests or explaining why the patient was seen more frequently in follow-up examinations. In these situations, report the V code as the secondary diagnosis. When the condition mentioned is still present, when there is a complication of previous care, or when a new disease is found during the encounter, a code for the specific disease should be listed as the primary diagnosis and the V code should be listed as the secondary diagnosis.

Codes from categories V42–V45 classify past surgical events that may influence a patient's current health status, such as a patient's status after a kidney transplant (V42.0) when the patient has a life-threatening condition in the remaining kidney.

Categories V51–V58 are used to report the purpose of the encounter, either to coordinate treatment or to prevent recurrence in a patient previously treated for a disease no longer present. If the disease is still present, use the V code as a secondary diagnosis. The codes for aftercare management are used for planned care, such as fitting and adjustment of a prosthetic device, attention to an artificial opening, or removal of a fixation device, and for chemotherapy (V58.1) or radiation therapy (V58.0) after cancer surgery.

Category V67 is reported when a patient is seen after treatment has been completed. Follow-up examinations are necessary but because the disease is no longer present, use a code from category V67 based on the most recent treatment modality as the primary diagnosis. If a patient has had surgery and treatment is completed, use V67.0.

Category V72 is reported as the primary diagnosis when a patient is seen only for tests and examinations which are routine and there is no suspected condition or symptom to be treated by the reporting physician. A patient receiving a preoperative examination from a primary care physician before surgery is reported by the physician as V72.84; when the surgeon has not specified a suspected condition, the surgical condition is reported as the secondary diagnosis by the primary care physician.

DIAGNOSTIC CODING OF DISORDERS OF THE CIRCULATORY SYSTEM

Diseases of the circulatory system are difficult to code because of their complexity and the lack of specific and accurate terminology that physicians use in specifying other diagnoses. Physicians who are not in cardiology-related fields are still likely to have some contact with codes referring to the circulatory system because of the widespread incidence of circulatory disease.

A common diagnosis is hypertension. The Alphabetic Index lists the codes applicable to this diagnosis in the form of a table. This table, which is shown in Figure 4-4, differentiates between benign and malignant hypertension. Malignant hypertension is characterized by elevated blood pressure which is life-threatening and requires immediate attention. Benign hypertension is not life-threatening if it is controlled.

Do not guess when selecting a code from the hypertension table. Ask the doctor to specify whether the patient has *malignant* or *benign hypertension.* The unspecified column in the table should be interpreted in the usual sense in which the ICD-9-CM system uses the term "unspecified" (the information is not specified). The treating physician should always be able to differentiate between the benign and malignant categories, and the office staff should never report from the column in the table labeled "Unspecified." To use the hypertension table or any table in ICD-9-CM, guide your eyes or a ruler down the alphabetic list of subterms and indent to the site of the patient's condition. From the columns in the table, select the patient's condition and guide your eyes down this column until the chosen indentation intersects with the column. This is the code which must be verified in the Tabular List. The code for benign essential hypertension is 401.1. The subindentations are not always clear. Code 642.0 (benign essential hypertension complicating pregnancy) is often selected for 401.1

The circulatory system codes include some combination codes. 642.0 is a combination code that reports that the patient is pregnant with a complication of essential hypertension.

	Malignant	Benign	Unspecified
Hypertension, hypertensive (arterial) (arteriolar) (crisis) (degeneration) (disease) (essential) (fluctuating) (idiopathic) (intermittent) (labile) (low renin) (orthostatic) (paroxysmal) (primary) (systemic) (uncontrolled) (vascular)	401.0	401.1	401.9
with			
heart involvement (conditions classifiable to 425.8, 428, 429.0–429.3, 429.8, 429.9 due to hypertension) (*see also* Hypertension, heart)............	402.00	402.10	402.90
with kidney involvement — *see* Hypertension, cardiorenal			
renal involvement (only conditions classifiable to 585, 586, 587) excludes conditions classifiable to 584	403.00	403.10	403.90
with heart involvement — *see* Hypertension, cardiorenal			
failure (and sclerosis) (*see also* Hypertension, kidney)	403.01	403.11	403.91
sclerosis without failure (*see also* Hypertension, kidney)....................	403.00	403.10	403.90
accelerated (*see also* Hypertension, by type, malignant)	401.0	—	—
antepartum — *see* Hypertension, complicating pregnancy, childbirth, or the puerperium			
cardiorenal (disease)........................	404.00	404.10	404.90
with			
heart failure (congestive)	404.01	404.11	404.91
and renal failure	404.03	404.13	404.93
renal failure....................	404.02	404.12	404.92
and heart failure (congestive)	404.03	404.13	404.93
cardiovascular disease (arteriosclerotic) (sclerotic)	402.00	402.10	402.90
with			
heart failure (congestive)	402.01	402.11	402.91
renal involvement (conditions classifiable to 403) (*see also* Hypertension, cardiorenal)............	404.00	404.10	404.90
cardiovascular renal (disease) (sclerosis) (*see also* Hypertension, cardiorenal)	404.00	404.10	404.90
cerebrovascular disease NEC	437.2	437.2	437.2
complicating pregnancy, childbirth, or the puerperium	642.2	642.0	642.9
with			
albuminuria (and edema) (mild)	—	—	642.4
severe.	—	—	642.5
edema (mild)....................	—	—	642.4
severe....................	—	—	642.5
heart disease	642.2	642.2	642.2
and renal disease	642.2	642.2	642.2
renal disease....................	642.2	642.2	642.2
and heart disease	642.2	642.2	642.2
chronic....................	642.2	642.0	642.0
with pre–eclampsia or eclampsia	642.7	642.7	642.7
fetus or newborn	760.0	760.0	760.0
essential....................	—	642.0	642.0
with pre–eclampsia or eclampsia	—	642.7	642.7
fetus or newborn	760.0	760.0	760.0
fetus or newborn	760.0	760.0	760.0
gestational....................	—	—	642.3
pre–existing....................	642.2	642.0	642.0
with pre–eclampsia or eclampsia	642.7	642.7	642.7
fetus or newborn	760.0	760.0	760.0
secondary to renal disease	642.1	642.1	642.1
with pre–eclampsia or eclampsia	642.7	642.7	642.7
fetus or newborn	760.0	760.0	760.0
transient....................	—	—	642.3
due to			
aldosteronism, primary....................	405.09	405.19	405.99
brain tumor....................	405.09	405.19	405.99
bulbar poliomyelitis....................	405.09	405.19	405.99
calculus			
kidney....................	405.09	405.19	405.99
ureter	405.09	405.19	405.99
coarctation, aorta....................	405.09	405.19	405.99

FIGURE 4-4 Hypertension table from the Alphabetic Index. (Context Software Systems, *ICD-9-CM 1995,* vols. 1 and 2, New York, McGraw-Hill Healthcare Management Group, 1995, p. 560.)

DIAGNOSTIC CODING
OF NEOPLASMS

The diagnostic coding of neoplasms is of special interest because of the complexity of this disease process. In medical terminology, *neo* means "new" and *plasm* means "tissue" or "growth." New growths may be either malignant or benign. A *benign neoplasm* is not characterized by the presence of cancer, while a *malignant neoplasm* includes cancer development.

Neoplasms are listed in Chapter 2 of the Tabular List under categories 140–239. A table of neoplasms, similar to the hypertension table, can be found under the letter N in the Alphabetic Index of Diseases; it lists the code numbers for neoplasms by body site. For each site, there are six possible code numbers, depending on whether the neoplasm is (1) malignant primary, (2) malignant secondary (metastasis), (3) malignant in situ, (4) benign, (5) of uncertain behavior, or (6) of unspecified nature. Figure 4-5 is a page from the Alphabetic List's table of neoplasms.

The *primary site* is the part of the body where the malignant neoplasm originated. The *secondary site,* or the metastatic site, is the body area where the cancer spread. The ICD-9-CM system uses the secondary malignancy column to deal with a cancer which has spread to any other part of the body as metastatic malignant carcinoma. *Carcinoma in situ* means that the cancer is self-contained and will not spread to other body parts. *Uncertain Behavior* means that the tumor cells do not look normal to the pathologist but that there are not enough changes to designate malignancy. It is borderline, indicating that the pathologist cannot determine whether the growth is benign or malignant. An unspecified code is used to classify a neoplasm when it is not known and has not been documented to fit a code from the other five classifications. The office staff should not use the "Unspecified" column of the table because the treating physician should be able to classify the patient's neoplasm into one of the five choices.

In addition to the table, neoplasms can be indexed by their specific names and can be specified by cell type. There are also numerous cross-references by specific disease. If you look through the neoplasm index, you will see code numbers beginning with M. For example, under the main term Lymphoma is

> Burkitt's type (lymphoblastic)
>   (undifferentiated) (M9750/3) 200.2

The diagnostic code used by a physician practice is 200.2. The M codes are morphology codes and are specific to tumor registrars, pathology departments, and other agencies involved in cancer and cancer research. Physician practices may ignore the M codes unless they are directly involved in reporting cancer research.

	Malignant				Uncertain	
	Primary	Secondary	Ca in Situ	Benign	Behavior	Unspecified
sphincter	154.2	197.5	230.5	211.4	235.5	239.0
aorta (thoracic)	171.4	198.89	—	215.4	238.1	239.2
abdominal	171.5	198.89	—	215.5	238.1	239.2
aortic body	194.6	198.89	—	227.6	237.3	239.7
aponeurosis	171.9	198.89	—	215.9	238.1	239.2
palmar	171.2	198.89	—	215.2	238.1	239.2
plantar	171.3	198.89	—	215.3	238.1	239.2
appendix	153.5	197.5	230.3	211.3	235.2	239.0
arachnoid (cerebral)	192.1	198.4	—	225.2	237.6	239.7
spinal	192.3	198.4	—	225.4	237.6	239.7
areola (female)	174.0	198.81	233.0	217	238.3	239.3
male	175.0	198.81	233.0	217	238.3	239.3
arm NEC*	195.4	198.89	232.6	229.8	238.8	239.8
artery — see Neoplasm, connective tissue						
aryepiglottic fold	148.2	198.89	230.0	210.8	235.1	239.0
hypopharyngeal aspect	148.2	198.89	230.0	210.8	235.1	239.0
laryngeal aspect	161.1	197.3	231.0	212.1	235.6	239.1
marginal zone	148.2	198.89	230.0	210.8	235.1	239.0
arytenoid (cartilage)	161.3	197.3	231.0	212.1	235.6	239.1
fold — see Neoplasm, aryepiglottic						
atlas	170.2	198.5	—	213.2	238.0	239.2
atrium, cardiac	164.1	198.89	—	212.7	238.8	239.8
auditory						
canal (external) (skin)	173.2	198.2	232.2	216.2	238.2	239.2
internal	160.1	197.3	231.8	212.0	235.9	239.1
nerve	192.0	198.4	—	225.1	237.9	239.7
tube	160.1	197.3	231.8	212.0	235.9	239.1
opening	147.2	198.89	230.0	210.7	235.1	239.0
auricle, ear	173.2	198.2	232.2	216.2	238.2	239.2
cartilage	171.0	198.89	—	215.0	238.1	239.2
auricular canal (external)	173.2	198.2	232.2	216.2	238.2	239.2
internal	160.1	197.3	231.8	212.0	235.9	239.1
autonomic nerve or nervous system NEC	171.9	198.89	—	215.9	238.1	239.2
axilla, axillary	195.1	198.89	234.8	229.8	238.8	239.8
fold	173.5	198.2	232.5	216.5	238.2	239.2
back NEC*	195.8	198.89	232.5	229.8	238.8	239.8
Bartholin's gland	184.1	198.82	233.3	221.2	236.3	239.5
basal ganglia	191.0	198.3	—	225.0	237.5	239.6
basis pedunculi	191.7	198.3	—	225.0	237.5	239.6
bile or biliary (tract)	156.9	197.8	230.8	211.5	235.3	239.0
canaliculi (biliferi) (intrahepatic)	155.1	197.8	230.8	211.5	235.3	239.0
canals, interlobular	155.1	197.8	230.8	211.5	235.3	239.0
contiguous sites	156.8	—	—	—	—	—
duct or passage (common) (cyst) (extrahepatic)	156.1	197.8	230.8	211.5	235.3	239.0
contiguous sites with gallbladder	156.8	—	—	—	—	—
interlobular	155.1	197.8	230.8	211.5	235.3	239.0
intrahepatic	155.1	197.8	230.8	211.5	235.3	239.0
and extrahepatic	156.9	197.8	230.8	211.5	235.3	239.0
bladder (urinary)	188.9	198.1	233.7	223.3	236.7	239.4
contiguous sites	188.8	—	—	—	—	—
dome	188.1	198.1	233.7	223.3	236.7	239.4
neck	188.5	198.1	233.7	223.3	236.7	239.4
orifice	188.9	198.1	233.7	223.3	236.7	239.4
ureteric	188.6	198.1	233.7	223.3	236.7	239.4
urethral	188.5	198.1	233.7	223.3	236.7	239.4
sphincter	188.8	198.1	233.7	223.3	236.7	239.4
trigone	188.0	198.1	233.7	223.3	236.7	239.4
urachus	188.7	—	233.7	223.3	236.7	239.4
wall	188.9	198.1	233.7	223.3	236.7	239.4
anterior	188.3	198.1	233.7	223.3	236.7	239.4
lateral	188.2	198.1	233.7	223.3	236.7	239.4
posterior	188.4	198.1	233.7	223.3	236.7	239.4
blood vessel — see Neoplasm, connective tissue						

FIGURE 4-5 Neoplasm table from the Alphabetic Index. (Context Software Systems, *ICD-9-CM 1995,* vols. 1 and 2, New York, McGraw-Hill Healthcare Management Group, 1995, p. 634.)

Sequencing Malignant Neoplasms

Use the following guidelines to sequence codes in this category.

1. If the patient's primary site is still present, the cancer has spread to a secondary site, and the patient is receiving treatment for both sites:
—Code the primary site from the first column in the neoplasm table.
—Code any secondary site that may be present from the second column.

Coding Tip
The primary site is always the primary diagnosis when it and other cancer sites are treated at the same time.

2. If the patient's primary site previously was excised but chemotherapy and/or radiotherapy continue and they are the only services provided during the visit, code V58.1, indicating chemotherapy, or V58.0, indicating a radiotherapy session, as the primary diagnosis.

Coding Tip
A malignant neoplasm is always the secondary diagnosis when the purpose of the visit was to receive chemo or radio therapy and the therapy is the only procedure reported on that day.

3. If only the patient's secondary site is being treated, the codes from the second column become the primary diagnosis.

Coding Tip
If the primary site is still active but is not receiving treatment, code it as the secondary diagnosis.

DIAGNOSTIC CODING FOR PREGNANCY, CHILDBIRTH, AND THE PUERPERIUM

Chapter 11 in the Tabular List deals with obstetrics/gynecology; it has extensive fifth-digit requirements. The only categories which do not require the use of a fifth digit are ectopic and molar pregnancy (630–633), failed attempted abortion (638), complications following abortion, ectopic and molar pregnancies (639), and delivery in a completely normal case (650). With the exception of 634–637, when fifth digits are required, these are the choices:

0 unspecified as to episode of care or not applicable
1 delivered, with or without mention of antepartum condition
2 delivered, with mention of postpartum complication
3 antepartum condition or complication
4 postpartum condition or complication

When a woman is pregnant, to report her condition, use the index under three main terms:

1. "Pregnancy" (to describe carrying a child or any problems before delivery)
2. "Delivery" (to describe the type of delivery)
3. "Puerperal" (to describe problems arising after the first stages of labor up to 6 weeks after the patient has given birth)

For example,

Main term	*Clinical Example*	*Index Words*	*Code*
Pregnancy	Antepartum bleeding, at 2 months	Pregnancy—complicated; hemorrhage—before 22 wks.	640.93
Delivery	Pregnancy, uterine, delivered twins	Delivery—twins NEC	651.01
Puerperal	Sepsis, 3 weeks post-partum of unknown origin	Puerperal—infection—generalized	670.04

For certain complications that occur during pregnancy, a combination code suffices for both the pregnancy and the complication. For such pregnancy-related complications, categories 642–648 are used to report pregnancy and conditions such as anemia, diabetes mellitus, and drug dependence, among others.

Category 655 should be used as an additional code when a condition in the fetus affects the care of the mother during pregnancy or is a cause for the termination of pregnancy. For example,

Clinical Example	*Index Words*	*Code*
Suspected damage to fetus due to drug dependence, 26 weeks gestation	Pregnancy—management affected by fetal damage from drugs	655.53

The *puerperium* is the period that elapses between the last stages of labor and the return of the reproductive organs to a nonpregnant state. It usually refers to the 6 weeks after labor. Puerperal conditions are usually coded in categories 670–676. For example,

Clinical Example	*Index Words*	*Code*
Puerperal mastitis, two weeks postpartum	Puerperal—mastitis	675.24

DIAGNOSTIC CODING FOR NEWBORNS AND CONDITIONS ORIGINATING IN THE PERINATAL PERIOD

All normal newborn charts are coded to categories V30–V37. These codes are the primary diagnosis in most cases for pediatricians treating normal newborns at birth in a hospital. Babies born in hospitals require a fifth digit noting whether the birth was or was not by cesarean delivery. For example,

Clinical Example	Index Word	Code
Full-term living newborn, male, by C section	Newborn	V30.01

Categories 760–763 classify conditions transferred to the baby and diagnosed in the first 28 days of life (the perinatal period). These codes should be used on the infant's chart. Many of the codes can be found with the main term "noxious" subindented to substances transmitted through placenta or breast milk.

Perinatal conditions are considered transitory in nature, and if permanent, they should be classified to a disease category or as a congenital anomaly.

DIAGNOSTIC CODING FOR INJURIES

All practices need a solid grounding in coding for injuries. Injuries are dealt with in Chapter 17 of the Tabular List. The note that begins Chapter 17 informs office personnel to use combination codes for multiple injuries when it is convenient and when one is listed.

Fractures

Categories 800–829, fractures, are the most common types of injuries listed under the general category of injuries in Chapter 17. Office personnel must know if the fracture is open or closed in order to code it accurately. With an *open fracture* the bone has broken through the skin; in a *closed fracture* the skin is intact. A compound fracture is synonymous with an open one. If the fracture type is unknown, ask the physician before selecting the code. Under the index word "Fracture," in a box, a comprehensive note lists the types of open and closed fractures.

Fractures are relatively simple to code once they are classified into the open or closed category. Then it is just a matter of subindenting to the name of the bone. An open fracture of the medial malleolus is indexed under Fracture—ankle (malleolus)—medial malleolus—open.

Open Wounds and Superficial and Internal Injuries

The main term index words are misleading when one is searching for codes to report animal bites, avulsions, cuts, lacerations, puncture wounds, and traumatic amputations. Most deep open wounds are indexed by the words "Wound, open"—subindent to the site of the wound on the body, such as muscle, eyebrow, hip, or elbow. Categories 870–897 describe open wounds. These categories require a fourth digit. Any time a fourth-digit descriptor is selected with the word "complicated," it refers to open wounds with delayed treatment, healing, a foreign body, or a major infection.

Superficial lacerations are defined as nonvenomous insect bites, blisters, scratches, and abrasions. They are indexed under the main term "Injury." Under this word there is a note with this helpful information. The box also gives information about the main terms for finding traumatic ruptures, tears, lacerations, and penetrating wounds of internal organs. Internal organ injuries are indexed under the word "Injury"—subindent to internal, then subindent to the body site, such as the heart, liver, spleen, or lungs.

Burns

Burns of specified sites or of multiple sites are classified under categories 940–949. These categories identify the site and severity (degree) of the burn. Burns of one site that exhibit multiple degrees (first degree, second degree, third degree) are coded to the most severe degree burn of that site. To index burns, use the main term "Burn"—subindent to body site.

The extent of total body surface involved in a burn is identified by using category 948. The fourth digits 0–9 identify the total percentage of body surface involved in any degree of burn. The fifth digits 0–9 identify the percentage of body surface with third-degree burns. To use category 948 correctly, add all the percentages of body surface involved in any degree of burn to assign the appropriate fourth digit and then use the percentage of body surface involved in third-degree burns to assign the correct fifth digit. The percentage of body surface with third-degree burns will never be larger than the percentage of body surface with all burns. If there are no third-degree burns, a fifth digit of 0 is used with category 948.

The Rule of Nines

The *rule of nines* is a simple method used in calculating the extent of body surface affected in a burn victim. This must be calculated in instances in which the doctor failed to do so in the medical record. Each area of the body represents a certain percentage of the total body area. These are multiples of 9. Each area's percentages must be added together to come up with the total body surface. Figure 4-6 shows the areas of the body and what percentage (%) they represent: The figure contains a picture of the layers of skin to help in coding the burns as first-, second-, or third-degree burns.

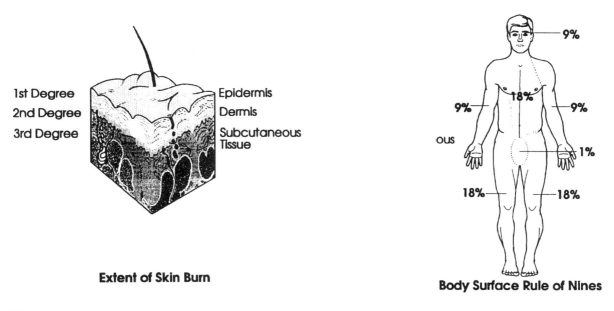

Extent of Skin Burn

Body Surface Rule of Nines

FIGURE 4-6   Body surface rule of nines and extent of skin burn. (Bradford, Billie C., *ICD-9-CM Coding For Physicians Offices*, McGraw-Hill Healthcare Management Group, 1993, p. 171.)

Late Effects

Late effects are the long-term effects of a traumatic injury which have left a patient with a residual problem. A malunion or traumatic arthritis can be a late effect from a fracture, and residual scarring can occur because of a severe burn, to cite a few examples. A late effect code is reported to explain the cause of a condition that is currently being treated. This sequencing of coding adds more detail to the diagnostic statement and adds more severity to the illness. Late effects are indexed under the word "late." For example,

Clinical Example	Index Words	Code
Contracture, left elbow following clavicle fracture	Contraction—joint—elbow	718.42
	Late effect—fracture	905.2

CODING FOR COMPLICATIONS

At times it may be necessary to report a complication to justify the medical necessity of seeing a patient more often than would be expected. Complication codes can be found within the disease and injury categories. However, there are categories 996–999, which classify complications of surgical and medical care that are not elsewhere classified. While it is always the rule to avoid not elsewhere classified codes, there are some general guidelines for reporting from these categories:

1. If a specific code cannot be found elsewhere classified, then use "Complications of Surgical and Medical Care, Not Elsewhere Classified." The 996–999 category range describes complications of internal prostheses, devices, implants, and grafts, either mechanical or body reactions.

2. Categories 996–999 are found under the main term "Complications" in the Alphabetic Index.

E CODES: EXTERNAL CAUSES OF INJURY AND POISONING

E codes are the external cause codes within ICD-9-CM. They describe events and situations which were the external cause of an injury or poisoning in a patient. They are seldom used by a physician practice because Medicare and other plans do not usually have them installed in their computer systems. However, some workers' compensation programs in certain states may request their use.

E codes follow V codes as other supplementary codes. E codes are indexed from their own index, beginning as Section 2 of the Alphabetic Index. Section 2 is a table that identifies drugs and chemicals. Figure 4-7 is a section of this table.

The first column may be helpful to the office staff because the drug or chemical which poisoned (overdosed) the patient can be identified and reported. Note that the codes in this column begin with the number 9 and are part of the Tabular List of diseases and injuries. Most insurance and managed care plans accept the overdose codes. This table is used in the same way as the hypertension and neoplasm tables mentioned earlier in this chapter. Directly following this table is Section 3, which is the E code index. Examples of main terms are as follows:

collision	fall	misadventure
crushed	fire	radiation
explosion	hit	shooting

Guidelines for Using E Codes

Use the following guidelines for reporting E codes.

- Never use E codes as the primary diagnosis.
- If they are reported, E codes are the last codes listed on a claim.
- The specific adverse effect of, reaction to, or localized toxic effect of a correct drug or substance properly administered in a therapeutic or prophylactic dosage must be coded from Chapters 1 through 17 in the Tabular List.

Substance	Poisoning	External Cause (E–Code)				
		Accident	Therapeutic Use	Suicide Attempt	Assault	Undetermined
Carbamide	974.4	E858.5	E944.4	E950.4	E962.0	E980.4
topical	976.8	E858.7	E946.8	E950.4	E962.0	E980.4
Carbamylcholine chloride	971.0	E855.3	E941.0	E950.4	E962.0	E980.4
Carbarsone	961.1	E857	E931.1	E950.4	E962.0	E980.4
Carbaryl	989.3	E863.2	—	E950.6	E962.1	E980.7
Carbaspirin	965.1	E850.3	E935.3	E950.0	E962.0	E980.0
Carbazochrome	972.8	E858.3	E942.8	E950.4	E962.0	E980.4
Carbenicillin	960.0	E856	E930.0	E950.4	E962.0	E980.4
Carbenoxolone	973.8	E858.4	E943.8	E950.4	E962.0	E980.4
Carbetapentane	975.4	E858.6	E945.4	E950.4	E962.0	E980.4
Carbimazole	962.8	E858.0	E932.8	E950.4	E962.0	E980.4
Carbinol	980.1	E860.2	—	E950.9	E962.1	E980.9
Carbinoxamine	963.0	E858.1	E933.0	E950.4	E962.0	E980.4
Carbitol	982.8	E862.4	—	E950.9	E962.1	E980.9
Carbocaine	968.9	E855.2	E938.9	E950.4	E962.0	E980.4
infiltration (subcutaneous)	968.5	E855.2	E938.5	E950.4	E962.0	E980.4
nerve block (peripheral) (plexus)	968.6	E855.2	E938.6	E950.4	E962.0	E980.4
topical (surface)	968.5	E855.2	E938.5	E950.4	E962.0	E980.4
Carbol–fuchsin solution	976.0	E858.7	E946.0	E950.4	E962.0	E980.4
Carbolic acid (see also Phenol)	983.0	E864.0	—	E950.7	E962.1	E980.6
Carbomycin	960.8	E856	E930.8	E950.4	E962.0	E980.4
Carbon						
bisulfide (liquid) (vapor)	982.2	E862.4	—	E950.9	E962.1	E980.9
dioxide (gas)	987.8	E869.8	—	E952.8	E962.2	E982.8
disulfide (liquid) (vapor)	982.2	E862.4	—	E950.9	E962.1	E980.9
monoxide (from incomplete combustion of) (in)						
NEC	986	E868.9	—	E952.1	E962.2	E982.1
blast furnace gas	986	E868.8	—	E952.1	E962.2	E982.1
butane (distributed in mobile container)	986	E868.0	—	E951.1	E962.2	E981.1
distributed through pipes	986	E867	—	E951.0	E962.2	E981.0
charcoal fumes	986	E868.3	—	E952.1	E962.2	E982.1
coal						
gas (piped)	986	E867	—	E951.0	E962.2	E981.0
solid (in domestic stoves, fireplaces)	986	E868.3	—	E952.1	E962.2	E982.1
coke (in domestic stoves, fireplaces)	986	E868.3	—	E952.1	E962.2	E982.1
exhaust gas (motor) not in transit	986	E868.2	—	E952.0	E962.2	E982.0
combustion engine, any not in watercraft	986	E868.2	—	E952.0	E962.2	E982.0
farm tractor, not in transit	986	E868.2	—	E952.0	E962.2	E982.0
gas engine	986	E868.2	—	E952.0	E962.2	E982.0
motor pump	986	E868.2	—	E952.0	E962.2	E982.0
motor vehicle, not in transit	986	E868.2	—	E952.0	E962.2	E982.0
fuel (in domestic use)	986	E868.3	—	E952.1	E962.2	E982.1
gas (piped)	986	E867	—	E951.0	E962.2	E981.0
in mobile container	986	E868.0	—	E951.1	E962.2	E981.1
utility	986	E868.1	—	E951.8	E962.2	E981.1
in mobile container	986	E868.0	—	E951.1	E962.2	E981.1
piped (natural)	986	E867	—	E951.0	E962.2	E981.0
illuminating gas	986	E868.1	—	E951.8	E962.2	E981.8
industrial fuels or gases, any	986	E868.8	—	E952.1	E962.2	E982.1
kerosene (in domestic stoves, fireplaces)	986	E868.3	—	E952.1	E962.2	E982.1
kiln gas or vapor	986	E868.8	—	E952.1	E962.2	E982.1
motor exhaust gas, not in transit	986	E868.2	—	E952.0	E962.2	E982.0
piped gas (manufactured) (natural)	986	E867	—	E951.0	E962.2	E981.0
producer gas	986	E868.8	—	E952.1	E962.2	E982.1
propane (distributed in mobile container)	986	E868.0	—	E951.1	E962.2	E981.1
distributed through pipes	986	E867	—	E951.0	E962.2	E981.0
specified source NEC	986	E868.8	—	E952.1	E962.2	E982.1
stove gas	986	E868.1	—	E951.8	E962.2	E981.8
piped	986	E867	—	E951.0	E962.2	E981.0
utility gas	986	E868.1	—	E951.8	E962.2	E981.8
piped	986	E867	—	E951.0	E962.2	E981.0
water gas	986	E868.1	—	E951.8	E962.2	E981.8
wood (in domestic stoves, fireplaces)	986	E868.3	—	E952.1	E962.2	E982.1
tetrachloride (vapor) NEC	987.8	E869.8	—	E952.8	E962.2	E982.8

FIGURE 4-7 Table of drugs and chemicals. (Context Software Systems, *ICD-9-CM 1995,* vols. 1 and 2, New York, McGraw-Hill Healthcare Management Group, 1995, p. 810.)

■ Although E codes may seem helpful in describing the severity of a patient's condition, they should not be used unless one is instructed to do so by a specific plan.

E codes are very specific in describing automobile accidents and trauma caused by machinery. E code categories E810–E819 describe motor vehicle traffic accidents, and at the beginning of this category there is a list of the correct fourth-digit numbers to use for specific situations.

Clinical Example
The injured patient was the driver of a vehicle involved in a collision with another car. The code E813 describes "collision with another vehicle"; the fourth-digit numeral for "driver of vehicle other than motorcycle" is .0. The correct E code is E813.0.

Coding Tip
The use of E codes from a medical-legal viewpoint is a sensitive issue. As with any code, because a code exists, that does not mean that you should report it. Suicide attempts and assaults may be highly confidential. The office staff should check with the physician before reporting any sensitive diagnosis.

A WORD ABOUT ICD-10

This chapter has discussed the basics of ICD-9-CM from the perspective of a physician's practice. All examples and answers were taken from the official version of ICD-9-CM, 9th revision, volumes 1 and 2. Traditionally, every 10 years the ICD is revised. ICD-10 is long overdue but in fact has already been drafted and is being used by coders in other professional settings.

When finished, ICD-10 will contain sweeping changes, such as total conversion to an alphanumeric system. In this system all codes will look like the V and E codes. The categories will be greatly expanded. Because of these sweeping changes, it will take insurance plans a long time to get their computer programs converted. It is unofficial, but the change to ICD-10 is predicted to be effective in physician practices around the year 2000.

EXERCISING KNOWLEDGE

Coding Conventions

Go to a medical library or obtain access to the Tabular List from ICD-9-CM. In the exercise, Alphabetic Index information is considered as given. Consult the Tabular List (volume 1) for the answers.

1. Identify the type of disease or condition that is excluded from code 716.2, Allergic Arthritis.

2. Look up code 011, Pulmonary tuberculosis. Does this category require the use of a fifth digit? What is the code that identifies pulmonary tuberculous pneumonia [any form] found by bacterial culture?

3. Code 330.3, Cerebral degeneration of childhood in other diseases, appears in italics. The purpose of the italics in this code is _____ .

4. Braces are located under code 836.0. These braces signify that _____ .

5. Code 420.99, Pericarditis (acute):, demonstrates the use of a colon. What does this colon signify?

6. Note code 443.1, Thromboangitis obliterans [Buerger's disease]. Of what significance are the brackets? Buerger's disease is an _____ .

7. Code 726, Peripheral enthesopathies and allied syndromes, includes a note. What purpose does this note serve?

8. The symbol □ precedes codes 016.1 and 016.2. What does this symbol signify?

9. See code 459.0. Is it correct to select a description with unspecified in this example? What does the abbreviation NOS mean?

10. A patient's diagnostic statement reads idiopathic ulcerative proctocolitis. Look up code 535.4. Must the patient have either allergic, bile-induced, and irritant gastritis or superficial or toxic gastritis for this code to be selected?

Basic Coding

Instructions for all coding exercises:

1. *Locate the main term in the Alphabetic Index of Diseases and record it as the index word(s).*
2. *Go to the Tabular List to verify that the code number selected is correct.*
3. *Read and be guided by the list of inclusions, exclusions, notes, and other coding conventions that may apply to the particular code.*
4. *If the code number selected is appropriate, record the code number.*
5. *If the first selection of an index word was not correct, note why it was not correct.*
6. *Consult the Alphabetic Index again to begin another code search.*

These instructions apply to all coding exercises.

		Index Word	*Code*
11.	Common cold	_____	_____
12.	Pneumonia, influenzal	_____	_____
13.	Chlamydia vaginitis	_____	_____
14.	Foreign body of right eyelid	_____	_____
15.	Cholelithiasis	_____	_____
16.	Chronic allergic otitis media	_____	_____
17.	Bleeding esophageal varices	_____	_____
18.	Acne	_____	_____
19.	Senile cataract, nuclear	_____	_____
20.	Charcot-Marie-Tooth disease	_____	_____

V Codes

21. Mr. Bank has been complaining of photophobia for the past several days. He is visiting an ophthalmologist to have his eyes examined. The physician cannot diagnose his problem at this time. The physician has ordered tests, but Mr. Bank cannot have the tests for a while. The physician noted in the medical record that Mr. Bank had a cataract extraction without lens implant 1 year earlier. The claim needs to be reported now. What are the two codes to use?

_____ _____

22. Jimmy was bitten by a dog last night while playing in the park. He had a complicated wound of the right forearm. His mother took him to the emergency room (ER) for stitches. When the ER physician wanted to give Jimmy a tetanus shot, his mother asked if they could wait until his pediatrician's office opened in the morning, as she was not certain when Jimmy had had his last tetanus shot. She is in the pediatrician's office now, and the doctor has elected to give Jimmy a tetanus injection. Code the pediatrician's diagnostic statement.

_____ _____

23. Mr. Aren came to the office today for routine management and cleansing of his urethrostomy. The results of the lab work confirmed that Mr. Aren had a urinary tract infection caused by *E. coli.*

_____ _____

24. Since Mrs. Reynolds had a pacemaker inserted 3 years ago for her chronic condition of arteriosclerotic cardiovascular disease (ASCVD), she comes in annually for a pacemaker check.

_____ _____

25. Jan Johnson came in today in a state of high anxiety. After a 45-minute session of psychotherapy, the doctor diagnosed Mrs. Johnson as having acute anxiety caused by the stress of conflicts at home with her 15-year-old son.

_____ _____

26. Mr. Hammond was referred to your office for a chest x-ray. The referring physician noted on the order form that Mr. Hammond has had a persistent cough for the past 3 weeks.

_____ _____

27. Submit a diagnostic statement to an HMO for Mr. White. Yesterday he had a vasectomy.

_____ _____

28. Mrs. Saldono had normal twins in the hospital. Code the diagnostic statement for each twin on behalf of the pediatrician attending them at birth.

_____ _____

Circulatory System Codes

29. Acute true posterior wall infarction (newly diagnosed)

_____ _____

30. Old healed anterior wall myocardial infarction

_____ _____

31. Hypertensive cardiorenal disease, malignant

_____ _____

32. Chest wall pain   _____ _____

33. Buerger's disease   _____ _____

34. Generalized chronic arteriosclerosis of heart and cardiovascular system   _____ _____

Neoplasm Coding

35. Carcinoma of splenic flexure (primary site)

_____ _____

36. Metastatic carcinoma of left lower lobe of lung

   from breast (female) _____   _____

37. Squamous esophageal carcinoma of contiguous sites

   with metastasis to stomach _____   _____

38. Carcinoma in situ of cervix _____   _____

Fracture Coding

39. Open fracture of medial malleolus _____   _____

40. Simple closed fracture of the neck of humerus _____   _____

41. Greenstick fracture, shaft, right upper femur _____   _____

Wounds and Injuries Coding

42. Laceration of foot (asphalt in wound) _____   _____

43. Uncomplicated avulsion of right thigh _____   _____

44. Infected skunk bite of hand _____   _____

45. Blister of nose _____   _____

46. Liver contusion _____   _____

Late Effects and Complications Codes

47. Chronic subdural hematoma after bacterial meningitis _____   _____

48. Residual dislocation of distal fibula (ankle) after a fracture 2 years ago _____   _____

49. Brain pacemaker malfunction _____   _____

50. Rejection of bone marrow graft _____   _____

▼ **TOOL 4-1**
COMMON INDEX WORDS FOR V CODES

ADMISSION
AFTERCARE
ATTENTION to
CHECKUP
CONFLICT
CONTACT
CONTRACEPTION
ENCOUNTER for
EXAMINATION

REFERRAL
REMOVAL
REPLACEMENT
SCREENING
STATUS POST
SUPERVISION
SURGERY
VACCINATION

HISTORY personal or family

Instructions for using this tool:

(Post in a handy place or place in a file labeled ICD-9-CM tips.)

Locate the main term, "History," in the Alphabetic Index of Diseases. Sub-indent once (two spaces) to endocrine disorder, V12.2. This is where History (personal of) ends. History (personal of) is where the patient's own personal history of a disease is indexed. History (personal of) begins again with genital disorder, V13.2, but it is deceiving to the eye. Draw a horizontal line under endocrine disorder V12.2. Directly under this line begin a new subterm, "family," which means that the patient never had the disorder but there is a family history of it. History (family) continues for several pages until visual loss (V19.0) appears. Draw a line under visual loss to note where History (family) ends. If the lines aren't drawn in the index, it is easy to report the wrong condition.

Draw the line as shown under History (personal) to mark where family history of begins:

History (personal) of—*continued*
  endocrine disorder   V12.2
  family

Draw the line as shown under family history of visual loss V19.0 to mark where family history ends and personal history of resumes:

History (personal) of—*continued*
  family—continued
  visual loss   V19.0

Procedure Coding and HCPCS

CHAPTER OVERVIEW

CPT (Current Procedural Terminology) and HCPCS (Health Care Financing Administration Common Procedural Coding System, pronounced "hick picks") are the coding systems used most frequently in the United States to report procedures to insurance and managed care plans. HCPCS has three levels. Level I of the HCPCS procedural coding system is CPT; Levels II and III are mandated by government plans for use when the CPT codes are insufficient. Ambulance companies, suppliers of durable medical equipment, dentists, and other types of providers need a procedural coding system to bill the government and use all three HCPCS coding levels for this purpose. All insurance and managed care plans accept CPT codes. All government plans and some private plans accept Level II of the HCPCS coding system. Only Medicare carriers accept Level III of this system. Practices must know which plans accept which levels of HCPCS codes and use them instead of CPT codes when HCPCS codes more accurately describe the services provided.

To use the CPT-4 book effectively, those reporting the codes must have an understanding of its structure, index, code ranges, format, wording of descriptions, notes, guidelines, code changes, symbols, and unlisted procedures.

The evaluation and management (E&M) section of CPT-4 is used extensively by all medical practices. Therefore, the medical personnel responsible for procedural coding must understand how the three major determinants of the level of service—history, examination, and medical decision making—are applied in choosing E&M codes.

After reading the material in this chapter, doing the exercises, and using the end-of-chapter tools, you will be able to:

■ Describe the structure of CPT and the use of its index
■ Apply CPT guidelines and other conventions to select and report accurate descriptions of physician procedures
■ Default to the correct use of the HCPCS system whenever it is applicable
■ Use CPT and HCPCS modifiers when appropriate

INTRODUCTION TO CPT

The current edition of CPT is the fourth edition, or CPT-4. The first edition was developed by the American Medical Association in 1966 for the purpose of establishing a system for obtaining payment for physician services. The AMA creates the code numbers and describes the intent of the codes. The AMA's Department of Coding and Nomenclature assumes the role of educator but has no jurisdiction over insurance and managed care plans in regard to how they interpret the codes and their payment amounts. The AMA has been successful in providing a national language for procedural coding which is acceptable to the majority of plans. The narrative descriptions of medical procedures, each assigned to one five-digit number help medical practices be consistent in reporting physician services. CPT-4's language of numbers also eliminates lengthy typographic descriptions of complicated operations, diagnostic tests, and other medical services. Claim processors at the plans do not have to read and decipher the meaning or extent of services attached to a five-digit code number. CPT-4 helps plans minimize incorrect interpretations. For example, the five-digit code number 10120 always describes the incision and removal of a foreign body in subcutaneous tissues by simple means. If 10120 has been properly installed in an insurance or managed care plan's computer, there should be minimal confusion in reporting what the physician did for the patient, although methods of payments may be different. The CPT procedural coding system is a welcome and well-used language in medical practices. Once it has been learned, only additions and revisions need to be learned each year.

As was mentioned in Chapter 1, a new CPT book should be purchased each year. New code numbers and revised descriptions of existing numbers should be ready for use at the beginning of each new calendar year. Medicare requests the use of additions and revisions every January 1. Other insurance and managed care plans may not have installed the changes until February, March, or even April. It is important that a practice keep abreast of when and how to use the changes in CPT for each plan. If plan newsletters do not give information on when changes will be effective, a practice must call frequently billed plans to learn when to apply the changes.

The AMA's editorial panel is responsible for the maintenance of CPT and must approve all changes. Most panel members are physician representatives of the AMA, but there are also physicians nominated by the Blue Cross and Blue Shield Association, the Health Insurance Association of America (a national association of private plans), the Health Care Financing Administration (the overseer of the Medicare program), and the American Hospital Association. As medical care changes and advances, this panel determines whether codes must be added or revised. As procedures become obsolete, they are deleted from the book. The panel is assisted by physician representatives from most national medical specialty societies. The foreword of the CPT book contains the names of the physicians on the panels and advisory committees. Practicing physicians, by writing their national medical specialty societies or writing directly to the Department of Coding and Nomenclature at the AMA, can have input into this annual publication. Before a code is added or revised, it must be introduced to the Relative Value Update Committee (RUC). The RUC is also composed of physician representatives from the national physician specialty societies. The RUC recommends relative value unit numbers for these codes to the RBRVS (Medicare Fee Schedule). Revisions to CPT involve a lengthy process and begin early in the calendar year, soon after the annual publication is printed and distributed by the AMA.

USES OF CPT CODES

While CPT codes are used by physician practices to report the services and procedures physicians have provided to their patients that are to be paid by a third-party payer, they have other uses as well. The organizations listed in Chapter 4 that use the ICD-9-CM coding system also use CPT data. CPT code data can be used to track the frequency of physician procedures and determine which procedures are traditionally performed in combination and in sequence with other procedures. CPT code data are also useful to insurance and managed care plans when they perform quality of care studies. Thus, CPT codes are useful in research concerning medical care.

THE STRUCTURE OF CPT-4

Some fundamental aspects in the structure of the CPT book have not changed since the first edition appeared in 1966; others have changed or may change in the future. However, once a practice has learned the fundamental structure of CPT-4, brushing up on annual changes will be sufficient to maintain a current mastery of the system.

CPT-4 has six sections:

Section	Code Range
1. Evaluation and Management (E&M)	99201–99499
2. Anesthesia	00100–01999
3. Surgery	10040–69979
4. Radiology	70010–79999
5. Pathology and Laboratory	80002–89399
6. Medicine	90700–99199

Sections are organized into categories and subcategories, often according to anatomic site and/or type of service. Boldface type is used to highlight important topics. Introductory pages contain instructions for using the book. These instructions inform the reader that use is not restricted to a section of any particular specialty, although the book is divided into different sections of medical procedures. Any physician can code from any section of the book if the service in question is provided and is documented in the patient's medical record.

The Index

An alphabetic index is located in the back of CPT. To find the code that most accurately describes a procedure, users must be familiar with the main terms in the alphabetic index and the content of each section. Main terms are located in four ways:

1.   Name of actual procedure (examples: Arthroscopy, Hemorrhoidectomy)
2.   Name of organ or anatomic site (examples: Liver, Femur)
3.   Condition (examples: Pregnancy, Colles Fracture)
4.   Synonyms (examples: Strapping or Splint); eponyms (examples: Maquet Procedure, Burrow's Operation); and abbreviations (examples: EKG, CAT Scan)

Main terms can be followed by up to three series of indented terms. Select the correct code by looking at each code description given in the main term or series.

Subcategories and Ranges

Sections of CPT are divided into categories and subcategories which appear in boldface type. Subcategories are further divided into headers according to body system, type of diagnostic test, or type of service. The code number ranges contained on a particular page are listed in the upper right corner. These notations allow for quick moving through the pages after using the index.

Format

CPT uses a unique format to list codes and their corresponding descriptions. For example,

33502	Repair of anomalous coronary artery; <u>by ligation</u>
33503	<u>by graft, without cardiopulmonary bypass</u>
33504	<u>by graft, with cardiopulmonary bypass</u>
33505	<u>with construction of intrapulmonary artery tunnel (Takeuchi procedure)</u>
33506	<u>by translocation from pulmonary artery to aorta</u>

To the far left of the page the codes are listed in order numerically. After each code there is a descriptive phrase. Some descriptive phrases begin with a capital letter directly after the five-digit code. These codes are the parent codes for a procedural family. The descriptions which are indented farther from the left margin and do not begin with a capital letter are the child codes in a procedural family. The child codes always refer back to a parent code whose description began with a capital letter.

In the example "Repair of anomalous coronary artery; by ligation" is the parent code. The words in the parent code which precede the semicolon are common to all the indented child codes which follow. "Repair of anomalous coronary artery" is dropped down before the words "by graft, without cardiopulmonary bypass" in code 33503. Code 33503 reads "Repair of anomalous coronary artery by graft, without cardiopulmonary bypass."

Wording of Descriptions

In the example above, we inserted underlining for the descriptions unique to each code to emphasize how important it is to read the descriptions carefully when selecting a code number. It may be helpful to highlight the differences in descriptions while learning the system. Everyone responsible for using the CPT system must become familiar with the descriptions of the codes used most frequently in the practice. Although the descriptions may be studied for differences very thoroughly, CPT has some terminology which can be subjective, such as "simple" versus "complicated" and "partial" versus "complete." Unless this information is documented in the medical record by the physician, it may be difficult to select the right code. Since "complicated" and "complete" are paid at a higher rate than are "partial" and "simple," an insurance or managed care plan can find fault during an audit if a code was used describing a case as "complicated" and the operative report documented that only a "simple" procedure was performed. In this case, the practice would be asked to repay the difference between the simple and complicated codes. With each printing, CPT attempts to refine these subjective terms.

Notes

Throughout CPT, there are helpful explanations for the use of each category and individual code. These explanations are known as notes. Notes can appear in parentheses after an individual code. They suggest other codes that should be reviewed before choosing a final code. Notes can appear in parentheses within a description of a code. The example below displays the common ways in which notes can appear. Read the note before code 93307. The note begins with Echocardiography and ends after the first set of parentheses. There are three sets of notes in the example.

Echocardiography

Echocardiography includes obtaining ultrasonic signals from the heart and great arteries, with two-dimensional image and/or Doppler ultrasonic signal documentation, and interpretation and report. When interpretation is performed separately use modifier '-26' or 09926.

(For fetal echocardiography, see 76825–76828)

(93300, 93305 have been deleted)

93307   Echocardiography, real-time with image documentation (2D) with or without M-mode recording; complete

93308   follow-up or limited study

(93309 has been deleted. To report, see 93307, 93308)

Guidelines

Guidelines explain the coding principles for a section and are found at the beginning of each section. An example appears in the Medicine section. The guideline—"MATERIALS SUPPLIED BY PHYSICIAN"—explains how supplies and materials over and above those usually included with an office visit should be reported separately. One of the most confusing guidelines is the *starred procedure* found as a guideline at the start of the Surgery section. If a CPT code is subject to this guideline, the star symbol (*) always appears to the right of the code number. A starred procedure means CPT does not recommend that the code have a global period or FUD. CPT refers to FUD as a package. A *package* includes a standard number of follow-up days (FUD) in which patient visits after the surgery are included in a package fee for the surgery. Starred procedures cannot be included in the package because a standard set of postoperative services cannot be determined. Services are variable, depending on the patient's needs. Starred procedures are not well understood by insurance and managed care plans. Medicare and other plans that are RBRVS payers have not always agreed with the CPT starred procedures. For example, 10160* is a starred procedure in CPT, but it has 10 days of FUD to an RBRVS payer.

Code Changes from Previous Editions

Code changes are marked by two symbols:

- ▲ A triangle indicates that the code number was present in the previous year's printing but that the description has changed with this year's printing. CPT has added or deleted words from the description. It is possible that the wording was changed enough that it is a code that no longer represents the service provided by the physician.
- ● A dot indicates that the code number and description are new to that year's printing.

Appendix B, which appears before the index, contains a summary of additions, deletions, and revisions in that year's printing.

Unlisted Procedures

Since medical technology is advancing rapidly and the CPT book is printed only once a year, CPT will never be complete for the needs of all physicians. An unlisted procedure code ending in the digits 9 or 99 exists after each category and within the guidelines of each section. An example of an unlisted procedure code is 90749 (Unlisted immunization procedure), which appears after the category Immunization Injections in the Medicine section.

Using Modifiers for Unlisted Procedures

Another method is used when the service has been altered by a circumstance which is not described exactly with a five-digit code number: A two-digit modifier may be added to a five-digit CPT code number which describes the service provided. Although modifiers may require a bit more work on the part of the office staff, they convey circumstances which alter the descriptions of the five-digit code numbers.

For example, 33736-22 modifies the circumstances of atrial septectomy, open heart with cardiopulmonary bypass, to report that the heart was extremely abnormal, the patient was not responding well, and 2 additional hours was required for this patient. -22 is Unusual Procedural Services: It is used when the services provided are greater than those usually required for the listed description. The use of modifiers may slow payment because allowances for these services are not usually established. The use of -22 by physician practices calls for a higher fee than does the listed procedure. The additional resources of the surgeon will increase the normal fee for that procedure code. The code will be reported as:

Code	Fee
33736-22	$3700.00

Adding two-digit modifiers to the five-digit CPT code is the preferred method for using modifiers. An alternative method is to report the modifier on a separate line of the claim with the prefix 099 and then list the two-digit modifier. For the example above:

Code	Fee
33736	$3700.00
09922	$ 200.00

Any time a new claim line with separate code numbers is used, another fee is reported. Each line on a claim requires a fee representing each code number.

There are several points to remember when using modifiers.

- Modifiers may require documentation (operative reports, cover letters of explanation, office/hospital progress notes, or even the reporting of a different diagnosis). A lengthy report is not needed, but it must justify the need for special consideration. Tool 5-1 is a guide showing which modifiers require documentation and which do not.
- Certain modifiers can be used only with physician visit codes, and certain other modifiers are used with surgery and diagnostic procedural codes.
- Use modifiers only when necessary. Overuse of modifiers may alert an insurance or managed care plan to inappropriate attempts to collect higher payments.

Some Frequently Used CPT Modifiers

When reading the following section, refer to Appendix A of the CPT book. We do not list all modifiers, and the descriptions do not appear exactly as they are written in CPT. Italic type has been used to emphasize important instructions which are often overlooked. Read each description carefully and compare it with the descriptions in Appendix A. For our purposes, a hyphen is used before each modifier. When reporting a claim, do not use hyphens. Because of the limited space on a claim or electronic field, there is no need to preface multiple modifiers with the -99 notation.

-20 Microsurgery. When the surgical service is performed using the techniques of microsurgery, including the aid of an operating microscope, -20 may be *added to the surgical procedure.* The use of this modifier is not warranted when the surgery is done with the aid of a magnifying loupe or magnifying binoculars worn by the surgeon. A special report may be appropriate to document the necessity of the microsurgical approach.

Coding Tip
Do not use this modifier on a code if the description already includes microsurgical use. Do not use -20 with "add on" codes such as 61712 Microdissection, intracranial or spinal procedure.

-21 Prolonged Evaluation and Management Services. When the service(s) provided is prolonged or otherwise greater than that usually required *for the highest level of evaluation and management service within a given subcategory and the physician is face to face with the patient continuously, add -21 to the highest level of evaluation and management code number.*

Coding Tip
Do not use this modifier in place of the CPT codes for prolonged physician service with direct face-to-face patient contact. Prolonged physician service codes can be used at any level of an E&M code and refer to noncontinuous services. They are more likely to produce payment than is the modifier -21.

-22 Unusual Procedural Services. A greater service than is usually required. A report must be included with the claim.

Coding Tip
Use -22 with any section except the evaluation and management section. Some plans feel that this modifier is overused and may not lead to the receipt of extra payment unless the cover letter is very convincing. The operating surgeon should sign the letter, which can be drafted by the office staff.

-23 Unusual Anesthesia. Occasionally, a procedure that usually requires either no anesthesia or only local anesthesia must be done under general anesthesia because of unusual circumstances.

Coding Tip
Provide a letter explaining these circumstances. For example, -23 should be reported if the patient was combative or very frightened of the surgery and unable to hold still during the procedure.

-24 *Unrelated Evaluation and Management Service by the Same Physician* During a Postoperative Period. Use of a different diagnosis code matched with an E&M code and -24, to the right of the E&M code. -24 will indicate that the visit was necessary for a diagnosis unrelated to the recent surgical procedure. The visit should not be denied as related to a visit for postoperative care.

Coding Tip
If the FUD is still in effect, the plan will have an edit to catch all E&M codes billed by the same physician during the period. If the patient visits the practice on day 28 of a 90-day postoperative period, the E&M code will be denied unless it is modified and matched with another diagnosis, other than the diagnosis originally reported for the surgery.

Clinical Example
Ted Jenkins, who had gallbladder surgery 28 days ago, comes to the practice for the treatment of bursitis. The claim reports 99212-24 matched with bursitis as the reason for this visit.

-25 *Significant, Separately Identifiable Evaluation and Management Service by the Same Physician on the Day of the Procedure or Other Service.* The physician may need to indicate that on the day of a minor surgical procedure with a global period, the patient's condition required a separate E&M service above and beyond the usual preoperative and postoperative care associated with the procedure performed that day. The modifier is also used to indicate E&M services were provided for an illness, injury, or problem on the same day of a Preventive Medicine E&M code.

Coding Tip
Do not use -25 to report the E&M service which resulted in the decision to perform surgery. Use -25 with E&M codes on the same date of a minor surgical procedure which has a global period of zero to eighty-nine FUD. -25 may not be required by certain plans when reporting a consultation, new patient visit, or emergency room codes. -25 is necessary with all hospital visits, established patient office visits, and any E&M code which implies a subsequent visit.

Clinical Example

Ted Jenkins's bursitis is still painful. He returns and receives a joint injection (code 20605) which has zero FUD to an RBRVS payer. 99212-25 is reported along with 20605 to enable the 99212 to pass through an edit.

Even if -25 is reported, these two services may be bundled by certain plans which have a policy of not allowing visits on the day of a minor surgical procedure. To alleviate this problem, try reporting a different diagnosis, such as a painful symptom of the bursitis (a frozen shoulder in the Ted Jenkins example), to justify a separate evaluation and management service.

Modifier -25 can also be used to report problem-oriented E&M services which were provided during a preventive medicine visit. -25 is added to codes 99201-99215 (office or other outpatient services) in addition to reporting an E&M code for Preventive Medicine Services.

Clinical Example

A 13-month-old female established patient visits the physician for a preventive medicine examination. During the visit the mother states the child has been pulling on her ears. The physician diagnoses an ear infection (otitis media), explains the illness to the mother, and prescribes treatment. These services are reported as:

Code	*Fee*
99392 and	$45.00
99212-25	30.00

-26 Professional Component. Certain procedures are a combination of a physician component and a technical component. When the physician interprets a test and writes a report of the findings, this service is reported separately *by adding the modifier -26 to the usual procedure code.*

Coding Tip

Do not use -26 with codes which describe the professional component only, such as (1) 93010 routine ECG with at least a 12-lead interpretation and report only or (2) with the supervision and interpretation codes (S&I) in the radiology section, 74350 is percutaneous placement of gastrostomy tube, radiologic supervision and interpretation.

-32 Mandated Services. These are services related to second opinions mandated by the insurance or managed care plan. *Add the modifier -32 to the E&M and any related services codes.*

Coding Tip

With use of this modifier, some plans will waive copayments and coinsurance payments on behalf of the patient. Some plans may require that a report be sent to them when this modifier is used.

-50 Bilateral Procedures. Unless the word "bilateral" is identified in the description written in CPT, use -50. Bilateral surgical procedures are performed during the same operative session. The first procedure should be identified by using the code that describes that procedure. The second (bilateral) procedure is identified by adding the modifier -50 to its number.

Coding Tip

If the plan is an RBRVS payer, the code is listed once with the modifier -50 on one line. For example,

49520-50   Bilateral repair of recurrent inguinal hernia, any age; reducible

-51   Multiple Procedures. When multiple procedures are performed at the same session, the major procedure may be reported without this modifier. The second, third, fourth, and fifth procedures are identified by adding the modifier -51 to each one.

Coding Tip

When five procedures have been performed on the same date, always submit an operative report. Report procedures in descending order of importance because plans prorate procedures. *Prorating procedures* refers to the reduction of the allowed amounts for the second, third, fourth, and fifth procedures, for example, 50 percent for the second, 25 percent for the third, 10 percent for the fourth, and 5 percent for the fifth. If the practice does not have a policy on whether multiple procedures are reported at the full charge or at a reduced charge, ask the manager and the accountant to produce one. Watch for newsletters from the plans; some plans do not require the use of -51.

-52   Reduced Services. Under certain circumstances, the service provided can be identified by its usual procedure number and the addition of the modifier -52, signifying that the service is reduced or was not completed. -52 provides a means of reporting reduced services without interfering with the identification of the basic service that was attempted.

Coding Tip

-52 is useful with a code such as 45378 Colonoscopy, diagnostic when the procedure was not completed because the doctor could not move the scope all the way through the colon.

-54   Surgical Care Only. When one physician performs a surgical procedure and another provides preoperative and/or postoperative management, surgical services may be identified *by adding the modifier -54 to the usual surgical procedure number.*

Coding Tip

-54 results in payment for preoperative and intraoperative (the actual surgery) care but no postoperative care. The payment equals a certain percentage of the total allowed amount.

-55   Postoperative Management Only. When one physician performs the postoperative management and another physician has performed the surgical procedure, the postoperative component can be identified *by adding the modifier -55 to the surgical procedure number.*

Coding Tip

The date when the care was assumed through the date when it was relinquished should be reported by the covering surgeon. -55 causes payment for postoperative care only, which represents a certain percentage of the allowed amount.

-56 Preoperative Management Only. When one physician performs the preoperative care evaluation and another physician performs the surgical procedure, the *preoperative component* can be identified by adding the modifier -56 to the surgical procedure number.

Coding Tip

If the plan is an RBRVS payer and you are billing for a primary care physician performing a preoperative history and physical, report an E&M code alone. -56 is rarely used, and then only with the codes located in the surgical section.

-57 Decision for Surgery. An evaluation and management service that resulted in the *initial* decision to perform the surgery may be identified *by adding -57 to the appropriate level of E&M service.*

Coding Tip

Watch plan newsletters for their interpretations. Medicare has said that practices should use -57 only with major surgical procedures. Medicare defines major surgical procedures as those having a preoperative period 1 day before the surgery and 90 days afterward in the postoperative period. Some plans may have adopted this Medicare coding rule, and some may have a totally different method of defining preoperative and postoperative periods.

-58 *Staged or Related Procedure by the Same Physician* During a Postoperative Period. There are three ways to use modifier -58:

1. For a surgery result planned in stages—a *staged procedure*

Clinical Example

54308-58 would be used for "Urethroplasty for second stage hypospadias repair; less than 3 cm" if this second stage was performed during the postoperative period of the first procedure.

2. To report a more extensive procedure performed during the postoperative period of a less extensive procedure

Clinical Example

54352-58 would be used for "Repair of hypospadias cripple requiring extensive dissection" if the procedure was performed during the postoperative period of 54308 above.

3. To report a therapy given after a diagnostic surgical procedure

Clinical Example

29870, "diagnostic knee arthroscopy," carries a 90-day FUD. If a claim is reported under the same surgeon's name for physical therapy, during the 90-day postoperative period, 97124-58 should be reported for the massage therapy.

Coding Tip

The uses of -58 described above may be required only by plans which are RBRVS payers, such as Medicare. Do not use -58 when a complication develops during the postoperative period after a surgery.

-62 Two Surgeons. Under some circumstances the skills of two surgeons (usually with different skills) may be required in the management of a specific surgical procedure. Under such circumstances the separate services may be identified *by adding the modifier -62 to the surgical procedure used by each surgeon re-*

porting the services. -62 may be used by the surgeon who opens the case and the surgeon who closes the incision.

Coding Tip
If the plan is an RBRVS payer, there are specific surgery codes which require that operative notes be submitted with this modifier. Check newsletters for the list or call your Medicare carrier. For Medicare, -62 causes a reduced allowance, usually 62.5 percent for each surgeon. Other payers may follow Medicare's lead on this. Use -62 only when two surgeons perform the same CPT code.

-76 Repeat Procedure *by Same Physician.* This is used to indicate that a procedure or service was repeated shortly after the original service.

Coding Tip
When a physician reports the same CPT code on the same patient *twice or more on the same date,* use -76 plus documentation of the medical necessity of repeating the procedure. Do not confuse -76 with -51. -76 is used for the same CPT code which was repeated, and -51 is used with different CPT codes.

-78 Return to the Operating Room for a *Related Procedure During the Postoperative Period.* The physician may need to indicate that another procedure was performed during the postoperative period of the initial procedure. When this subsequent procedure *is a complication of the first* and requires the use of the operating room, it is reported *by adding the modifier -78 to the related surgical procedure.*

Coding Tip
Do not confuse -78 with item 2 under -58 above, which is a more extensive procedure. While both are related to the original surgery and are performed within the postoperative period, a complication requiring a return to the operating room and the use of -78 usually occurs within a short time after the original surgery. RBRVS payers usually will not pay for complications unless the patient was cared for in an operating room.

Clinical Examples
Sutures break open and require secondary closure. In this case 13160-78 is reported. If a more extensive procedure is required as a result of failure to correct the problem with the original surgery, -58 is used.

52510, "Transurethral balloon dilatation of the prostatic urethra," was performed, and the problem was not cured. Within the postoperative period of 52510, the same physician and/or physician practice performed a 52601-58, "Transurethral electrosurgical resection of prostate," a more extensive procedure.

-79 *Unrelated Procedure or Service* by the Same Physician *During the Postoperative Period*

Coding Tip
Do not confuse -79 with -78 and -58, which are related to the first procedure. -79 is unrelated to the patient's first surgery and is usually matched with a different diagnosis.

Clinical Example
A patient fell and fractured his right wrist. While the global period was in effect, the patient fell and broke his left leg. To be paid for the fracture care for the left leg, the practice must report "27530-79 Closed treatment of tibial fracture, proximal; without manipulation."

-80   Assistant Surgeon. The first (primary) surgical assistant reports -80 with the code used by the attending surgeon.

Coding Tip
-80 is used when the surgery was performed at a hospital without a surgical residency program. Practices must keep lists of hospitals without these programs. Payment for the assistant surgeon ranges from 16 to 25 percent of the amount allowed for the attending surgeon. Medicare and other plans have lists of CPT codes which allow payment for the use of an assistant. Write to Medicare for a copy or watch plan newsletters to learn when payment is allowed.

-81   Minimum Assistant Surgeon. The second (secondary) surgical assistant adds -81 to the code used by the attending surgeon.

Coding Tip
Use modifier -81 when appropriate, but do not be surprised if the claim is denied with the reason being not medically necessary. Due to the availability of hospital personnel, i.e. scrub nurses, and physician assistants who act as second surgical assistants, many plans will not allow payment for physician minimum assistants. If the claim is denied as an exclusion in the patient's policy, then the patient may be billed for this service.

-82   Assistant Surgeon (when qualified resident surgeon not available). The first surgical assistant reports -82 when the surgery is performed at a hospital which has a surgical residency program but there were no residents available to assist with the case.

Coding Tip
-82, which indicates that there was no qualified resident at the time to assist with the surgery, should be used at hospitals which do have surgical residency programs.

Because the use of modifiers is such a difficult area, you may want to test your knowledge of this section by completing the "Exercising Knowledge of Fundamentals and Use of Modifiers" problems at the end of this chapter before going on to the next section.

NINE BASIC CPT CODING PRINCIPLES

Coding is a skill which can be developed with practice. When in doubt, refer back to these nine coding principles.

1. If the practice's encounter form or computer system does not contain the procedure name and code number, use the index of CPT to begin a code search. Depending on the type of service, it may be best to obtain a copy of the operative report and the laboratory and/or pathology report. The discharge summary or the office progress note may also be needed. After all the information has been obtained that indicates exactly what the doctor did, do the following.

2. Refer to the index to obtain a code number or series of code numbers.

3. Refer to the numeric order listing within a section of the book.

4. Read all the guidelines for that section.

5. Read up and down and all around the code(s) under consideration. Read the notes and notice semicolons, differences in descriptions, and any separate procedures. There may be a code which more accurately describes what the doctor did. Review a list of the HCPCS codes which apply to the services the practice provides. HCPCS may have a better code describing the service(s) than does CPT; if it does, choose a HCPCS code instead of a CPT code if the plan will accept HCPCS codes.

6. Select the code(s). When in doubt, send a note to the office manager and/or physician asking if they would also choose this code(s). Do not be afraid to ask questions of others. Coding and billing are an important aspect of the practice and are very difficult. No one will think you are unskilled. People will be more upset if the wrong code has been reported for many months before it is uncovered. More work is generated when a practice attempts to undo incorrect coding and must resubmit claims. Additionally, if incorrect coding is uncovered by an auditor, it can create financial liability for a practice.

7. When satisfied with the code number(s), consider the circumstances surrounding the procedure. Is a modifier needed because of altered circumstances?

8. List the primary or major procedure first. The *primary procedure* is the one provided for the primary diagnosis. It is usually the most expensive and extensive procedure.

9. When listing a code and/or modifier, always list a fee. *There must be a code for each fee.* For example,

Code	Fee
47480	$1200.00
47500-51	200.00
74320-51	100.00
Total	$1500.00

EVALUATION AND MANAGEMENT

This is the first section of the CPT. The first two digits in evaluation and management codes are 99, the third and fourth digits refer to the subcategories 20–43 for the type of encounter and location, and the last digit refers to the level of service. 99201 is an evaluation and management code for a new patient in the office or other outpatient location for the first level of service.

Evaluation and management (E&M) categories involve all types of physician encounters with patients in any location. The E&M section is used by physicians in all specialties and their employees who provide clinical services.

Certain terms and definitions are used throughout the evaluation and management section. Definitions are intended to reduce the potential for different interpretations and increase the consistency of reporting by physicians in different specialties. Each E&M category has a specific number of levels of service or code numbers from which to choose. The higher the level of service, the more physician work provided and, it is hoped, the greater the allowance. For example, there are three levels of codes for initial hospital care: 99221, 99222, and 99223, with 99223 being the code for the third, or highest, level of service. CPT instructions list the criteria *at each level* for documentation, and these should be noted in the medical record wherever the doctor provides care. The minimum set of criteria must be met or exceeded. It is the physician who must assume responsibility for this documentation. In the office, the clinical staff can help by taking a history or performing part of the examination, but the physician must countersign all documentation. Ideally, the physician and other direct caregivers should indicate the correct level of service on the encounter form, but the more knowledge other staff members have of this often misused system, the better they will be able to assist in choosing the correct code.

Components of E&M Encounters

Table 5-1 shows the seven components of E&M encounters and the way in which they are used in the code selection process. The first six are used in determining the level of care for a particular service. The three *key components*—history, examination, and medical decision making—are criteria which must be met and must appear in the documentation of the medical record. Three other components are *contributory factors,* which are not required to be provided with every patient visit. The seventh component—*time*—can be used as a guideline for the average length of time of the encounter, or it can be a controlling factor. Time is a *controlling factor* if more than 50 percent of the doctor's time with the patient is spent counseling or coordinating care. The code number is selected according to the total time listed for the level of service.

TABLE 5-1
Components of Evaluation and Management Encounters

Component	Description
History	Key component 1
Examination	Key component 2
Medical decision making	Key component 3
Counseling	Contributory factor
Coordination of care	Contributory factor
Nature of presenting problem	Contributory factor
Time	Guideline or controlling factor

Key Component 1: History

The levels of E&M codes recognize four types of history, defined as follows:

Problem-Focused—chief complaint; brief history of present illness or problem.

Expanded Problem-Focused—chief complaint; brief history of present illness; problem pertinent system review.

Detailed—chief complaint; extended history of present illness; pertinent extended system review; *pertinent* past, family, and/or social history directly related to the patient's problems.

Comprehensive—chief complaint; extended history of present illness; complete system review, *complete* past, family, and/or social history.

Key Component 2: Examination

The levels of E&M codes recognize four types of examinations, which are defined as follows:

Problem-Focused—an examination that is limited to the affected body area or organ system.

Expanded Problem-Focused—an examination that is limited to the affected body area or organ system and other symptomatic or related organ systems.

Detailed—an examination that is extended to the affected body area(s) and other symptomatic or related organ system(s).

Comprehensive—a complete single organ system specialty examination or a complete multisystem examination.

Key Component 3: Medical Decision Making

Medical decision making refers to the complexity of making a medical decision for the encounter. There are four types:

Straightforward
Low
Moderate
High

The physician must meet or exceed the criteria listed in two of three elements to arrive at the type of decision making. These elements are as follows:

The number of diagnoses or the number of management options

The amount and/or complexity of data to be reviewed (medical records, results of diagnostic tests or other information that must be reviewed and analyzed)

The risk of complications and/or morbidity or mortality as well as the degree of comorbidities which affect decision making

Using the Key Components

To understand how to use the key components and determine whether three key components or two key components are required, the subcategories of the E&M codes are used. For example, a new patient E&M code requires documentation to support three key components, while the established patient requires documentation for only two key components.

New patients   A *new patient* is one who has not received any professional services from the physician or another physician in the same specialty who belongs to the same group practice within the past 3 years. The new patient definition must be met and all three key components must be documented to select this subcategory and a certain level of E&M code.

Established patient   An *established patient* is one who has received professional services from the physician or another physician in the same specialty who belongs to the same group practice within the past 3 years. The established patient definition must be met and only two of the three key components must be documented to select this category and a certain level of E&M code.

The Contributory Factors

Counseling is a discussion with a patient and/or family member concerning one or more of the following areas:

- Diagnostic results, impressions, and/or recommended diagnostic studies
- Prognosis
- Risks and benefits of management (treatment) options
- Instructions for management (treatment) and/or follow-up

■ Risk factor reduction
■ Patient and family education

"Coordination of care" refers to time spent by the physician when the patient is in the office or on the hospital unit during which the physician phones other healthcare professionals or talks with them. If the patient is not present in the office or on the hospital unit, another category of codes, "Case management," should be used.

"Nature of presenting problem" refers to the reason the doctor sees the patient. It can be a disease, injury, condition, or other finding.

Time

Time is defined according to the place of service. In the office, time is defined as only that time which the physician spends face to face with the patient and/or family. *Face-to-face time* includes the time the physician spends documenting a patient's history or performing an examination or counseling and any other occasions when the doctor and patient are together. It does not include the time spent by other clinical employees of the physician. The time clock starts when the doctor encounters the patient face to face. In a hospital or nursing home, time is defined as unit or floor time. It begins when the doctor opens the door to the unit and includes time at the bedside, time at the nurses' station reviewing the chart, time writing notes, and time speaking with other professionals and the patient's family.

Level of Service

The nature of the patient's presenting problem and selected examples of clinical situations are provided in the descriptions accompanying each E&M code and in Appendix D. This is done to assist the physician in selecting the appropriate code for the level of service. Providing a *level of service* is defined as meeting the criteria for the key components. Figure 5-1 is a grid showing types of key components for each level of service for a new patient during an office or other outpatient visit. The grid in Figure 5-2 applies to an established patient for an office or other outpatient visit. You can refer to the key component requirements using these charts when you code from the E&M section of the CPT book. Below are examples of clinical situations which could be coded as levels 1 through 5 for a new patient seen in the office as long as there is adequate documentation in the medical record.

Clinical Examples—New Patient

99201   Initial office visit for severe rash and itching for the past 24 hours, positive history for contact with poison oak 48 hours before the visit, male child.

99202   Initial office visit for recurrent urinary infection in a female.

Levels & Time	Both: Hx and Exam	Types of: Decision Making (Select two or more from 4,5,6)	Patient Risk of Morbidity/ Mortality	Diagnostic Testing/ Data Review	Number of Diagnoses or Management Options
Level 1 99201 10 min.	**Problem Focused** Hx {•Chief complaint •Brief Hx present illness} Em {•One area or organ system}	**StraightForward** •Patient risk •# mgmt options or possible dx •Data review	minimal severity	minimal or none	minimal
Level 2 99202 20 min.	**Expanded Problem Focused** Hx {•CC, brief HPI •Problem **Pertinent** ROS} Em {•1 area or organ + related organs}	**StraightForward** •Patient risk •# mgmt options or possible dx •Data review	minimal severity	minimal or none	minimal
Level 3 99203 30 min.	**Detailed** Hx {•CC, extended HPI + limited ROS •1 **Pertinent** past MH, FH, or SH} Em {•Extended-areas + related organs}	**Low Complexity** •Patient risk •# mgmt options or possible dx •Data review	low severity	limited	limited
Level 4 99204 45 min.	**Comprehensive** Hx {•CC, extended HPI •**Complete** ROS, MH, FH + SH} Em {•Complete specialty or total PE*}	**Moderate Complexity** •Patient risk •# mgmt options or possible dx •Data review	moderate severity	moderate	multiple
Level 5 99205 60 min.	**Comprehensive** Hx {•CC, extended HPI •**Complete** ROS, MH, FH + SH} Em {•Complete specialty or total PE*}	**High Complexity** •Patient risk •# mgmt options or possible dx •Data review	high severity	extensive	extensive

Key Factors	Decision Making
Hx, Exam, and Decision Making must be provided (3 of 3).	If counseling and coordination of care involve 50% of doctor's time, use time factor alone to select the code. If coordination of care is provided alone, use case management codes

* Specialty exam is a complete single organ system specialty exam or a complete multi-system exam.
CPT codes, descriptions, and two digit numeric modifiers only are copyright 1994 American Medical Association.

FIGURE 5-1 New patient office/outpatient visits.

99203　　Initial office visit for recurrent low back pain radiating to the leg, 48-year-old male.

99204　　Initial office visit for chest pain on exertion, 63-year-old male.

99205　　Initial office visit for severe chronic obstructive pulmonary disease, congestive heart failure, and hypertension, 69-year-old male.

Note
The coding examples above were provided by the CPT Advisory Committee as guidelines only and may not be accurate examples when compared with the actual code choices in your practice.

Specific guidelines on the amount of documentation necessary for systems review, body areas, and organ systems will be addressed further in Chapter 7.

	1 + / or 2	or 3	4	5	6
Levels & Time	Hx and/or Exam	Types of: Decision Making Select two or more from 4,5,6	Patient Risk of Morbidity/ Mortality	Diagnostic Testing/ Data Review	Number of Diagnoses or Management Options
Level 1 99211 5 min.	Does not require Doctor to administer	Usually None	minimal severity		
Level 2 99212 10 min.	**Problem Focused** Hx {•Chief complaint •Brief Hx present illness Em ►One area or organ system	**StraightForward** •Patient risk •# mgmt options or possible dx •Data review	minimal severity	minimal or none	minimal
Level 3 99213 15 min.	**Expanded Problem Focused** Hx {•CC, brief HPI • Problem **Pertinent** ROS Em ►1 area or organ & related organs	**Low Complexity** •Patient risk •# mgmt options or possible dx •Data review	low severity	limited	limited
Level 4 99214 25 min.	**Detailed** Hx {•CC, extended HPI + limited ROS •1 **Pertinent** past MH, FH, or SH Em ►Extended-areas + related organs	**Moderate Complexity** •Patient risk •# mgmt options or possible dx •Data review	moderate severity	moderate	multiple
Level 5 99215 40 min.	**Comprehensive** Hx {•CC, extended HPI •**Complete** ROS, MH, FH + SH Em ►Complete specialty or total PE*	**High Complexity** •Patient risk •# mgmt options or possible dx •Data review	high severity	extensive	extensive

Key Factors	Decision Making
Hx, Exam, and Decision Making must be provided (2 of 3).	If counseling and coordination of care involve 50% of doctor's time, use time factor alone to select the code. If coordination of care is provided alone, use case management codes.

* Specialty exam is a complete single organ system specialty exam or a complete multi-system exam.
CPT codes, descriptions, and two digit numeric modifiers only are copyright
1994 American Medical Association.

FIGURE 5-2 Established patient office/outpatient visits.

Overview of the E&M Subcategories

Table 5-2 lists all the categories and subcategories in the evaluation and management section. It can be used in conjunction with Figures 5-1 and 5-2 which list the criteria to identify the four types of history, examination, and decision making, the key components of E&M coding.

The following sections describe important E&M categories and subcategories. Each time a subcategory contains such words as "new," "initial," "consultation," or "assessment" or if there is only one type of description in a category, all three key components (history, exam, and decision making) must be met with supporting documentation in the patient's medical record. When the subcategories contain such words as "established," "subsequent," or "follow-up," only two of the three key components must be met with supporting documentation in the patient's medical record. Keep referring to Table 5-2 as you read the following sections of the E&M codes to note the

TABLE 5-2
CPT-4 E&M Categories and Subcategories

Code Numbers	Category/Subcategory
	Office or Other Outpatient Services
99201–99205	New patient
99211–99215	Established patient
99217	Hospital observation discharge services
99218–99220	**Hospital observation services**
	Hospital Inpatient Care
99221–99223	Initial hospital care
99231–99233	Subsequent hospital care
99238	Hospital discharge services
	Consultations
99241–99245	Office consultations
99251–99255	Initial inpatient consultations
99261–99263	Follow-up inpatient consultations
99271–99275	Confirmatory consultations
99281–99285	**Emergency Department Services**
99291–99292	**Critical Care Services**
99295–99297	**Neonatal Intensive Care**
	Nursing Facility Services
99301–99303	Comprehensive assessments
99311–99313	Subsequent care
	Domiciliary, Rest Home, or Custodial Care Services
99321–99323	New patient
99331–99333	Established patient
	Home Services
99341–99343	New patient
99351–99353	Established patient
	Prolonged Services
99354–99357	With direct patient contact
99358–99359	Without direct patient contact
99360	**Standby Services**
	Case Management Services
99361–99362	Team conference
99371–99373	Telephone calls
99375–99376	Care plan oversight
	Preventive Medicine Services
99381–99387	New patient
99391–99397	Established patient
99401–99404	Individual counseling
99411–99412	Group counseling
99420–99429	Other preventive medicine services
99431–99440	**Newborn Care**
99450–99456	**Special E&M Services**
99499	**Other E&M Services**

subcategory names which will let you know if two or three key components are required to select a certain code number. Refer also to Table 5-2 for the code number ranges.

Hospital Observation

These codes are used to report E&M services provided to patients designated admitted as observation status in a hospital. These patients are not inpatients. To report services provided to a patient who is admitted to the hospital on the same date, after receiving hospital observation care services, use the initial hospital *inpatient care* codes, 99221–99223. For a patient admitted to the hospital after the date of observation status, the claim would be reported as:

> January 1   An observation status code
> January 2   Initial hospital care code

When a patient is admitted to observation status in the course of an encounter in another place of service, such as a hospital emergency room, all E&M services provided by the physician in conjunction with admission to observation status are reported under one hospital observation code when the services are performed on the same date as admission to observation status.

Hospital Inpatient

On a patient's hospital admission day, the initial hospital care code is reported only by the admitting physician. All visits after the admission day are reported by using subsequent hospital care codes. When you use the subsequent hospital care codes, keep in mind that only one code is used for each day of care. Therefore, if the doctor sees a patient more than one time per day, there will have to be a medically necessary reason for the second visit per day and documentation will have to be submitted. Many plans will deny a claim for a second hospital visit performed on the same date, especially with the same diagnosis.

Another code that is often ignored is the hospital discharge day management code, 99238. *Hospital discharge management* is reported by the doctor who discharges a patient after a multiple-day stay. The charge should reflect the time and effort expended by the doctor in the final examination of the patient, continuing care, instructions, and preparation of the medical records for discharge.

Consultation

A *consultation* occurs when a physician renders an opinion or advice regarding the evaluation and/or management of a specific problem at the request of another physician. A consultant may initiate diagnostic or therapeutic services. The request and need for the consultation must be documented in the patient's medical record. The consulting physician may begin the documentation by stating, "This patient was sent by Dr. Smith for consultation regarding recurring abdominal pain." The consultant's opinion and any services that were provided or ordered must also be documented in the patient's record by the consultant and communicated to the requesting physician. A doctor should never use the word "referral" in the medical record when a consultation has been requested. *Referral* is the delegation of care. Insurance and managed care plans may deny a consultation during an audit if a referral is documented. This would imply that the consulting doctor is assuming a portion of care for the patient, a situation which is referred to as concurrent care. *Concurrent care* is questioned by the payers mainly in a hospital setting when two physicians bill the same diagnosis code with subsequent hospital care codes. Concurrent care claims in a hospital setting are often denied. Plans use edits to detect when two or more physicians are billing for similar services for the same patient. During concurrent care, the office staff must communicate with other practices to determine which diagnosis codes they are using as the primary diagnosis. For example, suppose a family physician admits a patient with chest pain and requests a cardiologist's advice. The cardiologist diagnoses a myocardial infarction, and the family physician delegates care of the myocardial infarction to the cardiologist. The cardiologist uses an inpatient consultation code on the bill for the first visit and then uses the codes for subsequent hospital care thereafter. The diagnosis code for the cardiologist is myocardial infarction. The family physician bills the diagnosis of chest pain initially and then must find another diagnosis or reason to follow the patient for subsequent hospital care.

Confirmatory (Second Opinion Consultations)

Confirmatory consultations are not requested by physicians. Instead, confirmatory consultation codes are used when a patient or plan requests a second or third opinion to confirm the medical appropriateness of the treatment that was previously recommended by another physician. Use the modifier -32 with confirmatory consultations (mandated second opinions) requested by an insurance plan.

Emergency Room

All physicians who provide evaluation and management in an emergency room (ER) can use these codes. There is no distinction between a new patient and an established patient, and time is never a factor. An *emergency room* is defined as a hospital-based facility that is open 24 hours a day for the treatment of patients who present for immediate medical attention. If a physician is called to the emergency room by the ER doctor, it is a consultation within an emergency room (other outpatient service). If the patient is not admitted to the consultant's service, 99241–99245 may be used. Critical care codes are used in place of ER codes if the patient requires constant physician attendance.

Critical Care

Critical care codes are based on the time a physician spends providing critical care services for the entire day. Critical care can be provided in any location, not just in an intensive care unit. Critical care requires constant physician attendance because of the critical nature of the patient's condition. When reporting critical care codes, certain services are included and cannot be billed separately. There is a note in the CPT book listing these services. Any service performed which is not listed in the note should be reported separately. For example, a physician spent 25 minutes in the morning in constant attendance on a patient and 15 minutes in the afternoon. The office staff adds the minutes of the two visits together when coding. Forty minutes of critical care is coded 99291. A physician must spend at least 30 minutes per day providing critical care when using 99291 describing the first hour. Table 5-3 gives the timetable used in CPT whenever a code refers to time in hours or half hours (1 hour and each additional 30 minutes).

To avoid confusion when billing, ask the physician to give you the total number of minutes spent each day providing critical care services or any service for which the code specifies time.

Example

Physician spends 2½ hours providing critical care services on May 3. The services are reported as:

Code	Fee
99291	$170.00
99292	85.00
99292	85.00
99292	85.00

TABLE 5-3

Critical Care Time per Day

Total Duration of Critical Care	Codes
Less than 30 minutes (½ hour)	99232 or 99233
30–74 minutes (½ hr–1 hr 14 min)	99291 X 1
75–104 minutes (1 hr 15 min–1 hr 44 min)	99291 X 1 & 99292 X 1
105–134 minutes (1 hr 45 min–2 hr 14 min)	99291 X 1 & 99292 X 2
135–164 minutes (2 hr 15 min–2 hr 44 min)	99291 X 1 & 99292 X 3
165–194 minutes (2 hr 45 min–3 hr 14 min)	99291 X 1 & 99292 X 4

Nursing Facility Services

When coding nursing facility services, a distinction must be made between skilled nursing facilities and custodial care facilities. Skilled nursing facilities provide active medical professional care. In contrast, a custodial facility may intermittently provide medical professional care. When coding physician services provided at nursing facility services, the office staff should ask how the institution is licensed in the state. Services at facilities that are licensed as providing skilled, intermediate, or long-term care are coded 99301–99313, whereas physician services at facilities that are licensed for custodial care are coded 99321–99333.

Prolonged Services

Codes for *prolonged services* are used when a physician provides care involving face-to-face patient contact that lasts beyond the normally required time. The codes 99354–99357 are used in addition to other codes but are more commonly added to levels of E&M services which specify a typical time. Prolonged services codes represent the total duration of face-to-face time spent by the physician on a given date even if the time on that date is not continuous. 99354 is used for prolonged face-to-face service in an office or other outpatient setting, for 30–74 minutes, and 99355 represents each additional 30 minutes of prolonged service. 99356 represents prolonged physician service in the inpatient setting, for 30–74 minutes. 99357 is used for each additional 30 minutes. Remember that inpatient face-to-face time includes time spent by the physician on the floor or unit.

Use Table 5-3 to select the code(s) by time. Prolonged physician time must be at least 30 minutes beyond the typical time spent for an E&M service. Review Figures 5-1 and 5-2 for examples of typical time per level of service. See the CPT book for the time allotted for other E&M levels of service. Notice that ER, custodial care, hospital observation, and home visits have no typical times. Therefore, prolonged services codes cannot be used in addition to these E&M codes.

Coding Tip

Medicare will pay for 99354–99357 services in conjunction with office, hospital, or skilled nursing facility visits and consultations. It will not pay for prolonged services reported with other codes, such as monitoring electroencephalograms and intrathoracic pressures. Other insurance and managed care plans may follow Medicare's rules on this issue.

E&M Codes Which Are Not Always Covered

Insurance and managed care plans may not cover certain services, but this does not mean that their codes should not be reported. The office staff and physicians may want to create a practice financial policy to bill for these services if an extraordinary amount of physician time is spent providing them. Additionally, if these codes are not reported to the plans, the plans will never have a database for covering these services. If a plan denies a service because of an exclusion, the patient can be billed. The E&M codes which are not always covered are discussed below.

Code Ranges	Description
99358–99359	Prolonged physician services without direct (face-to-face) physician-patient contact are used when a physician provides prolonged service not involving direct face-to-face care that is beyond the usual service in either the outpatient or the inpatient setting. Example: the physician spends time reviewing charts before patients are initially evaluated.
99360	Physician standby service is used to report a service requested by another physician which involves prolonged physician attendance (detention time) without direct face-to-face patient contact. The code represents each 30 minutes of attendance. Example: the heart surgeon waits while the cardiologist performs an angioplasty. If the heart surgeon is not needed, 99360 is billed for each 30 minutes of detention time. If the heart surgeon is needed and performs major surgery, the code is not used.
99361–99373	Case management services are used when the physician is responsible for the direct care of a patient and for coordinating and controlling access to or supervising the medical services needed by a patient. The codes include team conferences (99361–99362) conducted by the physician with other professionals involved in a patient's case without the patient present. Case management services also include telephone calls (99371–99373). Telephone calls are reported when the physician initiates a telephone call to a patient for medical care or telephones other healthcare professionals to coordinate management. These codes cannot be used when the patient initiates the call.
99375–99376	Care plan oversight services are reported separately from other E&M codes. Physician time spent in care plan oversight provided within a 30-day period for 30–60 minutes is code 99375. If the physician spends 61 minutes in the period, 99376 is used. All physician time spent must be documented in the medical record. Figure 5-3 is a sheet which can be placed in a patient's record to keep track of the doctor's time spent in each 30-day period. Medicare considers payment for 99375. The office staff should begin suggesting ways to keep track of excessive amounts of the doctor's time spent on the phone caring for homecare patients.
99381–99387	These codes refer to preventive medicine. Insurance plans that do not cover preventive care will not cover these E&M codes. HMOs do cover preventive care. Preventive medicine services occur when a patient makes an appointment for a checkup, desiring a comprehensive examination. There are seven codes describing ages 1 year or less to 65 years and over. Immunizations and diagnostic tests are coded separately. Counseling about risk factors on the same date of the preventive care examination is included in codes 99381–99387.

Date	Service	Jimmy Lane	Time
1/6/XX	Coumadin	2 tabs in a.m. every day omitting Tuesday	5 minutes
1/13/XX	P.T.T. results	Review of report	3 minutes

FIGURE 5-3   Care plan oversight tracking sheet.

99401–99412   Counseling and/or risk factor reduction intervention are used to report counseling services provided to patients to reduce risk factors which might cause health problems later in life. The codes are reported only when this counseling occurs on a separate date from the preventive medicine codes. Risk factor counseling can include such topics as family problems, diet, exercise, substance abuse, sexual patterns, dental health, and injury prevention. There are individual, group, and other counseling codes that are based on the time the physician spends counseling patients.

MEDICINE

The medicine section is the last section of the CPT book. It includes diagnostic, therapeutic, and unique specialty services in the following order:

Immunization injections
Therapeutic or diagnostic infusions
Therapeutic or diagnostic injections
Psychiatry
Biofeedback
Dialysis
Gastroenterology
Ophthalmology
Special otorhinolaryngologic services
Cardiovascular
Noninvasive vascular diagnostic studies
Pulmonary
Allergy and clinical immunology
Neurology and neuromuscular procedures
Chemotherapy administration
Special dermatological procedures
Physical medicine and rehabilitation
Osteopathic manipulative treatment
Special services and reports

Medicine section codes are used by all physicians and other professionals who provide these services. An overview of a few of these categories will help you understand this section.

Immunizations

Immunizations are listed by the type of vaccines administered. Each code includes the syringes, bandages, or cotton swabs normally found in the doctor's office. Plans which cover preventive immunizations at specified intervals in a patient's life will cover certain injections, such as a tetanus shot (90703) every 10 years for an adult. However, vaccinations for cholera (90725) for travel to another country most likely will not be covered. Since preventive medicine is becoming widespread, even Medicare has expanded traditional indemnity benefits to include preventive vaccinations for influenza (90724), pneumonia (90732), and hepatitis B (90731). With hepatitis B immunizations, the patient's risk factors must be listed on the claim, such as a hemophiliac, a dialysis patient, and hepatitis in the household.

Coding Tip

Note that the descriptions of the CPT vaccine codes do not specify a dosage amount. If less than the normal dose is given, the practice still reports the full code. Read newsletters of the major payers for their immunization coding and benefit rules. Clip and place articles in a scrapbook for reference by plan name.

Therapeutic and Diagnostic Injections

Therapeutic and diagnostic injections include injections given for the treatment of a condition but do not include allergy injections (see codes 95115–95134). Injection codes are selected in accordance with the method of administration, such as subcutaneous or intramuscular. Most plans cover injections for patients who are ill. Rules differ in terms of how plans want the services reported. Government plans, Medicare, Medicaid, and plans that accept the HCPCS J codes pay separately for the cost of a generic injectable medication with a J code. J2060 is the HCPCS code for Lorazepam, the generic name for Ativan. The J code must be reported to recover the practice's expense in purchasing the medication. With plans that do not accept J codes, the injection will be billed specifically as stated in CPT. The note in parentheses in code 90782 says "(specify material injected)," which means that you should list the medication's name and dose. The example below shows the different coding rules when the patient receives an injection at the time of an office visit with the physician for plans accepting J codes and those who do not accept them.

Plans Accepting J Codes	Plans Not Accepting J Codes
99213 E&M code, level 3	99213 E&M code, level 3
J2060 lorazepam	90782 therapeutic injection,
(generic name for Ativan) 2 mg	intramuscular Ativan 2 mg

If the patient does not see the doctor, but receives an injection from a nurse, 99211 can be reported instead of 99213, as in the example above. When using 99211, the nurse must document more than just the administration of the injection. The nurse must provide professional services, such as patient history taking and vital signs, which are medically appropriate to the situation and which must be documented in the patient's chart. If the nurse provides no professional services other than the administration of the injection, codes 90782 or 90788 (antibiotic injection) are the appropriate codes to use.

Cardiovascular Services

Cardiovascular services include therapeutic services such as cardiopulmonary resuscitation (CPR) and percutaneous transluminal coronary angioplasty (PTCA) and diagnostic services such as cardiography, Holter

TABLE 5-4

Special Services Codes

Code	Description	Example of Use
99000	Handling of a specimen	To report medical office's time spent labeling a 24-hour urine specimen and sending it to a lab
99024	Postoperative follow-up visit, included in global (package) service	To report the encounter postoperatively so that the plan has a record of care and data for the collection of capitation rates and the performance of quality of care studies
99050–99052	Services requested after hours and/or at night	To report inconvenient times by the physician rendering care
99054	Services provided on Sundays and holidays	To report inconvenient time spent by the physician rendering care, such as 2 a.m. on Thanksgiving.
99058	Office services provided on an emergency basis	To report the extra time used in rearranging the schedule or extended hours to see a patient in the office for an emergency
99070	Supplies dispensed from the office beyond what is normally included in the office visit	To report drugs, surgical trays, and other supplies to plans which do not accept HCPCS codes. When using 99070, the name of the supply and the practice's cost for the supply must be noted with a copy of the invoice; some plans do not allow the reporting of 99070 because it is not specific; plans want specific data
99075	Medical testimony	To bill a law firm for the medical testimony of the physician
99080	Special reports such as insurance forms or reports which are not conveyed as per usual communication	To bill for special reports, such as insurance forms
99082	Unusual travel	To report the physician's time spent escorting the patient from one location to another

monitors, echocardiography, cardiac fluoroscopy, cardiac catheterization, analysis of pacemaker functioning, and other vascular services. Cardiography codes distinguish between the inclusion of a tracing only and an interpretation and report. For example,

93000	Electrocardiogram; routine ECG with at least 12 leads; with interpretation and report
93005	tracing only, without interpretation and report
93010	interpretation and report only

Special Services and Reports

The codes 99000–99199 are indexed under the words "Special Services." Special services codes describe special circumstances that may be reported in addition to the basic service provided. They are never reported alone. The basic service could be any type of E&M service, diagnostic service, or therapeutic service. Medicare does not cover these codes with the exception of 99082, which is by special review. Other plans may cover some of them. Table 5-4 lists code numbers, descriptions, and examples of special services.

Exercises that will help you select codes from the medicine section are located at the end of this chapter.

RADIOLOGY

The radiology section of the CPT book is divided into these categories of procedures:

Diagnostic Radiology (Diagnostic Imaging). Begins with code 70010. Headings are also listed according to anatomic body part.

Diagnostic Ultrasound. Begins with code 76506. Headings are listed according to anatomic body part.

Radiation Oncology. Begins with code 77261 for radiology treatment planning. Headings include treatment, delivery, and management.

Nuclear Medicine. Begins with code 78000. Headings are arranged by body system.

Diagnostic radiology procedures contain technical and professional components unless the description states otherwise. The *technical component* includes the use of the equipment and materials and the actual taking of an x-ray by a technician. The *professional component* includes the reading of the film, the interpretation of the x-ray findings, and the writing of a report. The professional component is often identified with the words "radiological supervision and interpretation" within the description. For example, 74220 is for radiologic examination of the esophagus. The description assumes this code includes the use of the equipment to take the x-ray and its maintenance as well as the radiologist's interpretation and report. If the x-ray was taken at another hospital or location and the radiologist is only reading and writing the report, 74220 is modified with -26 (professional component).

Physicians other than radiologists also use this section. For example, surgeons who place catheters, inject contrast material, and remove foreign bodies with the aid of radiologic equipment use codes from the radiology section. A surgeon removing a foreign body of the esophagus and using x-rays to guide a balloon catheter would use "74235 Removal of foreign body(s), esophageal, with use of balloon catheter, radiological supervision and interpretation (S&I)." The radiologist at the hospital in which the procedure was performed should not report this code. The surgeon would report this code in addition to the actual surgery, 43215, which is the code for esophagoscopy with removal of a foreign body. There is a helpful note below 43215 to use 74235 for radiologic supervision and interpretation. Throughout the surgery section, there are notes suggesting to add the S&I codes if the surgeon provides this service.

Medical practices code from the radiology section when x-ray procedures are done in their offices, such as chest x-rays and knee x-rays. "71010 Radiologic examination, chest; single view, frontal" is used by the practice that films this x-ray, reads the findings, and writes a formal report. You can find the correct code either by first looking under the anatomic site and then looking for the subentry for the radiologic procedure (e.g., first "chest" and then subindent to "x-ray") or by first finding the procedure and then subindenting to the anatomic part (find "x-ray" first and then subindent to "chest").

Exercises for radiology coding appear at the end of this chapter.

PATHOLOGY AND LABORATORY

The pathology and laboratory section is subdivided into the following categories of procedures:

■ Automated, Multichannel Tests. Begins with the code 80002 for the reporting of chemistry tests performed as groups on automated multichannel equipment. A complete list of the chemicals in the blood being analyzed, such as chloride, cholesterol, and potassium, appears in the CPT book in the note introducing this category. If glucose and creatinine chemistry levels were analyzed from one blood sample, the code is 80002. If three chemistry tests from the list in CPT were analyzed, the code is 80003. 80019 is the last code in the series and describes 19 or more clinical chemistry tests.

■ Organ or Disease Oriented Panels. Begins with code 80050 and lists individual tests included in the reporting of codes from panels. If a practice performs a test that is not listed in the panel, the test is reported in addition to the panel.

Example
80061 is a lipid panel which includes a total cholesterol (82465), HDL cholesterol (83718), and triglycerides (84478). If the physician also performs a manual complete blood count (85031), this code is reported in addition to the panel.

■ Drug Testing. Begins with code 80100 and used to test for the presence of a drug.

■ Therapeutic Drug Assays. Begins with code 80150 and used to test the quantity of a drug.

■ Evocative/Suppression Testing. Begins with code 80400 and do not include the physician work in administering the agents. Code 90780–90784 are used. The laboratory reports evocative/suppression testing codes.

■ Consultations (Clinical pathology). Begins with code 80500 and are reported by pathologists for their consultations.

■ Urinalysis. Begins with code 81000 for the examination of urine.

■ Chemistry. Begins with code 82000. Descriptions under this heading are considered quantitative (the exact amount of the substance) unless specified otherwise.

■ Hematology and Coagulation. Begins with code 85002 and contains all types of tests performed on blood cells.

■ Immunology. Begins with code 86000 for body reactions to disease.

■ Transfusion Medicine. Begins with code 86850 for use in the transfusion of blood and blood products.

■ Microbiology. Begins with code 87001 and covers isolation of organisms and fungi which cause disease.

■ Anatomic and Surgical Pathology. Begins with codes 88000 and 88300 for use by pathologists dealing with specimens.

■ Other Procedures. Begins with code 89050 and includes any procedure which does not fit under the other headings.

Within each major heading, the procedures are listed alphabetically according to the name of the test.

Within the descriptions of the codes, the words *qualitative,* meaning the presence of a substance, and *quantitative,* meaning the total amount of a substance, are often used. If these meanings are not understood, it is difficult to select the correct code. Insurance and managed care plans have strict rules for billing laboratory services performed in a physician practice. Medicare will allow only the laboratory in which the test was performed to bill it directly for payment. If a physician performs a laboratory test in the office laboratory, the practice must accept Medicare's payment as payment in full: The patient cannot be billed for the difference. If the practice does not perform the test, Medicare does allow payment for a venipuncture (drawing blood from a vein into a tube) after which the specimen is sent out to a laboratory that will interpret the result. Medicare will not accept 36415 from CPT for this purpose because its description contains the words, "finger, heel, ear stick" in addition to the word "venipuncture." There is a special Level II HCPCS code for billing Medicare for a venipuncture; G0001.

Many managed care plans have restricted the types of tests which can be performed in a physician's practice. These plans have lists describing which tests they will pay for. Managed care plans contract with large commercial laboratories to get better rates. Participating physicians must send specimens or direct patients to the managed care plan's laboratories for services that are not on this list. If a claim is reported for a test that is not on the list, the claim will be denied.

Exercises for the pathology and laboratory section appear at the end of this chapter.

SURGERY

The surgery section is by far the longest section of the CPT book. It includes procedures ranging from minor excisions of skin neoplasms performed in the office to organ transplants performed in a hospital. The categories of the surgery section are listed in the following order:

Code Ranges	Categories
10040–19499	Integumentary system
20000–29909	Musculoskeletal system
30000–32999	Respiratory system
33010–37799	Cardiovascular system
38100–38999	Hemic and lymphatic systems
39000–39599	Mediastinum and diaphragm
40490–49999	Digestive system
50010–53899	Urinary system
54000–55899	Male genital system
55970–55980	Intersex surgical procedures
56300–56399	Laparoscopy/Peritoneoscopy/Hysteroscopy
56405–58999	Female genital system
59000–59899	Maternity care and delivery
60000–60699	Endocrine system
61000–64999	Nervous system
65091–68899	Eye and ocular adnexa
69000–69979	Auditory system

Because of the size of the surgery section, we will not discuss all the categories. The surgery section is arranged primarily by

1. Body system
2. Anatomic site
3. Procedure performed

Procedural headings generally follow anatomic headings in the following order, although this is not always consistent.

Incision
Excision
Introduction/removal
Repair/reconstruction
Endoscopy
Grafts
Other or miscellaneous procedures

Listed Surgical Procedures

The listed surgical procedure guideline addresses surgical follow-up days (FUD). In the beginning of this chapter, under "Guidelines," we mentioned that the starred procedures are not predictable enough to set a standard number of postoperative follow-up visits to be included in the surgeon's fee as a package. The *listed surgical procedures guideline* is the opposite of the starred procedure guideline. The surgeon is not paid for E&M codes during normal followup unless there is an unusual circumstance or complication. The guideline also includes local infiltration, digital block, or topical anesthesia if the procedure is performed in the office. At times, medical practices are confused about when a package begins and ends for each payer. There is no universal way in which each insurance or managed care plan determines the number of pre- and postoperative visits included in its package payment. As was mentioned in Chapter 1, many plans have adopted the RBRVS global periods for follow-up days. In an attempt to establish a single universal method for charging all plans, many physician practices have adopted the RBRVS global periods as internal office policy. Under this policy, the practice also knows when to use the global surgery modifiers (-24, -25, -57, -58, -78 and -79). The practice then has one method for charging postoperative visits after the global period or package expires.

Although many insurance and managed care plans have adopted the RBRVS postoperative global periods, variations among plans still exist in regard to what is included in the package fee for preoperative visits. Plans may include all visits 6 weeks before surgery or include only visits 1 day before the surgery.

> **Coding Tip**
> Medicare exempts consultations, new patient visits, and emergency room visits from any preoperative global fee. Medicare pays the attending surgeon for critical care services during the global period for seriously ill or burned patients. Codes 99291 and 99292 with the modifier -24 should be reported in these circumstances. Regardless of a plan's policy for establishing its package fee, a claim can be reported for visits resulting from complications or unusual circumstances. The use of modifiers and a diagnosis different than the reason for surgery can justify the additional payment.

Separate Procedure Guideline

Another confusing guideline that appears at the beginning of the surgery section is the *separate procedure guideline*. It is the only guideline CPT has for a bundling rule. Throughout CPT, the words "(separate procedure)" are contained in the descriptions. For example,

44005   Enterolysis (freeing of intestinal adhesion) (separate procedure)

It is common for the attending surgeon to perform more than one procedure within the same operative session. In some instances the additional procedures are considered to be part of the major procedure, especially if they are related. In other instances the additional procedures are unrelated and distinctly different. When the phrase "separate procedure" appears in parentheses in the description, a coding and billing decision must be made. If a procedure is carried out at the same time as another procedure and is normally part of a major procedure, report only the major procedure, not the one which has "separate procedure" in its description. A *separate procedure* is a procedure that is ordinarily done as a part of a larger procedure, but if it is performed alone for a specific purpose, it is considered a separate procedure that is reported by itself or in addition to another procedure(s). In the enterolysis example, the procedure can be reported by itself if it is the only procedure the attending surgeon performed on the intestines during that operative session. Otherwise, because 44005 has the words "(separate procedure)," it cannot be added to a claim with other procedures for intestinal surgery.

It is possible to report two codes that contain within their descriptions "(separate procedure)" during one operative session if they are performed on two separate body systems. For example,

19100*   Biopsy of breast; needle care (separate procedure)
44312   Revision of ileostomy; simple (release of superficial scar) (separate procedure)

These procedures are unrelated and are performed on two different body systems. With all the different edits being sold to plans to bundle services, the office staff should consult with the physicians and set a single standard policy for when to report separate procedures. The AMA's bundling rules are easily adopted as an internal office policy and are defendable if there is a claim denial for unbundling. Medicare's bundling list is published in their newsletters. Some practices use that list.

INTEGUMENTARY SYSTEM

In the integumentary section, under the headings "Excision—Benign Lesions" and "Excision—Malignant Lesions," size and pathology are used in selecting the code numbers. Not only does CPT classify excision of skin lesions into benign and malignant types, it goes further by specifying lesion size in centimeters and anatomic location. All this information must be conveyed by the physician to the office staff so that the lesion can be coded correctly. When you are selecting the code for the size of the lesion, use the longest portion of the lesion before the lesion is removed as the diameter. An introductory note defines an excision as including a simple nonlayered closure. If the excision involves deeper layers of skin or requires reconstructive surgery, an intermediate or complex repair code is used in addition to the excision code.

Wound Repairs

There are three types of wound repair codes:

> *Simple repair* refers to the closing of superficial wounds which involve the skin and/or subcutaneous tissues applying in one layer of sutures.
>
> *Intermediate repair* involves the application of a second layer of sutures to close one or more of the subcutaneous tissues and nonmuscle tissues or the use of a single-layer closure of heavily contaminated wounds requiring extensive cleaning or removal of foreign material.
>
> *Complex repair* applies to scar revision, debridement, extensive undermining, stents, and retention sutures.

Follow these steps when reporting repair codes:

1. Measure and record the wound size in centimeters (1 inch = 2.54 cm).
2. Sum the lengths according to repair type and use one code to report a patient with two or more wounds of the same repair type and when the areas are in the same description of the code.

Clinical Example

Jeff Slater has an open wound to the leg which is 8 cm long and a 3-cm wound on the scalp. Both wounds require intermediate repair. The sum of the lengths is 11 cm. Code 12034 is the correct code for reporting both repairs because extremities and scalp areas are described within this code.

3. Do not report an extra code for debridement and cleansing when they are provided unless the debridement is performed independently of the closure or when prolonged cleansing is required and/or large amounts of tissue are removed.

MUSCULOSKELETAL SYSTEM

In the musculoskeletal section, the care of fractures is coded on the basis of what the physician did to treat the fracture, not by the type of fracture. CPT descriptions reference types of treatment and arrange the descriptions into a template for different types of treatment.

Closed fracture treatment occurs when the fracture site is not surgically opened. *Open fracture treatment* occurs when the fracture is surgically opened. The bone ends are visualized, and internal fixation may be used.

The descriptions used to describe closed and open treatment of fractures are as follows:

Without manipulation
With manipulation
With or without manipulation.

Manipulation is the physical alignment of broken bones.

Percutaneous skeletal fixation is a fracture treatment that is neither open nor closed. The fracture fragments are not visible, but fixation is placed across the fracture site, usually under x-ray imaging.

Coding Tips: Casting and Strapping a Fracture

The application of a cast in conjunction with a surgical procedure is included in the package fee and should *not* be reported separately.

For casts reapplied during or after the global period, use the codes 29000–29799 and Level II HCPCS code(s) for Cast Supplies if the payer accepts them. Otherwise, use 99070 for cast supplies.

If no surgery was performed but a splint, strap, or cast was applied, use the appropriate E&M service and Level II HCPCS code(s) for the casting materials used as long as the payer accepts them. Otherwise use 99070 for the casting supplies.

THE HCPCS SYSTEM

The HCPCS coding system is utilized primarily by Medicare and Medicaid, the major government plans, and contains codes for physician and nonphysician services. The HCPCS codes were developed as an extension of the AMA's CPT-4 codes. They were implemented in 1983 by the Health Care Financing Administration. HCFA, in conjunction with the AMA, developed this single coding system to replace the variety of coding systems used by processors of Medicare claims. HCFA developed HCPCS for coding services, materials, drugs, and procedures which are not contained in the CPT-4 or when CPT's descriptions are insufficient.

HCPCS is a five-digit, alphanumeric coding system made up of one letter from the letters A–Z followed by four numeric digits. A2000 is an example of a HCPCS code. HCPCS has two-letter modifiers that may be added. The modifiers are used exactly as the two-digit CPT modifiers are used.

Three Levels in HCPCS Coding

Level I is the CPT book and all the codes in it. Level II is developed and maintained by HCFA. Level II codes are recognized nationwide by Medicare carriers and many others, such as the Blue Shield plans. The alphanumeric range for Level II codes is A0010–V9999. In some instances Level II provides codes for procedures not included in CPT. In other instances it provides codes to be used instead of or in addition to CPT codes. Level II codes affect payment. An example of Level II category codes frequently used by physician practices are the codes beginning with the letter J. J codes are for injections of specific medications, as was mentioned earlier in this chapter. An example of Level II category codes not generally used by physicians are D codes. They are used primarily by dentists who report services to Medicare and Medicaid.

Level III codes approved by HCFA and maintained by each Medicare carrier beginwith the letter W and end with the letter Z and four digits (W0001 through Z9999). Medicare carriers issue these codes, which are specific to the individual carrier. They should be reported only to the carrier that issues them and are used only for Medicare claims.

Steps for Using HCPCS When Billing Medicare and Other Government Plans

1. Always use a Level III code or modifier first when one exists for the service.
2. Use a Level II code or modifier if it gives a more specific description.
3. Use CPT if there is no Level III or Level II code describing the service more specifically.

Steps for Using HCPCS Level II Codes When Billing Nongovernment Plans

1. Make a list of the HCPCS codes which describe services the practice provides.
2. Check with your major payers to see if they accept those codes.
3. Use a HCPCS code if it is more specific. The A and J codes are always more specific than CPT, and many private plans now accept them.

Levels I, II, and III may be used together on the same claim. Another way in which Levels I, II, and III are used together is by using a CPT code (Level I) with a Level II modifier.

Clinical Example

A Medicare patient visits his family physician to have a foreign body removed from his right eye. The physician's office is in a rural health professional short-age area (HPSA). During that visit the patient mentions that he is experiencing severe pain in a hip joint. Although the primary reason for the visit to the doctor was for removal of the foreign body, the physician also provided evaluation and management of pain in the hip joint. The situation justifies billing for an office visit. Modifier -25 should be used along with the correct codes to indicate that the patient's condition required a separately identifiable E&M service.

The correct codes are as follows:

Second level office visit, established patient: 99212-25-QB. (QB denotes a rural health professional shortage area.)

Removal of foreign body, external eye; conjunctival superficial, 65205-RT-QB. (RT denotes the right side of a bilateral body part.)

Categories of HCPCS in Level II

There are general ranges of categories under which a specific service may be listed. Table 5-5 should be reviewed by the office staff in regard to the service categories provided by the practice. Most often a physician practice is interested only in the A4000–A5999 (for supplies) and J0110–J9999 (injectable medication) codes. Each year, while the practice is installing the new CPT codes, the additions, deletions, and revisions of HCPCS should be reviewed. Next, the office staff makes a list of HCPCS codes which are more specific than CPT codes. A survey is then conducted of the most frequently billed plans to determine whether they will accept the HCPCS codes. If the plans respond favorably, allowances should be made for the addition of these codes to the encounter form and/or computer system.

TABLE 5-5
HCPCS Level II Ranges

Category Ranges	Description
A0010–A0999	Transportation Services including Ambulance
A2000–A2999	Chiropractic Services Only
A4000–A4599	Medical and Surgical Supplies
A9000–A9999	Administrative, Miscellaneous and Investigational
B4000–B9999	Enteral and Parenteral Therapy
D0110–D9999	Dental Procedures
E0100–E9999	DME (Durable Medical Equipment)
G0001–G9999	Procedures/Professional Services (temporary codes)
H5000–H9999	Rehabilitative Services
J0110–J3999	Drugs Administered other than Chemotherapy—Subcutaneous, Intramuscular, or Intravenous Injections
J6000–J6999	Immunization Injections
J7010–J7399	Miscellaneous Drugs and Solutions
J7500–J8499	Immunosuppressive Drugs
J8500–J8999	Chemotherapy Drugs (Oral)
J9000–J9999	Chemotherapy Drugs (Other)
K0001–K9999	Durable Medical Equipment Regional Carrier Codes
L0100–L9999	Orthotic and Prosthetic Procedures
M0005–M9999	Medical Services
P2000–P9999	Pathology and Laboratory Services
Q0034–Q9999	Miscellaneous Services (temporary codes)
R0070–R0076	Diagnostic Radiology Services
V2020–V2799	Vision Services
V5000–V5999	Hearing Services

Examples Using Level II Codes with CPT Codes

99212	Level 2, established patient E&M in the office
J2060	Injection; Lorazepam, 2 mg
99211	Level 1, established patient E&M in the office (History taken by nurse)
J0290	Injection, Ampicillin, up to 500 mg
20605	Injection of intermediate joint
J3302	Units Injection, triamcinolone diacetate, 10 mg
x 2	
19120	Excision of breast cyst
A4550	Surgical tray
99203	Level 3, new patient E&M in the office
A4572	Rib Belt

Temporary HCPCS Codes

The codes beginning with the letters, G, K, and Q are temporary codes. Their categories and code numbers may be deleted in the next printing of the HCPCS codes so it is important to watch these categories especially from year to year. Table 5-6 lists examples of temporary codes.

TABLE 5-6

Examples of Temporary HCPCS Codes

Code	Description
G0001	Venipuncture
G0002	Office procedure: temporary urinary catheter (separate procedure)
Q0103	Physical therapy evaluation, initial
Q0104	Physical therapy reevaluation, periodic
Q0109	Occupational therapy evaluation, initial
Q0110	Occupational therapy reevaluation, periodic
Q0111	Wet mounts, including preparations of vaginal, cervical or skin specimens
Q0112	All potassium hydroxide (KOH) preparations
Q0113	Pinworm examinations
Q0114	Fern test
Q0115	Postcoital direct, qualitative examinations of vaginal or cervical mucous

Level II

HCPCS level II modifiers are reported only on Medicare claims. Table 5-7 displays the HCPCS level II modifiers that are of interest to a physician practice. Level II modifiers are essential when billing Medicare electronically.

Level III

Level III codes are for the processing and screening of certain services and are made known to physician practices through newsletters. Level III codes can be obtained by writing to the Freedom of Information Division (Disclo-

TABLE 5-7

Examples of Level II Modifiers

Modifier	Description
-AA	Anesthesia services performed personally by anesthesiologist
-AH	Clinical psychologist
-AJ	Clinical social worker
-AS	PA services for assistant-at-surgery, nonteam member
-EJ	Subsequent claim [claim for injection of the drug Epoetin Alfa (EPO)]
-EM	Emergency reserve supply (for ESRD benefit only)
-LT	Left side (used to identify procedures performed on the left side of the body)
-QB	Physician providing service in a rural HPSA
-QU	Physician providing service in an urban HPSA
-QX	CRNA (certified registered nurse anesthetist) with medical direction by a physician
-QZ	CRNA without medical direction by a physician
-RT	Right side (used to identify procedures performed on the right side of the body)
-SF	Second opinion ordered by a professional review organization (PRO) por section 9401, P.L. 99-272 (100 percent reimbursement—no Medicare deductible or coinsurance)
-TC	Technical component; under certain circumstances, a charge may be made for the technical component alone; in those cirumstances, the technical component charge is identified by adding modifier -TC to the usual procedure
-VP	Aphakic patient; absence of the lens of the eye is reported to alert the plan that the first pair of glasses or contact lenses should be a covered benefit
-YY	Second surgical opinion
-ZZ	Third surgical opinion

sure Unit) of any Medicare carrier. Y3000 is an example of a level III code for injection of vitamin B_{12} and estrogen.

Level III modifiers consist of two letters or one letter and a number. Like Level III codes, Level III modifiers appear in newsletters and are also available by writing to the Freedom of Information Division of your Medicare carrier. Use these modifiers when appropriate, as they are vital for proper Medicare payment.

The following examples are just a small number of the many local modifiers created by carriers. These are subject to change and are purely examples.

-NP   No purchased diagnostic tests (to convey that all tests were performed within the practice)

-WR   Coumadin check (add to telephone calls made by a physician to check results, 99371-WR)

-WI   Advanced notice has been given to beneficiary (waiver letter signed regarding conditional coverage)

-Z9   Psychiatric service by physician

EXERCISING KNOWLEDGE

Fundamentals and Modifiers

You will need a copy of the CPT book to complete the following exercises.

1. Name the six sections of the CPT book.

2. What words drop down before the indented child codes in 63300?

3. 35701 is the _____ code in a procedural family.

4. What does a triangle to the left of a code number mean?

5. What does a dot to the left of a code number mean?

6. Which modifier is added to the E&M code to report that the decision to perform surgery was made during this encounter?

7. Which modifier is added to second opinion codes when an insurance or managed care plan requires the patient to have a second opinion?

8. Is 93010-26 correct? Explain your answer.

9. In what three circumstances is modifier -58 used?

10. What is the difference between the modifiers -78 and -79?

E&M Codes

Fill in the blanks. Complete questions 11 through 20 using Figures 5-1 and 5-2.

11. The physician has documented an expanded problem-focused history and examination and a low complexity of decision making for a new patient. What is the appropriate code? _____

12. The physician has documented a detailed history and a low complexity of decision making for an established patient. What is the appropriate code number? _____

13. The physician has documented an expanded problem-focused history and a low complexity of decision making, which took 10 minutes. Fifteen minutes was spent face to face with this established patient, discussing recommended tests and instructions for treatment. This consumed over 50 percent of the physician's total time spent with the patient. What is the appropriate code number? _____ Does the physician need to document the number of minutes spent counseling when time is the controlling factor for selecting the code? _____

14. If the physician has documented a comprehensive history and examination for an established patient, does the doctor have to spend about 40 minutes with the patient to report 99215? _____

15. Jimmy Jones was stung on the arm by a bee and developed an immediate rash. The pediatrician provided a 99212 service that took about 10 minutes. He placed Jimmy in a room for 60 minutes of observation. The physician checked on Jimmy six times, 5 minutes each time, before releasing him. What codes should be used?

    _____   _____

16. In order to report risk factor reduction intervention on another date, a code from _____ _____ services must be reported first.

17. Critical care services can be reported when the physician spends _____ minutes in constant attendance on a critically ill patient.

18. If hospital observation codes are reported, all E&M codes provided on the _____ _____ are included in the observation code.

19. Hospital discharge day management is code _____.

20. A physician consultant _____ initiate therapeutic service.

Your physician has asked you to read and recommend codes from this discharge summary. Review the summary and answer the physician's questions at the end of the summary.

DISCHARGE SUMMARY

Admission Date:	3/20	Discharge Date:	4/4
Patient:	Roberts, John	Physician:	Piper, Audrey, M.D.

FINAL DIAGNOSIS:
1. Acute staphylococcal endocarditis.
2. Idiopathic thrombocytopenic purpura.
3. Diabetes mellitus, insulin-dependent.
4. Hypertension, benign.
5. Ischemic heart disease, status post aortocoronary bypass grafts.

DISCHARGE PLAN:
1. Diet: 1550-calorie diabetic, fat-controlled.
2. Activity: sedentary
3. Human Lente insulin 35 units q.d.

ADMISSION FINDINGS: This 67-year-old married man, a retired teacher, was hospitalized as an emergency with fever, myalgia, and polyarthritis of 3 days' duration. He had been taking Prednisone for 3 months because of idiopathic thrombocytopenic purpura. Back in December he had a dental abscess. At that time he was treated with penicillin in addition to local dental care. When first seen on 3/21, he was diffusely toxic and could hardly move. His memory was impaired. His temperature was 102 degrees, pulse 110 and regular, BP 180/100. He appeared acutely ill with dry skin. There was a vesicular hemorrhagic lesion of the heel of the left foot. Heart sounds were clear with an S4 gallop and grade II systolic ejection murmur. Echocardiogram at that time did not show evidence of vegetative lesions, with calcification of the aortic root and mitral annulus. Chest x-ray was normal.

HOSPITAL COURSE: The patient was started on Nafcillin 6.0 gm. a day, and the dose was increased to 12.0 gm. a day within 24 hours because of continued toxicity and continued positive blood cultures on therapy. Nafcillin was continued for 1 week. Peak and trough antibacterial titers were greater than 1:8. Then, because of the appearance of morbilliform rash, antibiotic was switched to Vancomycin 2.0 gm. a day.

Prednisone was discontinued rapidly during the first hospital week. Because of this, the patient remained extremely toxic, unstable, and with severe myalgia. He could hardly move, even with assistance of a walker. Myalgia gradually abated. Mental clarity slowly returned.

During the last 3 days of hospitalization he worked intensively with physical therapy. At the time of discharge, the patient was weak and rational. There are no new heart murmurs. Blood pressure and diabetes are well controlled. Three blood cultures were drawn on the day before discharge, his first day without antibiotic therapy.

Audrey Piper, M.D.

Place a checkmark next to the answers which require yes or no.

		Yes	No
21.	Do I have the correct primary diagnosis listed first?	_____	_____
22.	I first saw the patient on 3/21 and can bill a 99223 for this date as the admitting physician.	_____	_____
23.	If Mr. Roberts was unstable and toxic for the first week, should I bill Level 3 subsequent hospital care visits?	_____	_____
24.	How many hospital visits can I report?		
25.	When the patient starts physical therapy, are these Level 2 visits?	_____	_____
26.	What code is used for the last day?		

Use the CPT book to code these procedures. Record the index word(s) used to find the code(s). There may be several ways to index the procedure code.

		Index Word(s)	Code(s)
27.	Cardiopulmonary resuscitation	_____	_____
28.	Initial IPPB, with one subsequent treatment	_____	_____
29.	Intradermal allergy testing, 20 tests, immediate reaction	_____	_____
30.	Tetanus toxoid injection by the nurse (nurse checked wound and recorded vital signs)	_____	_____
31.	Electrocardiogram (ECG) tracing	_____	_____
32.	Left and right heart catheterization with left ventricular angiography	_____	_____
33.	Physical therapy in Hubbard tank, 45 minutes	_____	_____
34.	Psychotherapy for one person, 20 minutes	_____	_____

Medicine Section

35. Intramuscular injection of antibiotic, Rocephin 250 mg
(billing a plan which does not accept HCPCS J codes)

_____ _____

36. Escort of a cardiac patient from ER to a heart hospital

_____ _____

37. Level 2 ER visit   _____ _____

Radiology Section   **38.** X-ray of calcaneous, three views_____ _____

39. Ultrasound of pregnant uterus, limited for gestational age

_____ _____

40. X-ray with contrast of bile duct with guided stone removal,
postoperative, by Burhenne technique by the surgeon

_____ _____

41. MRI of knee   _____ _____

42. Screening mammography, bilateral

_____ _____

43. Angiography of brachial artery, S&I only

_____ _____

44. Thyroid uptake, multiple determinations

_____ _____

Laboratory Section   **45.** Routine urinalysis with microscopy

_____ _____

46. Thyroid panel (TSH, T_3, thyroxine)

_____ _____

47. Stool for occult blood   _____ _____

48. Urine culture with colony count_____ _____

49. Skin test for *Candida*   _____ _____

50. List the tests included in a general health panel.

51. List the 19 substances which can be coded which are included in
automated, multichannel tests of either urine or blood.

Surgery Section

Obtain a copy of CPT-4. Write the index word(s) used to select the most appropriate procedure code. There may be several ways to index the code. Use the anatomy diagrams of the skin, bones, heart, and gastrointestinal tract, Tools 5-2 through 5-5.

Index Word(s)   *Code(s)*

Integumentary System

52. Chemical peel of the dermal layer of the forehead

    _____   _____

53. Removal of facial lesion (1.5 cm) by shaving

    _____   _____

54. Excision of benign lesion, 0.8 cm of arm

    _____   _____

55. Breast reconstruction for immediate insertion of breast prosthesis after mastectomy   _____   _____

56. Excision of 3.5-cm malignant neoplasm on cheek

    _____   _____

57. Complex repair of 6-cm defect left from excision of 3.5-cm lesion on cheek   _____   _____

Musculoskeletal System

58. Whitman procedure with resection of the femoral head

    _____   _____

59. Reapplication of Velpeau cast, arm   _____   _____

60. Closed reduction of nasal bone fracture, no manipulation

    _____   _____

61. Medial meniscectomy (knee) via arthroscopy

    _____   _____

62. Bone graft for nonunion, femoral neck fracture

    _____   _____

Cardiovascular System

63. Percutaneous transluminal aortic atherectomy

_____ _____

64. Upgrade of implanted pacemaker system

_____ _____

65. Repair of aorta without cardiopulmonary bypass machine

_____ _____

Digestive System

66. Colonoscopy with biopsy and cauterization of polyps

_____ _____

67. Laparoscopic cholecystectomy with cholangiography

_____ _____

68. Repair of recurrent, strangulated, incisional hernia with Marlex mesh

_____ _____

69. Percutaneous placement of gastrostomy tube with S&I

_____ _____

Urinary and Female System

70. Laser hysteroscopy with removal of polyps

_____ _____

71. Transurethral electrosurgical resection of the prostate

_____ _____

72. Low cervical cesarean section including prenatal and postpartum care

_____ _____

Level II National Codes

Use the information given in the chapter to answer these questions.

73. Which Level II national categories are used most frequently by physician practices?

74. List the letters of other Level II national categories which may be of interest to physicians.

75. When are HCPCS Level III codes used in Medicare billing?

76. In what order are HCPCS levels used in Medicare billing?

77. When are HCPCS Level II national codes used for other plans?

78. Which two HCPCS Level II categories are always more specific than CPT?

79. What is the temporary Level II code for venipuncture?

80. Which Q code reports a Fern test?

▼ TOOL 5-1
DOCUMENTATION WITH CPT MODIFIERS

When a service or procedure is performed which does not exactly fit the description in CPT, modifiers are used to indicate that it has been altered by a specific circumstance. Modifiers are placed after the code number, making it a seven-digit code number to report. Appendix A of the CPT book contains a listing of all CPT modifiers.

When using modifiers today, most third-party payers require documentation to review the altered circumstances, such as with -20, -21, -22, -23, and -62. When using any of these modifiers, prepare and submit documentation with your claim. Suggested documentation includes the following:

- Operative reports (underline in pencil the documentation to note the special circumstances)
- Admission history and physicals
- Discharge summaries
- Progress notes
- Brief form letter explaining altered circumstances

All documentation should contain the following:

- Patient name
- Patient plan ID number
- Physician's name and address
- Physician's provider number for that payer.

Note: The commonly used and understandable modifiers usually do not require documentation in this age of electronic claims submission. They are -50, -51, -26, -32, -52, -78, -79, -80, -24 and -25 (as long as you use a diagnosis code different from the surgical diagnosis with modifiers -24 and -25). Documentation of -57 and -58 varies by payer. Multiple modifier -99 is considered obsolete and should not be used. It only takes up space in the claim fields.

▼ **TOOL 5-2**
INTEGUMENTARY SYSTEM

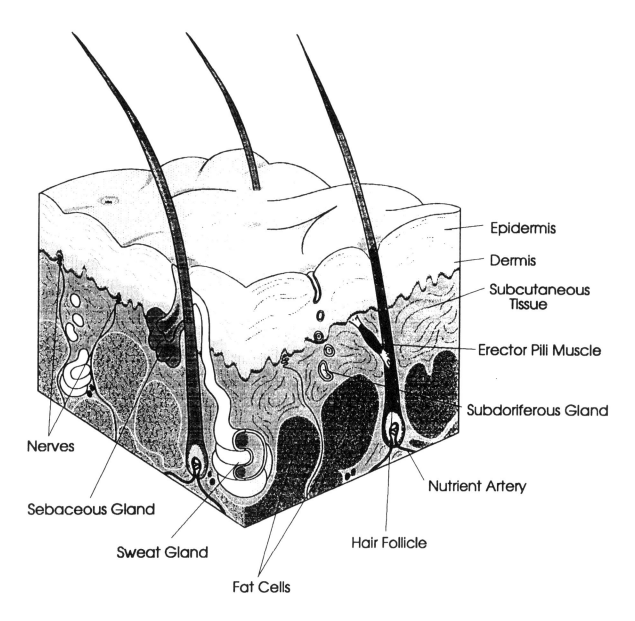

From Bradford, Billie C., *ICD-9-CM Coding For Physicians Offices,* New York, McGraw-Hill Healthcare Management Group, 1993, p. 134.

▼ TOOL 5-3
MUSCULOSKELETAL SYSTEM

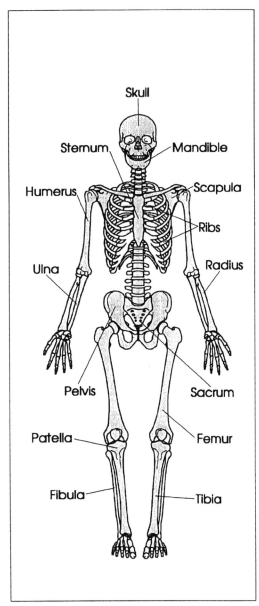

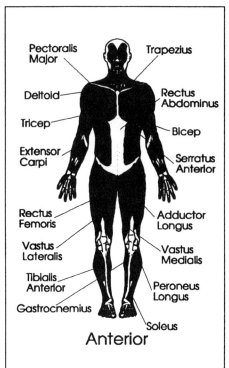

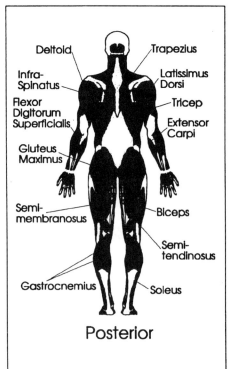

From Bradford, Billie C., *ICD-9-CM Coding For Physicians Offices,* New York, McGraw-Hill Healthcare Management Group, 1993, p. 140.

▼ **TOOL 5-4**
ANTERIOR AND POSTERIOR HEART

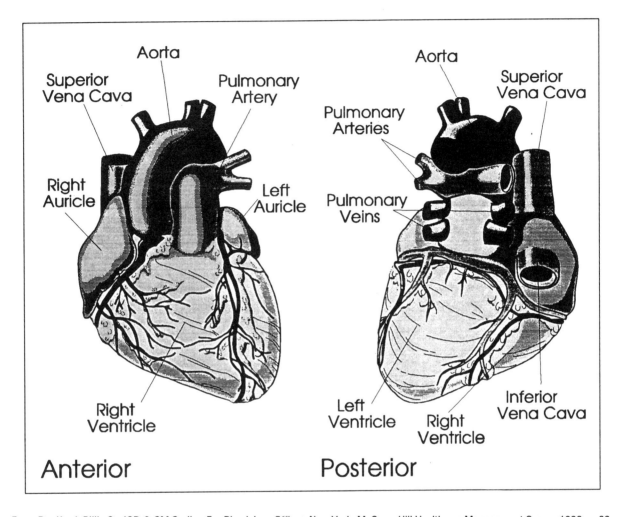

From Bradford, Billie C., *ICD-9-CM Coding For Physicians Offices,* New York, McGraw-Hill Healthcare Management Group, 1993, p. 89.

▼ TOOL 5-5
GASTROINTESTINAL SYSTEM

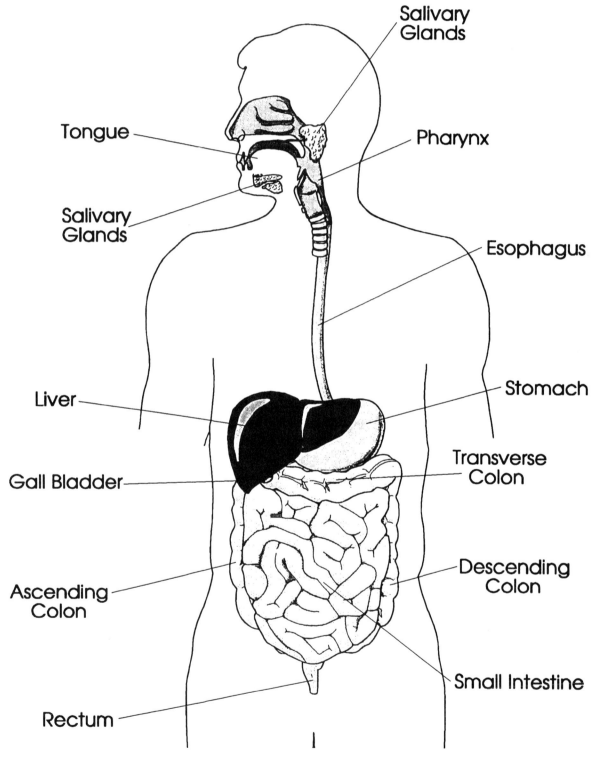

From Bradford, Billie C., *ICD-9-CM Coding For Physicians Offices,* New York, McGraw-Hill Healthcare Management Group, 1993, p. 102.

Completing the Universal Claim Form

CHAPTER OVERVIEW

In the past it was sufficient to give a patient a copy of the encounter form, and the patient would submit his or her own medical claim for payment. Today patients are often overwhelmed when they attempt to complete the paperwork. With the change in healthcare delivery, contracts with insurance and managed care plans maintain that it is the physician's responsibility to report patients' claims in an accurate and timely manner. Managed care plans often use claims filing as a selling point in their advertisements: "No more claim forms." Even without a contract, Medicare, as of October 1, 1990, has mandated that physicians must submit claims for Medicare beneficiaries.

When a physician practice is not required to file a claim, it often makes sense for it to do so. The practice is the coordinator of all services and is best able to submit claims related to those services. The filing rules for insurance and managed care plans today are often complicated and detailed. Not only do patients appreciate being relieved of this duty, but under fee for service reimbursement, the practice is likely to be paid faster.

After reading the material in this chapter, doing the exercises, and using the end-of-chapter tools, you will be able to:

- *Describe the various billing options available to a physician practice*
- *List the universal requirements for each item and the specific requirements for Medicare, Medicaid, Champus, and most private plans*
- *Describe the prerequisites for optical scanning a claim*
- *Explain the basic steps in electronic claims reporting*
- *Explain the significance of ANSI Standard 837 for electronic claims and the planned Medicare Transaction System*

OPTIONS IN BILLING

When one is working with many types of insurance and managed care plans, claims submission constitutes a considerable task in a medical practice. Reporting services to the plans can be handled in many different ways. Some practices elect to contract with a billing service to do all the claims reporting outside the practice. All data and information that are needed to file a claim are forwarded to the service. Any other transactions, such as payments received on patient's accounts, occurring in the practice are also forwarded. The billing service is often responsible for coding services, monitoring payment, handling appeals, billing patients, and collecting delinquent accounts. Periodically, a billing service reports on accounts receivable to the practice. By employing such a service, the practice eliminates a great deal of paperwork and reduces staffing costs. If the practice chooses this option, it is vital to the physician that billing services be thoroughly investigated for their effectiveness before they are employed. Accountants can advise the practice on the economic feasibility of using a billing service.

There are two options when billing is done within a medical practice: a manual system (information is recorded by hand) and a computer system (information is entered into a computer).

Under a *manual system,* charges from the encounter form are entered on a ledger card. Ledger cards provide a complete record of the total charges and payments for each patient. A *pegboard,* or *write-it-once, system* is a common manual system used by medical practices. When a patient visits the office, the patient's name, the service provided, the charges made, and any payment are recorded on a numbered patient encounter form. Information is taken from the form, which has carbon strips on the back. This information is simultaneously recorded by a carbon impression on the day sheet and on the patient's ledger card. A *day sheet* is the summation of all the activities of the practice for each day. Figure 6-1 shows a typical day sheet used in manual billing systems, and Figure 6-2 shows a typical *ledger card.*

If the plan's rules allow it, a copy of the ledger card or encounter form

Date		Fee	Payment	Adjustment	Balance	Previous Balance	Claim Number	Receipt Number	Deposits	Daily A/R	
										A/R=	$32115
7/3	Mark Jones	125		14	111	0	2189			Fees	$1505
7/3	Mary Smith	30	30		0	0	2190	R215	$30	Payment	$1176
7/3	Carol Harris	250	235		15	265	2191	R216	$235	Adj.	$55
7/3	Lisa Hohler	245	45		200	134	2192		$45	A/R Balance	$32389
7/3	Jack Koenig	124	38	41	45	0	2193	R217	$38		
7/3	Kathy Loch	131	828		0	956	2194	R218	$828	Month A/R	
7/3	Lisa Fox	600			600	0	2194			Begin Month	$38193
										Month to date Fees	$5257
										Month to date Payment	$5558
										Month to date Adjustments	$5503
										Total A/R	$32389
Page Total		$1505	$1176	$55	$971	$1355			$1176		

FIGURE 6-1 Typical day sheet for manual billing.

<table>
<tr><td colspan="6">Medical Healing Arts Practice
4915 Muirwoods Lane
Green Ash, Ohio 45299</td></tr>
<tr><td colspan="4">Mark Jones
123 Apple Lane
Green Ash, Ohio 45299</td><td colspan="2">Balance Forward</td></tr>
<tr><td>Date</td><td>Description</td><td>Fee</td><td>Payments</td><td>Adjustments</td><td>Balance</td></tr>
<tr><td>7/3/xx</td><td>99205</td><td>$125.00</td><td>$15.00</td><td></td><td>$110.00</td></tr>
<tr><td></td><td></td><td></td><td></td><td></td><td></td></tr>
<tr><td></td><td></td><td></td><td></td><td></td><td></td></tr>
</table>

FIGURE 6-2 Typical ledger card used in manual billing.

can be attached to an HCFA 1500, the universal claim form, and sent to the insurance plan.

Medicare does not permit the attachment of an encounter form to an HCFA 1500. Medicaid and some private plans have similar rules. When a manual system is used, each claim must be typed or handwritten on a form. Voluminous paperwork often causes delays in reporting claims and mistakes in entries; poor financial reporting often results. If more than 200 monthly statements are sent, the manual method is not cost-effective or financially beneficial to a physician practice, and it is advisable to computerize the reporting and billing process.

Computerized billing and filing systems, which are tied in with the patient information database, can record and process information quickly, print billing statements and claim forms, and generate reports on aged accounts receivable and other financial information.

THE UNIVERSAL CLAIM FORM, HCFA 1500 (12-90)

A universal claim form is used by physician practices to standardize the submission of claims. When one attaches an encounter form to a claim form, mistakes are more likely to occur. Each encounter form has a different format. Claim processors who enter data information from encounter forms find that no two forms look alike or have the same codes in the same places.

On universal claim forms, by contrast, all the codes are consistently located in the same place.

The version of HCFA 1500 (12-90) is the form approved for use by HCFA for the Medicare program for claims submitted by physicians and other providers. It is known as the *universal claim form*. In addition to Medicare and the Office of Civilian Health and Medical Program of the Uniformed Services (OCHAMPUS), most Blue Cross/Blue Shield plans and the majority of managed care plans also accept this form. When one is reporting claims, it is best to check with your major third-party payers to see if they have specific requirements for claim forms. The current version of the health insurance claim form (HIC), the HCFA 1500 (U2)(12-90), was under development since 1986 and the final version was approved as of December 1990.[1] Most insurance plans adopted it shortly afterward, and it became mandatory to use for reporting services provided to Medicare beneficiaries on April 1, 1992.

REQUIREMENTS FOR COMPLETING INFORMATIONAL ITEMS ON THE UNIVERSAL CLAIM FORM

Specific requirements for government plans are noted in red type. Obviously Medicare, a complicated government program, has the most extensive requirements. Most insurance and managed care plans provide basic instructions for completing items on the claim form in the physician manual. If there are no special requirements, the item should be completed according to the requirements stated on the form. If the claim forms are not computer-generated, it is best to type them. If they are handwritten, the staff should print the requirements using all capitals and black ink.

The claim form is divided into two major sections: patient information, items 1–13, and physician information, items 14–33. Refer to Figure 2-6 to see an HCFA 1500 form in its entirety.

Patient and Insured Information

Items 1 through 13 ask for information about the patient and the insured, and for a determination of whether the patient is a dependent. This is information that was completed on the registration form at the patient's initial office visit or at the hospital. Figure 6-3 shows items 1 to 13 on a health in-

---

1. Medicare Carrier Manual, Section 2010.1, August 1993. The primary difference between HCFA 1500 (U2)(12-90) and the earlier versions is the complete use of coding systems: ICD-9-CM, CPT, and HCPCS. There is no space on the current claim form to describe procedures. All services, procedures, and diagnoses are represented by codes. In addition, there are spaces for reporting secondary coverage of the patient.

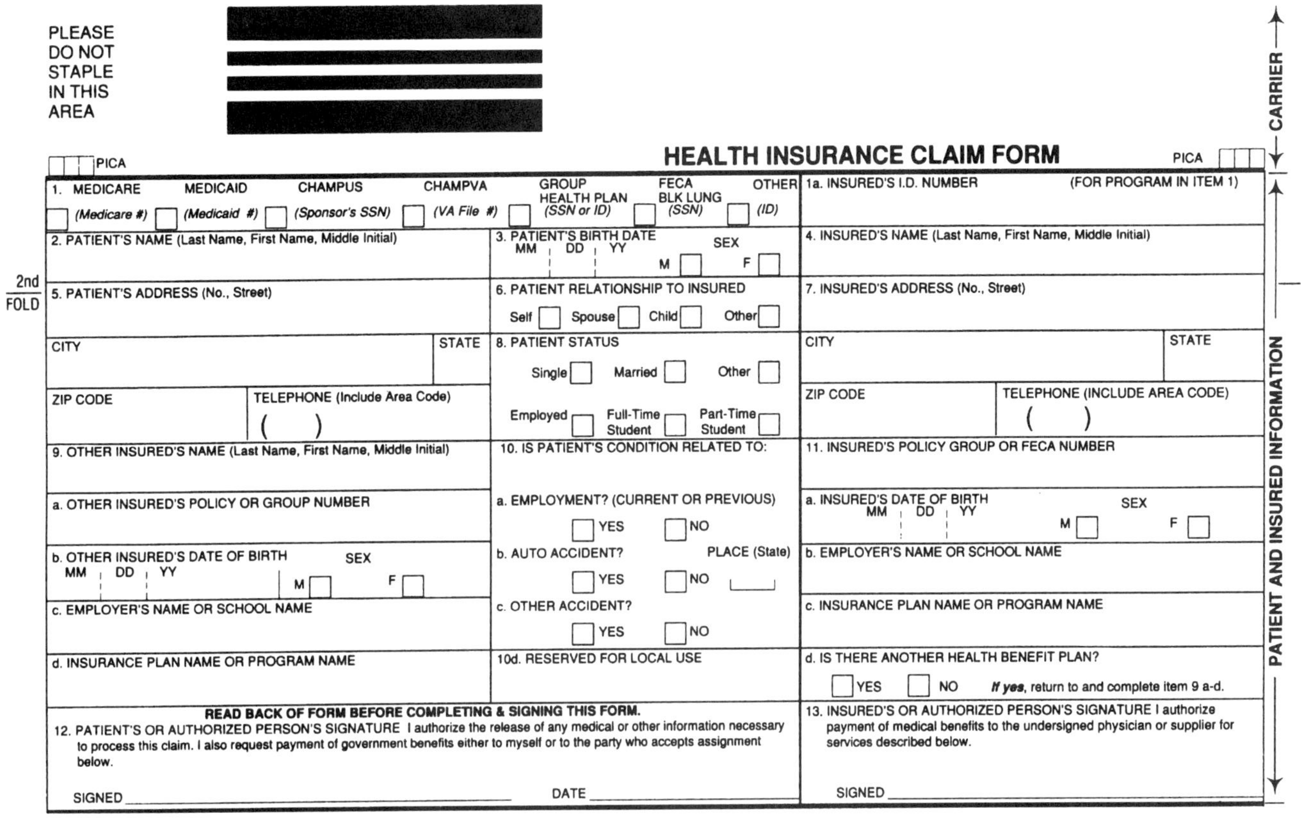

FIGURE 6-3 Health insurance claim form (top half).

surance claims form. In practices that use computerized patient information–accounting systems this information can be generated automatically by entering a single patient identification number assigned by the practice.

The following sections describe each of these 13 items; below the general explanation, where applicable, there are descriptions of the special requirements for Medicare, Medicaid, CHAMPUS, CHAMPVA, and private plans.

Item 1: Type of Insurance

Indicate the type of insurance coverage applicable to a claim by checking the appropriate box. For example, if a Medicare claim is being submitted, check the Medicare box; for the Federal Employment Compensation Act/Black Lung, check FECA. For private plans such as a Blue Shield claim, check OTHER.

Item 1a: Insured's ID Number

Enter the insured's primary identification number, including all letters. This is the number that appears on the plan identification card.

Medicare Enter the Health Insurance Claim Number (HICN) from the Medicare card, including all the letters.

Medicaid   Enter the Medicaid number from the current Medicaid card. It is sometimes called the billing number or recipient number.

CHAMPUS   Enter the sponsor's Social Security number (SSN). Do not provide the patient's SSN unless the patient and sponsor are the same. If a sponsor is an active-duty security agent, enter "SECURITY." Additional information about sponsors is given in Chapter 9.

CHAMPVA   Provide the sponsor's SSN; add the number in item 5 of the CHAMPVA authorization card if there is no SSN.

Private Plans   Enter the insured's subscriber, enrollee, or member number. This may be the certificate number or the insured's number, and it is copied directly from the plan's identification number. Frequently this number is the insured's SSN.

Item 2: Patient's Name

Enter the patient's last name, first name, and middle initial, if any, as shown on the identification card. The practice may know the patient by a nickname or the individual may want to be known by his or her middle name, but enter the name exactly as it appears on the card.

Item 3: Patient's Birthdate

Enter the patient's birthdate and sex. The format should be month, day, and year. Generally, this is written as 01-09-90; however, some plans do not permit the use of punctuation marks, and in this case the birthdate should be 010990.

Item 4: Insured's Name

Enter the full name of the insured.

Medicare   If there is a plan primary to Medicare, through the patient's or spouse's employment or any other source, list the name of the insured on that policy. When the insured and the patient are the same, enter the word "SAME" or leave the box blank.

Medicaid   Enter the full name of the insured.

Private Plans   Enter the full name of the insured if it is different from that of the patient.

Item 5: Patient's Address

Enter the patient's mailing address on the first line, the city and state on the second line, and the ZIP Code and telephone number on the third line.

CHAMPUS   Do not provide a post office box number; enter the actual place of residence. If this is a rural address, the address must contain the route and box number. An APO/FPO address should not be used for a patient's mailing address unless that person is actually residing overseas.

Item 6: Patient Relationship to Insured
Check the appropriate box for the patient's relationship to the insured after item 4 has been completed.

Medicare   Enter the relationship of the individual whose coverage is the primary plan for the Medicare beneficiary.

CHAMPUS   If the patient is the sponsor, check the "self" block. If "other" is checked, indicate how the patient is related to the sponsor, for example, former spouse, parent. Parents, parents-in-law, stepparents, and parents by adoption are not CHAMPUS/CHAMPVA-eligible. These categories of dependents may have ID cards with privileges for the military treatment facility but not for CHAMPUS/CHAMPVA benefits. Grandchildren are not eligible unless they are legally adopted. Be certain that an ID card authorizes "CIVILIAN" medical benefits. Review the reverse side of the dependent's ID card (DD Form 1173, Block 15.b) or the reverse side of the retiree's ID card (DD Form 2. Retired). An unnumbered block provides a date when civilian military care is no longer authorized; for example, the CHAMPUS beneficiary becomes eligible for Medicare. If the child is a stepchild, check the "child" box.

Private Plans   If the patient is the insured, check "self."

Item 7: Insured's Address
Enter the insured's address and telephone number. When this address is the same as the patient's address, enter the word "same." Complete this item only after items 4 and 11 have been completed.

CHAMPUS   Enter the address for the active duty sponsor's duty station or the retiree's mailing address. If the address is the same as the patient's address, enter "same." If the sponsor resides overseas, enter the APO/FPO address.

Private Plans   If the insured is the patient, enter "same."

Item 8: Patient Status
Check the appropriate box for the patient's marital status and indicate whether the patient is employed or is a full-time or part-time student.

Item 9: Other Insured's Policy or Group Number
Enter the insured's last name and their first name for a plan that is secondary to the patient's primary insurance plan listed in item 2.

Medicare   Enter the last name, first name, and middle initial of the enrollee in a Medigap policy if it is different from that shown in item 2. Otherwise, enter "same" or enrollee's name. If no Medigap benefits are assigned, leave this space blank.

Medigap is medical insurance offered by a private plan to individuals covered by Medicare and is designed to supplement Medicare benefits. It fills in some of the gaps in Medicare coverage by providing payment for charges which Medicare does not cover, such as deductibles, coinsurance, and other limitations imposed by Medicare. It does not include limited benefit coverage available to Medicare beneficiaries such as a "specific disease," i.e., cancer, or "hospital indemnity" per day coverage. Medigap excludes policies offered by an employer to employees or former employees as well as policies offered by a labor union to members or former members.

Note
Only participating physicians are to complete items 9 and 9a–d and only when the beneficiary wishes to assign benefits under a Medigap policy.

Participating physicians and suppliers must enter the information required in item 9 and its divisions if this is requested by the beneficiary. A claim for which a beneficiary elects to assign benefits under a Medigap policy to a participating physician/supplier is called a *mandated Medigap transfer or crossover.*

Do not list other supplemental coverages which are not Medigap policies in item 9a–d when a Medicare claim is submitted. Other supplemental claims are forwarded automatically if the private plan contracts with a Medicare carrier to send Medicare claim information electronically. If there is no such contract, the beneficiary must file his or her own supplemental claim.

CHAMPUS Enter the name of the insured if it is different from that shown in item 2 (patient). For example, the patient may be covered under a plan held by a spouse, parent, or other person. (Item 11a–d should be used to report insurance plans covering the patient.)

Note
Item 11d should be completed before the office staff determines the need for completing items 9a–d. If Item 11d is checked, items 9a–d must be completed.

Private Plans Enter the name of the insured for secondary insurance plans to the patient's primary plan listed in item 2.

Item 9a: Other Insured's Policy or Group Number
Enter the plan ID number which is the policy or group number of the secondary insurance plan.

Medicare Enter the policy number of the Medigap enrollee preceded by Medigap, Medicaid, Employee–Supplement; also enter the policy number of the other insured's plan. Patients may have coverage because of their own or their spouse's former employment.

CHAMPUS Enter the policy number of the other insured's plan.

Private Plans   List the policy number of the secondary plan.

Item 9b: Other Insured's Date of Birth
Enter the birthdate and sex of the other (secondary) insured.

Item 9c: Employer's Name or School Name
Enter the employer's name or school name for the secondary insurance plan.

Medicare   Disregard the employer's name or school name which is printed on the form. Enter the claims-processing address for the Medigap insurer. Use an abbreviated street address, two-letter state postal code, and ZIP Code copied from the Medigap enrollee's Medigap identification card. For example,

> 1257 Anywhere Street
> Baltimore, MD 21204

is shown as

> 1257 Anywhere St. MD 21204

CHAMPUS   Enter the name of the employer or school.

Item 9d: Insurance Plan Name or Program Name
Enter the name of the insurance program or plan which receives the claim after the plan noted in item 1.

Medicare   Enter the name of the Medigap enrollee's insurance plan or the Medigap insurer's unique identifier provided by the local Medicare carrier. If you are participating and the beneficiary wants Medicare payment data forwarded to a Medigap insurer, all other information in items 9a–d must be complete and correct.

CHAMPUS   Enter the name of the insurance plan or the program name where the individual has other health insurance benefits. On an attached sheet, provide a complete mailing address for all other insurance information and enter the word "attachment."

Item 10: Is Patient Condition Related to:
If the services listed on the claim form are for a work-related injury or accident-related injury, check the "yes" box.

Medicare   Check "yes" or "no" to indicate whether employment, auto liability, or other accident involvement applies to one or more of the services described in item 24. Any item checked "yes" indicates that there may be subrogation primary to Medicare. Identify primary insurance information in item 11.

CHAMPUS Check "yes" or "no," but if this service was the result of an automobile accident, indicate the state where the accident occurred. The contractor will contact the patient for potential third-party liability information. When a third-party liability is involved, the beneficiary is required to complete DD Form 2527, Statement of Personal Injury—Possible Third Party Liability.

Private plans Provide information concerning potential third-party liability.

Item 10d: Reserved for Local Use

Medicaid If the patient is entitled to Medicaid, enter the patient's Medicaid number preceded by the letters *MCD*.

CHAMPUS Use this block to indicate that there is other health insurance.

Item 11: Insured's Policy Group or FECA Number

Enter the insured's policy group or FECA number. If it is the same as in item 4, write "same."

Medicare This item must be completed by the physician, who acknowledges having made a good faith effort to determine whether Medicare is the primary or secondary plan. If there is insurance primary to Medicare, enter the insured's plan ID number and complete items 11a–c. If there is no insurance primary to Medicare, enter the word "none."

CHAMPUS If the patient has other insurance, enter the plan ID number and indicate whether the patient is covered by Medicare. (Block 9a–d should be used to report another primary insurance plan.)

Item 11a: Insured's Date of Birth

Enter the insured's birthdate and sex if they are different from item 3.

CHAMPUS Complete the insured's date of birth (MM/DD/YY) and sex (check box). Enter the date of birth and sex if they are different from item 3.

Item 11b: Employer's Name or School Name

Medicare Enter the employer's name, if applicable. If there is a change in the insured's insurance status, for example, retired, enter the retirement date preceded by the word "retired."

CHAMPUS Enter the employer's or school's name if applicable.

Item 11c: Insurance Plan Name or Program Name

Enter the complete primary insurance plan or program name, such as Blue Shield of Illinois. If the primary payer's EOB does not contain the claims-processing address, record the primary payer's claims-processing address directly on the EOB.

CHAMPUS Enter the insurance plan or program name. If the patient has supplemental CHAMPUS coverage, it is not necessary to report a claim with that insurance first unless the insurance can be considered a primary plan. For CHAMPUS purposes, supplemental policies are those which are specifically designed to supplement CHAMPUS benefits, for example, payment of the beneficiary's cost share or deductible liability. Remember, CHAMPUS is secondary to all other medical insurance except Medicaid. When you submit the claim to the other insurer, attach a copy of the EOB from the primary insurance plan to the CHAMPUS claim.

Item 11d: Is There Another Health Benefit Plan?

Medicare Leave blank. Not required by Medicare.

CHAMPUS Check yes or no to indicate whether there is or is not another primary insurance plan. If the patient is covered by secondary insurance, Medicare, or Medicaid, enter that plan ID number. If the patient is covered by Medicaid, enter the word "Medicaid," followed by the Medicaid number.

Private Plans Place an X in the yes box to indicate patient coverage by a third insurance plan. Enter the group number or group name if the patient is covered by an employer-paid medical insurance plan.

Item 12: Patient's or Authorized Person's Signature

The patient or authorized representative must sign the item unless the signature is on file in the practice or at the hospital. The signed authorization for the patient that is on file at the hospital should cover all inpatient and outpatient hospitalization services related to the services on the claim form. When the patient's representative signs, the relationship to the patient must be indicated. The patient's signature authorizing the release of medical information is necessary to process the claim.

Medicare The program allows the obtaining of a lifetime authorization one time, which is kept on file. This is found in Chapter 8. The registration form in Chapter 2 contains the terminology required by Medicare, and so a separate authorization is not necessary if the form is used. If a signature is obtained, enter "Signature on File" in item 12.

Signature by Mark (X). When an illiterate or physically handicapped patient signs by mark, the patient's name and address must be entered next to the mark.

CHAMPUS   If a patient is under 18 years of age, either parent should sign unless the services are confidential. If the patient is 18 or older but cannot sign the claim, the person who signs must be either the legal guardian or, in the absence of a legal guardian, the spouse or parent of the patient. The signer should write the patient's name in item 12, followed by the word "by" and his or her own signature. A statement must be attached to the claim giving the signer's full name and address, the signer's relationship to the patient, and the reason the patient is unable to sign. Also included must be documentation of the signer's appointment as a legal guardian, an indication of whether a power of attorney has been issued, or a statement that a legal guardian has not been appointed if such is the case.

Private Plans   It is very important to maintain current signatures for patients and/or insureds. Use the words "signature on file" if a valid signature is available. Most insurance and managed care plans will accept this but have the right to request a copy of the actual signature.

Item 13: Insured's or Authorized Person's Signature

The signature in this item authorizes payment of medical benefits to the physician or provider for services listed on the claim.

Private Plans   If a plan has offered a contract for participation in its program and the doctor has not signed the contract, even though the signature is in item 13, payment may not be sent to the practice.

Physician or Supplier Information

These items describe diagnoses, procedures, and charges and give a history of the patient's condition. Most of this information is found on the patient's encounter form. Figure 6-4 shows the bottom portion of the universal claim form.

Item 14: Date of Current Illness, Injury, Pregnancy

Enter the date when the first symptoms began for the current illness, injury, or pregnancy (date of last menstrual period).

Medicare   For chiropractic services, enter the date of the initiation of the course of treatment and then enter the x-ray date in item 19.

Private Plans   This information is used in determining benefits or exclusions for preexisting conditions.

Item 15: If Patient Has Had Same or Similar Illness

Medicare   Leave blank.

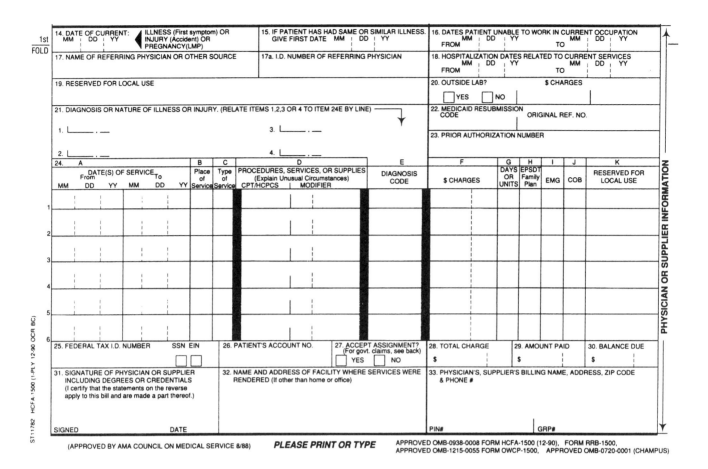

FIGURE 6-4   Health insurance claim form (bottom half).

CHAMPUS   Enter the date when the patient first consulted the physician for a similar condition.

Private Plans   Enter the date when the patient first consulted the physician for a similar condition.

Item 16: Dates Patient Unable to Work in Current Occupation

Enter the dates the patient is employed and unable to work in his or her current occupation. This is important if the patient has employment-related insurance coverage or workers' compensation.

Item 17: Name of the Referring Physician or Other Source

Medicare   Enter the name of the referring or ordering physician if the service or item was ordered or referred by a physician.

A *referring physician* is a physician who requests an item or service for the beneficiary for which payment may be made under the Medicare program. An *ordering physician* is a physician who orders nonphysician services for the patient, such as diagnostic laboratory tests, clinical laboratory tests, pharmaceutical services, and durable medical equipment.

The ordering/referring requirement became effective on January 1, 1992. *All* claims for Medicare-covered services and items that result from a physician's order or referral must include the ordering/referring physician's name and *Unique Physician Identification Number* (UPIN). A UPIN is a unique number assigned to each physician or other practitioner who bills the Medicare program. This includes parenteral and enteral nutrition, immunosuppressive drug claims, and the following:

- Diagnostic laboratory services
- Diagnostic radiology services
- Consultative services
- Durable medical equipment

Claims for other ordered/referred services that are not included in the preceding list must also show the ordering or referring physician's name and UPIN. For example, a surgeon must complete items 17 and 17a when a physician sends a patient for a consultation. When the ordering physician is also the performing physician (as is often the case with in-office clinical laboratory tests), the performing physician's name and assigned UPIN must appear in items 17 and 17a.

All physicians must obtain a UPIN even though they may never bill Medicare directly. A physician who has not been assigned a UPIN must contact the Medicare carrier.

When a patient is referred to a physician who also orders and performs a diagnostic service, a separate claim is required for the diagnostic service.

- Enter the original ordering or referring physician's name and UPIN in items 17 and 17a of the first claim form.
- Enter the ordering (performing) physician's name and UPIN in items 17 and 17a of the second claim form.

CHAMPUS Provide the name and address of the physician, institutional provider, or other source who referred the patient to the provider of the services identified on this claim. This is required for all consultation services. If your patient was referred from a military treatment facility (MTF), enter the name of the MTF and attach part DD2161 of SF 513, "Referral for Civilian Medical Care."

Item 17a: ID Number of Referring Physician

Medicare Enter the HCFA-assigned UPIN of the referring or ordering physician listed in item 17. The first position of the UPIN must be alphabetic, the second and third alphabetic or numeric, and the last three numeric. For example, a UPIN may be A70759 or AAA123.

When a claim involves multiple referring or ordering physicians, a separate HCFA 1500 must be used for each ordering or referring physician.

If the ordering or referring physician has not been assigned a UPIN, one of the *surrogate UPINs* listed below must be used in item 17a. The surrogate UPIN that is used depends on the circumstance and is used only until the physician is assigned a UPIN. Enter the physician's name in item 17 and the surrogate UPIN in item 17a. All surrogate UPINs, with the exception of retired physicians (RET000), are temporary and may be used only until a UPIN is assigned.

Use the following surrogate UPINs for physicians who have not been assigned individual UPINs. Claims received with surrogate numbers will be tracked and may be audited.

- Residents who are issued a UPIN in conjunction with activities outside their residency status must use a UPIN. For interns and residents without UPINs, use the six-character surrogate UPIN RES000 for residents and INT000 for interns.
- Retired physicians who were not issued a UPIN may use the surrogate RET000.
- Physicians serving in the Department of Veteran Affairs or the U.S. armed services may use VAD000.
- Physicians serving in the Public Health or Indian Health services may use PHS000.

Medicare extends coverage and direct payment in certain areas to practitioners who are state-licensed to order medical services including diagnostic tests or refer patients to Medicare providers without a supervising physician. Use the surrogate UPIN NP0000 on claims involving services ordered or referred by nurse practitioners, clinical nurse specialists, and all nonphysician practitioners.

When the ordering or referring physician has not been assigned a UPIN and does not qualify to use one of the surrogate UPINs, use the surrogate UPIN OTH000 until an individual UPIN is assigned.

Item 18: Hospitalization Dates Related to Current Services
Complete this item when a medical service is furnished as a result of or subsequent to a related hospitalization. Enter the admission and discharge dates. If the patient is still hospitalized at the time of billing, enter 0 in the "to" item.

Item 19: Reserved for Local Use

Medicare   Enter the date when the patient was last seen and the UPIN of the patient's attending physician when an independent physical therapist, psychotherapist, or physician providing routine foot care submits claims. Enter the x-ray date for chiropractic services.

Item 20: Outside Lab?

Medicare   Complete this item when billing for diagnostic tests subject to purchase price limitations. A "yes" check indicates that the diagnostic test was performed outside the entity billing for the service. When yes is annotated, item 32 must be completed. Enter the purchase price under charges (item 24f) if the yes block is marked. A check in the "no" box indicates that the tests were performed by the reporting physician.

Private Plans   Leave blank unless instructions are given by a specific plan.

Item 21: Diagnosis or Nature of Illness or Injury

Enter the patient's diagnosis and/or condition by using ICD-9-CM code numbers. Enter up to four codes in priority order (primary condition, secondary condition, comorbid conditions, and complications).

Item 22: Medicaid Resubmission

Leave this blank. It is required by some Medicaid agencies if the agency is going to resubmit a claim. Show the resubmission code and the original claim reference number.

Item 23: Prior Authorization Number

Enter the authorization number for procedures that require preauthorization.

CHAMPUS   Attach a copy of the authorization, for example, mental health preauthorization, heart-lung transplant authorization.

Private Plans   If required, enter the preauthorization number.

Item 24A: Dates of Service

Enter the month, day, and year for each procedure, service, or supply. When "from" and "to" are shown for a series of identical services, enter the number of days or units in column 24G. Do not use ditto marks for dates of service for additional services and/or procedures.

Item 24B: Place of Service

There are variations in the codes used for place of service (POS). The previous HCFA form (1-84) had specific codes printed on the reverse side for use in column 24B. HCFA (12-90) has no such codes printed. Some insurance plans still require the old (1-84) POS codes, and many require the new (12-90) ones. Tool 6-1 is a comprehensive list of places of service, giving both the old codes and the new ones.

Medicare   Use the new POS codes.

CHAMPUS   Use the new POS codes.

Private Plans   Check with the plan's billing instructions to determine which POS codes are required.

Item 24C: Type of Service
The type of service code is listed here when this is required. Tool 6-2 provides a list of services and their numeric codes.

Medicare   Providers are not required to complete this item.

Private Plans   Some plans require the use of type of service codes. Otherwise, leave it blank.

Item 24D: Procedures, Services, Supplies
Enter the five-digit CPT code or the HCPCS Level II/III number for the service. Up to three modifiers can be used in the spaces next to the code. The first modifier is added between the solid line and the dotted line on the form. If three modifiers are necessary, there should be two blank spaces between the second and third in the item to the right of the dotted line.

Medicare   Enter the procedures, services, or supplies, using the HCPCS codes. When applicable, show the HCPCS modifier with any procedure code.

Private Plans   Not all modifiers are accepted. It is best to check with the individual plan to see which modifiers it recognizes.

Item 24E: Diagnosis Code
Enter the diagnosis code reference number, as shown in item 21, to relate the date of service and the procedures performed to the appropriate diagnosis.

Medicare   Enter only one reference number per line. When multiple services are performed, enter the corresponding reference number for each service. Try to use all reference numbers.

Item 24F: $ Charges
Enter the charges for each listed service. Medicare Diagnostic tests, if not personally performed and "yes" is checked in Item 20, are billed at the purchased price.

Item 24G: Days or Units

Enter the number of days or units.

Some services require that the actual number or quantity provided be clearly indicated on the claim form as units of service (e.g., multiple ostomy or urinary supplies, medication dosages, or allergy testing procedures). When multiple services are provided, enter the actual number provided.

For anesthesia services, show the elapsed time in minutes in item 24G. Convert hours into minutes and enter the total minutes required for this procedure.

Item 24H: EPSDT Family Plan

Medicaid   Use a checkmark or X if preventive services were provided under Medicaid.

Item 24I: EMG (Emergency)

CHAMPUS   It is best to mark this block to indicate that the service was provided in a hospital emergency room.

Private Plans   Some plans may require that this item be marked to indicate that the service was provided in a hospital emergency room.

Item 24J: COB (Coordination of Benefits)

Private Plans   Check this item if the patient is covered by one or more private plans. These plans are identified in items 11 and 11a–d.

Item 24K: Reserved for Local Use

Medicare   Enter the carrier-assigned Provider Identification Number (PIN) when the performing physician is a member of a group practice.

CHAMPUS   Enter the state license number of the provider.

Private Plans   Not required.

Item 25: Federal Tax ID Number

Enter the physician/supplier federal tax ID (employer identification number) or Social Security number.

Medicare   The participating physician or supplier's federal tax ID number is required for a mandated Medigap transfer.

Item 26: Patient's Account No.

Enter the patient's account number that was assigned by the practice's accounting system. This is an optional way to enhance patient identification by the physician. Some private plans, Medicaid, and some Medicare include this information on their EOBs. It is easier to identify the patients and post the payments.

Item 27: Accept Assignment?

Medicare   Check the appropriate box to indicate whether the physician accepts assignment of benefits. If Medigap is indicated in item 9 and Medigap payment authorization is given in item 13, the physician must also be a Medicare participating physician and must accept assignment of Medicare benefits for all covered charges for all patients.

The following services can be paid only on an assignment basis:

- Clinical diagnostic laboratory services
- Physician services provided to individuals entitled to both Medicare and Medicaid
- Services of physician assistants, nurse practitioners, clinical nurse specialists, nurse midwives, certified registered nurse anesthetists, clinical psychologists, and clinical social workers
- Ambulatory surgical center services
- Home dialysis supplies and equipment paid under Method II

CHAMPUS   Check "yes" if you accept assignment; check "no" if you do not. Failure to complete this block results in nonacceptance of assignment. "Accept assignment" means that the provider has agreed to be a CHAMPUS participating provider on the claim and will accept the allowable amount as the total amount payable. When a provider accepts assignment, payment will be made to the provider. If the provider does not accept assignment, payment will be made to the patient and/or sponsor.

Private Plans   Not applicable to plans with which the doctor has a contract.

Item 28: Total Charge

Enter total charges for the services reported on the claim (i.e., the total of all charges in item 24F).

Item 29: Amount Paid

Enter the total amount the patient or other medical plan paid toward charges in item 28.

Medicare   Enter the amount received by the provider from the patient toward charges in item 28. If the amount includes payment by another insurance plan, include the EOB or denial showing the amount paid or denied.

CHAMPUS Enter the amount received by the provider or supplier from the other plans or insurances. If the amount includes payment by any other insurance, the other insurance EOB, worksheet, or denial showing the amounts paid or denied must be attached to the CHAMPUS claim. Payment from the beneficiary should not be included.

Item 30: Balance Due

Enter the balance due (item 28 minus item 29).

Item 31: Signature of Physician or Supplier Including Degrees or Credentials

Enter the signature of the physician and/or his or her representative and the date when the form was signed. Most plans will accept a stamped or computer-generated signature.

CHAMPUS The signature of physician or supplier, including degree(s) or credentials and the date of the signature, is necessary unless other authorized signatures are on file with the contractor.

Item 32: Name and Address of Facility Where Services Were Rendered (If Other Than Home or Office)

Enter the name and address of the facility if services were furnished in a hospital, clinic, laboratory, or facility other than the patient's home or the physician's office.

Medicare Physicians must identify any supplier's name, address, and carrier-assigned PIN when billing for purchased diagnostic tests. When more than one supplier is used, list each name and carrier-assigned PIN. Complete this item for all laboratory work performed outside a physician's office. If an independent laboratory is billing, enter the place where the test was performed.

Item 33: Physician's, Supplier's Billing Name, Address, ZIP Code, and Telephone Number

Enter the physician and/or supplier's billing name, address, ZIP Code, and telephone number.

Medicare Enter the carrier-assigned PIN (not the HCFA-assigned UPIN) for the performing physician who is not a member of a group practice. Enter the group number for a physician who is a member of a group practice.

CHAMPUS Enter the provider number.

Private Plans Enter the provider number for the plan.

THE ROLE OF COMPUTERIZED SYSTEMS IN THE INSURANCE CLAIMS PROCESS

In an age of computerized technology, several methods are used to automatically report claims into the data systems of insurance and managed care plans.

Optical Character Recognition

Optical character recognition devices (OCR scanners) are being used more frequently in the entry phase of claims processing. The red-inked HCFA 1500 (12/90) is designed to be used with OCR scanners. These scanners transfer the data from printed or typed forms to computer data storage. Processors no longer have to type or key in the information. These scanners can read 2400 claims per hour, about 20 times the volume of a data entry operator[2] and with very few, if any, entry errors.

For a claim form to be optically scanned, very specific techniques must be employed when the medical office personnel is preparing a paper claim. These techniques include the following:

- Align the form as illustrated at the top of the form.
- Use the most common type (font) styles. Script, italic, proportional spacing, and minitype fonts *cannot* be used.
- Dot-matrix printers may be used, but only letter-quality dot-matrix impressions will allow successful scanner processing.
- Capitalize all letters on the form (do not use lowercase letters).
- Type only within the white areas (characters or parts of characters in the shaded areas are not scannable).
- Use only black ink (light print or blue or other colored ink will not scan).
- Do not strike over or use correction fluid to correct an error (this may result in rejection of the claim).
- Do not use separators such as a slash (/) in dates, hyphens, $ in amounts, periods, or commas.
- All dates should be six numeric digits with spaces between each set of two digits. May 23, 1996, is written 05 23 96.
- Do not fold claims.
- Use only original forms.
- Do not highlight (OCR scanners do not recognize highlighted information).

---

2. Ohio Medicaid Provider Handbook, Chapter 3336, Section III, p. III-1.

Electronic Claims

The electronic revolution has further automated claims processing. One technological advance is electronic claims reporting, a paperless way to report insurance claims. It is a method for communication between the physician's computer and the computer of the insurance or managed care plan. Data are transmitted by means of magnetic tape, diskette, or direct transmission over telephone lines to a plan using a modem. The claim information is transmitted directly into the computer of the insurance plan.

Advantages

There are many advantages to this kind of reporting for plans. Electronic transmission aids plans by reducing their administrative costs per claim, since it takes fewer people to process a claim. Electronic transmission of claims also offers significant benefits for physician practices.

It is the most direct route for sending claims to the databanks of plans. No claims are lost in the mail.

The information sent is the information entered, as there are no data entry personnel to make errors in the transposition of a CPT or ICD-9-CM code number.

Rejections are decreased with this method. If an incomplete claim is sent electronically, the claim will not be accepted. Claim edits in the software used in sending the data assure that the claims are properly completed with appropriate codes and accurate patient and physician information. Figure 6-5 shows a sample rejection list report generated by the computer system of a plan to which electronic claims have been transmitted. The remarks in the Comment column in the figure tell why the claim was not accepted. For example, the Medicare claim for Karl Brown was rejected because the ID number was missing the UPIN. Beth Witte's claim to Prudential was missing a valid primary CPT code. Such reports are generated immediately after the information has been transmitted. In contrast, when claims are sent on paper, it typically takes many days or even weeks before notification of rejection is received.

In many cases electronic claims decrease office expenses. For a medical practice, reporting claims electronically reduces time spent completing insurance forms, cuts postage costs, and provides better management of accounts receivable. Personnel can spend their time doing more productive activities.

Another advantage of transmitting claims electronically is that status reports on all electronic claims can be generated by the computer system of the practice. Figure 6-6 shows a typical status report on the electronic claims sent to a plan on a specific day. Two claims were received for Medicare, one claim for Metropolitan, and two for Prudential, totaling $807.00. Tracking paper claims is much more difficult.

Many plans which pay physicians under fee for service pay claims faster

Dr. Jones/April 15

Please correct and resubmit the claims listed below and send them back in the next file. You will not be charged for these claims until they are processed completely.

Payer: Medicare

Account #	Patient Name	ID Number	Comment
A123456	Jones, Betty	46802468	Missing alpha ID#
A45678	Brown, Karl	24680135D	Missing UPIN#

Payer: Blue Cross/Blue Shield

Account #	Patient Name	ID Number	Comment
A13579	White, Tom	1470293	Need last two digits ID
A369246	Green, Mary	12345234	Date of birth missing

Payer: Prudential

Account #	Patient Name	ID Number	Comment
A1579034	Witte, Beth	24635467	CPT code #1 invalid

FIGURE 6-5 Rejected list report.

if the claims are submitted electronically. Medicare pays electronic claims within 14 days after the date of receipt; paper claims are paid in 27 days. If 90 percent of the claims sent by a practice are electronic, the check can be deposited directly into the bank account of the practice through an *electronic funds transfer (EFT)* method. Instead of paper EOBs, electronic remittance notices documenting the payment are sent. Some managed care plans will return a larger portion of the money withheld, and, in some cases, an additional bonus is paid to those providers using electronic claims.

Disadvantages

There are some disadvantages to electronic claims submission. If there is a transmission failure, claims will be lost. Failures during transmission may be due to power failure or hardware and/or software failure. Many clearinghouses use a download report; this is a listing of the claims that were processed on a particular date.

Date 4/15/xx					
Account #	Patient Name	D. O. S.	Charges	Status	Payer Name
A357903	Davis, Jeff	4/12	134.00	Batch	Medicare
A35798	Lewis, Lisa	4/10	45.00	Batch	Medicare
Total Medicare Claims		2	Total Charges $179.00		
A130495	Hoffman, Becky	4/10	168.00	Wait	Metropolitan
Total Metropolitan Claims		1	Total Charges $168.00		
A4385943	Lambers, Albert	4/12	285.00	Batch	Prudential
A98340293	Weber, Carolyn	4/11	175.00	Batch	Prudential
Total Prudential Claims		2	Total Charges $460.00		
TOTAL CLAIMS: 5			Total Charges $807.00		

FIGURE 6-6   Detailed claim listing.

Figure 6-7 is a download report for the same practice whose detailed claim listing for April 15 is shown in Figure 6-6. According to the download report, only four claims were transmitted on that day. An interruption occurred when the last claim, Carolyn Weber, was being transmitted. Her name does not appear on this report. The detailed claim listing is shown in Figure 6-6. The office personnel are able to check the names that appear on this report against the claims that were sent. If the download report does not contain all the patients who were to be billed, the office staff merely retransmits those claims again rather than retyping or regenerating them, collating them, stuffing them into an envelope, putting on the postage stamp, and mailing them.

There are circumstances in a medical practice when a letter or operative note is sent along with the claim. Perhaps the office staff has used a modifier on the claim and the report will better explain its use. In this instance the claim should be sent on paper rather than electronically. However, Medicare carriers in some states recommend sending the claim electronically and faxing the report separately. In this case the carrier will match the report with the claims. There are also plans that allow a practice to fax the report with a cover letter in addition to sending the claim electronically. These plans will correlate the fax with the electronic claim.

| | Download Report | |
| | Dr. Jones/April 15 | |
Patient Name	Account #	Patient ID#
Davis, Jeff	A357903	49785045
Lewis, Lisa	A35798	09485062
Hoffman, Becky	A130495	40592834
Lambers, Albert	A 4385943	76432087
Total # of Claims	4	

FIGURE 6-7 Sample report.

Workgroup for Electronic Data Interchange (WEDI)

As a result of a congressional mandate, all hospitals must have standardized electronic billing systems in place by 1995, and most other healthcare providers by the year 2000. An advisory body known as the *Workgroup for Electronic Data Interchange (WEDI)* was formed at the request of a former secretary of health and human services, Louis Sullivan, M.D. Through the use of automation of claims reporting and payments made between the hospitals, physicians, employers, and the insurers, healthcare costs could be reduced by several billion dollars. Two things must be in place before this system is successful: There must be national rules for protecting the confidentiality of electronic records, and there must be uniform formats for transmitting enrollment, eligibility, claims, and payment information.

Uniform Formats

Medicare has been accepting electronic claims for almost 25 years. Each state or regional office and other insurance and managed care plans have developed their own versions of the federally recommended format for sending information. By the mid-1980s there were over 400 different formats for electronic claims submission (ECS) across the country. This is the principal reason why ECS has taken so long to be put into effect. If, for example, a claim is sent to Medicare, Medicaid, Blue Shield, and Prudential, four different data sets, user's guides, and operating formats are needed. This is not practical for a physician practice.

National Electronic Information Corporation (NEIC)

In 1981 the *National Electronic Information Corporation (NEIC)* was founded by 10 major insurance plans as a clearinghouse for electronic claims submission. This clearinghouse accepts data from the computer in a single format and then edits, sorts, and distributes the data into formats that are acceptable by various plans. Only one format is needed by a medical practice: the one accepted by the clearinghouse. There is generally a monthly fee charged by the clearinghouse for its services; it includes a cost per claim. Some clearinghouses charge a start-up fee, and then the cost is per claim sent.

ANSI Format

NEIC and other industry representatives have worked to reduce the number of formats to 200, down 50 percent since the 1980s. In 1993, the *American National Standards Institute (ANSI) Standard 837* for electronic claims was approved by industry leaders, establishing a national standard that will be used by all payers. These standards were developed for major business transactions, such as eligibility, claims, and payments. Although it will take some time to implement this sytem, at least there is now one standard to be used.

Medicare Transaction System

In January 1994, HCFA awarded a contract for the development and implementation of the *Medicare Transaction System (MTS)*. The purpose of MTS is to provide better service to beneficiaries, their families, and providers of medical services at a lower cost.[3] MTS will consolidate the automated claims-processing functions of the 79 carriers that use 14 different systems to process Medicare claims at 62 sites throughout the United States.

MTS will utilize a national standard system linking regional processing centers with local carriers. It is predicted that implementation of the Medicare Transmission System will begin by late 1996 and will be fully implemented in 1998. The system will process over 1 million claims by the turn of the century, saving the Medicare program an average of $200 million a year.

Aside from the cost-saving aspect of MTS, the program will decrease paperwork and confusion through improved coordination of benefits and sharing of other payment claims information.

With the development of national standard formats for electronic claims submission, it is conceivable that paper claims will be eliminated.

3. Bruce Vladeck, Ph.D., *JAMA*, March 2, 1994, vol 271, no 9, p. 649.

EXERCISING KNOWLEDGE

Fill in the Blanks

1. If the patient has Blue Cross/Blue Shield, _____ should be checked in item 1.

2. The patient's _____ is entered in item 3.

3. If the form is being completed for injuries suffered in an automobile accident, that information is entered in item _____ .

4. If the patient is covered as a dependent, that information is entered in item _____ .

5. The birthdate of the insured is found in item _____ .

6. The assignment of benefits is found in item _____ .

7. The dates of hospitalization are found in item _____ .

8. The diagnosis or nature of an illness or injury belongs in item _____ .

9. If a laboratory test was sent to an outside laboratory, that should be indicated in item _____ .

10. The procedure codes for the services are found in item _____ .

11. If the provider accepts assignment, item _____ will indicate it.

12. The number of services is indicated in item _____ .

13. The amount the patient paid while in the office can be found in item _____ .

14. The place of service, if it is different from the office or home, is indicated in item _____ .

15. If the plan has issued the provider a special ID number, that can be found in item _____ .

Define These Terms

16. ECS

17. OCR

18. MTS

19. ANSI format

20. NEIC

21. WEDI

Applying Concepts   **22.** Using the information on the registration form completed by Ronald Sample, fill in items 1–13 on HCFA 1500.

PLEASE
DO NOT
STAPLE
IN THIS
AREA

☐☐ PICA	**HEALTH INSURANCE CLAIM FORM** PICA ☐☐☐

1. MEDICARE MEDICAID CHAMPUS CHAMPVA GROUP HEALTH PLAN FECA BLK LUNG OTHER	1a. INSURED'S I.D. NUMBER (FOR PROGRAM IN ITEM 1)
☐ (Medicare #) ☐ (Medicaid #) ☐ (Sponsor's SSN) ☐ (VA File #) ☐ (SSN or ID) ☐ (SSN) ☐ (ID)	

2. PATIENT'S NAME (Last Name, First Name, Middle Initial)	3. PATIENT'S BIRTH DATE MM DD YY SEX M☐ F☐	4. INSURED'S NAME (Last Name, First Name, Middle Initial)
5. PATIENT'S ADDRESS (No., Street)	6. PATIENT RELATIONSHIP TO INSURED Self☐ Spouse☐ Child☐ Other☐	7. INSURED'S ADDRESS (No., Street)
CITY STATE	8. PATIENT STATUS Single☐ Married☐ Other☐	CITY STATE
ZIP CODE TELEPHONE (Include Area Code) ( )	Employed☐ Full-Time Student☐ Part-Time Student☐	ZIP CODE TELEPHONE (INCLUDE AREA CODE) ( )
9. OTHER INSURED'S NAME (Last Name, First Name, Middle Initial)	10. IS PATIENT'S CONDITION RELATED TO:	11. INSURED'S POLICY GROUP OR FECA NUMBER
a. OTHER INSURED'S POLICY OR GROUP NUMBER	a. EMPLOYMENT? (CURRENT OR PREVIOUS) ☐YES ☐NO	a. INSURED'S DATE OF BIRTH MM DD YY SEX M☐ F☐
b. OTHER INSURED'S DATE OF BIRTH MM DD YY SEX M☐ F☐	b. AUTO ACCIDENT? PLACE (State) ☐YES ☐NO ☐	b. EMPLOYER'S NAME OR SCHOOL NAME
c. EMPLOYER'S NAME OR SCHOOL NAME	c. OTHER ACCIDENT? ☐YES ☐NO	c. INSURANCE PLAN NAME OR PROGRAM NAME
d. INSURANCE PLAN NAME OR PROGRAM NAME	10d. RESERVED FOR LOCAL USE	d. IS THERE ANOTHER HEALTH BENEFIT PLAN? ☐YES ☐NO *If yes*, return to and complete item 9 a-d.

READ BACK OF FORM BEFORE COMPLETING & SIGNING THIS FORM.

12. PATIENT'S OR AUTHORIZED PERSON'S SIGNATURE I authorize the release of any medical or other information necessary to process this claim. I also request payment of government benefits either to myself or to the party who accepts assignment below. SIGNED _____ DATE _____	13. INSURED'S OR AUTHORIZED PERSON'S SIGNATURE I authorize payment of medical benefits to the undersigned physician or supplier for services described below. SIGNED _____

2nd FOLD

CARRIER

PATIENT AND INSURED INFORMATION

PATIENT REGISTRATION FORM

PLEASE PRINT Physician or person who sent you to us _Ted Jones, M.D._

PATIENT INFORMATION (TO BE COMPLETED BY PATIENT OR RESPONSIBLE PARTY)   DATE _5/4/XX_

NAME: _Ronald Sample_

ADDRESS: _26 Maple Street_

CITY: _Green Ash_ STATE: _AM._ ZIP: _45299_

HOME PHONE: (_593_) _666-4444_

WORK PHONE: (   )

DRIVER'S LICENSE: _CA 10958_

SEX: ☒M ☐F   AGE: _75_   BIRTHDATE: Month _8_ Day _4_ Year _21_

MARITAL STATUS (✓ ONE): ☐Single ☐Married ☐Divorced ☒Widowed

SSN: _281-45-6000_

EMPLOYER: _Retired_
ADDRESS:
CITY: STATE: ZIP:

TO BE COMPLETED BY RESPONSIBLE PARTY (IF OTHER THAN PATIENT)

NAME:
ADDRESS:
CITY: STATE: ZIP:
HOME PHONE: (   )
WORK PHONE: (   )

RELATIONSHIP TO PATIENT: ☐Spouse ☐Child ☐Other
BIRTHDATE: SSN.:
EMPLOYER:
ADDRESS:
CITY: STATE: ZIP:

BLUE SHIELD ☐ PRUDENTIAL ☐ HMO/CARE ☐ MEDICARE ☒ MEDICAID ☐ WORKERS' COMP. ☐ PPO/CARE ☐ OTHER ☐

Please give us all information regarding your insurance plan(s). Please show all numbers on your card(s). IF YOUR BENEFITS DEPEND ON **PRE-AUTHORIZATION, IT IS YOUR RESPONSIBILITY TO INFORM US, UNLESS WE ARE A PROVIDER FOR YOUR PLAN(S).**

Primary Plan Name: _Medicare_
Address: _Columbus, AM_
Insured (Name on ID Card): _Ronald Sample_
Relationship to Patient: ☒Self ☐Spouse ☐Child ☐Other
Insured ID No.: _281-45-6000T_
Group No. or Company Name: Plan #
Effective Date: _08-01-87_

Secondary Plan Name: _AARP_
Address: _Pennsylvania_
Insured (Name on ID Card): _Ronald Sample_
Relationship to Patient: ☒Self ☐Spouse ☐Child ☐Other
Insured ID No.: _281-45-6000_
Group No. or Company Name: Plan No.
Effective Date: _08-01-87_

Signature of patient or authorized person
I hereby authorize release of medical information necessary to report a claim to my plans(s). A copy of this signature is valid as the original. SIGNATURE _Ronald Sample_

Signature of insured or authorized person to ASSIGN BENEFITS OTHERWISE PAYABLE TO THE INSURED TO THE PHYSICIAN INDICATED ON THE CLAIM. I understand I am financially responsible for benefits not covered by my insurance plan. A copy of this signature is valid as the original   SIGNATURE _Ronald Sample_

TO BE COMPLETED BY PATIENTS COVERED BY MEDICARE and /or those with a Medigap
Name of Beneficiary _Ronald Sample_   HI Claim Number _281-45-6000T_
I request that payment of authorized Medicare benefits be made either to me or on my behalf to _Dr. Lewis_ for any services furnished me by that physician. I authorize any holder of medical information about me to release to the Health Care Financing Administration and its agents any information needed to determine these benefits or the benefits payable for related services. I hereby authorize Medicare to furnish to the above-named doctor any information regarding my Medicare claims under Title XVIII of the Social Security Act.   SIGNATURE _Ronald Sample_
I request that payment of authorized Medigap benefits be made to me or on my behalf to _Dr. Lewis_ for any services furnished me by that physician/supplier. I authorize any holder of medical information about me to released to _AARP_ (name of Medigap insurer) any information needed to determine these benefits or the benefits payable for related services. Medigap Policy Number _281-45-6000_ SIGNATURE _Ronald Sample_

23. Using the information on the registration form completed by Mary Lanes, fill in items 1–13 on HCFA 1500.

PLEASE DO NOT STAPLE IN THIS AREA

2nd FOLD

CARRIER

PATIENT AND INSURED INFORMATION

HEALTH INSURANCE CLAIM FORM

PICA   PICA

1. MEDICARE   MEDICAID   CHAMPUS   CHAMPVA   GROUP HEALTH PLAN   FECA BLK LUNG   OTHER

(Medicare #)   (Medicaid #)   (Sponsor's SSN)   (VA File #)   (SSN or ID)   (SSN)   (ID)

1a. INSURED'S I.D. NUMBER   (FOR PROGRAM IN ITEM 1)

2. PATIENT'S NAME (Last Name, First Name, Middle Initial)

3. PATIENT'S BIRTH DATE   MM | DD | YY   SEX   M   F

4. INSURED'S NAME (Last Name, First Name, Middle Initial)

5. PATIENT'S ADDRESS (No., Street)

6. PATIENT RELATIONSHIP TO INSURED   Self   Spouse   Child   Other

7. INSURED'S ADDRESS (No., Street)

CITY   STATE

8. PATIENT STATUS   Single   Married   Other

CITY   STATE

ZIP CODE   TELEPHONE (Include Area Code)   ( )

Employed   Full-Time Student   Part-Time Student

ZIP CODE   TELEPHONE (INCLUDE AREA CODE)   ( )

9. OTHER INSURED'S NAME (Last Name, First Name, Middle Initial)

10. IS PATIENT'S CONDITION RELATED TO:

11. INSURED'S POLICY GROUP OR FECA NUMBER

a. OTHER INSURED'S POLICY OR GROUP NUMBER

a. EMPLOYMENT? (CURRENT OR PREVIOUS)   YES   NO

a. INSURED'S DATE OF BIRTH   MM | DD | YY   SEX   M   F

b. OTHER INSURED'S DATE OF BIRTH   MM | DD | YY   SEX   M   F

b. AUTO ACCIDENT?   PLACE (State)   YES   NO

b. EMPLOYER'S NAME OR SCHOOL NAME

c. EMPLOYER'S NAME OR SCHOOL NAME

c. OTHER ACCIDENT?   YES   NO

c. INSURANCE PLAN NAME OR PROGRAM NAME

d. INSURANCE PLAN NAME OR PROGRAM NAME

10d. RESERVED FOR LOCAL USE

d. IS THERE ANOTHER HEALTH BENEFIT PLAN?   YES   NO   *If yes*, return to and complete item 9 a-d.

READ BACK OF FORM BEFORE COMPLETING & SIGNING THIS FORM.

12. PATIENT'S OR AUTHORIZED PERSON'S SIGNATURE I authorize the release of any medical or other information necessary to process this claim. I also request payment of government benefits either to myself or to the party who accepts assignment below.

SIGNED _____ DATE _____

13. INSURED'S OR AUTHORIZED PERSON'S SIGNATURE I authorize payment of medical benefits to the undersigned physician or supplier for services described below.

SIGNED _____

PATIENT REGISTRATION FORM

PLEASE PRINT   Physician or person who sent you to us *William Brown*

PATIENT INFORMATION (TO BE COMPLETED BY PATIENT OR RESPONSIBLE PARTY)   DATE _____

NAME: Mary Lanes	SEX: ☐ M ☒ F AGE: 50 BIRTHDATE: Month 1 / Day 30 / Year 44 MARITAL STATUS (✓ ONE) ☐ Single ☒ Married
ADDRESS: 1123 Apple Lane	
CITY: Green Ash STATE: AM ZIP: 45299	SSN: 614-34-5897 ☐ Divorced ☐ Widowed
HOME PHONE: (513) 333-4444	EMPLOYER: none
WORK PHONE: ( )	ADDRESS:
DRIVER'S LICENSE: CB 8560765678	CITY: STATE: ZIP:

TO BE COMPLETED BY RESPONSIBLE PARTY (IF OTHER THAN PATIENT)

NAME: Raymond Lanes	RELATIONSHIP TO PATIENT: ☒ Spouse ☐ Child ☐ Other
ADDRESS: Same	BIRTHDATE: 5/8/40 SSN.: 7890-45-9780
CITY: STATE: ZIP:	EMPLOYER: ABC Cement
HOME PHONE: ( )	ADDRESS: 1 Concrete Way
WORK PHONE: ( )	CITY: Green Ash STATE: AM ZIP: 45299

BLUE SHIELD	PRUDENTIAL	HMO/CARE	MEDICARE	MEDICAID	WORKERS' COMP..	PPO/CARE	OTHER
☒	☐	☐	☐	☐	☐	☐	☐

Please give us all information regarding your insurance plan(s). Please show all numbers on your card(s). **IF YOUR BENEFITS DEPEND ON PRE-AUTHORIZATION, IT IS YOUR RESPONSIBILITY TO INFORM US, UNLESS WE ARE A PROVIDER FOR YOUR PLAN(S).**

Primary Plan Name: Blue Shield of Florida	Secondary Plan Name:
Address: PO Box 1796 Jacksonville, Fl 32231	Address:
Insured (Name on ID Card): Raymond Lanes	Insured (Name on ID Card):
Relationship to Patient: ☐ Self ☒ Spouse ☐ Child ☐ Other	Relationship to Patient: ☐ Self ☐ Spouse ☐ Child ☐ Other
Insured ID No.: ABC 19064	Insured ID No.:
Group No. or Company Name: ABC Cement Plan #	Group No. or Company Name: Plan No.
Effective Date: 08-05-95	Effective Date:

Signature of patient or authorized person
I hereby authorize release of medical information necessary to report a claim to my plans(s).
A copy of this signature is valid as the original.   SIGNATURE *Mary Lanes*

Signature of insured or authorized person to ASSIGN BENEFITS OTHERWISE PAYABLE TO THE INSURED TO THE PHYSICIAN INDICATED ON THE CLAIM I understand I am financially responsible for benefits not covered by my insurance plan.
A copy of this signature is valid as the original   SIGNATURE *Mary Lanes*

TO BE COMPLETED BY PATIENTS COVERED BY MEDICARE and /or those with a Medigap
Name of Beneficiary _____ HI Claim Number _____
I request that payment of authorized Medicare benefits be made either to me or on my behalf to _____ for any services furnished me by that physician. I authorize any holder of medical information about me to release to the Health Care Financing Administration and its agents any information needed to determine these benefits or the benefits payable for related services. I hereby authorize Medicare to furnish to the above-named doctor any information regarding my Medicare claims under Title XVIII of the Social Security Act.   SIGNATURE_____
I request that payment of authorized Medigap benefits be made to me or on my behalf to _____ for any services furnished me by that physician/supplier. I authorize any holder of medical information about me to released to _____(name of Medigap insurer) any information needed to determine these benefits or the benefits payable for related services. Medigap Policy Number _____ SIGNATURE _____

24. Using the following sample office visit (99212), complete items 14–33 on the universal claim form for Ruth Brown. Set your own charges for questions 24, 25, and 26.

Ruth Brown   April 25, 199X

DOB: 01-02-29—age 67

CHIEF COMPLAINT
(1) Osteoarthritis of the Knees, 1989 (715.9)

SUBJECTIVE
Ruth complains of aches and stiffness in joints, especially the left knee. She has been taking ibuprofen and/or aspirin. She is discouraged. She wants her knees to be well.

OBJECTIVE
Wgt. 107 lb.; BP 130/80; P 80 and regular. The synovium is slightly thickened, more so on the left, with medial inferior tenderness.

MEDICAL DECISION MAKING
The joint problem is beginning to limit her lifestyle. She will be started on a regular dose of an anti-inflammatory drug. Complete evaluation will be done in 2 months.

PLAN

Diagnostic: Nothing further at this time.

Therapeutic:
(1) Diet—Step-One Low Fat, Low cholesterol.
(2) Activity—encouraged as able.
(3) Naproxen 375 mg. Bid. START.

Counseling: The plan was reviewed.

TL/rl   *Tracy Lewis, M.D.*

25. Using the following information, complete items 21-33 for Dr. Lewis.

Marvin Friedman

DOB: 01-17-42—age XX   January 19, 19XX

The Olympus OSF-2/OSF-2-35 was placed in the rectum and advanced 60 cm. The endoscope was then slowly withdrawn, examining the colonic mucosa circumferentially. A moderate number of fairly uniform diverticula were noted in the middle and high sigmoid colon. The mucosa appeared normal. No polyps were found. On retroflexion, the proximal rectum was normal.

IMPRESSION: Sigmoid diverticula.

tl/im   *Tracy Lewis, M.D.*

1st FOLD

14. DATE OF CURRENT: ILLNESS (First symptom) OR INJURY (Accident) OR PREGNANCY(LMP) MM DD YY	15. IF PATIENT HAS HAD SAME OR SIMILAR ILLNESS. GIVE FIRST DATE MM DD YY	16. DATES PATIENT UNABLE TO WORK IN CURRENT OCCUPATION FROM MM DD YY TO MM DD YY
17. NAME OF REFERRING PHYSICIAN OR OTHER SOURCE	17a. I.D. NUMBER OF REFERRING PHYSICIAN	18. HOSPITALIZATION DATES RELATED TO CURRENT SERVICES FROM MM DD YY TO MM DD YY

19. RESERVED FOR LOCAL USE

20. OUTSIDE LAB?　　$ CHARGES　　☐ YES　☐ NO

21. DIAGNOSIS OR NATURE OF ILLNESS OR INJURY. (RELATE ITEMS 1,2,3 OR 4 TO ITEM 24E BY LINE)

1. |___.__|　　　3. |___.__|

2. |___.__|　　　4. |___.__|

22. MEDICAID RESUBMISSION CODE　　ORIGINAL REF. NO.

23. PRIOR AUTHORIZATION NUMBER

24. A DATE(S) OF SERVICE		B Place of Service	C Type of Service	D PROCEDURES, SERVICES, OR SUPPLIES (Explain Unusual Circumstances) CPT/HCPCS MODIFIER	E DIAGNOSIS CODE	F $ CHARGES	G DAYS OR UNITS	H EPSDT Family Plan	I EMG	J COB	K RESERVED FOR LOCAL USE
From MM DD YY	To MM DD YY										
1											
2											
3											
4											
5											
6											

25. FEDERAL TAX I.D. NUMBER ☐ SSN ☐ EIN	26. PATIENT'S ACCOUNT NO.	27. ACCEPT ASSIGNMENT? (For govt. claims, see back) ☐ YES ☐ NO	28. TOTAL CHARGE $	29. AMOUNT PAID $	30. BALANCE DUE $

31. SIGNATURE OF PHYSICIAN OR SUPPLIER INCLUDING DEGREES OR CREDENTIALS (I certify that the statements on the reverse apply to this bill and are made a part thereof.) SIGNED　　DATE	32. NAME AND ADDRESS OF FACILITY WHERE SERVICES WERE RENDERED (If other than home or office)	33. PHYSICIAN'S, SUPPLIER'S BILLING NAME, ADDRESS, ZIP CODE & PHONE # PIN#　　GRP#

PHYSICIAN OR SUPPLIER INFORMATION

ST11782　HCFA-1500 (1-PLY 12-90 OCR BC)

(APPROVED BY AMA COUNCIL ON MEDICAL SERVICE 8/88)　**PLEASE PRINT OR TYPE**　APPROVED OMB-0938-0008 FORM HCFA-1500 (12-90),　FORM RRB-1500, APPROVED OMB-1215-0055 FORM OWCP-1500,　APPROVED OMB-0720-0001 (CHAMPUS)

1st FOLD

14. DATE OF CURRENT: ILLNESS (First symptom) OR INJURY (Accident) OR PREGNANCY(LMP) MM DD YY	15. IF PATIENT HAS HAD SAME OR SIMILAR ILLNESS. GIVE FIRST DATE MM DD YY	16. DATES PATIENT UNABLE TO WORK IN CURRENT OCCUPATION FROM MM DD YY TO MM DD YY
17. NAME OF REFERRING PHYSICIAN OR OTHER SOURCE	17a. I.D. NUMBER OF REFERRING PHYSICIAN	18. HOSPITALIZATION DATES RELATED TO CURRENT SERVICES FROM MM DD YY TO MM DD YY

19. RESERVED FOR LOCAL USE

20. OUTSIDE LAB?　　$ CHARGES　　☐ YES　☐ NO

21. DIAGNOSIS OR NATURE OF ILLNESS OR INJURY. (RELATE ITEMS 1,2,3 OR 4 TO ITEM 24E BY LINE)

1. |___.__|　　　3. |___.__|

2. |___.__|　　　4. |___.__|

22. MEDICAID RESUBMISSION CODE　　ORIGINAL REF. NO.

23. PRIOR AUTHORIZATION NUMBER

24. A DATE(S) OF SERVICE		B Place of Service	C Type of Service	D PROCEDURES, SERVICES, OR SUPPLIES (Explain Unusual Circumstances) CPT/HCPCS MODIFIER	E DIAGNOSIS CODE	F $ CHARGES	G DAYS OR UNITS	H EPSDT Family Plan	I EMG	J COB	K RESERVED FOR LOCAL USE
From MM DD YY	To MM DD YY										
1											
2											
3											
4											
5											
6											

25. FEDERAL TAX I.D. NUMBER ☐ SSN ☐ EIN	26. PATIENT'S ACCOUNT NO.	27. ACCEPT ASSIGNMENT? (For govt. claims, see back) ☐ YES ☐ NO	28. TOTAL CHARGE $	29. AMOUNT PAID $	30. BALANCE DUE $

31. SIGNATURE OF PHYSICIAN OR SUPPLIER INCLUDING DEGREES OR CREDENTIALS (I certify that the statements on the reverse apply to this bill and are made a part thereof.) SIGNED　　DATE	32. NAME AND ADDRESS OF FACILITY WHERE SERVICES WERE RENDERED (If other than home or office)	33. PHYSICIAN'S, SUPPLIER'S BILLING NAME, ADDRESS, ZIP CODE & PHONE # PIN#　　GRP#

PHYSICIAN OR SUPPLIER INFORMATION

ST11782　HCFA-1500 (1-PLY 12-90 OCR BC)

(APPROVED BY AMA COUNCIL ON MEDICAL SERVICE 8/88)　**PLEASE PRINT OR TYPE**　APPROVED OMB-0938-0008 FORM HCFA-1500 (12-90),　FORM RRB-1500, APPROVED OMB-1215-0055 FORM OWCP-1500,　APPROVED OMB-0720-0001 (CHAMPUS)

26. Using the following information, complete items 14–33 for Tim Levy.

Tim Levy

DOB: 08/10/31   July 2, 199X

PROBLEM/COMPLAINT
1. Chronic pressure ulceration right foot. (ICD-707.0)
2. Diabetes Mellitus/Insulin Dependent 1987 with peripheral vascular disease. (ICD-250.71)
3. Arteriosclerotic cardiovascular disease. (ICD-429.2)

HISTORY
Healing of the dorsal lesion at the base of the toes continues. He is developing a pressure ulceration on the right lateral heel through thick layers of callused skin. His feet are clean. He still soaks them in Epsom salts twice daily. His diabetes mellitus is under control as well as his arteriosclerotic cardiovascular disease.

EXAMINATION
Wgt. 165½ lbs; BP 100/70. Neck veins are flat; lung fields are clear. Heart rhythm is regular with a loud S3 systolic murmur at the apex. There is a Grade II apical systolic murmur and little pedal edema at this time, although his peripheral circulation is impaired. The thin slit of a lesion on the dorsum of the foot is healed. A 1-cm round tender ulcer is developing on the right lateral heel.

MEDICAL DECISION MAKING
Tim must be meticulous about preventing any undue pressure to any area of the foot because of his chronic ulcers. His feet need to be better lubricated. The antibiotic will be discontinued.

PLAN

Diagnostic: Nothing further at this time.

Therapeutic:
(1) Diet—Step-One Low Fat, Low Cholesterol.
(2) Activity—sedentary.
(3) Human Lente Insulin 15 U s.c., q.d.
(4) Lisinopril 10 mg b.i.d.
(5) Furosemide 40 mg b.i.d.
(6) Metolazone 2.5 mg q.o.d.
(7) Allopurinol 300 mg q.d.
(8) Aspirin 80 mg q.o.d.
(9) Digoxin 0.25 mg q.d.
(10) Ciprofloxacin 500 mg b.i.d.

Counseling: He was advised after soaking to rub his foot gently with cocoa butter twice daily.

TAL/im   Tracy Lewis, M.D.

1st FOLD

14. DATE OF CURRENT: ILLNESS (First symptom) OR INJURY (Accident) OR PREGNANCY(LMP) MM DD YY	15. IF PATIENT HAS HAD SAME OR SIMILAR ILLNESS. GIVE FIRST DATE MM DD YY	16. DATES PATIENT UNABLE TO WORK IN CURRENT OCCUPATION MM DD YY MM DD YY FROM TO
17. NAME OF REFERRING PHYSICIAN OR OTHER SOURCE	17a. I.D. NUMBER OF REFERRING PHYSICIAN	18. HOSPITALIZATION DATES RELATED TO CURRENT SERVICES MM DD YY MM DD YY FROM TO
19. RESERVED FOR LOCAL USE		20. OUTSIDE LAB? $ CHARGES ☐ YES ☐ NO

21. DIAGNOSIS OR NATURE OF ILLNESS OR INJURY. (RELATE ITEMS 1,2,3 OR 4 TO ITEM 24E BY LINE) ⟶

1. └─ . ─   3. └─ . ─

2. └─ . ─   4. └─ . ─

22. MEDICAID RESUBMISSION CODE   ORIGINAL REF. NO.

23. PRIOR AUTHORIZATION NUMBER

24. A DATE(S) OF SERVICE From To MM DD YY MM DD YY	B Place of Service	C Type of Service	D PROCEDURES, SERVICES, OR SUPPLIES (Explain Unusual Circumstances) CPT/HCPCS | MODIFIER	E DIAGNOSIS CODE	F $ CHARGES	G DAYS OR UNITS	H EPSDT Family Plan	I EMG	J COB	K RESERVED FOR LOCAL USE
1										
2										
3										
4										
5										
6										

25. FEDERAL TAX I.D. NUMBER SSN EIN ☐ ☐	26. PATIENT'S ACCOUNT NO.	27. ACCEPT ASSIGNMENT? (For govt. claims, see back) ☐ YES ☐ NO	28. TOTAL CHARGE $	29. AMOUNT PAID $	30. BALANCE DUE $
31. SIGNATURE OF PHYSICIAN OR SUPPLIER INCLUDING DEGREES OR CREDENTIALS (I certify that the statements on the reverse apply to this bill and are made a part thereof.) SIGNED DATE	32. NAME AND ADDRESS OF FACILITY WHERE SERVICES WERE RENDERED (If other than home or office)		33. PHYSICIAN'S, SUPPLIER'S BILLING NAME, ADDRESS, ZIP CODE & PHONE # PIN# GRP#		

PHYSICIAN OR SUPPLIER INFORMATION

ST111782   HCFA-1500 (1-PLY 12-90 OCR BC)

(APPROVED BY AMA COUNCIL ON MEDICAL SERVICE 8/88)   ***PLEASE PRINT OR TYPE***   APPROVED OMB-0938-0008 FORM HCFA-1500 (12-90), FORM RRB-1500, APPROVED OMB-1215-0055 FORM OWCP-1500, APPROVED OMB-0720-0001 (CHAMPUS)

▼ TOOL 6-1
PLACE OF SERVICE CODES

Place of Service	New Codes	Old Codes
Office	11	3 (O)
Home	12	4 (H)
Inpatient Hospital	21	1 (IH)
Outpatient Hospital	22	2 (OH)
Emergency Room	23	2 (OH)
Ambulatory Surgical Center	24	B (ASC)
Birthing Center	25	0 (OL)
Military Treatment Facility	26	0 (OL)
Skilled Nursing Facility	31	8 (SNF)
Nursing Home	32	7 (NH)
Custodial Nursing Facility	33	0 (OL)
Hospice	34	0 (OL)
Inpatient Psychiatric Facility	51	0 (OL)
Psychiatric Facility—Day	52	5 or 6
Community Mental Health Center	53	5 or 6
Intermediate Care Facility/Mentally Retarded	54	D (STF)
Residental Substance Abuse Treatment Center	55	C (RTC)
Psychiatric Residential Treatment Center	56	C (RTC)
Comprehensive Inpt. Rehabilitation Facility	61	0 (OL)
Comprehensive Outpt. Rehabilitation Facility	62	F (COR)
End-Stage Renal Disease Treatment Facility	65	E (EDC)
State or Local Public Health Clinic	71	0 (OL)
Rural Health Clinic	72	0 (OL)
Independent Laboratory	81	A (IL)
Other Unlisted Facility	99	0 (OL)

▼ **TOOL 6-2**
TABLE OF NUMERIC SERVICE CODES

Service	Numeric Type of Service
Medical care	1
Surgery	2
Consultation	3
Diagnostic x-ray	4
Diagnostic laboratory dialysis	5
Radiation therapy	6
Anesthesia	7
Assistant at surgery	8
Other medical service	9
Blood or packed cells	0
Used DME	A
Ambulatory surgical center	F
Hospice	H
Renal supply in home	L
Alternate payment for maintenance	M
Kidney donor	N
Pneumococcal vaccine	V
Second opinion in elective surgery	Y
Third opinion in elective surgery	Z

CHAPTER 7

Backing Up the Codes with Documentation

CHAPTER OVERVIEW

Documentation is defined as the chronological recording of pertinent facts and observations regarding a patient's health status in a logical sequence. The structure of the medical record must be consistent, and the information must be recorded in a format that allows the physician to access it easily and quickly. Documentation helps in making a proper diagnosis and formulating a sound therapeutic plan. For those who work with a patient, it provides a means to understand quickly the patient's history and current medical status. Documentation promotes continuity of care among physicians and other healthcare providers. The medical record is also a collection of information that may be useful for research and education.

It is also important to maintain a record of all the treatments received by a patient to reflect what has been reported to third-party payers. Concomitantly, the CPT/ICD-9 codes reported to payers should reflect the documentation in the chart. An unwritten rule states that if it is not documented, it is not done; if it is not done, it cannot be reported or billed. A properly documented medical record provides the legal means of verifying care. Millions of dollars are paid in malpractice cases annually because the care was good but the medical record was not.

After reading the material in this chapter, doing the exercises, and using the end-of-chapter tools, you will be able to:

- *Understand the importance of documentation*
- *Describe the structure and content of a medical record*
- *Use specific tools that simplify the record-keeping procedure, including master problem sheet, the master medication sheet, the preventive medicine record, and the laboratory summary sheet*
- *Relate medical record-keeping procedures to physician payment*

THE IMPORTANCE OF DOCUMENTATION

With the increase in malpractice claims during the mid-1970s, patient charts assumed an important role outside the clinical setting. In the event of a lawsuit, the medical record provides a historic perspective on treatment that can be measured in terms of standards of care. *Standards of care* are the minimum sets of services which should be provided for the treatment of a patient's condition. When a physician does not use the standard of care which others in the profession would employ, that physician has breached a duty to the patient. The medical record is a legal document which helps reconstruct the sequence of care.

Quality of Care and Utilization of Resources

In the late 1980s physicians found that more and more of their income was coming from third-party payers. Those organizations then began to assess the quality of care their patients were receiving. Most managed care contracts require the physician to maintain adequate medical records and give the employees of the managed care organization access to medical records to conduct utilization and quality improvement studies.

Clinical site surveys conducted by managed care organizations include a review of medical record documentation. Plans conduct these evaluations not only to measure the quality of care but also to determine whether medical resources are being utilized effectively.

Fines for Inadequate Documentation

In the 1992 and 1994 CPT-4 books, the American Medical Association revised the way in which physician encounters should be documented. Each level of encounter now requires certain types of documentation which were developed by the AMA and HCFA. Data from HCFA obtained through a random review of charts indicate that the primary difficulty in reporting evaluation and management codes is inadequate documentation. Physician practices must cooperate with random medical record reviews under the Social Security Act, which created the Medicare program. Practices which do not cooperate can be referred to the Office of the Inspector General (OIG), and payment can be denied if a practitioner fails to provide patient care data that are pertinent to the review. The OIG was established at the Department of Health and Human Services by Congress in 1976 to identify and eliminate fraud, abuse, and waste in departmental operations. The OIG may exclude a practitioner from participation in the Medicare program. Under the act, Medicare must conduct retrospective audits to determine whether a treatment is reasonable and necessary. Other plans are following Medicare's lead and are also conducting retrospective audits. During these audits, questions are asked. If a plan determines that the documentation does not agree with a claim it has paid, large fines may be assessed. For example, if Dr. Tracy Lewis billed a Level 4 office visit, 99214, but the chart documentation reflects a Level 3 office visit, 99213, the fine may be as follows:

Code	Fee, $
99214	68.00
99213	31.00
Difference	37.00

Thus, this sum is owed to Medicare for each incidence of billing 99214 instead of 99213.

In the past 2 years, Dr. Lewis billed approximately 4000 Level 4 visits. The difference between the visits billed and the visits documented is $37.00, and so 4000 × $37.00 = $148,000.

Dr. Lewis was overpaid $148,000 by Medicare, and that sum must be repaid. Dr. Lewis may have done the work of a Level 4 service, but his medical record documentation did not support the work.

Although there is no "right way" to document medical care which will satisfy the audits of every plan, there are recommended principles of medical record documentation.

Principles of Medical Record Documentation

While the office staff is not responsible for documentation, it is responsible for the organization and maintenance of charts. There are accepted principles of medical record keeping, and the office staff members should encourage physicians to document properly and provide them with the necessary equipment and supplies.

Development of Principles of Documentation

In 1992, at a meeting attended by representatives of the AMA, the American Hospital Association, the American Managed Care and Review Association, the American Medical Peer Review Association, the Health Insurance Association of America, the American Health Information Management Association, and the Blue Cross/Blue Shield Association, certain principles of medical record documentation were developed. All seven groups agree that the fundamental reason for maintaining an adequate medical record should be its contribution to quality medical care. Let us examine several aspects of medical record documentation.

Individual Charts Are Kept for Each Patient

A separate chart is maintained for each individual receiving medical care. Although the physician may be treating siblings as well as parents, it is appropriate to separate a child's record from that of the child's parent.

The Charts Are One Size with Secured Pages

It is best to use a standard $11\frac{3}{4}$-inch by $9\frac{1}{2}$-inch folder with permanent fasteners that can hold material or information securely. If the document is dropped, it can be easily reassembled in a chronological sequence without much time being wasted. A chart smaller than that size does not allow the storage of standard size letters or reports without folding. Fasteners are usually made of metal and can be attached at the top or the left-hand portion of a folder. All documents to be placed in the chart are punched with two holes and attached to the fastener. Smaller items, such as laboratory results, medical release forms, and notations of telephone calls, can be taped to a full-size sheet and kept in the folder.

A Consistent Labeling System Is Used

The outside of the chart should contain a color-coded alphabetic label that lists the patient's name and birthdate in case there is more than one patient with the same name. Chart labels are of two varieties. In one system, a color is assigned to each letter of the alphabet; for example, A is red, B is green, and C is yellow. Some practices double code each chart by matching two letters of the patient's last name with two different colored labels; for example, the chart for John Smith has a red label for S and a green one for M. These color-coded alphabetic labels make filing the record easier; if a chart is misfiled, it can easily be located and identified because of the different colors that are used.

In a third option, full colored folders indicate the first letter of the patient's last name. These folders usually come in several different colors but tend to be more expensive than traditional folders. Under this system all patients with a last name beginning with S have red folders.

Although there are many ways to file charts, the alphabetic system seems to work best. If this system is used, the patient's last name must be written first on the label or outside jacket of the chart. This is followed by a comma and then the first name and middle initial. Titles such as "Doctor" are not included in the alphabetic sequence. If the surname has a prefix, as in MacArthur, the chart is filed under the name of the first letter of that prefix, in this case the letter M.

Yearly aging of the labels kept on the outside of charts allows frequent purging of inactive records. *Purging* is a method for reducing the number of inactive documents in the medical record. Every medical practice should have a policy for the definition of an inactive period so that patients who have not received treatment can have their charts removed from the active file. Yearly aging labels on the outside of a chart folder also facilitate more timely *recalls* (notifying the patient that it is time to schedule an appointment or procedure).

Other labels may be attached to the outside of a patient's chart to identify situations that are of critical importance, such as allergies, pacemaker implantation, and the presence of a living will, as well as insurance information. Their use varies with the individual physician's needs.

A Consistent Structure Is Maintained

Sections or chart dividers are very helpful in maintaining a consistent structure because they allow for easy access to x-ray and laboratory reports, hospital discharge summaries, and consultation reports. All the sheets within each category relate specifically to the section in which they are stored. If sectioning is not done, all office notes should be filed together and all laboratory and x-ray reports should be filed together in a chronologic sequence. This filing system makes it possible to find information quickly. It is also helpful if there is some cross-referencing of the information. For example, if a patient comes to the office for a treatment after being in the hospital, there should be some mention in the office notes that the patient was hospitalized so that the physician can refer back to the hospital report section for additional information. Other services, such as x-ray and lab reports, are kept with the records of the patient's last encounter.

Entries Are Made in Permanent Black Ink

All entries in the medical record should be made in ink to give permanency to the record and make it difficult to alter. If the medical record must be changed, the information is crossed out and the new information is written above it and marked with the initials of the staff person who made the alteration. Never use white-out material in the medical record.

Entries Are Made in a Timely Fashion

Most insurance plans require that entries be recorded in a timely fashion. The patient may be receiving a series of services over a brief period of time from a number of different physicians, and the chart allows for communication between the physicians. If the physician is unable to write legibly, he or she might consider dictating the findings. If only the doctor is able to interpret the notes, the notes should be dictated and transcribed.

Busy physicians tend to postpone dictation. The quality and accuracy of observations and treatment are enhanced when dictation is done on the date of service. There are many dictation systems; it is best to select one which encourages prompt dictation. Some practices have a central dictation unit in the hallway between treatment rooms where the physician can pause between seeing patients, with the chart in hand, to dictate notes about the current visit. Others prefer to use small hand-held dictating machines. These small units are portable and can be used at the hospital, in the car, or at home.

All Entries Must Be Authenticated by the Responsible Caregiver

The responsible physician and the other clinical caregivers must sign or initial entries in the medical record. The signature includes the title of the individual, such as M.D., R.N. or P.A. If the encounter is dictated and the transcriptionist uses stenographic initials at the end of the report, this merely indicates the individual who dictated the information and did the transcription. If the physician signs or initials the note, he or she is agreeing that what has been recorded is accurate.

Summary Sheets of Clinical Situations Improve Patient Care

A master problem sheet (see Tool 7-1) for both acute and chronic disorders is a useful tool in medical record documentation. This is a summary list of problems that affect the patient at a particular time and may affect the patient's current care. The sheet may also list patient allergies and adverse reactions to medications. All previous surgeries are noted on the problem sheet. The value of the master problem sheet is decreased if it is not kept up to date. Notations must be made on a regular basis whenever the physical or mental situation of the patient changes.

A master medication sheet (see Tool 7-2) is vital for monitoring the drugs prescribed, the doses, the number of drugs dispensed, the dates started, and the dates stopped. This sheet allows the doctor to quickly see the medication history of the patient and to review the last renewal and amount of a medication, its effectiveness, and its relationship to the health of the patient. Some practices note dates of immunizations on the problem sheet, while others create a preventive medicine record (see Tool 7-3) to document this information. Summary sheets give the physician an overall view of a patient's health status. When all summary sheets are placed on the left side of the patient's chart, the information can be seen immediately when the chart is opened and the physician can review the patient's clinical condition before entering the treatment room.

A summary sheet of laboratory tests (see Tool 7-4) is valuable in tracking the progress of a chronic disease. This sheet is most useful in visually identifying the values for tests done in the office which can be expressed numerically and are measured on a regular basis, for example, the blood glucose levels of an unstable diabetic patient whose medication is being adjusted. A graphic illustration of values gives the physician an overall view of the patient's progress and the effectiveness of the medication.

Each Medical Record Should Stand by Itself

A separate record for each patient should contain the following data:

> Patient's name
> Address and telephone number
> Date of birth

Sex

Occupation and employer's name, address, and telephone number

Next of kin

Previous medical history, family history, and personal history

Relevant health risk factors

Referring physician's name, address, and telephone number

An emergency contact (someone not living with the patient), including name, address, and telephone number

These data are part of the registration process.

Financial and Billing Data Should Be Included

In the past, financial and billing information were separated from the medical information and maintained in a different area. Because so many patients are enrollees of insurance and managed care plans, this information is now kept in the medical record. It allows for easy accessibility if the patient needs precertification or authorization for a referral to another physician.

METHODS OF DOCUMENTATION

A wide variety of methods are used in medical documentation. In the past, when information about a patient was obtained because the patient informed the physician or through the doctor's actual findings (blood pressure, temperature), the information was noted in the chart. Each visit was recorded in sequence in the patient's medical history as the patient saw the physician.

When other physician practices or insurance plans requested information, it became difficult for a practice to retrieve the data. There was no organized logical sequence for entering information in the patient's chart.

Documenting Face-to-Face Encounters with the Physician/Caregiver

The following information should be documented after each face-to-face encounter with a patient:

- The patient's name on each page of the medical record
- The date
- The reason for the encounter (chief complaint of the patient or problem)

■ A diagnosis or impression, as well as the comorbidity or complications which contribute to the patient's problem or a notation that the problem sheet has been reviewed

■ Notations of all diagnostic tests ordered

■ All therapies administered by the doctor and/or employees

■ Recommendations or instructions to the patient

■ Signature or initials of professional

SOAP Format of Record Keeping

The method of documentation most widely used by physicians is the SOAP (subjective, objective, assessment, plan) format for record keeping. It is taught in medical schools and can be adapted to the evaluation and management section of the CPT-4 book. With the SOAP format, the patient's treatment is recorded in an organized and consistent sequence. Otherwise, the physician may not document important components of the E&M codes. The SOAP format can be described as follows:

S Subjective (E&M history): the chief complaint or the reason for the medical encounter. Generally includes the history of the present illness (HPI) and a review of systems. This is usually information the patient tells the doctor. The subjective format also includes past, family, and/or social history.

O Objective (E&M examination): the physical examination of the patient, including vital signs, height, weight, and blood pressure.

A Assessment (E&M decision making): the doctor's diagnosis at the time of the encounter or a recording of the impression if a diagnosis cannot be made.

P Plan (E&M medical decision making): a recording of recommended treatment, testing ordered or other workup contemplated, new medications or adjustments of medications, therapies, and planned surgical procedures.

Documentation Guidelines

In 1994, HCFA collaborated with the AMA to publish Documentation Guidelines for E&M Services. These guidelines will be used to review medical records and determine the appropriate level of E&M services. The components of E&M coding were described in Chapter 5 and are history, examination, medical decision making, counseling, coordination of care, nature of presenting problem, and time. The first three components are the key components in the selection of a level of service of an E&M code. Documentation Guidelines provide definitions and guidelines for the three key components of E&M services and not for visits which are predominately based on counseling and coordination of care.

Subjective (Documentation of History)

The history is a record of the patient's medical problems and treatment. The history should be documented in a chronologic sequence, starting with the current episode, and relevant past information should also be entered in the chart. Components of the history are the chief complaint, history of the present illness (HPI), review of patient body systems (ROS), and information about past, family, and/or social history (PFSH). Table 7-1 shows the elements required for each type of history. To select a level of history, all three elements in the figure must be met.

TABLE 7-1
Documentation of a History[1]

Type of History	History of Present Illness (HPI)	Review of Systems (ROS)	Past, Family, Medical and/or Social History (P, F, M, SH)
Problem-focused	Brief 1–3 elements	N/A	N/A
Expanded problem-focused	Brief 1–3 elements	Problem pertinent system(s) directly related to HPI	N/A
Detailed	Extended 4+ elements	Extended system(s) directly related to HPI 2–9 elements	Pertinent 1 item from any history element
Comprehensive	Extended 4+ elements	Complete system(s) directly related to HPI 10+ elements	Complete 1 item from 2 of 3 elements—established patient and ER 1 item from each of 3 elements—new patient and consultation
	HPI Elements Location Quality Severity Duration Timing Context Modifying factors Associated signs and symptoms	**ROS Elements** Constitutional symptoms Eyes Ears, nose, mouth, throat Cardiovascular Respiratory Gastrointestinal Genitourinary Integumentary (skin and/or breast) Neurologic Psychiatric Endocrine Hematologic/lymphatic, allergic/immunologic	**P, F, M, S History Elements** Past medical history (items: illnesses, operations, injuries, and treatments) Family history (items: medical events in family) Social history (items: age-appropriate review of past and current activities)

[1]CPT Assistant: 1995 Coding Symposium, November 11, 1994, pp. 6–8.

Stated in the patient's own words, the chief complaint is a concise statement describing the symptom, the problem, the condition, a physician's recommendation for return, or another factor that is the reason for the encounter. It is included in all types of history.

The history of the present illness (HPI) includes the following elements:

Location
Quality
Severity
Duration
Timing
Context
Modifying factors
Associated signs and symptoms

The requirements for the types of history are as follows:

Brief   1–3 elements
Extended   4 or more elements

The review of systems (ROS), or information the patient provides about himself or herself, helps identify the problems or symptoms the patient is experiencing. The doctor documents systemic problems, and although *positive* data are usually recorded, *negative* data that will help the physician come to a medical conclusion also should be recorded. If the physician asks the patient, "Have you ever had chest pain?" and the patient responds no, "denies chest pain" should be recorded in the patient's history. If the information is not recorded, it cannot be used in future encounters to determine treatment. The systems recognized for the purpose of the ROS are as follows:

Constitutional symptoms (e.g., fever, weight loss)
Eyes
Ears, nose, mouth, throat
Cardiovascular
Respiratory
Gastrointestinal
Genitourinary
Musculoskeletal
Integumentary (skin and/or breasts)
Neurologic
Psychiatric
Endocrine
Hematologic/lymphatic
Allergic/immunologic

A problem pertinent ROS includes documentation about the system directly related to the problem(s) identified in the HPI.

An extended ROS documents the problem-pertinent ROS and the patient's positive and pertinent negative responses for two to nine additional systems.

A complete ROS includes individual documentation about the system directly related to the problem(s) identified in the HPI plus positive and negative response to at least ten organ systems.

The past, family, and/or social history consist of a review of three areas:

1. Past medical history, which is the patient's past experience with illnesses, injuries, and treatment and includes information about
   —Prior major illnesses and injuries
   —Prior operations
   —Prior hospitalization
   —Current medications
   —Allergies (food, drug)
   —Age-appropriate immunization status
   —Age-appropriate feeding/dietary status
2. Family history, which is a review of medical events in the patient's family, including diseases which may be hereditary or place the patient at risk.
3. Social history, which consists of an age-appropriate review of past and current activities. The social history should include information about the marital status and/or living arrangements, level of education, and other relevant social factors. In the case of adults, it is helpful to document the current occupation and associated health risks, if applicable. Current use of tobacco, dangerous drugs, and alcohol should also be noted.

For the categories of E&M services that include only an interval history, it is not necessary to record information about the PFSH. These categories are subsequent hospital care, follow-up inpatient consultations, and subsequent nursing home care.

A *pertinent PFSH* is a review of the history area(s) directly related to problem(s) identified in the HPI. At least one specific item from any of the three history areas must be documented in a pertinent PFSH.

A *complete PFSH* is a review of two or all three of the PFSH history areas, depending on the category of the code. A review of all three history areas is required for services that include a comprehensive assessment or reassessment of the patient, as in the category nursing home assessment. A review of one item from two of the three history areas is sufficient for all other services.

For office or other outpatient services, established patients, emergency department, subsequent nursing facility care, domiciliary care, and home care for an established patient, one specific item from two of the three history areas must be documented for a complete PFSH.

At least one specific item from *each* of the three history areas must be documented for a *complete PFSH* for the categories of office or other outpatient services, hospital observation services, hospital inpatient services, initial care, consultations, comprehensive facility assessments, domiciliary and home care, and new patient.

Objective

The *objective* portion of the SOAP method of documentation relates to the physical examination section of the E&M code. For purposes of examination, the following are considered body areas:

- Head, including face
- Neck
- Chest, including breast and axillae
- Abdomen
- Genitalia, groin, buttocks
- Back, including spine
- Each extremity

For purposes of examination, the following organ systems are recognized:

Constitutional (e.g., vital signs, general appearance)
Eyes
Ears, nose, mouth, and throat
Cardiovascular
Respiratory
Gastrointestinal
Genitourinary
Musculoskeletal
Skin
Neurologic
Psychiatric
Hematologic/lymphatic/immunologic

There are four levels of examination. The physician may perform a *problem-focused examination,* which is an examination of one area of the body or one organ system. When one area of the body along with a related organ system is examined and noted, this is an *expanded problem-focused examination;* this could be an examination of the chest and the cardiovascular system. A *detailed examination* consists of an examination of one area plus the related organ systems, such as an examination of the chest and the respiratory system. The highest level of examination consists of a complete specialty or multi-system examination known as a *comprehensive examination*. A complete specialty examination may be done on one organ system, such as the eyes, because an ophthalmologist treats only diseases of the eyes and his or her comprehensive examination thus would include only the eyes. In contrast, a family practitioner or medical internist would document the findings of eight or more organ systems for a comprehensive examination.

Specific abnormal and relevant negative findings from the examination of the affected or symptomatic body area(s) should be documented. Any abnormal findings of the unaffected or asymptomatic body areas(s) or organ symptoms should be described. *Negative* or *normal* is sufficient to document normal findings related to unaffected area(s) or organ systems. When a pelvic or rectal examination in an adult is deferred, the reason(s) should be documented.

Assessment

The *assessment* and *plan* portions of the SOAP documentation relate to the medical decision-making components of the E&M codes. Medical decision making is guided by the complexity of establishing a diagnosis or selecting a management option. The terminology for this component ranges from straightforward, to low complexity, to moderate complexity, to high complexity. These four types of decision making (Table 7-2) are measured by

■ Number of possible diagnoses and/or number of management options to be considered
■ Amount and/or complexity of medical records, diagnostic tests, and/or other information that is addressed, reviewed, and analyzed
■ The risk of significant complications, morbidity, and mortality

To select a given type of decision making, two of the three elements in the table must be met or exceeded.

TABLE 7-2
Complexity of Medical Decision Making

No. of Diagnoses or Management Options	Amount and/or Complexity of Data to be Reviewed	Risk of Complications and/or Morbidity or Mortality	Type of Decision Making
Minimal	Minimal or none	Minimal	Straightforward
Limited	Limited	Low	Low complexity
Multiple	Moderate	Moderate	Moderate complexity
Extensive	Extensive	High	High complexity

Number of Diagnoses or Management Options The number of diagnoses and/or management options depends upon the number and types of problems seen during the encounter, the complexity of establishing a diagnosis, and the management choices made by the physician. For each encounter, an assessment, clinical impression, or diagnosis should be documented. For a problem with an established diagnosis, the medical record should indicate whether the problem is

1. Improved, well controlled, resolving, or resolved
2. Inadequately controlled, worsening, or failing to change with treatment as expected
3. Inadequately controlled, worsening, or failing to change as anticipated

Without an established diagnosis, the assessment or clinical impression may be stated in the form of a differential diagnosis or as "probable," "possible," or "rule out." However, do not code these terms as the diagnosis on a claim form; use symptoms instead. The initiation of or changes in treatment must be documented, including medications, therapies, and patient instructions. If referrals are made or consultation or other advice is sought, the medical record must indicate where the referral or consultation is made or from whom the advice is requested.

Amount and/or Complexity of Data to Be Reviewed The amount and complexity of data to be reviewed are based on the specific types of diagnostic testing ordered or reviewed. If old medical records are obtained from other sources or additional history is obtained from the family, a caretaker, or another source, this increases the amount and complexity of data to be reviewed and should be documented. The review of diagnostic tests should be documented. A simple notation such as "glycohemoglobin within normal limits" is acceptable. Discussion of unexpected test results with the physician who performed or interpreted the test is an indication of the complexity of the data reviewed and should also be noted.

Risk of Significant Complications and/or Morbidity or Mortality The risk of significant complications, morbidity, and/or mortality is based on the risks associated with the presenting problem(s), the diagnostic procedure(s), and the management options. Underlying or comorbid conditions or other factors that increase the complexity of medical decision making by increasing the risk of complications, mortality, morbidity, should be documented.

Medicare has developed its own table for determination of risk of complications, and/or morbidity or mortality. The table uses clinical examples rather than absolute measures of risks. The highest level of risk in any one category (presenting problems, diagnostic procedures ordered, or management options scheduled) determines the level of risk for Medicare patients. Once the level of risk is selected, Table 7-2 can be used to determine the complexity of decision making.

Plan

Any diagnostic services planned, scheduled, or performed at the time of an E&M service must be documented.

If a surgical or invasive diagnostic procedure is performed at the time of an E&M encounter, the procedure should be documented. If the procedure is planned, ordered, or scheduled, this also should be noted in the medical record. If the procedure was performed on an urgent or acute basis, document this.

Counseling

There are instances where counseling and/or coordination of care involve more than 50 percent of the physician's time. Time is considered the controlling factor in the selection of a proper level of service; thus, the total duration of the face-to-face encounter, or floor time, should be documented in the medical record. The type of counseling and/or coordination of care also should be noted.

Documentation of the key components, history, examination, and decision provides support for the selection of the appropriate level of E&M codes. Proper documentation can be used to defend the practice in an audit or a lawsuit. Contact that is not face to face also must be documented.

Cancellations and missed appointments should be entered in the chart. If the patient is not doing well and claims that his or her status has resulted from the doctor's treatment, the physician is in a much better situation if he or she can show that the patient did not comply with the recommendations and was not seen as the doctor requested.

Telephone Calls

One of the more time-consuming entries in the medical record is the documentation of telephone calls. The time, date, subject, and disposition of the call should be entered in the chart. This is especially valuable when instructions for care and appointment making and recommendations for additional treatment are suggested. Patients may attempt to use the telephone instead of making appointments and seeing the doctor face to face. If treatment is prescribed on the telephone and the result is not good because the patient misunderstood the instructions, the recommendations documented in the chart will show the appropriate care.

Use of Templates

Many physicians prefer to use preprinted forms or dictation templates such as the one shown in Tool 7-5. These forms supply prompts or reminders while the doctor is working with the patient so that appropriate documentation is noted.

These forms include the past medical history, social history, and chief complaint of present illness. They allow the clinical staff to take the history portion of the examination by asking the questions listed on the history sheet. It must be emphasized that whoever enters this information into the medical record must sign or initial his or her work. If the physician delegates history taking to clinical staff, the physician must sign or initial the entry to indicate agreement with the staff's work.

Certain specialties use anatomic forms to illustrate the areas they are treating. The physician indicates on the body site what the examination shows, thus saving a great deal of writing. The major problem with this type of notation is that only the problems are documented; the normal part of the examination is not, and this is often necessary for future care.

Obtaining a Patient Release

The medical record remains the property of the treating physician. The physician must maintain an accurate medical record, but the patient can obtain copies upon request (see Tool 7-6). Requests for copies of the chart may be done to obtain health and/or life insurance, in cases of accident or personal injury, for admission to schools, and to determine fitness for sports or employment. The Hippocratic oath and the AMA's Principles of Medical Ethics require the physician to maintain the confidentiality of the medical record. Therefore, a signed medical release must be obtained from the patient before these records can be released to another party. The release must also be maintained in the patient's chart. In the case of minors, the signature of a parent or guardian is appropriate. Sometimes the policy of the practice requires a payment for copying records; this payment should be received before the record is sent. When information is released, only copies of the record should be released. This can be difficult when there is a request for x-rays or other tracings, such as an ECG, but the originals must be maintained unless there is a legal request for them. In malpractice cases and other forms of litigation, the court may subpoena the original records. It is best to check with the doctor's legal counsel before these records are released. If anything happens to the original documents, there is no medical record. The integrity and confidentiality of the medical record must be maintained by the practice. If calls are received from individuals who are not directly involved in the patient's care, medical information should never be given verbally.

Use of the Fax

Many medical institutions use facsimile (fax) machines for healthcare communications. If a patient is treated in a medical practice, the doctor may request a diagnostic test result or the record of a consultation performed in the hospital. Such information can be transmitted immediately by faxing it to the office. However, this method of communication poses a problem in regard to confidentiality. Since not all states have laws that pertain to this situation, it is prudent to obtain a properly completed and signed authorization before releasing patient information. This authorization is transmitted before the release of the medical records. To limit the opportunity for breach of patient confidentiality, specific guidelines must be developed by each practice, including guidelines stating that the information is to be sent only in emergency situations. It is also very important to ensure that the information is received by the authorized individual; if it is received by someone else, instructions on what to do with the information should be included. The information received by fax becomes part of the medical record.

Length of Time Medical Records Are Kept

The question of how long a practice keeps a patient's medical record can best be answered by checking with the medical association in your state or the practice's legal counsel. Statutes of limitation vary from state to state, and no specific period of time can cover every state requirement. When there is a large number of inactive medical records and storage becomes a problem, these records can be microfilmed or stored elsewhere. These records must be easily retrievable for review.

Termination of the Physician-Patient Relationship

After a patient decides to terminate a relationship with a physician, the physician is still required to maintain the medical record. It is prudent for the physician to send a communication to the patient to reinforce the termination and describe the nature of unfinished treatments. A letter of termination should be sent by certified mail with return receipt requested (see Tool 7-7). Copies of the medical record can be sent to the patient's new doctor after the receipt of a properly signed request from the former patient. If the physician terminates the relationship with the patient, the patient must be informed in writing by certified letter with a return receipt and there should be ample time for the patient to find another physician to continue the care. A copy of the letter should be kept in the chart, along with the patient's signature. If the patient refuses to sign for the letter, the unopened letter is maintained in the patient's medical record, showing the doctor's intent to release the patient.

Consent for Medical Treatment

Another document that should be kept in the patient's medical record is a properly signed consent form for medical treatment (see Tool 7-8). This form states that the patient has been informed of the possible risks of a certain procedure and has given consent for the treatment.

Conducting a Documentation Audit

To learn if the medical records in your practice are proper, have a member of the office staff pretend to be an auditor and conduct a mock audit on randomly selected charts. This staff member can assess the completeness of the entries and the accuracy of documentation and find sources of lost revenue. To conduct a mock audit, select at least 15 charts at random per physician. Use a site review checklist (Tool 7-9) to conduct the audit. This is a good way to improve the medical documentation in the practice.

Smart Card

In the future there will be a revolution in medical record keeping. Medical records will be computerized, and each patient will be given a *smart card*. A healthcare provider will use this card to (1) retrieve the patient's medical history, (2) review the patient's treatment, (3) verify the eligibility of the patient as an enrollee, and (4) report a claim to the insurance plan. All this information will be transferred to a central database. This database will allow communication between providers and payers and will be instrumental in the analysis of outcome studies as well as utilization management studies. Although there will be changes in the laws to protect the confidentiality of the information, the basic format of documentation will remain the same.

EXERCISING KNOWLEDGE

Fill in the Blanks

1. The definition of documentation is _____ .

2. The purposes of medical record documentation are _____ , _____ , and _____ .

3. The most widely used format for medical record documentation by physicians is _____ .

4. The components each patient encounter must contain are

    _____ , _____ , _____ , _____ ,
    _____ , _____ , and _____ .

5. Each family member should have _____ chart.

6. The purpose of a master problem sheet is _____ .

7. The importance of a master medication sheet is _____ .

8. A physician terminates the relationship with a patient by

    _____ .

9. All entries in the medical record must be _____ ,
    _____ , and _____ .

10. It is important to have a patient _____ before faxing
    patient information to another source, such as a hospital.

Define These Terms or Abbreviations

11. SOAP

12. Standards of care

13. Master problem sheet

14. Preventive medicine sheet

15. Subjective portion of the SOAP format

16. Objective portion of the SOAP format

17. Assessment portion of the SOAP format

18. Plan portion of the SOAP format

Applying Concepts

19. This afternoon, on July 7, Mrs. Jones called to tell the doctor that her fever was down to 100°, her throat was not as sore, but her ears were still ringing. Document this as though you were writing it in the chart.

20. Document the telephone call from Mrs. Jones the next day canceling her appointment for July 10.

▼ TOOL 7-1
MASTER PROBLEM SHEET

Name _____ Date of Birth (D.O.B.) _____

Primary Diagnosis/Surgeries	Secondary Diagnosis	Date	Date	Date	Date Resolved

Instructions for Master Problem Sheet:

Each significant problem the patient presents should be entered on this form, and the form should be placed in the patient's medical record.

The record should be revised when medical problems affect the current treatment.

▼ **TOOL 7-2**
MASTER MEDICATION SHEET

Name _____ Date of Birth (D.O.B.) _____

Date Onset	Date Given	Drug Name/Dosage	Refill/Date	Refill/Date	Refill/Date	Refill/Date	Date Resolved

Instructions for Master Medication Sheet:

Record each new medication at the time it is prescribed. When refills are given, enter the date and the number of refills authorized. Place in the patient's medical record and revise as appropriate.

▼ TOOL 7-3
PREVENTIVE MEDICINE RECORD

Patient Name _____

	Date/Signature of Healthcare Professional	Dose	Inj. Site Given	Mfg./Brand	Lot #
DTP					
TOPV					
MMR					
HIB					
TB Skin					
Hepatitis B					
Pneumococcal					
Influenza					
Tetanus					
Tonometry					
Pap Smear					
Physical Exam					
Chest X-ray					
ECG					
Stool Occ. Bld.					
Blood Type/RH					
Mammogram					
Sigmoidoscopy					

Instructions for Preventive Medicine Record:

Each time the patient receives a preventive medicine service, a notation is made in the appropriate column(s). Maintain record in the patient's chart.

▼ TOOL 7-4
SUMMARY SHEET OF LABORATORY TESTS

Date	Hgb	WBC	Hct	Grans %	Lymph %	Mid%	Plat	MCV	MCH	RDW	MCHC	Lymph	MID	Gran	MPV	TECH

Date	Color	Sp.Gr	PH	Sugar	Protein	Ketone	Uro	Nitrate	Leuko	Micro	EPI	Mucous	Amorph			Tech

Date	Misc.	Tech		Date	Misc.	Tech		Date	Misc.	Tech		Date	Misc.	Tech		

Instructions for Laboratory Summary Sheet:

Enter the date, type of lab test, initials of the technician, and the results in the appropriate column. This sheet is maintained in the patient's medical record.

▼ **TOOL 7-5**
OFFICE PROGRESS NOTE

Date _____ Ht. _____ Wt. _____ BP _____ P _____

Name _____ Appearance _____

HISTORY   EXAM

Chief complaint   *Body areas:*
                                                           Head   _____
HPI   Neck   _____
                                                           Chest   _____
ROS   Abdomen   _____
Eyes   _____   Genitalia and buttocks   _____
E.N.M.T.   _____   Back and spine   _____
Cardiovascular   _____   Each extremity
Respiratory   _____
Gastrointestinal   _____   *Organ Systems:*
Genitourinary   _____   Eyes   _____
Musculoskeletal   _____   E.N.M.T.   _____
Integumentary   _____   Cardiovascular   _____
Neurological   _____   Respiratory   _____
Psychiatric   _____   Gastrointestinal   _____
Endocrine   _____   Genitourinary   _____
Hematologic/Lymphatic   _____   Musculoskeletal   _____
Allergic/Immunologic   _____   Skin   _____
                                                           Neurologic   _____
Medical Hx   Psychiatric   _____
                                                           Hematologic/lymphatic/
Family Hx   /immunologic   _____

Social Hx

                                                           Counseling & Coordinating Care
DECISION MAKING   _____ minutes

Plan—Tests & Therapies

Impression/Diagnosis(s)

                                                           NEXT APPOINTMENT

_____
Signature or initials   (license title)

▼ **TOOL 7-6**
RELEASE OF MEDICAL INFORMATION LETTER

Medical Healing Arts
4915 Muirwoods Lane
Green Ash, America 45299

Authorization for Release of Medical Records of

_____

I, the undersigned, authorize _____ to disclose the following medical records:

Dates: From _____ To _____

( ) My diagnosis   ( ) Hospital admission summary
( ) My prognosis   ( ) Hospital discharge summary
( ) Dr. _____'s office notes   ( ) Hospital notes
( ) Emergency Treatment   ( ) Operative report(s), findings, and complications
( ) Other documents

To ____(Name and address)____ for the purpose of _____ .

This authorization specifically authorizes Dr. _____ to disclose records of alcohol abuse and substance abuse.

This authorization specifically authorizes Dr. _____ to disclose HIV test results or diagnosis and AIDS and AIDS-related conditions.

This consent is subject to revocation at any time except to the extent that Dr. _____ has already taken action in reliance upon it. If not previously revoked, this consent will terminate on [specific date] [event] [or other condition].

_____   _____
Witness   Patient, Parent, Guardian, or Authorized Person

Date: _____   Date: _____

                                                   Birthdate: _____

                                                   SSN: _____

▼ **TOOL 7-7**
LETTER INFORMING PATIENT OF TERMINATION OF MEDICAL CARE

Medical Healing Arts Practice
4915 Muirwoods Lane
Green Ash, America 45299

Date

Dear Patient,

I find it necessary to discharge you as a patient because you have regularly failed to keep your appointments and have failed to follow proper medical advice to improve your health status. Therefore, as of (date), I can no longer be responsible for your medical care.

This letter is sent to you so that you will have time to find another physician to provide you with care. We will be able to suggest other physicians to you if you encounter any difficulty in finding a new doctor.

Sincerely,

Tracy Lewis, M.D.
TAL/ml

▼ TOOL 7-8
CONSENT FORM FOR PROCEDURE OR SURGERY

Medical Healing Arts
4915 Muirwoods Lane
Green Ash, America 45299

Patient's Name _____ Date _____

The nature of this procedure has been explained to me in general terms; all my questions were answered. I understand there may be risks as a result of this procedure

_____ , _____ , and _____ .

The alternatives include _____

_____

and were explained in detail to me.

I understand that during this procedure it may be necessary to perform additional services which are unforeseen and not known to be needed at this time. I consent to and authorize my physician to make the decisions concerning such treatment.

I voluntarily consent to proceed with this procedure, having been explained all the risks.

Patient _____ Witness _____

(Relationship to patient if patient unable to sign)

Date: _____ Date: _____

▼ **TOOL 7-9**
SITE REVIEW CHECKLIST FOR HEALTH SERVICE RECORDS

		YES	NO
A.	Are all health service records maintained in the same basic format?	_____	_____
B.	Is a separate single medical record kept for each patient?	_____	_____
	Are all medical records completely legible?	_____	_____
	Does each medical record for a patient contain		
1.	An identification sheet?	_____	_____
	With the patient's:		
	Name?	_____	_____
	Birthdate (or age on a given date)?	_____	_____
	Sex?	_____	_____
	Next of kin or person to contact in case of emergency?	_____	_____
	Address?	_____	_____
2.	A medical history?	_____	_____
3.	A family history?	_____	_____
4.	Social history?	_____	_____
5.	Intake/periodic physical exam finding?	_____	_____
	With all entries dated?	_____	_____
	With all entries signed or initialed?	_____	_____
6.	A problem list, prominently displayed?	_____	_____
	With all important surgeries noted?	_____	_____
	With all chronic or recurrent conditions noted?	_____	_____
7.	Dated notations of immunizations?	_____	_____
8.	Entries for all ambulatory encounters with the patient included?	_____	_____
	a. The date?	_____	_____

▼ **TOOL 7-9 (CONTINUED)**

SITE REVIEW CHECKLIST FOR HEALTH SERVICE RECORDS

    b.   The chief complaint or purpose?   _____ _____

    c.   A diagnosis or medical impression?   _____ _____

    d.   Notations of all diagnostic tests ordered?   _____ _____

    e.   All therapies administered by the doctor or his/her employees?   _____ _____

    f.   Recommendations or instructions to the patient?   _____ _____

    g.   The signature or initials of the service provider, along with his/her professional title (e.g., MD, DO, RN, PA, PT, etc.) on the first entry?   _____ _____

  9. Dated reports for any lab, x-ray, or other diagnostic studies ordered for the patient?   _____ _____

  10. Dated, signed consultative reports for any specialty physician services noted ordered for the patient?   _____ _____

  11. Discharge summaries for each episode of inpatient care noted for the patient?   _____ _____

  12. Dated, signed reports for any other ambulatory services, performed by nonphysician health professionals (e.g., educators, medical social workers, nutritionists, physical therapists, speech therapists, visiting nurses, psychologists, clinical social workers)?   _____ _____

  13. A drug list, prominently displayed, noting any ongoing medication, if the patient has a chronic health problem (e.g., hypertension, diabetes)?   _____ _____

C. Does one person on the physician's staff bear responsibility for assuring that other physicians may gain necessary access to patients' health service records, on file in the physician's office, if he/she should be inaccessible?   _____ _____

Medicare: A Complicated Government Program

CHAPTER OVERVIEW

This chapter deals with the federal medical insurance program known as Medicare. Medicare's highly structured, federally regulated method for submitting and appealing claims procedures must be adhered to for physicians to be paid. The rules governing Medicare change each year; most changes are effective on January 1, but changes occur throughout the year.

In addition to formulating the regulations that govern the claims procedure, Medicare identifies specific criteria for fraud and abuse and monitors those criteria closely. The Medicare program has a great influence on private plans because of the cost containment efforts on the part of the federal government. When Medicare acts, other payers follow.

After reading the material in this chapter, doing the exercises, and using the end-of-chapter tools, you will be able to:

- *Describe the enrollment procedures of the Medicare program*
- *Describe the benefits of the Medicare program*
- *Recognize and be able to implement the major program changes that have occurred*
- *Describe Medigap's benefit options*
- *Understand and apply the Resource Based Relative Value Scale (RBRVS)*
- *Explain the volume performance standard used by Medicare to adjust fee schedules*
- *Recognize claims-processing issues that are specific to Medicare*
- *Follow correct procedures when Medicare claims are not paid appropriately*

ENROLLMENT

Medicare became an entitlement program in 1965. Under Title XVIII of the Social Security Act, two insurance programs were established: *Part A* (hospital insurance) and *Part B* (voluntary medical insurance). Both Part A and Part B are available to the groups of persons listed in Table 8-1.

Persons who fulfill the requirements listed in the table are eligible for Part A benefits. Since Part B is a voluntary program requiring the payment of a monthly premium, those who do not want these benefits may refuse enrollment. Each individual has 3 months before and 7 months after the time he or she first meets the eligibility requirements to enroll in Part B (Table 8-2). For example, Mr. Brown will be 65 years old on December 2, 1996. Currently he is a dependent on his wife's contract and does not want to enroll in Medicare. He has from September 1996 (3 months before) to July 1997 (7 months after) to inform Social Security of his decision. If a person fails to enroll or refuses automatic enrollment during the *initial enrollment period,* that person may enroll at a later time during a *general enrollment period,* but with a monetary penalty. A *special enrollment period* (SEP) exists for persons who did not enroll initially in Part B because they were covered under an *employer group health plan (EGHP).*

When individuals are not eligible for Part A or Part B, they may purchase the insurance from the Social Security Administration.

TABLE 8-1

Types of Individuals Entitled to Medicare Benefits

Type of Person	Entitlement
Individuals 65 years of age or older	Have paid FICA (Federal Insurance Contributions Act) taxes or Railroad Retirement taxes for at least 40 calendar quarters (QCs). QCs are 3-month periods beginning January 1 each calendar year
Adults disabled before age 18	Parents are either disabled or eligible for retirement Social Security (SS) benefits
Disabled individuals	Entitled to Railroad Retirement or SS benefits due to disability. There is an additional 5-month waiting period for Medicare after disability has been determined.
Spouse of a deceased, disabled, or retired worker	Spouse of an entitled individual
Individuals of any age who receive dialysis or a renal transplant for end-stage renal disease (ESRD)	Entitlement begins the first day of the month after an individual begins renal dialysis. For those in self-dialysis training, entitlement begins with the first month of training. Entitlement begins the month the individual is admitted to the hospital for a renal transplant, provided that the transplant is performed within 2 months. If this does not occur, entitlement begins the second month before the month of the transplant.

TABLE 8-2
Enrollment Periods

Enrollment Period	Benefits Begin
Three months before 65	Month eligible (turns age 65)
Fourth month after age 65	Month after month of enrollment
First month after EGHP disenrollment (SEP)	First day of that month
Two to six months after EGHP dis-enrollment	Month after month of enrollment
General enrollment period	July 1

Funding for Part A and Part B

The funds for Part A come from taxes paid by employees and self-employed persons with matching contributions from employers. The premiums for Part B are determined by Congress each year at 25 percent of the Part B costs and are collected by the Social Security Administration, the Railroad Retirement Board, or the Office of Personnel Management.

Medicare Trust Funds

Two separate trust funds for paying claims made by providers exist for Part A and Part B in the United States Treasury. The trust fund for Part A is financed by hospital insurance taxes paid by individuals who are currently employed and premiums from those who are not automatically enrolled in Part A. The trust fund for Part B is financed by monthly premiums paid by enrollees in the program and contributions from general federal revenues.

MANAGEMENT AND RESPONSIBILITY
OF THE MEDICARE PROGRAM

The overall responsibility for the management of the Medicare program lies with the Secretary of Health and Human Services. The management of the program is delegated to the Health Care Financing Agency (HCFA). HCFA maintains 10 regional offices in the United States (see Tool 8-1). HCFA contracts with private plans to process claims, provide payment, and perform other program functions. Part A companies are called fiscal intermediaries. *Fiscal intermediaries* are organizations that are responsible for processing claims from hospitals and skilled nursing facilities. Part B claims, such as those from physicians and durable medical equipment (DME) providers, are processed by insurance plans known as *carriers*. Carriers are private insurance companies with contracts subject to renewal by HCFA.

Benefits for Part A

Although a physician practice does not usually send claims to Part A, patients sometimes bring questions about their hospital coverage to the practice. The benefits for Part A are listed in Table 8-3.

Benefits for Part B

A physician practice primarily reports claims for Part B services. Table 8-4 lists the benefits of Part B of the Medicare program.

Excluded Services

There are a number of *noncovered services* (Medicare's term for "excluded"). The office staff can collect payment for such services at the time of service,

TABLE 8-3
Benefits for Part A

A semiprivate bed in a hospital (up to 90 hospital days for each 90-day *benefit period*) and services associated with inpatient confinement. Benefit periods (*spell of illness*) begin the first day a Medicare patient is given inpatient hospital services and end when the patient has been out of a hospital or skilled nursing facility for 60 consecutive days.

A semiprivate bed patient in a skilled nursing facility (SNF)

Care in a psychiatric hospital (up to 90 days in a lifetime)

Hospice care and respite care when a terminally ill patient can be admitted to a hospice (a public or private organization that provides respite care, support, and symptom management to the patient and his or her family)

Nursing home care (provided that a patient spent at least 3 days in a benefit period as an inpatient)

Home health services such as intermittent nursing care and physical, occupational, or speech therapy; part-time services of home health aides, medical supplies, and equipment (no drugs). These patients are generally confined to their homes by injury or illness.

TABLE 8-4
Benefits for Part B

Physician services including surgery, consultations, home, office, and institutional services and supplies incidental to physician services; drugs and biologicals that cannot be self-administered; physical therapy; speech pathology; blood and blood transfusions

Outpatient hospital services, including outpatient diagnostic services and physical and occupational therapy or speech pathology services furnished by certain approved institutions and public agencies; outpatient physician and occupational therapy services (up to a monetary limit per calendar year) furnished by an independently practicing therapist in the patient's home or the therapist's office (no dollar limit applies to the therapist's services in an institution); hospital services furnished to outpatients in connection with a doctor's services; outpatient (ambulatory) surgery; and emergency hospital outpatient services

Diagnostic x-ray and laboratory tests and other diagnostic tests, including in certain cases diagnostic x-rays taken in a patient's home

X-ray, radium, and radioactive isotope therapy

Durable medical equipment such as oxygen, hospital beds, and walkers for use in the home, whether furnished on a rental basis or purchased

Artificial devices (other than dental), such as pacemakers, that replace all or part of an internal body organ; colostomy or ileostomy bags and related supplies are also covered; one pair of glasses or contact lenses after cataract surgery is covered if an intraocular lens has been inserted

Braces and artificial legs

Rural and community health clinic services performed by licensed nurses and physician assistants, plus similar services provided to homebound patients in certain areas

Certified registered nurse anesthetist (CRNA), nurse midwife, and physician assistant services

Psychologist and social worker services provided in connection with a physician's service

Limited chiropractic services, pediatric and optometric services

Ambulance service (when the patient's condition rules out other means of transportation)

Home dialysis supplies and equipment, self-care home dialysis support services, and institutional dialysis services and supplies and unless the patient requests it, these claims do not have to be submitted to Medicare. In addition to what most other plans exclude, Medicare excludes several services and items under Section 1862 of the Social Security Act, as follows:

- Services that are not reasonable and necessary (not *medically necessary* in Medicare's terminology).
- Immunizations other than pneumococcal, hepatitis B, and influenza vaccinations.
- Routine physician checkups, including lab tests and x-rays. *Routine* means that there is not an underlying disease or symptoms for which the service is provided. *[handwritten: Limited Routine]*
- Eye exams for the purpose of prescribing or fitting eyeglasses or contact lenses when eye disease or injury is not present. Refraction lenses are noncovered.
- Hearing aids or exams for the purpose of prescribing hearing aids.
- Routine dental care.
- Routine appliances.
- Self-administered drugs or biologicals except for oral anticancer drugs.
- Supportive devices for feet.
- Charges for services provided by immediate relatives or members of the household.
- Services not provided in the United States
- Services for which the individual has no legal obligation to pay
- Nonphysician services provided to a hospital inpatient which were not provided directly or arranged for by the hospital
- Services rendered by a provider who has been found guilty of Medicare fraud and abuse.
- Services provided by Christian Science practitioners.

Claims Denied as Not Reasonable and Necessary

Services which are not reasonable and necessary for the diagnosis and treatment of an illness or injury or to improve the treatment of a malformed body part can be denied. Whenever Medicare denies a claim, the ultimate liability for payment for the service lies with the beneficiary unless the beneficiary did not know and did not have reason to know that the service would not be covered. In this instance, the beneficiary does not have to pay for that service. To determine whether a denial of services was made under the "not reasonable and necessary" exclusion, the following must be validated:

1. The service or item is covered, that is, it is not listed as a specific exclusion.
2. The service must be reasonable or necessary for the diagnosis or treatment of an illness or injury.

For a nonparticipating physician, the carrier is required to notify the practice of the possible denial and provide an opportunity for the physician to submit additional clinical documentation to justify the situation before the patient is notified of the denial. Otherwise, the nonparticipating physician would not know that the claim was denied since it is the patient who receives the explanation of benefits containing the denial. If the patient already paid for the denied services, the practice is not required to make a refund if

- The physician did not know and could not reasonably have been expected to know that Medicare would not pay for those services
- The physician notified the patient in advance that Medicare probably would not pay for the specific service. If, after being informed, the patient signed a waiver of liability, the patient is responsible for paying for the service.

Thus, it is necessary to have the patient sign a waiver of liability letter whenever the practice believes that a service may not be covered. A *waiver of liability letter* is a statement advising the patient that the physician believes that Medicare will not cover the service. A waiver of liability letter must indicate the services, the dates of the services, and the specific reasons why payment may be denied. Generic statements such as "I never know what Medicare pays or doesn't pay" are not acceptable. A waiver of liability letter is shown in Tool 8-2. The office staff enters the name of the service in the area marked "specify particular service," and the appropriate reasons for the denial must be marked. The patient signs and dates the document, which is kept in the patient's record for future reference. Some Medicare carriers have mandated that a Level III HCPCS modifier be added to the procedure code to indicate that this letter is signed. Check with your Medicare carrier to determine if such a modifier is applicable when reporting claims.

LOOK AT pg 260

Conditional Coverage

In addition to coverage provided by Medicare for services that are "reasonable and necessary," some benefits are based on criteria which are appropriate in certain medical situations. Payment of benefits for certain procedures is based on the condition or diagnosis of the patient.

An example of *conditional coverage* would be

Carotid Body Resection/Denervation Procedure
Covered for the following conditions:
    Evidence of a mass in carotid
    Hypersensitive carotid sinus
Not covered for:
    Relief of pulmonary problems.

Medicare carriers are very specific in defining the medical necessity of conditional coverage. Their newsletters list the procedure codes and the matching ICD-9-CM codes.

Another example: benefits for control of a hemorrhage [HCPCS (CPT–Level I) codes 45317, 45334, 45382, 46614] are paid if one or more of these ICD-9-CM codes are used:

562.12
562.13
569.3
569.85
578.2–578.9

Medicare catches these claims through edits.

Prepayment Screens

Medicare calls its edits prepayment screens and uses them to prevent unnecessary utilization of services. Examples of these screens are given in Tool 8-3. Medicare EOBs will contain the reason for a prepayment screen denial, such as reason code 16.24: "We do not pay for this many services within this period of time." With clinical documentation upon appeal, services may be paid.

Preventive Medicine Benefits

not Read

While Medicare began as an indemnity benefit plan, it is moving toward covering preventive care. In 1989 preventive medicine benefits were first provided for screening vaginal Pap smears. In 1992 benefits were extended to breast mammography, and in 1993 flu, pneumococcal, and hepatitis B immunizations were added. Therapeutic shoes for patients with severe diabetic foot disease began to be covered in 1994.

In many areas Medicare patients may choose to join a managed care plan. These beneficiaries tend to receive benefits greater than those provided in the traditional Medicare package. When these beneficiaries join a managed care plan, the rules of that plan, not Medicare's rules, must be followed.

THE ID CARD

Upon enrollment in the Medicare program, a patient receives a red, white, and blue ID card (Figure 8-1). The patient is called a beneficiary. This card gives the name of the patient exactly as it appears in the Social Security records. When the name on the Medicare ID card is not the name the patient

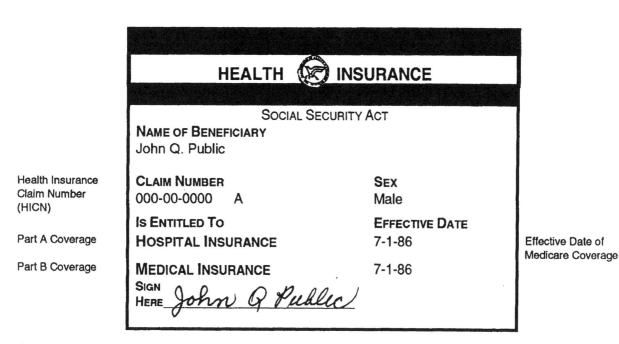

FIGURE 8-1 Medicare identification card.

is usually called, it is important to use the name exactly as it appears on the card because this is the way the patient is identified by the Social Security Administration. The *health insurance claim number (HICN)* (generally the beneficiary's nine-digit Social Security number followed by an alphabetic character, such as 123-45-6789 A) is followed by the patient's sex, the effective date of coverage, and the type of benefits to which the patient is entitled. A beneficiary whose HICN begins with a letter followed by numerals (e.g., MA 12345678) are railroad retirees who are entitled to Medicare. The Travelers Insurance Company is the designated carrier for processing claims for all railroad beneficiaries. Tool 8-4 lists Travelers offices by region.

OUT-OF-POCKET COSTS

Under Part A of the program, for each day (up to a maximum of 90 days) in any *benefit period*, beneficiaries pay a deductible and an additional coinsurance equal to 25 percent of the deductible amount for hospitalization for the sixty-first day through the ninetieth day of hospitalization. If, for example, the deductible for an admission to the hospital is $716.00, this is paid on the first day of admission. For each day of the sixty-first day through the ninetieth day of hospitalization, the Medicare beneficiary is responsible for 25 percent of $676.00. There are 60 lifetime reserve days that are available to beneficiaries, and the coinsurance for those inpatient days is equal to 50 percent of the initial inpatient hospital deductible. There are also deductibles for the twenty-first day to the hundredth day at skilled nursing facilities.

The Part B program has a yearly deductible (e.g. $100.00). Once the deductible has been met, Medicare covers 80 percent of its allowed amount, with the remaining 20 percent as out-of-pocket costs for the beneficiary. The out-of-pocket costs will be larger when services are provided by a physician not participating in the Medicare program.

Medigap Coverage

Many people who are entitled to Medicare benefits purchase secondary insurance to supplement Medicare's coverage. Secondary insurance usually covers Medicare deductibles and coinsurance and other services not covered by the Medicare program. Frequently, the office staff is asked which Medigap insurance plans are best. *Medigap*, or gap filler, policies have been standardized by the government so that it is easy to make comparisons between plans.

Figure 8-2 lists the letters A–J, signifying the types of Medigap supplemental benefit options. Plan A contains only the basic benefits, while plan J has the most options.

It is important to maintain Medigap information in a patient's financial record. This information should be updated on a yearly basis as patients tend to change these policies.

Benefit Plan	A	B	C	D	F	G	H	I	J
Basic Benefits	X	X	X	X	X	X	X	X	X
Skilled Nursing Coinsurance		X	X	X	X	X	X	X	X
Part A Deductible		X	X	X	X	X	X	X	X
Part B Deductible		X			X				
Part B Excess 100%					X	X		X	X
Foreign Travel Emergency		X	X	X	X	X	X	X	X
At-Home Recovery				X		X		X	X
Extended Drugs ($3000 limit)							X	X	X
Preventive Care				X					X

FIGURE 8-2 Medicare supplemental benefit coverage.

One-Time Authorization for Medicare Beneficiaries

In Chapter 2 we discussed the necessity of having a patient sign a medical release to report a claim. Medicare has a one-time authorization for medical release (Figure 8-3). Figure 8-4 shows a signature form for Medigap coverage. A lifetime signature of the Medicare beneficiary should always be obtained for release of medical information. If the patient has Medigap coverage, release of medical information to Medigap must also be signed.

This language, as designated by Medicare, was used in the registration form shown in Figure 2-2, eliminating the need for a separate signature sheet for Medicare beneficiaries.

NAME OF BENEFICIARY _____ HICN _____

I request that payment of authorized Medicare benefits be made to me or on my behalf to Dr. _____ for any service furnished me by that physician. I authorize any holder of medical information about me to release to the Health Care Financing Administration and its agents any information needed to determine these benefits or the benefits payable for related services.

_____
Beneficiary or his/her representative

FIGURE 8-3 Lifetime signature for release of medical information.

NAME OF BENEFICIARY _____ HICN _____

I request that payment of authorized Medigap benefits be made either to me or on my behalf to Dr. _____ for any services furnished me by that physician or supplier. I authorize any holder of medical information about me to release to (name of Medigap insurer) any information needed to determine these benefits or the benefits payable for related services.

_____
Beneficiary or his/her representative

FIGURE 8-4 Signature for Medigap coverage.

CHANGES IN MEDICARE RULES
AND REGULATIONS

Medicare differs from private plans because it is a government plan. The Deficit Reduction Act and the Omnibus Reconciliation Acts (OBRAs) passed by Congress have brought changes in the rules. Congress passes OBRAs near the end of its fiscal year, September 30, in an effort to control the cost to the federal budget.

The Medicare Participation
Program

One of the first major changes in the Medicare program enacted by Congress was the development of the *Medicare Participation Program.* This is a program in which physicians voluntarily sign a contract, beginning January 1 each year, and then accept assignment on all Medicare claims. When in this program, participating physicians are paid more by Medicare directly than are providers who do not sign the contract. The names of participating physicians appear in the *Medpard Directory of Participating Physicians,* which is distributed to hospitals, senior citizen groups, retirement communities, physicians, suppliers, clinics, and to requesting beneficiaries. It is a form of advertising. Another benefit of participation is that Medicare carriers crossover claims to the supplemental plans. *Crossover* means that the Medicare carrier coordinates benefits by forwarding paid claims to supplemental plans for the payment of the remaining balances.

Nonparticipating Physicians

Physicians who do not sign a Medicare contract are known as *nonparticipating physicians.* The *limiting charge* is the highest fee a nonparticipating physician can charge a Medicare beneficiary. This amount currently is 115 percent of the nonparticipating fee schedule. The patient is responsible for the entire limiting charge unless the physician takes assignment on the claim. Tables 8-5 through 8-7 illustrate three different payment situations.

A nonparticipating physician has the option of accepting assignment on a claim-by-claim basis. If item 27 of the HCFA 1500 form is checked yes, the doctor accepts Medicare's allowed payment amount for nonparticipating physicians. In Table 8-7, the check for $76.00 (80 percent of the allowed $95.00) is sent directly to the practice, and the difference between the limiting charge and what Medicare allows is written off ($109.25 − $95 = $14.25). If the nonparticipating physician does not accept assignment (Table 8-6), the check goes to the patient and the practice can collect the entire limiting charge, or $109.25.

TABLE 8-5

Participating Physician

Physician fee	$110.00
Medicare fee schedule	100.00
Medicare pays 80%	80.00
Check goes to doctor	
Patient/second insurance pays	20.00
Total amount doctor can collect	100.00
Doctor must write off	$ 10.00 ($110.00 – $100.00)

TABLE 8-6

Nonparticipating Physician Not Accepting Assignment

Participating physician fee schedule	$100.00
Nonparticipating fee schedule (NPFS)	95.00
Limiting charge (115% of NPFS)	109.25
Limiting charge billed to patient	109.25
Medicare fee schedule for nonparticipating physicians (95% of participating fee schedule)	95.00
Medicare pays 80%	76.00
Check goes to the patient	
Patient/second insurance responsible for 20%	19.00
Total amount patient owes or doctor can collect	$109.25
There is no write-off (patient out-of-pocket cost, $14.25)	

TABLE 8-7

Nonparticipating Physician Accepting Assignment

Limiting charge	$109.25
Medicare fee schedule for nonparticipating physicians	95.00
Medicare pays 80% of $95.00	
Check goes to doctor	76.00
Patient/second insurance is responsible for 20% ($95.00)	19.00
Doctor can collect no more than	95.00
Doctor writes off	$ 14.25 ($109.25 – $95.00)

Several states have passed laws making it mandatory for all physicians to take assignment on claims for Medicare patients with incomes at a certain level. For example, if a patient has a taxable income below $12,000, the state mandates that a physician must accept assignment on the claim even though the physician does not participate in the Medicare program. Vermont, Connecticut, Rhode Island, New York, and Ohio require physicians to take assignment in similar situations. In Massachusetts, license renewal is contingent upon acceptance of assignment. The office staff must be familiar with the legislation in the practice's state.

The percentage of physicians participating in Medicare has been increasing since the beginning of the program. Over one-half of all physicians now participate in Medicare.

Other Rules When a Claim Is Not Assigned

Nonparticipating physicians who provide a nonemergency surgical procedure and do not accept assignment must inform patients in writing if the charges exceed $500. This is called a *surgical financial disclosure*. An emergency surgical procedure is one that is performed for conditions which afford no alternatives for the physician or the beneficiary and, if delayed, could result in death or permanent impairment of the patient's health. Figure 8-5 is a worksheet for determining the patient's estimated Medicare payment for elective surgery. The surgical financial disclosure should contain

1. The limiting charge for the procedure
2. The Medicare allowed amount
3. The difference between the physician's limiting charge and the allowed amount
4. The coinsurance amount if applicable

A surgical disclosure letter is shown in Tool 8-5.

Physician Payment for Purchased Diagnostic Services

OBRA of 1986 amended the Medicare program to pay laboratory services performed in a physician's office on an assigned claim basis only; there is no balance billing to the patient. The law permits the practice to bill Medicare for personally performed tests. If the practice did not perform the laboratory

---

Assume that the annual deductible has already been met.

1. The doctor's limiting charge   _____
2. Medicare allowed amount for procedure   _____
3. The difference between the limiting charge and the
   Medicare allowed amount (no. 1 – no. 2)   _____
4. Twenty percent coinsurance (.20 × no. 2)   _____
5. Beneficiary's out-of-pocket expense (no. 3 + no. 4)   _____

FIGURE 8-5 Worksheet for surgical financial disclosure.

test, it can bill only for the routine venipuncture. Later, Medicare's payment rules were amended to apply to all purchased diagnostic services, such as cardiac and pacemaker monitoring, ultrasound, noninvasive vascular studies, and x-rays. The term "purchased diagnostic services" refers specifically to the component of a test not provided by the billing physician. The claim form must indicate that the tests were performed by the physician or the physician's staff. If the services were purchased from an outside source, "purchased from a supplier" is noted on the claim form. In addition to the supplier's name and address and the provider number, the net charge for the purchased portion of the test must be included on the HCFA 1500 form (item 32). There can be no markup on purchased services when one is billing Medicare.

Payment for Ancillary Professional Services

Since January 1, 1987, Medicare has paid for physician assistant (PA) services when they are licensed in the state and the service is provided under the supervision of a physician. Payment is made on assignment only to the PA's employer. Since 1989 payment has been made for the services of certified registered nurse anesthetists (CRNAs) and anesthesia assistants (AAs). CRNAs may work with or without the supervision of a physician, but AAs must work under direct physician supervision. Both are given a provider identification number (PIN) and may bill Medicare directly for their services or have the payments sent to their employers.

In 1990 payment was authorized for a nurse practitioner (NP) or clinical nurse specialist (CNS) who provides legally authorized services in collaboration with a physician in a skilled nursing facility or nursing home. When they provide service incident to a physician, nurse practitioners in skilled or intermediate nursing facilities are reimbursed separately by Medicare Part B. *Incident to service* means that the service is

- An integral part of a doctor's diagnosis or treatment
- Provided under the direct supervision of a physician
- Performed by an employee of that doctor
- Ordinarily done in a doctor's office or clinic

Other categories of nonphysician practitioners are also covered for payment, such as physical, occupational, and speech therapists. Clinical psychologists (CPs) and clinical social workers (CSWs) are paid only as incident to the physician's services. CPs and CSWs must accept assignment on their claims.

Health Professional Shortage Areas

Health Professional Shortage Areas (HPSAs) are designated areas—a specific county, a portion of a county, or even a specific street—where there is a shortage of doctors and other practitioners. Carriers make the determination on the basis of census data. An extra 10 percent of the 80 percent that Medicare allows is paid on a quarterly basis for assigned and unassigned claims. In order to be paid the bonus, modifiers QU (urban HPSA) or QB (rural HPSA) must be written on the claim for the services.

Assistants at Surgery

Payment for physicians who assist in surgery is 16 percent of the intraoperative amount for the surgical procedure. When billing for a nonparticipating physician, the office staff must reduce the limiting charge. Not all surgical procedures can have an assistant at surgery. Surgical procedures excluded from Medicare payment for an assistant at surgery number almost 1700, and if Medicare does not pay for the service, the patient cannot be billed.

Site of Service Differential

Certain procedures are subject to a site of service differential. *Site of Service (SOS)* is a reduction in payment that is made because of where the service is provided (the site). In this case, the physician does not provide payment for the use of the facility or for any of its overhead. For example, if a consultation is provided in a hospital emergency room, the reimbursement for the consultation will be reduced because the doctor did not pay for use of the room or its expense. Each year the SOS requirements change. Request the current year's list of procedures involving SOS from your Medicare carrier or watch for a list in newsletters each January. The reductions do not apply to rural health clinic services, surgical procedures designated by Medicare as ambulatory surgery procedures, anesthesiology services, and diagnostic or therapeutic radiology services.

MEDICARE'S FEE SCHEDULE: THE RESOURCE BASED RELATIVE VALUE SCALE (RBRVS)

Public Law 99-272 and Public Law 100-203 mandate that physicians be paid by Medicare according to a Resource Based Relative Value Scale. Commissioned by the Department of Health and Human Services, Dr. William

Hsaio and a team of researchers at Harvard developed an RBRVS whose goal is to

- Provide a uniform Medicare payment system on a national basis
- Assure a more equitable allocation of funds between the undervalued E&M services and the sometimes overvalued surgical procedures
- Reduce unacceptably large increases in total physician payments
- Control beneficiary liability for unassigned claims

There are three major components of the Medicare's RBRVS fee schedule:

1. Relative value units (RVUs) for procedure codes
2. Variations in practice costs in different areas of the country
3. The conversion factor

Medicare was the first to use the RBRVS and maintains its annual revisions. Adjustments to RVUs are made because of changes in medical practices, coding changes, and new data on relative values.

Relative Value Units for Procedure Codes

The first component of the fee schedule, for each procedure code, is the relative value unit. Table 8-8 shows changes in the work column for the most commonly used code, 99213, from the inception of RBRVS in 1991 (proposed) to 1995. The decreasing RVUs in this column indicate relatively less physician work in the 99213 category from 1991 to 1995. Note that the relative overhead unit for the years 1992–1995 is a fraction lower, not higher, than the figure for 1991.

TABLE 8-8

Relative Value Unit Changes in the Work Column of 99213

RVU	Work	Expense	Malpractice	Total
1991 (proposed)	0.58	0.39	0.03	1.00
1992	0.59	0.38	0.03	1.00
1993	0.59	0.38	0.03	1.00
1994	0.56	0.38	0.03	0.97
1995	0.55	0.38	0.03	0.96

Geographic Practice Cost Indices

Geographic practice cost indices (GPCIs) are used in the RBRVS to account for variances in the cost of medical practice across the country. GPCIs are composed of three factors for each procedure code. The work factor represents one-fourth of the difference between the relative value of a physician's work in a particular locality and the national average. The practice factor measures its expenses for rent, wages, and other costs. The malpractice factor compares variations in malpractice in relation to the national average.

The GPCI components for determining payments for the locality Green Ash, America, might appear like this:

Work	*Practice Expense*	*Malpractice*
0.981	0.943	0.845

The national average is 1. Thus, in Green Ash, America, the work, practice expense, and malpractice costs are lower than the national average. The original locales used for GPCIs generally were existing Medicare carrier localities. Some states have requested the statewide use of GPCIs.

The Conversion Factor

The third component of the fee schedule is the conversion factor that applies to services paid under the RBRVS. This is a national factor that generates a dollar amount of payment for a physician's work. In 1994 three conversion factors were mandated: for surgical, nonsurgical, and primary care services. There is also a separate national conversion factor for anesthesia. Since anesthesia is reported in "time," not in RVUs, there is a need for this separate conversion factor.

All RVUs and GPCIs are published in the *Federal Register.* Figure 8-6 shows a page from the *Register.* Let us analyze this figure.

Column 1, HCPCS: This is the HCPCS code.

Column 2, MOD: A modifier such as -26 or TC in this column denotes that payment will be made separately for professional and technical services.

Column 3, Status: The current status of the HCPCS code:

A = active code which can be processed and paid by Medicare.

B = payments for covered services are always bundled into payment for other procedure codes.

C = carrier priced code (the Medicare claims processor for the area determines the payment).

D = deleted code for Medicare payment year.

E = excluded code from RBRVS payment for Medicare.

G = code not valid for Medicare purposes.

N = noncovered services.

P = bundled (no payment for these services).

Federal Register / Vol.59, No. 235 /   Thursday, December 8, 1994 /   Rules and Regulations   63491

ADDENDUM B			RELATIVE VALUE UNITS (RVUs) and RELATED INFORMATION-Continued						
HCPCS	MOD	Sta-tus	Description	Work RVUs	Practice Expense RVUs	Mal-practice RVUs	Total	Global period	Updates
29126		A	Apply forearm splint	0.77	0.4	0.06	1.23	0	S
29130		A	Application of finger splint	0.5	0.17	0.02	0.69	0	S
29131		A	Application of finger splint	0.55	0.39	0.06	1	0	S
29200		A	Strapping of chest	0.65	0.27	0.03	0.95	0	N
29220		A	Strapping of low back	0.64	0.38	0.05	1.07	0	S
29240		A	Strapping of shoulder	0.71	0.27	0.03	1.01	0	S
29260		A	Strapping of elbow or wrist	0.55	0.23	0.03	0.81	0	S
29280		A	Strapping of hand or finger	0.51	0.21	0.02	0.74	0	S
29305		A	Application of hip cast	2.03	1.88	0.31	4.22	0	S
29325		A	Application of hip casts	2.32	1.94	0.28	4.54	0	S
29345		A	Application of long leg cast	1.4	1.02	0.16	2.58	0	S
29355		A	Application of long leg cast	1.53	1.1	0.17	2.8	0	S
29358		A	Apply long leg cast brace	1.43	1.84	0.33	3.6	0	S
29365		A	Application of long leg cast	1.18	0.86	0.14	2.18	0	S
29405		A	Apply short leg cast	0.86	0.79	0.12	1.77	0	S
29425		A	Apply short leg cast	1.01	0.97	0.14	2.12	0	S
29435		A	Apply short leg cast	1.18	1.18	0.18	2.54	0	S
29440		A	Addition of walker to cast	0.57	0.23	0.03	0.83	0	S
29445		A	Apply rigid leg cast	1.78	1.7	0.28	3.76	0	S
29450		A	Application of leg cast	1.02	0.39	0.04	1.45	0	S
29505		A	Application long leg splint	0.69	0.57	0.07	1.33	0	S
29515		A	Application lower leg splint	0.73	0.47	0.06	1.26	0	S
29520		A	Strapping of hip	0.54	0.36	0.03	0.93	0	S
29530		A	Strapping of knee	0.57	0.35	0.05	0.97	0	S
29540		A	Strapping of ankle	0.51	0.3	0.03	0.84	0	S
29550		A	Strapping of toes	0.47	0.28	0.03	0.78	0	S
29580		A	Application of paste boot	0.57	0.79	0.04	1.4	0	S
29590		A	Application of foot splint	0.76	0.28	0.03	1.07	0	S
29700		A	Removal/revision of cast	0.88	0.32	0.05	1.25	0	S
29705		A	Removal/revision of cast	1.12	0.35	0.05	1.52	0	S
29710		A	Removal/revision of cast	1.34	0.45	0.07	1.86	0	S
29715		A	Removal/revision of cast	0.94	0.86	0.12	1.92	0	S
29720		A	Repair of body cast	0.68	0.23	0.04	0.95	0	S
29730		A	Windowing of cast	0.75	0.26	0.04	1.05	0	S
29740		A	Wedging of cast	1.12	0.38	0.06	1.56	0	S
29750		A	Wedging of clubfoot cast	1.26	0.5	0.07	1.83	0	S
29799		C	Casting/strapping procedure	0	0	0	0	YYY	S
29800		A	Jaw arthroscopy/surgery	5.28	4.01	0.46	9.75	90	S
29804		A	Jaw arthroscopy/surgery	7.99	11.75	1.46	21.2	90	S
29815		A	Shoulder arthroscopy	5.74	4.84	0.76	11.3	90	S
29819		A	Shoulder arthroscopy/surgery	7.33	9.38	1.73	18.4	90	S
29820		A	Shoulder arthroscopy/surgery	6.81	8.72	1.73	17.3	90	S
29821		A	Shoulder arthroscopy/surgery	7.43	10.36	2.13	19.9	90	S

(1)   (2)   (3)   (4)   (5)   (6)   (7)   (8)   (9)   (10)

FIGURE 8-6   RVUs from the Federal Register.

R = restricted coverage (special coverage restrictions apply).

T = injections. There are RVUs and payment amounts for these services if no other services are payable under the physician fee schedule billed on the same date by the same provider.

X = exclusion by law (no payment made).

Column 4, Description: This is a narrative description of the code.

Column 5, Work RVUs.

Column 6, Practice Expense RVUs.

Column 7, Malpractice RVUs.

Column 8, Total: This gives the sum of all RVUs for a code.

Column 9, Global Period: This shows the number of days in a global period for the code (0, 10, 90 days). The alpha codes are as follows:

MMM = service furnished in uncomplicated maternity cases, including antepartum care, delivery, and postpartum care. The usual global concept does not apply.

XXX = global concept does not apply.

YYY = global period set by carrier.

ZZZ = code is part of another service and falls within the global period for the first service.

Column 10, Update: This indicates whether the appropriate conversion factor (CF) for surgical, primary care, or nonsurgical services applies to the HCPCS code in column 1:

O = code deleted in the past year and not paid.

N = CF for nonsurgical services applies.

P = CF for primary care applies.

S = CF for surgical procedures applies.

The geographic practice cost indices by Medicare carrier and locality are also published in the *Federal Register* (see Figure 8-7). Let us analyze this figure.

Column 1 indicates the HCFA assigned carrier number.

Column 2 lists the locality number, which is the locality area within the carrier's jurisdiction.

Column 3 gives the locality/area name.

Columns 4, 5, and 6 show work, practice expense, and malpractice RVUs for the locale.

Working with the Formula

To understand how Medicare arrives at its fee schedule for each code, the office staff must learn how to apply Medicare's formula:

Payment = {(work RVU × adjusted work RVU)
+ (expense RVU × adjusted expense RVU)
+ (malpractice RVU × adjusted practice RVU)}
× conversion factor

Federal Register / Thursday,   Vol. 59, December 8, 1994 / Rules and Regulations   63491

ADDENDUM D -1995 GEOGRAPHIC PRACTICE COST INDICES BY MEDICARE			CARRIER AND LOCALITY- Continued		
Carrier Number	Locality number	Locality Name	Work	Practice expense	Mal-practice
528	1	New Orleans, LA	0.996	0.974	1.091
528	50	Rest of LA	0.968	0.865	0.868
21200	2	Central Maine	0.952	0.916	0.738
21200	1	Northern Maine	0.956	0.916	0.738
21200	3	Southern Maine	0.968	1.007	0.738
991	1	Baltimore/Surr. Cntys, MD	1.024	1.038	1.021
901	3	South & E. Shore, MD	0.998	0.991	0.841
901	2	Western MD	0.994	0.972	0.852
700	2	MA Suburbs/Rural Cities	1.006	1.086	0.916
700	1	Urban, MA	1.016	1.149	0.916
623	1	Detroit, MI	1.051	1.064	2.394
720	0	Minnesota (Blue Shield)	0.994	0.968	0.671
10240	0	Minnesota (Travelers)	0.994	0.968	0.671
10250	1	Rest of Mississippi	0.955	0.826	0.688
10250	2	Urban Mississippi	0.965	0.885	0.688
740	3	K.C. (Jackson Cnty), MO	0.954	0.956	1.193
740	3	N.K.C. (Clay/Platte), MO	0.984	0.956	1.192

   (1)   (2)   (3)   (4)   (5)   (6)

FIGURE 8-7   GPCIs from the Federal Register.

To calculate the payment amount, use the following formula:

$$\text{Payment} = [(RVUw \times GPCIw) + (RVUpe \times GPCIpe) + (RVUm \times GPCIm)] \times CF$$

RVUw = physician work RVUs for the procedure
GPCIw = geographic practice cost index for physician work in a locality
RVUpe = practice expense RVUs for the procedure
GPCIpe = geographic practice cost for expenses in a locality
RVUm = malpractice RVUs for the procedure
GPCIm = geographic practice costs for malpractice in a locality
CF = uniform national conversion factor

Figure 8-8 illustrates the method used to compute a Medicare MAF for a Level 5 consultation performed in Green Ash, America.

Since the code is a nonsurgical code, the nonsurgical conversion factor must be used. Medicare will pay $151.44 for a consultation (Level 5) in Green Ash when the fee schedule is fully implemented (assuming that no other adjustments are made).

```
99245                                      GPCI (Green Ash, AM)

RVU work = 2.96                            GPCI work = 0.951

RVU expense = 1.69                         GPCI expense = 0.857

RVU malpractice = 0.16                     GPCI malpractice = 0.688


                    FEE SCHEDULE WORKSHEET

                       Nonsurgical Care

Using the formula:

LOCALITY: Green Ash, AM

PROCEDURE: 99245

  1. Work RVU        2.96  ×  work GPCI       0.951  =    2.814

  2. Expense RVU     1.69  ×  expense GCPI    0.857  =    1.448

  3. Malpractice RVU 0.16  ×  malpractice GPCI 0.688 =    0.110

A. Total of  1 + 2 + 3                              =    4.372

B. Conversion factor (CF)                          =   34.616

Payment = A × B = 4.372 × 34.616 = $151.341 or rounded off to $151.34
```

FIGURE 8-8   Calculation of the Medicare fee schedule for 99245 in Green Ash.

Phase-in-Period

The Medicare fee schedule (MFS) was phased in over a 5-year period through 1995. From 1992 to 1995 there was a blend of the MFS and what was reimbursed the year before. This method was used for all services that are being increased as well as those which were being decreased by the fee schedule. However, if the fee schedule amount for a service in a particular locality was between 85 and 115 percent of the *adjusted historical payment base (AHPB)* in that locality, the service was paid at the fee schedule amount of the first year. To arrive at the AHPB, all 1991 charges from specialists, surgeons, primary care physicians, and anyone else using the code were weighted by the speciality of the physician who used the code the most. For example,

```
1991 AHPB for a code    = $ 95.00
1992 MFS for same code  = $103.00    $95/$103 = 92%
```

The code was on MFS the first year, and payment = $103.00 since it was between 85 and 115 percent. Also:

```
1991 AHPB for code      = $103.00
1992 MFS for same code  = $ 95.00    $103/$95 = 108%
```

This code was on the MFS the first year, and payment = $95 (between 85 and 115 percent).

When the AHPB is greater than the MFS:

```
Code XXXXX
AHPB       $67.00
1992 MFS   $54.50  67/54.50 = 122.9%
```

The following phase-in occurred:

```
1992  15% decrease $67.00 (54.50 × 15%) = 67 - 8.18 = $58.82
1993  75%/25% blend = (58.82 × 75%) + (54.50 × 25%) = 44.12 + 13.63 =
      $57.76
1994  67%/33% blend = (57.76 × 67%) + (54.50 × 33%) = 38.70 + 17.99 =
      $56.69
1995  50%/50% blend = (56.69 × 50%) + (54.50 × 50%) = 28.35 + 27.25 =
      $56.30
1996  100% of fee schedule = $54.50
```

The reimbursement for the code each year is as follows:

```
1991  $67.00     1994  $56.69
1992  $58.82     1995  $56.30
1993  $57.76     1996  $54.50
```

These calculations are based on no changes in the MFS. Using the same phase-in formula, the payment for a code increased in the following manner:

```
1991  $160.00    1994  $194.88
1992  $190.00    1995  $197.49
1993  $192.50    1996  $200.00
```

The MFS disclosure report sent to all physicians in the late fall contains a list of all current HCPCS codes and their allowed fees. Although the fee schedule for each carrier may look somewhat different, it should resemble the one shown in Figure 8-9.

If the physician is a nonparticipating physician, the office staff should change the limiting charges each January 1 using this report.

Volume Performance Standard

The Omnibus Budget Reconciliation Act of 1989 established *volume performance standard (VPS)* rates of increase in expenditures for Medicare physician services. VPS is a medical resource mechanism for slowing the rate of

(1)	(2)	(3)	(4)	(5)	(6)	(7)
				Nonpar		Limiting
	Par	Par SOS	Nonpar	SOS	Limiting	Charge
Proc	Amount	Amount	Amount	Amount	Charge	SOS
10080	68.56	60.72	65.13	57.68	74.90	66.33
96408	39.36	0.00	37.39	0.00	43.00	0.00
99212	21.60	17.27	20.52	16.41	23.60	18.87
99214	41.90	34.58	39.81	32.58	45.78	37.78

Date 00/00/9X

Notes:
Column 1 = procedure code
Column 2 = participating physician fee schedule amount of payment
Column 3 = participating physician fee schedule amount is subject to the site of service (SOS) reduction
Column 4 = nonparticipating fee schedule amount of payment
Column 5 = nonparticipating fee schedule amount of payment for service subject to the site of service reduction
Column 6 = limiting charge amount for the nonparticipating physician for the service
Column 7 = limiting charge amount for service subject to the site of service reduction
Codes 96408 and 99214 will increase in payment until 1996.
Code 10080 will decrease in payment until 1996.

FIGURE 8-9   Medicare locality fee schedule report.

increase in the cost of physician services. The annual update (increase or decrease) in the surgical, nonsurgical, and primary care conversion factors is dependent on the VPS and the Medicare Economic Index. The *Medicare Economic Index (MEI)* is used by Medicare in adjusting for inflation and the cost of medical resources. VPS uses information on services provided 2 years before the update of the MFS since all claims have already been processed (see Figure 8-10). The data collected from 1994 will be used to update the MFS in 1996.

	Surgical	Nonsurgical	Primary Care
MEI (%)	2.1	2.1	2.1
VPS (%)	+12.8	+5.8	+5.8
	14.9%	7.9%	7.9%
Congressional legislation update			
OBRA to balance the budget	−2.7	−2.7	0
Update factor	12.2%	5.2%	7.9%

In 1995 the physician fee schedule updates were 12.2 percent increase for surgical services, 5.2 percent increase for nonsurgical services, and 7.9 percent increase for primary care.

FIGURE 8-10   Calculation of the conversion factor updates.

If there are increases in the MFS totaling $20 million or more, such as in 1994, when payment for ECG interpretation was reinstated, the update factors will be reduced to keep Medicare's budget in balance.

MEDICARE CLAIM RULES

There are special exceptions for Medicare claim reporting. All claims for Medicare beneficiaries must be submitted by the practice within 1 year from the date of service. If the service was provided in October, November, or December, a practice has until the following December 31 to submit the claim for payment without a 10 percent penalty reduction. No superbills or encounter forms can be attached to the claim form.

Medicare as a Secondary Payer

pgs 266-268

There are instances when Medicare liability for payment is secondary to another insurance plan. Among these are:

- The "working aged" or patient is covered by an Employer Group Health Plan (EGHP) or spouse is employed with coverage by an EGHP
- Disability beneficiaries
- Automobile no-fault insurance or other liability
- Patient is covered under workers' compensation

Tool 8-6, with four flow charts with "yes" or "no" questions for these situations, is useful in determining the proper payer.

Medicare has specific rules that apply to beneficiaries over age 65 who are still working and are covered by their employers and those who are over age 65 with an employed spouse of any age. Medicare is the secondary insurance plan for individuals who are covered by an employer who has 20 or more employees during the course of the previous or current calendar year. These employers must offer an aged worker the same medical insurance benefits that are offered to any other employee. If the employee rejects the coverage, Medicare remains the primary insurer. If Medicare is the primary insurer, the employer cannot offer insurance that would supplement the Medicare benefits. Figure 8-11 shows how to determine whether Medicare is the primary or secondary insurance plan.

The office staff must ask a patient about his or her injury or illness to be able to file the claim with the primary insurance plan. When it is determined that Medicare is the secondary plan, the practice must report a claim to the primary plan first. Medicare can be billed for any balance not covered by the primary insurer. Include with your claim a copy of the EOB from the primary plan. Medicare will then pay the amount it would have paid if the

Employment/ Age Status	Primary	Coverage Status Spouse 65 or Older
Employee 65 or older	Group health plan	Medicare secondary
Employee 62–64 Not Medicare eligible	Family health plan	Medicare secondary
Employee under 62 Not Medicare eligible	Family health plan	If has no Part A and purchases Part B, Medicare coverage is primary; if has Part A and purchases Part B, Medicare is secondary
Retiree 65 or older	Medicare primary	Medicare primary
Retiree under 65 Not Medicare eligible	Individual health plan	Medicare primary

FIGURE 8-11   Determining Medicare as a secondary payer for spouses.

services were not covered by the employer's plan or the employer plan's allowable fee minus the amount actually paid by the employer plan or the MFS amount minus the amount paid by the employer's plan. Figure 8-12 is an illustration of payment when Medicare is the secondary insurance plan.

Determine which is greater, the balance after the primary insurance plan has paid or the amount if Medicare had paid as primary insurance plan. The balance of $24.00 is lower than the $88.00 that Medicare would have paid as the primary insurer. Medicare becomes the gap filler and pays the difference between what the primary insurance allows and what it pays ($24.00). When

Primary insurance plan allows	$120.00
Primary plan pays	$ 96.00
Patient owes	$ 24.00 ($120.00 – $96.00)
MFS allows	$110.00
Medicare payment @ 80%	$ 88.00
Since $88.00 is more than $24.00, Medicare will pay $24.00	

FIGURE 8-12   Calculation of the Medicare secondary payment.

the practice sends the claim to the section of the Medicare carrier known as the Medicare as a secondary payer department, the balance of $24.00 will be paid.

Medicare is the secondary payer for disabled beneficiaries who are covered by a "large group health plan" (an employer with 100 or more employees) as a current employee or as a family member of a current employee. When an employee or a member of the employee's family becomes disabled, the large group health plan is primary.

Automobile Liability and Work-Related Injuries

Medicare is also considered to be the secondary payer if the claim is for injuries related to an automobile accident, a fall, or another liability situation. Because there is often a delay before a liability situation is settled, Medicare will pay claims on a conditional basis unless no-fault insurance is involved. When settlement is received from the primary liability party, Medicare must be reimbursed for the accident-related services for which it paid (see Tool 8-6).

If the injury or illness is work-related, the services provided for the treatment of that injury or illness should be covered by workers' compensation or federal black lung benefits. It is necessary to state on a claim that the treatment is related to an illness or injury related to the patient's work. While waiting for the decision from workers' compensation, Medicare will issue a conditional payment, which must be refunded if the claim is subsequently paid by workers' compensation.

It is important to ask your patients about their injuries or illnesses so that you can report the claim with the appropriate payer. Tool 8-7 is a list of basic questions to use in determining the appropriate source.

Regionalization of DMEPOS Claims Filing

The transition to regional processing for durable medical equipment, prosthetics, orthotics, and supplies (DMEPOS) began on October 1, 1993. HCFA has selected four Medicare contractors designated as *durable medical equipment regional carriers (DMERCs)* that will be responsible for processing all DMEPOS claims. The address where the Medicare beneficiary resides for more than 6 months of the year determines which DMERC will process the claim. See Tool 8-8 for the names of DMERCs and areas of coverage.

Appeals

Each carrier determines the reimbursement for Part B benefits when a claim is reported. An explanation of Medicare benefits (EOMB) is sent to the practice or, if the claim is unassigned, to the patient. If either the patient or the practice feels that the denial or the payment of the claim is incorrect, a request can be made for review of the claim. A review is another look at the original claim. The request for a review must be in writing and must be sent to the carrier within 6 months of the original determination. Some carriers have specific forms which must be used for this request and some carriers are implementing telephone communications for appeals.

When requesting a review by mail, include a copy of the EOMB, a copy of the original claim, and any additional clinical documentation which supports the request for additional payment. Be specific. Additional documentation may include x-ray reports, consultation reports, medical histories, test results, and hospital discharge summaries. A letter from the physician clarifying the charges can be helpful.

The review is made on the basis of the new documentation. The individuals who made the original determination of the claim do not take part in the review.

After the review has been completed, the practice receives a review determination letter, generally within 45 days, stating the reasons behind the decision. If the supporting documentation was favorable in regard to the review, a check is included with the letter. If the denial was upheld, the letter gives the doctor an explanation and includes the regulations of laws that were used in making the decision. The letter also informs the practice of the next course of action which is available. The next level of action for requesting additional payment is known as a *fair hearing*. Medicare's appeal process is the same whether the practice or the patient initiates the appeal.

Carrier Fair Hearing

If the practice is dissatisfied with the review of the claim and the amount in controversy is at least $100, a fair hearing may be requested within 6 months of the date of the review determination letter. The dollar amount represents the amount you feel should have been paid, but it does not have to be a single claim. If, for example, the original claim in dispute was for $50 but there are three similar denials, the practice may combine the claims from several patients to meet the $100 minimum. Some state carriers require a HCFA 1965 form to request a hearing, while others permit the physician to write a letter relating dissatisfaction with the review determination and desire to appeal further. The request for a hearing should be acknowledged to the practice within 2 weeks of the date of Medicare's receipt of the request. There are three options for the fair hearing.

In-person Hearing   The claimant, either the physician or a representative such as the office manager or the practice's legal counsel, appears in person before the hearing officer (HO). A hearing officer may be employed by the carrier or may be a qualified individual such as a local attorney. The HO has knowledge of the Medicare program and its regulations, such as policy statements, HCFA instructions, and rulings by the courts. The HO is an impartial adjudicator. Appearing in person allows the office representative to answer the HO's questions immediately, present new evidence, and ask witnesses to testify.

Telephone Hearing   Testimony is given over the telephone, with an opportunity for question and answers by the HO. This is less time-consuming than an in-person hearing.

On-the-Record Decisions   No verbal arguments are given. The decision is based on past information and new information presented by the practice in writing. The HO will inform the practice or, if the patient requested the hearing, the patient of the decision within 30 days with a decision letter.

If the practice and/or patient have gone through a review and a fair hearing without success, the next level of appeal is to a federal administrative law judge (ALJ).

Administrative Law Judge

Administrative law judges (ALJs) are lawyers who work for the Social Security Administration. At this level of appeal, the amount in controversy must be at least $500 and no more than 60 days must have elapsed since the decision from the review process was notified. A letter should be sent within 60 days of the receipt of an unfavorable decision from the HO to the carrier or the local Social Security Administration (SSA) office, requesting to be heard by the ALJ. The informal hearing can be based on additional documentation, on-the-record decisions, or in-person testimony and will generally be held at one of the SSA offices located throughout the United States.

Carriers report the ALJ's decision within 15 days of its receipt by the HCFA regional office. If the practice is dissatisfied with the ALJ process, a request for a review can be filed with the appeals council within 60 days of the ruling by the ALJ.

Appeals Council

The appeals council will hear cases that represent an abuse of discretion by the ALJ or an error of law; cases whose evidence or conclusions are not supported; and cases that represent a broad policy or procedural issue.

If the practice or patient has not been successful, a judicial review in a federal district court is the last resort. The amount in controversy must be at least $1000. Tool 8-9 shows an outline of the claims appeal process.

FRAUD AND ABUSE

Medicare has a complicated system of regulations. Ignorance or willful violation of these regulations can lead to imprisonment, financial penalties, and loss of the privilege of treating Medicare beneficiaries. It is the responsibility of every Medicare carrier to identify violations of the Medicare law and refer them to the Office of Inspector General (OIG) of the Department of Health and Human Services for disposition. This office is responsible for detecting, investigating, and punishing providers who commit fraud and abuse. There are basically two violations Medicare identifies: fraud and abuse. *Abuse* is employed by the Medicare program to describe incidents involving providers which, although not usually considered fraudulent, are inconsistent with accepted medical or business practices. These violations include:

- A breach of assignment which results in the patient being billed for amounts disallowed by the carrier on the basis that such charges exceeded the allowed fee schedule amount
- Claims for services not medically necessary or, if medically necessary, not needed at the level or extent provided
- Excessive charges for services or supplies
- Claims that exceed the "limiting charge"

Fraud, as it applies to the Medicare program, is an intentional deception or misrepresentation which an individual makes, knowing that it is false and that deception could result in an unauthorized benefit to the provider or to another person.

Examples of fraud include the following:

- Billing for services or supplies that were not provided
- Billing for noncovered services as services which are covered
- Claims involving collusion between the physician and the patient, resulting in higher costs or charges to the Medicare program
- Soliciting, offering, or receiving a kickback, bribe, or rebate

Federal law provides for the exclusion from coverage of services rendered by providers who have engaged in certain forms of program abuse. In addition, civil monetary penalties as high as $2000 per service can be imposed. Upon conviction for fraud, a physician can incur substantial monetary penalties and/or imprisonment as well as exclusion from the Medicare and Medicaid programs.

Patient complaints, overutilization of services, and retrospective reviews can result in audits in which these problems are identified. Documentation must be maintained in the medical records to support the medical necessity for the services provided and substantiate that they were furnished. All medical records of Medicare beneficiaries are subject to audit for verification of Medicare billings.

Avoidance of Fraud and Abuse

Here are a few ways for a physician practice to prevent fraud and abuse:

- Report claims with the correct CPT codes and place of service.
- Participate in continuing education about the Medicare program.
- Warn the physicians of any agreement which might affect referrals, consultations, and equipment kickbacks.
- Be aware of the laws and policies regarding Medicare.

As we discussed in Chapter 1, the regulations and policies of Medicare are public information. The Freedom of Information Act of 1966 allows an individual to request internal operating policies of government agencies. A practice may be unable to obtain information about specific services or issues from the Medicare Part B Medical Policy Manual or their carrier newsletter. An inquiry to the Medicare carrier using a letter similar to Tool 8-10 can request the policy on a specific issue. It is necessary to describe in detail the specific information requested. If there is a question that must be researched, there can be fees imposed for copying costs or for the time required for the research. Figure 8-13 is an example of a Medicare Policy Bulletin about stress testing and resting ECGs obtained under the Freedom of Information Act.

MEDICARE MEDICAL POLICY BULLETIN

Freedom of Information

Subject: Stress Testing and Resting   BULLETIN NO. M-26
Electrocardiogram (ECG)   EFFECTIVE June 17, 199X
                                                          PREPARED BY C.A. JONES
                                                          APPROVED BY Tom Brown

PROCEDURE CODES   **ISSUED** June 17, 199X

Stress Testing and ECG

A resting ECG (codes 93000, 93005, 93010) is considered to be an inherent part of a stress test (codes 93015, 93017, 93018), and as such, warrrants no separate payment in addition to that for the stress test.

Consequently, when a resting ECG is reported in conjunction with a cardiac stress test, the service should be combined and processed under the appropriate code for the cardiac stress test.

FIGURE 8-13 Example of a Medicare policy bulletin.

EXERCISING KNOWLEDGE

Fill in the Blanks

1. There are two parts to the Medicare program: _____ and _____ .

2. Beneficiaries can enroll during the _____ , _____ , and _____ enrollment periods.

3. The funds for the hospital part of the Medicare program come from _____ .

4. Premiums for Part B are paid by _____ and are set at _____ .

5. A spell of illness _____ .

6. Coverage for physician services includes _____ , _____ , and _____ , and _____ calls and _____ .

7. _____ physical checkups are _____ from coverage.

8. Payment of certain benefits based on the condition or diagnosis of the patient is called _____ .

9. Three preventive medicine benefits are _____ , _____ , and _____ .

10. HICN beginning with a letter followed by numerals refers to _____ .

11. Medicare beneficiaries can sign a _____ time authorization for the practice to submit claims.

12. There are _____ and _____ physicians in the Medicare program.

13. _____ physicians must take assignment on all Medicare claims.

14. _____ physicians can take assignment on a claim-by-claim basis.

15. A _____ is the most a physician who has not signed a contract with Medicare can charge the patient.

16. Payment for physicians who assist in surgery is _____ .

17. The three components of the RBRVS are _____ , _____ , and _____ .

18. The phase-in period for the Medicare fee schedule is _____ .

19. Four types of appeals are _____ , _____ , _____ , and _____ .

20. Two categories Medicare identifies that can lead to fines, imprisonment are _____ and _____ of the program.

Define These Terms

21. EGHP

22. Hospice or respite care

23. HICN

24. Surgical disclosure letter

25. SOS

Applying Concepts

26. Mr. Smith is a Medicare beneficiary since 1990. His wife works at the local automobile plant and has XYZ family coverage. Who do I bill for Mr. Smith's recent surgery?

27. The recent office visit for Mrs. James was $225.00. The doctor is a participating physician with the Medicare program. The bill:

		Medicare allows
Office Visit	$150.00	94.00
Electrocardiogram	45.00	28.00
Spirometry	30.00	21.00

Mrs. James has not met her $100.00 deductible for the year.

Medicare pays _____

Mrs. James pays _____

Doctor writes off _____

28. Mr. James was in the office in July 1991. Today it is August 1, 1992, and he informs you that he has Medicare and wants his July service submitted to Medicare. Will there be any payment from Medicare? If so, to whom?

29. True or False:

    a. A nonparticipating physician can accept assignment on a case-by-case determination. _____

    b. All Medigap policies pay all deductible and copayments. _____

    c. All claims to Medicare are submitted on an HCFA 1500. _____

    d. All Medicare patients are over age 65. _____

    e. Medicare is always the primary insurer when there is a sudden illness.

    _____

    f. Everyone is entitled to Part A and Part B of the Medicare program.

    _____

    g. As a nonparticipating physician, I can charge Medicare patients any fee I choose. _____

    h. Medicare pays for all annual routine examinations. _____

    i. All checks from Medicare for physician services are sent to the patient. _____

    j. The provider must always accept what Medicare pays. _____

    k. Medicare pays 100 percent of the cost of laboratory tests. _____

30. Mrs. Freedman had a hernia repair. The bill from Dr. Glauser was $760.00. The primary insurance company paid $400.00 of their allowed fee of $600.00. Medicare's allowed fee is $330.00. Should the office submit a claim to Medicare as secondary payer? Will they pay any additional reimbursement?

Doctor Bill	$760.00
Auto Insurance allowed	600.00
Auto Insurance Paid	400.00
Medicare allowed	330.00
Additional Reimbursement	_____

▼ TOOL 8-1
HEALTH CARE FINANCING ADMINISTRATION (HCFA) REGIONAL OFFICES

BOSTON
John F. Kennedy Federal Building
Room 2325
Boston, MA 02203
(617) 565-1188
Maine, Vermont, New Hampshire,
 Massachusetts, Connecticut, Rhode Island

NEW YORK
26 Federal Plaza
Room 3811
New York, NY 10278
(212) 264-4488
New York, New Jersey (north), Puerto Rico,
 Virgin Islands

PHILADELPHIA
3535 Market Street
PO Box 7760
Philadelphia, PA 19104
(215) 596-1351
Pennsylvania, Maryland, Delaware, District
 of Columbia, New Jersey (south)

ATLANTA
101 Marietta Tower
Suite 701
Atlanta, GA 30323
(404) 331-2329
No. Carolina, So. Carolina, Kentucky,
 Tennessee, Mississippi, Alabama, Georgia,
 Florida

CHICAGO
105 West Adams
15th Floor
Chicago, IL 60603
(312) 886-6432
Minnesota, Wisconsin, Michigan, Illinois,
 Indiana, Ohio

DALLAS
1200 Main Tower Building
Room 2000
Dallas, TX 75202
(214) 767-6428
Texas, New Mexico, Oklahoma, Arkansas,
 Louisiana

KANSAS CITY
Federal Office Building
Room 235
601 East 12th Street
Kansas City, MO 64106
(816) 426-5233
Kansas, Missouri, Iowa, Nebraska

DENVER
Federal Building
1961 Stout Street
Room 574
Denver, CO 80294
(303) 844-2111
Colorado, Utah, Wyoming, South Dakota,
 North Dakota, Montana

SAN FRANCISCO
75 Hawthorne Street
4th Floor
San Francisco, CA 94105
(415) 744-3502
California, Nevada, Arizona, Hawaii, Guam,
 Samoa

SEATTLE
2201 Sixth Avenue
Seattle, WA 98121
(206) 615-2306
Washington, Oregon, Idaho, Alaska

▼ TOOL 8-2
WAIVER OF LIABILITY LETTER

Tracy Lewis, M.D.
4915 Muirwoods Lane
Green Ash, America 45299

Physician Notice

Medicare will pay only for services that it determines to be "reasonable and necessary" under Section 1862 (a) (1) of the Medicare law. If Medicare determines that a particular service, although it would be otherwise covered, is not "reasonable and necessary" under Medicare program standards, Medicare will deny payment for that service. I believe that in your case, Medicare is likely to deny payment for the following reasons:

Specify Particular Service(s)

_____

(Give Your Reason(s) For Your Belief)
Statements of reasons similar to those listed below are acceptable:

___ Medicare usually does not pay for this many visit treatments.
___ Medicare usually does not pay for this service.
___ Medicare usually pays for only one nursing home visit per month.
___ Medicare usually does not pay for this shot.
___ Medicare usually does not pay for this many shots.
___ Medicare usually does not pay for services by more than one doctor during the same time period.
___ Medicare does not usually pay for this many services within this period of time.
___ Medicare usually does not pay for more than one visit per day.
___ Medicare usually does not pay for like services by more than one doctor of the same specialty.
___ Medicare usually does not pay for such an extensive procedure.
___ Medicare does not pay for this because it is a treatment that has yet to be proved effective.
___ Medicare does not pay for this office visit unless it was needed because of an emergency.
___ Medicare usually does not pay for this equipment.
___ Medicare usually does not pay for this lab test.

Beneficiary Agreement

I have been notified by my physician that he/she believes that in my case Medicare is likely to deny payment for the service(s) identified above for the reason(s) stated. If Medicare denies payment, I agree to be personally and fully responsible for the payment.

Signed,

_____   _____
(Beneficiary Signature)   (Date)

▼ **TOOL 8-3**
PREPAYMENT SCREENS

Service	Explanation
A-mode scans	Verifies that the A-mode scan was performed in conjunction with cataract surgery (HCPCS 76516, 76519)
Chiropractic	Identifies claims involving an unusually large number of manipulations of a beneficiary's spine (HCPCS A2000)
Concurrent care	Identifies claims in which more than one doctor of the same specialty or subspecialty bills for in-hospital service to a beneficiary on the same date (HCPCS 99221–99223, 99238, 99231–99233, 99291, 99292)
Epoetin alfa (EPO)	Identifies claims of unusual dosages and/or contraindicated use of EPO (HCPCS EO720–EO730)
Inpatient rehabilitation medicine visits	Identifies claims for unusually large number of psychiatric visits to a patient in a rehabilitation facility (HCPCS 99221, 99222, 99223, 99231, 99232, 99233)
Replacement of postcataract external prosthetic contact lenses	Identifies claims involving replacement of an unusually large number of postcataract external prosthetic lenses (HCPCS V2500-V2599, 92326)
New patient office visits	Identifies, for new patients, multiple high-level office visits (HCPCS 99205)
Nursing home visits	Identifies claims involving an unusually large number of nursing home visits (HCPCS 99311, 99312, 99313)

▼ **TOOL 8-4**
TRAVELERS INSURANCE COMPANY OFFICES

Travelers Insurance Company
PO Box 10066
Augusta, GA 30999
(706) 855-1386

Travelers Insurance Company
PO Box 30990
Salt Lake City, UT 84130
(801) 364-0548

▼ **TOOL 8-5**
SAMPLE LETTER TO BENEFICIARY FOR SURGICAL DISCLOSURE

Tracy Lewis, M.D.
4915 Muirwoods Lane
Green Ash, America 45299

I do not plan to accept assignment for your nonemergency surgery. The law requires that where assignment is not taken and the charge is $500 or more, the following information must be provided prior to surgery. These estimates assume that you have met the $100 annual Part B Medicare deductible.

Type of surgery _____

*Estimated charge   _____

**Medicare estimated payment   _____

***Your estimated payment   _____

(This includes your Medicare coinsurance.)

_____   _____
Patient Signature   Date

*From 1 of worksheet
**From 2 of worksheet
***From 3 of worksheet

▼ **TOOL 8-6**
MEDICARE AS A SECONDARY PAYER

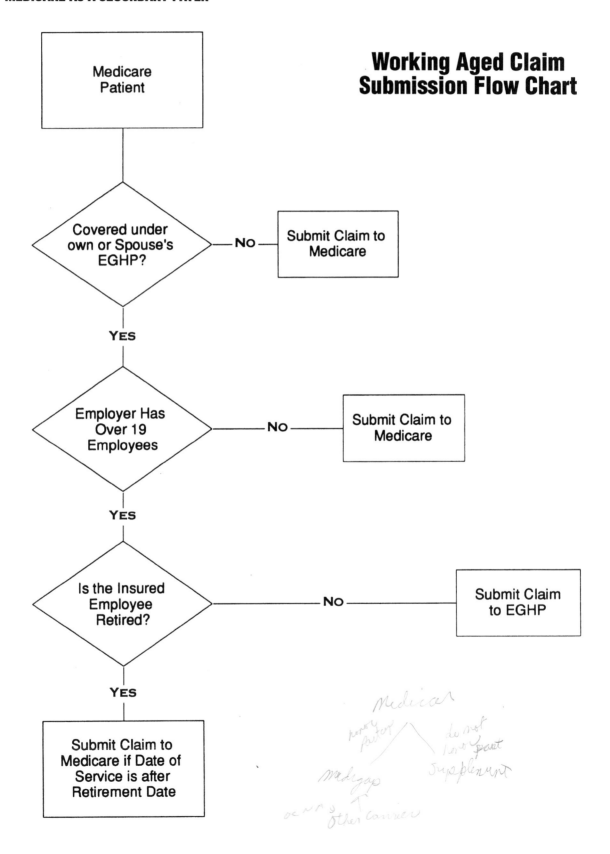

Working Aged Claim
Submission Flow Chart

▼ **TOOL 8-6 (CONTINUED)**
MEDICARE AS A SECONDARY PAYER

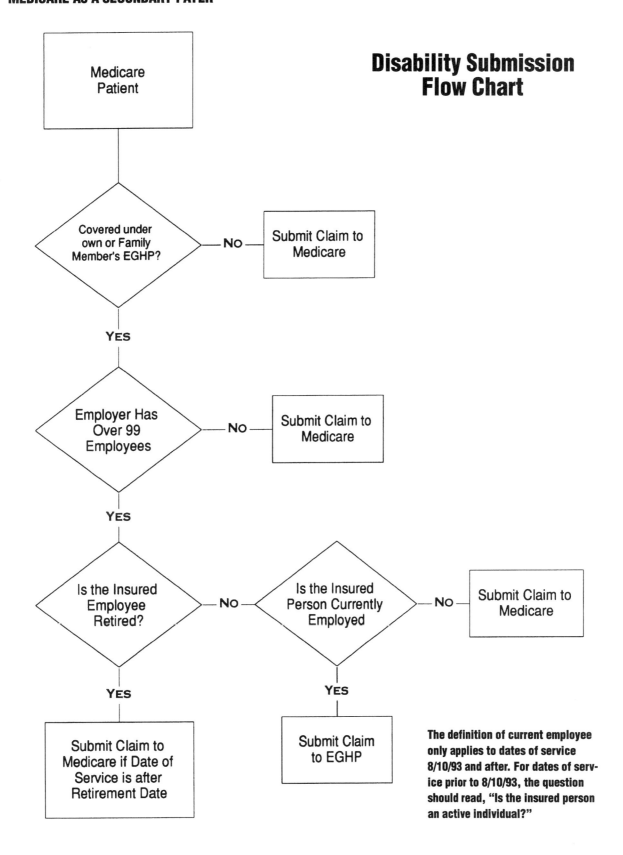

Disability Submission Flow Chart

Medicare Patient

Covered under own or Family Member's EGHP? — NO — Submit Claim to Medicare

YES

Employer Has Over 99 Employees — NO — Submit Claim to Medicare

YES

Is the Insured Employee Retired? — NO — Is the Insured Person Currently Employed — NO — Submit Claim to Medicare

YES — Submit Claim to Medicare if Date of Service is after Retirement Date

YES — Submit Claim to EGHP

The definition of current employee only applies to dates of service 8/10/93 and after. For dates of service prior to 8/10/93, the question should read, "Is the insured person an active individual?"

▼ TOOL 8-6 (CONTINUED)
MEDICARE AS A SECONDARY PAYER

Auto Insurance pays 1st

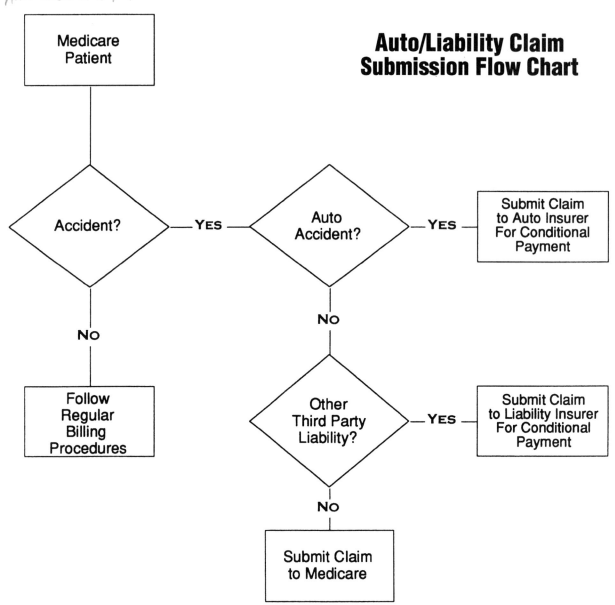

**Auto/Liability Claim
Submission Flow Chart**

▼ TOOL 8-6 (CONTINUED)
MEDICARE AS A SECONDARY PAYER

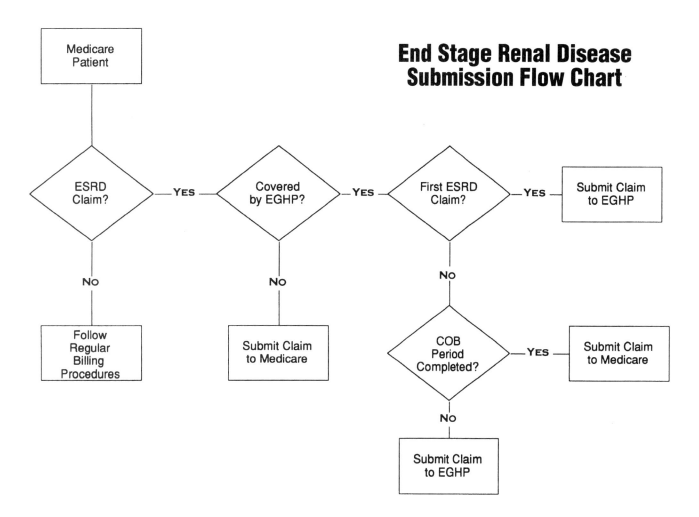

**End Stage Renal Disease
Submission Flow Chart**

▼ **TOOL 8-7**

QUESTIONS TO ASK TO DETERMINE MEDICARE AS A SECONDARY PAYER

1. Do you or your spouse work for a company that provides you with health insurance?

2. Are you entitled to Medicare benefits because of disability or end-stage renal disease?

3. Was this illness or injury the result of an automobile accident or another injury?

4. Was this illness or injury the result of an accident that occurred at work?

5. Has treatment for this accident or illness been authorized by the Veterans Administration?

▼ **TOOL 8-8**
DURABLE MEDICAL EQUIPMENT CARRIERS

Region A
Travelers Insurance Company
Government Operations 5RS
One Tower Square
Hartford, CT 06183

States

Connecticut	New Jersey
Delaware	New York
Maine	Pennsylvania
Massachusetts	Rhode Island
New Hampshire	Vermont

Region B
AdminaStar Federal, Inc.
P.O. Box 7078
Indianapolis, IN 46207-7078

States

District of Columbia	Minnesota
Illinois	Ohio
Indiana	Virginia
Maryland	West Virginia
Michigan	Wisconsin

Region C
Palmetto Government Benefits Administrators
P.O. Box 100141
Columbia, SC 29202-3141

States

Alabama	New Mexico
Arkansas	North Carolina
Colorado	Oklahoma
Florida	Puerto Rico
Georgia	South Carolina
Kentucky	Tennessee
Louisiana	Texas
Mississippi	Virgin Islands

Region D
CIGNA
P.O. Box 690
Nashville, TN 37202

States

Alaska	Montana
Arizona	Nebraska
California	North Dakota
Guam	Oregon
Hawaii	Samoa
Idaho	South Dakota
Kansas	Utah
Marianna Islands	Washington
Missouri	Wyoming

▼ TOOL 8-9
SUMMARY OF APPEALS PROCESS

Medicare Claim Submission ⟨ Resubmission (use only when original claim is completely denied)

Inquiry (use when some items are paid and others are denied)

Medicare Appeal	Must Be Filed	Dollar Limit	Personal Appearance	Type of Response	Completion
Written Review (HCFA form or letter)	Within 6 months of date of EOMB	None	No	Written	Within 45 days of request
Hearing (HCFA form 1965 or letter)	In writing, within 6 months of review result	$100 (total multiple claims)	On-the-record or telephone or in person	Written (request transcript)	Within 120 days of request or within 30 days of hearing
Administrative law judge (ALJ)	In writing, within 60 days of hearing decision	$500.00	Yes	Written	Takes up to 365 days to assign case
Appeals council	In writing, within 60 days of ALJ decision or at its own discretion	$500.00	Varies	Written	Unknown
Federal district court	Within 60 days of appeals council notice	$1000	Yes, and attorney	Transcript	Unknown

▼ **TOOL 8-10**
LETTER REQUESTING INFORMATION UNDER THE FREEDOM OF INFORMATION ACT

Tracy Lewis, M.D.
4915 Muirwoods Lane
Green Ash, America 45299

Medical Director
Medicare
P.O. Box 12345
Green Ash, AM 45299

Date

Dear Dr. Director,

Under the Freedom of Information Act, please provide, in writing, the proper ICD-9-CM codes to ensure correct and timely processing of our claims for diagnostic sigmoidoscopies,

(CPT codes 45300, 45302, 45303, 45305, 45330, 45331).

Your earliest response would be greatly appreciated.

Sincerely,

Tracy A. Lewis, M.D.
TAL/ml

Other Government Plans

CHAPTER OVERVIEW

The frequency with which a medical practice works with government plans other than Medicare—such as Medicaid, CHAMPUS, CHAMPVA, and workers' compensation—varies with the location of the practice, the policy of the physician, and the medical specialty. Congress makes the laws and sets the regulations for these plans, but the guidelines are specific for the state or region in which a practice is located.

As a result of increasing healthcare costs, Medicaid, CHAMPUS, and workers' compensation are moving toward managed care. All three are either developing HMOs and PPOs or contracting with existing ones to implement some form of managed care. With healthcare reform legislation, Medicaid and workers' compensation may be restructured, combined, or replaced. This chapter discusses eligibility, restrictions on benefits, and physician contracts common to Medicaid, CHAMPUS, and workers' compensation as they are currently structured.

After reading the material in this chapter, doing the exercises, and using the end-of-chapter tools, you will be able to:

■ *Follow the guidelines for claims processing under Medicaid, CHAMPUS, CHAMPVA, and workers' compensation*
■ *List the major components governing determination of eligibility and benefits under Medicaid, CHAMPUS, CHAMPVA, and workers' compensation*
■ *Describe the unique features of these government plans*
■ *Understand the significance to practices of three CHAMPUS-related terms:*
    — DEERS (the Defense Enrollment Eligibility Reporting System), a worldwide database of military families
    — TriCare, a new CHAMPUS program which offers eligible families a choice of three types of coverage
    — Inpatient nonavailability statements (INASs)
■ *Discuss the interrelationship of workers' compensation plans, the Bureau of Workers' Compensation, the Industrial Commission, varying forms of disability, and payment to the physician on record*

THE MEDICAID PROGRAM

Medicaid is a unique program in that it is a payer mechanism which involves both state governments and the federal government; rules and regulations come from both the federal and state levels. Since many of the rules are state-specific and change frequently, this chapter provides information about Medicaid in general.

The Medicaid program was established under Title XIX of the Social Security Act in 1965. It is meant to fund medical, rehabilitative, and other health-related services which are furnished to families with dependent children, the aged, the blind, and the disabled whose income and resources are insufficient to meet the cost of medical care. Most Medicaid programs are for the *categorically needy;* a person eligible for Medicaid must be eligible for financial assistance, such as assistance for food and housing, under the category of Title IV Aid to Dependent Children (ADC) or Title XVI Supplemental Security Income (SSI).

Physician Contract Requirements

To be paid by Medicaid, physicians must sign a contract. This contract is between the Department of Health and Human Services and the physician. Medicaid contracts are no different from contracts with insurance and managed care plans. Charges which differ from the allowed amount must be written off the patient's account.

A trend in Medicaid contracting is for the state to contract with managed care plans to deliver services. When this occurs, the practice is offered a contract with a managed care plan to deliver medical care to Medicaid recipients (Medicaid's terminology for enrollees).

Administration of Medicaid

The Health Care Financing Administration (HCFA) of the Department of Health and Human Services is responsible for determining the federal minimum requirements for Medicaid eligibility and the minimum benefit packages. Each state implements additional benefits as it feels they are needed. Therefore, benefits vary from state to state. Specific information can be obtained from your state's department of health and human services.

Federally required benefits include:

- Inpatient hospital services
- Outpatient hospital services
- Physician services
- Laboratory and x-ray services
- Skilled nursing facility services and home health services for individuals age 21 or older
- Early and periodic screening, diagnosis and treatment (EPSDT) for individuals under 21 years of age. EPSDT benefits include complete screening examinations, immunizations, and laboratory and other tests according to developmental age. EPSDT programs have other names in many states.
- Rural healthcare services

■ Family planning services
■ Nurse midwife services

Other services that may be available in some states include dental care, prescription drugs, and vision care, including eyeglasses.

Eligibility

Three categories of individuals are covered under Medicaid:

1. *ADC.* These are persons who receive financial assistance under the Aid to Families with Dependent Children Act (AFDC, sometimes shortened to ADC) because their income and resources are insufficient to cover the cost of necessary medical care. Local county departments determine eligibility on the basis of the following criteria:
   —Age of at least one child 18 or under
   —Absence, incapacity, or unemployment of at least one parent
   —Total personal and property resources of the family equal to or less than state standards
   —Possession of a Social Security number and birth certificate
   —Assignment of child support
   —Registration for employment
   —Countable income below the ADC payment standards
2. *ADC-related.* These recipients meet many of the ADC eligibility requirements but do not receive ADC financial assistance. ADC-related eligibles include pregnant women, children covered under Healthy Start, foster care children, and individuals and/or families who receive adoption assistance. These recipients may be under 21 years of age or pregnant.
3. *Aged, blind, and totally disabled.* These recipients are those age 65 and over, the legally blind, and the permanently and totally disabled who may or may not receive Supplemental Security Income (SSI). These recipients can be *medically indigent (MI),* or individuals who cannot pay for medical expenses because of the cost of previous care and have medical plans that do not cover the expenses.

ID Card or Form

Because recipients meet eligibility requirements which are state-specific, Medicaid programs renew or reissue cards or forms on a monthly basis, every 2 months or every 6 months. This time period is not standard in all states. The Medicaid card should be examined by the office staff each time a patient is seen to determine eligibility. In some cases, patients must pay a certain amount toward their monthly medical expenses to be eligible for the program. Figure 9-1 shows a typical Medicaid card.

```
┌─────────────────────────────────────────────────────────────────┐
│                    MEDICAID CARD            DHS 6488              │
│                                                                   │
│   Billing      Eligible      Date of                             │
│   Number     Individuals      Birth    Medicare No.   TPL Codes   │
│  ┌─────────┬─────────────┬──────────┬──────────────┬───────────┐ │
│  │1034569  │ Doe, John   │ 3/12/70  │              │           │ │
│  ├─────────┼─────────────┼──────────┼──────────────┼───────────┤ │
│  │         │             │          │              │           │ │
│  ├─────────┼─────────────┼──────────┼──────────────┼───────────┤ │
│  │         │             │          │              │           │ │
│  ├─────────┼─────────────┼──────────┼──────────────┼───────────┤ │
│  │         │             │          │              │           │ │
│  ├─────────┼─────────────┼──────────┼──────────────┼───────────┤ │
│  │         │             │          │              │           │ │
│  └─────────┴─────────────┴──────────┴──────────────┴───────────┘ │
└───────────────────────────────────────────────────────────────────┘
```

Case Name/Address

	Case Category	Sequence
John Doe	500-222 ADC	01
987 Any Street	**County**	Franklin
Columbus, AM 43296	**Print seq. no.**	567
	Eligibility Begins 06/01/9X	**Void After Date** 06/30/9X

Note: Use Billing Number for All Medicaid Billing

Signature _____

This card indicates person(s) eligible for health services up to the date shown in "Void After Date" block. Only those recipients whose name appears and recipient nos. are listed under "Eligible Individuals" are eligible for the service. Use the recipient's listed name in billing regardless of present name.

THIS CARD INSURES PAYMENT ONLY TO ELIGIBLE PROVIDERS WHO HAVE SIGNED A PROVIDER AGREEMENT WITH THE DEPARTMENT OF HUMAN RESOURCES. MEDICAID PAYMENT SHALL BE PAYMENT IN FULL, AND RECIPIENT SHALL NOT BE REQUIRED TO MAKE ADDITIONAL PAYMENT. If there is evidence of tampering or if card is mutilated, contact the local county Department of Human Services.

Column 1: the recipient or identification number used to bill Medicaid. If multiple family members were listed on the card, they generally each have their own identification numbers.
Column 2: the name of the eligible individual.
Column 3: date of birth of the recipient.
Column 4: the Medicare number, if applicable.
Column 5: any other third-party liability or insurance plans that must be billed before Medicaid.

The eligibility dates are on the right-hand side.

Each card should be signed, but often this is not a requirement of the state.

FIGURE 9-1 A typical Medicaid card.

If a recipient does not present a Medicaid card at the time of service, office staff must call the local department of health and human services to verify eligibility. Some states have eased this burden by issuing a card with magnetic tape that can be run through a machine to verify eligibility. A few states have programs which retroactively determine eligibility, but this is primarily for obstetric cases. The Medicaid card in many states does not require a signature or contain any identification other than name, address, and claim numbers. Care should be taken to ensure that the person presenting the card is the one to whom the card was issued.

DIFFERENCES IN MEDICAID

Medicaid has certain restrictions on benefits and certain unique eligibility requirements that distinguish it from other government plans.

Restricted Benefits

Sometimes there are restricted benefits that patients impose on themselves. An example of such benefits is restricted status. *Restricted status* requires the recipient to see a specific physician or have his or her prescriptions renewed at a specific pharmacy. The office staff must check the Medicaid card for restricted status; the doctor named on the card must be a doctor in the practice or the claim for services will be denied. Figure 9-2 illustrates a restricted Medicaid card.

On the right side of the figure there is the category "Physician." The patient can be treated only by the physician listed on the card. Also appearing on the card is the category "Pharmacy." The patient can refill prescriptions only at that pharmacy; no other pharmacy will be reimbursed. Usually, restricted cards are issued because the Medicaid program determined that there was abuse by the patient but realizes the patient needs care; thus, access is restricted to a specific physician and pharmacy.

Spend-Down

Spend down (share of cost) obligates recipients to incur a certain amount toward monthly medical expenses because their income is too high or because other criteria make them ineligible. A recipient who has income in excess of the maximum amount allowed for Medicaid may be eligible for Medicaid under the spend-down provision. Spending down means that the individual must incur medical expenses up to or higher than a certain amount before Medicaid eligibility is established. Spend-down amounts vary with the individual's income. Any medical service after the spend-down amount is met is billed to Medicaid and is subject to the fee schedule of the Medicaid pro-

RESTRICTED STATUS

Primary Alternative Care & Treatment Program (PACT)

Billing Number	Eligible Individual	Date of Birth	Medicare No.	TPL
1234567876	Mary J. Doe	05/28/68		

Eligibility Begins Date	Void After Date	County	For County Use Only	Case Category
09/01/9X	09/30/9X	Jefferson		

Mailing Address	Print Sequence No.
37 Main Street Green Ash, AM 45298	0000192

PHARMACY
Medicine Shop
1 Same Street
Green Ash, AM 45299

PHYSICIAN
Tracy Lewis, M.D.
4915 Muirwoods
Green Ash, AM 45299

NOTICE TO PROVIDERS: If there is evidence of tampering with data or card is mutilated, contact the local department of Human Services for the county shown above. Questions regarding the restricted program should also be directed to the local county Department of Human Services, Provider Relations Section.

EXPLANATION OF RESTRICTED STATUS: This individual is restricted to the physician and/or pharmacy providers shown on this card. Payments for covered pharmacy/physician services are available only for services provided by the designated provider unless referred by the designated physician. The limitations of the restricted status program do not apply to emergency services.

NOTICE TO RESTRICTED RECIPIENTS: Present this card to providers whenever you receive medical services. If this card is lost or stolen, contact the Department of Human Services at once. This care ensures the provider payment and the recipient shall not be required to make further payments.

FIGURE 9-2 Restricted Medicaid card.

gram. Starting with the first day of the following month, the spend-down process is repeated. For example,

Mary Brown is a Medicaid patient who has a spend-down of $75. She saw Dr. Jones on July 2 and incurred charges of $75. Mary takes a copy of the receipt to the Department of Health and Human Services office, where she will receive her Medicaid card with benefits effective July 3. Any other service during the month (after July 3) is reported to the Medicaid program and will be subject to the program's fee schedule.

Payment for Services

Payment from Medicaid constitutes payment in full for any covered service. The recipient may not be billed for the difference between the physician's charge and Medicaid's payment for covered services. The amount of payment is determined by the provisions of Title XIX of the Social Security Act, the regulations of the U.S. Department of Health and Human Services, and state statutes. The physician may bill the recipient for services not covered by the Medicaid program.

If a Medicaid claim is denied for payment because of lateness in claim submission, because a preauthorization was not requested, or because there is no medical necessity for that service, the patient cannot be billed for that service.

Claim Reporting

In 1986 federal law mandated the HCFA 1500 be adopted for the processing of Medicaid claims in all states that do not optically scan such claims. Some states use the HCFA 1500, and some have their own claim forms which can be optically scanned. If Medicaid processors require their own form, it must be obtained from the state processor and completed according to those specifications. In Chapter 6, specific guidelines were listed for the completion of a claim that is optically scanned. In some states physicians report claims to the county department of welfare; in others, to the department of human services; and in others, to a government-designated fiscal intermediary. Refer to the *Medicaid Provider Handbook* in your state for the claims reporting specific requirements. Most states require claims to be reported *one year from date of service.* Since this too varies from state to state, the office staff must be aware of the specific deadline.

In reporting claims to Medicaid, it is important to be certain that there is no other insurance plan for patients. Medicaid is the payer of last resort. If patients are covered by another insurance, such as Medicare, that plan must be billed first. After another plan pays, any balance of payment is reported to Medicaid.

Many states now automatically cross over claims from Medicare to Medicaid. After being paid by Medicare, the claim is sent to the Medicaid agency, usually electronically, for payment. A code appears on the Medicare EOB indicating that this was done.

Coding Systems Accepted by Medicaid

All Medicaid processors require the use of HCPCS codes to describe the procedures and/or services provided to a recipient. Each Medicaid processor has the option of issuing its own Level III local codes and modifiers. These codes can be used on claims for the Medicaid processor in that state and nowhere else.

The International Classification of Diseases, 9th Revision, Clinical Modification (ICD-9-CM) also can be used to describe the diagnosis or condition of a recipient.

CHAMPUS

CHAMPUS (the Civilian Health and Medical Program of the Uniformed Services) is a cost-sharing medical insurance program for the dependents of uniformed personnel, retirees and their families, some former spouses, and survivors of deceased military members. The program is administered by the Office for Civilian Health and Medical Program of the Uniformed Services (OCHAMPUS). CHAMPUS information and bulletins can be obtained by writing to or phoning OCHAMPUS, Aurora, CO 80045-6900, (303) 361-1000. Keep this information handy whenever you need more information about CHAMPUS.

CHAMPUS covers all seven uniformed services (Army, Navy, Marine Corps, Air Force, Coast Guard, Public Health Service, and National Oceanic and Atmospheric Administration). CHAMPUS is similar to other third-party payers in that it has a defined benefits package and requires out-of-pocket expenses for enrollees. It is an indemnity benefit plan that pays for medically necessary services and supplies for the treatment of an illness or injury, including maternity benefits. CHAMPUS is intended as a supplement to services provided by a military hospital or clinic. Under CHAMPUS, enrollees are called beneficiaries.

Eligibility

Individuals eligible to enroll in CHAMPUS include the following:

- Active-duty family members (spouses and children to age 21 if unmarried, to age 23 if full-time students, and beyond age 21 if disabled and unmarried).
- Retired service personnel and their dependents. If the former military member dies, the eligibility of the spouse does not change unless the spouse remarries. The eligibility of the children remains unchanged if a spouse remarries.
- Dependents (the spouse, children, and/or stepchildren) of service personnel who die while on active duty.

Identification Cards

Children under age 10 will probably not have an ID card; in this case, the office staff would be wise to check the parent's card. Each branch of service has its own color-coded CHAMPUS identification card (Figure 9-3). The cards can be colored green, orange, blue, or gray, depending on the status and service of the sponsor.

DEERS

The Department of Defense in the federal government maintains an enrollment system to check eligibility for CHAMPUS benefits. *DEERS* (the Defense Enrollment Eligibility Reporting System) is a worldwide database of military families. In the United States, active-duty and retired military personnel are automatically enrolled in DEERS but their family members must be registered by their sponsor. *Sponsors* are service personnel, on active or inactive duty, retired or deceased, whose relationship enables the patient to be eligible for CHAMPUS. Patients can verify their enrollment by calling a

FAMILY MEMBER (ORANGE)

UNITED STATES	UNIFORMED		SERVICES	
	ISSUING AUTHORITIES WILL PERMIT RECIPIENT'S SURNAME HERE PRIOR TO REQUISITIONING ACTUAL PHOTOGRAPH		RETIRED	
			SERVICE U.S.NAVY	
			SSN/SERVICE NO. 123 45 6789	
GRADE OFFICER			EXPIRATION DATE 01 JAN 9x	
SIGNATURE	*FREDERICK DAVIS*			

DD FORM 1173

DATE OF BIRTH	WEIGHT	HEIGHT	COLOR HAIR	COLOR EYES
29 APR 3X	175	6'	BROWN	BLUE
SIGNATURE OF ISSUING OFFICER *GARY METZGAR*			DATE OF ISSUE 01 JAN 8X	
MEDICAL NO CIV MED CARE AUTHORIZED	WARNING ISSUED FOR OFFICIAL USE OF THE HOLDER DESIGNATED. MEDICAL USE OR POSSESSION EXCEPT AS PRESCRIBED IS UNLAWFUL AND WILL MAKE THE OFFENDER LIABLE TO HEAVY PENALTY...U & C			
AFTER 01 JAN X0 SAMPLE	CARD NO 2768888			
PROPERTY OF THE UNITED STATES GOVERNMENT.IF FOUND, DROP IN NEAREST U.S. MAIL BOX.	POSTMASTER: RETURN TO DEPARTMENT OF DEFENSE WASHINGTON, D.C. 20301			

FIGURE 9-3 CHAMPUS ID card.

DEERS center. These numbers (listed below) are not to be used by a physician practice.

United States: 1-800-538-9552   Hawaii and Alaska: 1-800-527-5602
California only: 1-800-334-4162

Family members lose their eligibility at midnight on the day when the active-duty sponsor is discharged from service unless they have extended benefits. Congress has granted eligibility for limited periods to several categories of former active-duty service members and their family members. The ID cards of those granted extensions are stamped *TAMP* (Transitional Assistance Management Program).

Benefits

CHAMPUS provides benefits for most services that are medically or psychologically necessary. It may include family planning and benefits for well baby examinations and immunizations for the first 2 years of life. After age 2, examination and immunizations are excluded unless the enrollee is being transferred overseas. Mammograms and Pap smears are covered for adults at periodic intervals. Typical exclusions are anesthesia by the attending physician and chiropractic services.

COST SHARING (DEDUCTIBLES AND COINSURANCE)

CHAMPUS shares most of the cost of care provided by civilian hospitals and doctors when that care cannot be obtained through a military hospital or clinic. However, there are out-of-pocket costs for beneficiaries which CHAMPUS calls *cost sharing;* they consist of deductibles and coinsurance.

The amount of the enrollees' cost share depends on whether the sponsor is active-duty, retired, or deceased and on the site where the service is provided. For outpatient care which includes a physician practice, there is a yearly deductible of $150 for one person or $300 for a family on the allowed amounts for services per fiscal year. The deductible for family members of active duty E-4s and below is $50 for an individual and $100 for a family. Figure 9-4 shows a summary of benefits.

Differences in CHAMPUS

When patients have CHAMPUS as their primary insurance plan, there are times when nonavailability forms are required. Beneficiaries who live within the healthcare zone (postal ZIP Code zone) around a uniformed services

General Medical Services

Patients	Place of Service Inpatient	Place of Service Outpatient	Program for Persons with Disabilities
Active-duty service members	No	No	No
Active-duty families	Yes, but may need non-availability statement	Yes, but may need nonavailability statement	Yes
Retirees and their family dependents	Yes, but may need non-availability statement; Medicare exceptions for ESRD	Yes, but may need non-availability statement; Medicare exceptions for ESRD	No
Certain former spouses, dependent families	Yes, but may need non-availability statement; Medicare exceptions for ESRD	Yes, but may need non-availability statement; Medicare exceptions for ESRD	No
Dependent parents and parents-in-law	No	No	No

PATIENT RESPONSIBILITY (COST SHARING)
General Medical Services

Patients	Inpatient Hospital	Outpatient	Program for Persons with Disabilities
Active-duty family members	Small daily fee or $25 per admission, whichever is more to hospital	After deductible, 20% of allowed charges	Depends on pay grade of service member
Retirees, their families, and survivors and former spouses	Daily fee or 25% of billed charges whichever is less	After deductible, 25% of allowed charges	Not eligible
Dependent parents and parents-in-law		Not eligible for CHAMPUS	

FIGURE 9-4 CHAMPUS summary of benefits.

hospital or clinic need an *inpatient nonavailability statement (INAS)* (DD Form 1251) issued by the uniformed services hospital before receiving non-emergency inpatient civilian care. No payment will be made without an INAS.

The *ZIP Code zone* is a catchment area approximately 40 miles in radius surrounding a Uniformed Services Medical Treatment Facility (USMTF). CHAMPUS will share the cost of nonemergency inpatient care without a nonavailability statement when the patient has another plan that is primary. Families that are eligible for CHAMPUS but live outside the ZIP Code zone of the nearest uniformed services hospital do not have to get an INAS to receive inpatient civilian care. Obtaining an INAS is the responsibility of the patient.

A group of selected outpatient procedures require outpatient nonavailability statements (ONASs). Remember that this applies only to patients who live within the ZIP Code area around a military facility. These procedures are as follows:

GYN laparoscopy
Cataract removal
GI endoscopy; excludes removal of foreign bodies and decompression of colon
Myringotomy or tympanostomy
Arthroscopy (shoulder, elbow, wrist, knee ligaments, ankle)
Dilation and curettage for diagnostic or therapeutic reasons
Tonsillectomy or adenoidectomy
Cystoscopy
Hernia repair; excludes repair of inguinal hernia, incarcerated hernia, or strangulated hernia
Nose repair (rhinoplasty and septoplasty)
Ligation or transection of fallopian tubes
Strabismus repair
Breast mass or tumor excision
Neuroplasty (decompression or freeing of nerve from scar tissue)

The following services do not require a nonavailability statement:

Inpatient services in specialized treatment facilities, skilled nursing facilities, student infirmaries, and residential treatment centers
Inpatient care under the program for Persons with Disabilities
Maternity care and birthing services at a CHAMPUS authorized birthing center or hospital-based birthing room.
Admission for heart-lung, liver, and lung transplants

INAS and ONAS statements remain valid for care within 30 days of issuance and for 15 days after discharge for any additional inpatient treatment directly related to the original admission. These statements must be entered electronically in the DEERS computer at the patient's request at the nearest military facility. For this reason, the practice does not have to send the nonavailability statement with the claim.

Catastrophic Out-of-Pocket Limit

There is a catastrophic medical expense cap or limit on patient out of pocket cost provided by civilian physicians and hospitals. The limit for active-duty families is $1000; for all others it is $10,000. This cap applies only to the amount of money required to meet the family's annual deductibles and cost sharing based on CHAMPUS charges for covered medical care received in any fiscal year (October 1 to September 30). Once that limit is passed, CHAMPUS will reimburse 100 percent of the CHAMPUS allowable charge for the year.

It is important for CHAMPUS beneficiaries to keep accurate record of their medical expenses in a fiscal year. The best way to do this is to keep copies of the CHAMPUS explanations of benefits. The CHAMPUS claims processor maintains a record, but if the patient moves from one claims processor's jurisdiction to another, the patient must provide documentation to the new processor of how much has been paid toward meeting the limit or deductible. The *claims processor* is the contractor that handles the CHAMPUS and CHAMPVA claims received within a state or county. Claims processors are also called *fiscal intermediaries*. The office staff should ask the patient if the patient has met the deductible for the fiscal year. If the patient has, the practice can collect the 20 or 25 percent at the time of service.

Secondary Coverage

When a beneficiary has coverage under another medical insurance plan, CHAMPUS is always secondary except for Medicaid, the Indian Health Service, and any plan that is specifically designated as a CHAMPUS supplement.

Health Benefits Adviser

A physician practice must be aware of the many rules of the CHAMPUS program because service families frequently do not understand their plans. These families have a *health benefits adviser (HBA)* available to answer their questions; this is especially helpful for families that are new to the program. These advisers are generally found at uniformed services hospitals and clinics, and it is their responsibility to help individuals understand the program. Refer patients with questions to their HBA.

TriCare

CHAMPUS is implementing a program called TriCare in selected areas; this program will be nationwide. TriCare includes managed care and offers CHAMPUS service families three types of coverage:

1. TriCare Standard, which includes the traditional CHAMPUS benefits.
2. TriCare Extra, which consists of a PPO network panel with discounted cost sharing.
3. TriCare Prime, which is a managed care program with annual enrollment requirements and the lowest out-of-pocket costs.

Payment

Participating Providers or Accepting Assignment

There is no formal contract to sign to become a participating physician in either the CHAMPUS or the CHAMPVA programs (except for TriCare). The physician can choose to participate on a claim-by-claim basis. When a physician decides to participate, item 27 of HCFA 1500 is checked "yes" for assignment. By participating in the program, the physician agrees to accept the CHAMPUS allowable charge as the full fee for a service. Payment goes directly to the physician. Participating physicians also can file appeals and have a right to receive information on the status of their claims.

The Department of Defense has authorized reductions in maximum allowable fees to physicians and other professional providers, such as clinical laboratories, for certain overpriced procedures. These are procedures for which the prior year's national CHAMPUS maximum allowable charge (CMAC) exceeds the Medicare fee schedule. The payment is the lower of 15 percent of the Medicare fee schedule for the prior year or the percentage by which the procedure exceeds the fee schedule. For example, the MFS for a procedure is $100. Last year the CHAMPUS maximum allowable fee for that procedure was $125. Payment is $115, which is 15 percent of the MFS.

Nonparticipating Providers or Not Accepting Assignment

If a physician does not accept assignment, there is a limitation on the amount that can be billed to the patient; it is 115 percent of the allowed amount. Failure to comply with this requirement, which went into effect on January 1, 1994, is considered abuse and will result in exclusion from the CHAMPUS program. Here is an example of the calculation of the limiting charge.

CMAC (allowed amount)	$500
Limiting charge $ 500 × 115%	$575

A doctor who does not accept assignment (nonparticipating provider) can bill the patient for only $575.

Claims Reporting

All claims must be filed within 1 year of the date of service. Claims received after the filing deadline are denied unless sufficient documentation is sub-

Anyone not using the original source for CPT coding may want to consider procedure 70450.

When it comes to the most up-to-date CPT coding information, there is only one source you can always rely on. The American Medical Association—the originators of CPT codes.

As the true experts behind medical coding, the AMA is unsurpassed in depth of knowledge and insight. That, coupled with a dedicated staff, equates to the most comprehensive line of CPT products and services available today.

In addition to our CPT, ICD-9-CM, and HCPCS code books, we also offer *CPT Assistant*, a monthly newsletter filled with the latest updates and information on coding procedures. A must in any office.

Also, our recently developed CodeManager software provides five essential coding products on CD-ROM—all at your fingertips.

Plus, our new CPT Information Services can answer any of your coding questions quickly and accurately by phone, fax or mail.

With so many ways to ensure coding accuracy, the AMA is the only source you need. Ever. So call **800 621-8335** to place an order or to speak with one of our coding specialists. That way, you won't have to consider having your head examined.

Mention priority code AHQ.

We cover the codes.

How to avoid a paper cut when using our coding books.

mitted by the practice during an appeal. Appeals are considered when coordination of benefits is involved.

There are five contractors for claims reporting:

Palmetto Government Benefits Administrators (Palmetto GBA)
AdminaStar Defense Services, Inc.
Wisconsin Physicians Service (WPS)
Foundation Health Federal Services (FHFS)
Office of CHAMPUS, Europe (OCHAMPUS EUR)

The HCFA 1500 is used for reporting claims. If a patient elects to submit his or her own claim form, DD2642 is used by the patient; claims for the handicapped are filed on form DA1863-3. Itemized superbills or encounter forms may be attached to the claim form if they include the following:

Name of the patient
Date and charge
Name and address of physician
Diagnosis (ICD-9-CM) codes
HCPCS codes for each service
Related dates of hospitalization
Surgical procedure and duration of anesthesia
Maternity care (including the estimated or actual date of delivery)

Item 31 of the HCFA 1500 must be signed by the provider. A designated representative may sign for the physician if the physician has previously filed a notarized signature authorizing a representative or a computer-generated signature for the claims. Tool 9-1 shows the proper documentation for a designated signature. Contact the claims processor in your region to obtain an actual form if your doctor wants a staff member or the computer to sign CHAMPUS claims.

Coding

CPT-4 and ICD-9-CM are used for the completion of the claim form. CHAMPUS has designated a list of V codes which are acceptable as a primary diagnosis. It does not require additional diagnosis codes to process a claim. Here are the V codes that are acceptable to CHAMPUS:

V01.0–V01.9   V72.0
V22.0–V26.9   V72.2
V28.0–V39.0   V72.3*
V42.0–V45.89   V76.1
V50.0–V56.8   V76.2
V59.0

* Only when Pap smear is billed.

All other V codes require additional diagnosis codes describing a disease or injury or the claims will be denied because of an insufficient diagnosis. The office staff must be aware that this list is updated at least annually and should watch CHAMPUS newsletters for additional codes.

Rebundling

CHAMPUS has added a software edit to its claims-processing system for the bundling of surgical procedures and laboratory charges. This became effective in 1994.

Appeals

When a *proper appealing party* (a physician accepting assignment) disagrees with the payment of a claim, an appeal may be made. Physicians cannot appeal determinations relating to the issuance of a nonavailability statement (INAS and ONAS).

There are three levels of review in CHAMPUS appeals.

Reconsideration

Reconsideration is the first level of appeal. It is conducted by the claims processor. To initiate reconsideration, do the following:

■   Write to the address on the EOB within 90 days of the date on the EOB. Include a copy of the EOB and other information or papers to support the claim.
■   The CHAMPUS contractor will send a written acknowledgment of the receipt of the claim within 10 days of receiving it.
■   The contractor will review the case and send a reconsideration decision about the claim.

If the amount is $50 or less, the reconsideration decision is final. If there is further disagreement and the amount is over $50, ask for a review at OCHAMPUS headquarters. This request must be postmarked or received by OCHAMPUS headquarters within 60 days of the date of the written reconsideration.

Formal Review

The second level of appeal is a formal review conducted at CHAMPUS headquarters. To request a formal review, write to CHAMPUS Appeals, Aurora, CO 80045-6900. Include a copy of the reconsideration notice and any additional clinical information about the treatment that is appropriate. It is acceptable to write CHAMPUS for a formal review to meet the filing deadline and send the supporting documentation later.

CHAMPUS headquarters will review the case and issue a formal review decision. If the amount in dispute is less than $300, the formal review decision is final. If there is still disagreement and if the amount is $300 or more, the next step is an independent hearing at CHAMPUS headquarters.

Hearing

A hearing held by CHAMPUS is conducted by an independent hearing officer at a location convenient to both the requesting party and the government. A request for this hearing must be postmarked or received within 60 days of the date on the formal review decision. This is the last step in the review process, and both parties must abide by the decision of the independent hearing officer.

CHAMPVA

The Civilian Health and Medical Program for the Veterans Administration (*CHAMPVA*) is a medical benefit plan for the families of veterans with a 100 percent service-connected disability and the surviving spouses or children of veterans who die from a service-connected disability. These beneficiaries have similar benefits under the same conditions and cost-sharing plans as dependents of retired and deceased uniformed services personnel under CHAMPUS. The same claims processors handle both CHAMPUS and CHAMPVA claims and have the same requirements. Questions concerning CHAMPVA can be sent to: CHAMPVA Registry Center, 4500 Cherry Creek Drive South, Box 64, Denver, CO 80222.

Eligibility

The Veterans Administration is solely responsible for the determination of eligibility. Those eligible for benefits include:

■ The husband, wife, or unmarried child of a veteran with a total and permanent disability resulting from a service-connected injury or a veteran who died as a result of a service-connected disability
■ The husband, wife, or unmarried child of a person who died in the line of duty in the military, naval, or air service

When an individual is deemed eligible for CHAMPVA benefits, an ID card is issued to identify the home station where the beneficiary's case file is maintained. On the bottom right corner of the card is the veteran's VA file number. Figure 9-5 shows a CHAMPVA ID card.

1. NAME OF BENEFICIARY	
Samuel Smith	

2. DATE OF BIRTH	3. SEX
00/00/9X	M

4. EXP. DATE	5. I.D. NUMBER
XX/XX/9X	XXXXXXX

Use the identification number in block 5 when submitting CHAMPVA CLAIMS to the Fiscal Intermediary. If you have any questions regarding the use of this card, call the CHAMPVA Center at 1-800-331-0999.

6. ISSUE DATE	
XX/XX/9X	000238

CIVILIAN HEALTH AND MEDICAL PROGRAM
OF THE VETERANS ADMINISTRATION (CHAMPVA)

POSTMASTER: RETURN TO:
CENTRAL CHAMPVA
REGISTRY CENTER
VAMC DENVER, CO 80222

DEPENDENT OR SURVIVOR
DEPENDENT

BENEFICIARY OF VA
IDENTIFICATION CARD

SIGNATURE OF BENEFICIARY (*If age 12 or older*)
Samuel Smith

VA FORM 10-7959. DEC 1988

FIGURE 9-5   A CHAMPVA ID card.

Benefits

The benefits are the same for CHAMPVA beneficiaries as they are for dependents of retired or deceased CHAMPUS personnel (Figure 9-4). Dependents, survivors, and certain spouses have deductible and coinsurance requirements. As opposed to CHAMPUS beneficiaries, CHAMPVA beneficiaries never need to file a nonavailability statement. A beneficiary can get care in a VA hospital if space is available, but not in a military facility.

Payment and Claims Reporting

Completion of HCFA 1500 for CHAMPVA is identical to the process used for CHAMPUS. Payment for CHAMPVA is accepted as payment in full for the billed services less deductible and coinsurance.

WORKERS' COMPENSATION

Workers' compensation (WC) is a form of medical insurance that pays benefits only for occupational illnesses and injuries. WC differs from insurance and managed care plans because it begins on the first day of employment; there is no enrollment or waiting period. WC has no cost sharing. The purpose of this insurance is to provide the best medical care directed toward the prompt return of an injured or ill employee to work with a maximum recovery.

Benefits

WC generally covers all services for the medically necessary care of illnesses and injuries once it has been established that they resulted from employment.

Federal workers' compensation laws provided benefits for job-related injuries first to federal employees and later to coal miners. States have enacted compensation laws to cover workers not protected by the federal statutes. Each state has its own laws and programs which supersede federal laws. In some states WC may be mandated for employers with only one employee.

Within each state there are two parts to the workers' compensation system: the Bureau of Workers' Compensation (BWC) and the Industrial Commission (IC). The BWC is the administrative branch of the workers' compensation system. It is responsible for paying claims and may administer safety programs to prevent work-related accidents. The Industrial Commission determines levels of disability, resolves disputed claims, and establishes workers' compensation policy.

Payment for Coverage

An employer may provide coverage through a state fund or a qualified carrier or may be self-insured. State laws determine how an employer can provide coverage. *State fund employers* are public and private employers who pay premiums into a state insurance fund for workers' compensation coverage. Employers who have been granted the privilege by BWC of administering their own workers' compensation programs and who pay compensation and benefits directly are known as *self-insured employers*. In many states employers pay premiums to an insurance or managed care plan to administer their workers' compensation funds. An employer's premium amounts for each employee depend on the risk involved in the job. The more hazardous the job, the higher the premium. This encourages maximum employer interest in safety through an experience rating mechanism.

Compensation for Employees

There are five types of compensation for on-the-job injuries and illnesses:

1. Medical treatment and rehabilitation
2. Loss of wages (disability payments)
3. Permanent disability (payments in one sum or weekly or monthly payments)
4. Vocational rehabilitation
5. Compensation to the dependents of employees who are fatally injured (death benefits)

It is the responsibility of a medical practice to submit claims for the services provided to a patient and to supply reports concerning the disability of an injured worker.

Physician on Record

The initial physician whom an employee sees for treatment is known as the *physician on record*. The physician on record may be selected by the employee or be participating in a panel selected by the employer or managed care plan. The physician on record is responsible for promptly completing a report on the disability so that the employee can receive payments during this period of disability. In addition, the physician on record evaluates the rehabilitation potential in cases of actual or expected lengthy disability. If injured workers decide to change the physician on record, they must inform claims processors or the employer (see Tool 9-2).

Different Forms to Complete

There are three types of forms that must be completed by a medical practice for a WC patient.

Establishing an Allowed Condition

Employees injured on the job must report the illness or accident to the employer immediately. The employer sends an *employers' report of occupational injury or illness* form to the state office, informing it of the nature of the illness or injury and giving details about when, where, and how the injury or illness occurred. The number of days the employer has to submit this report varies with state law. The employer may also complete a *medical service order,* which the worker takes to the physician or hospital when receiving treatment. The employee receives a claim number, which correlates with the reported injury or illness and must be used when submitting all medical claims. The reported injury is known as the *allowed condition;* this condition must be a direct result of the industrial injury or occupational disease. There is also the diagnosis on record, which is the actual injury or illness received on the job and reported to the employer. Services for any other diagnosis are considered noncovered and are the responsibility of the patient. For example, a patient with diabetes mellitus sees the physician for a back strain suffered on the job while loading boxes. The only diagnosis that can be used in submitting a claim for workers' compensation payment is back strain. If recovery is delayed because of the diabetes mellitus, a letter explaining the delay can be sent to the claims processor of the employer.

When an injury occurs, there is a waiting period before temporary disability (and reimbursement for lost wages) can begin.

Temporary Disability

Temporary disability is the recovery period following a job-related injury or illness, after which an employee is able to resume normal job activities. This period varies from state to state; it is generally 1 to 7 days. Sometimes the period of temporary disability is difficult to predict because of the nature of the accident. For example, a simple laceration can become infected, leading to gangrene and amputation. Patients do recover, and once care is completed and the patient is well enough to return to work, a *doctor's final report* is submitted to indicate that there is no permanent disability. Benefits for lost wages then cease. If an individual has an illness or injury that prohibits that individual from performing his or her former job functions, this is a *permanent disability.*

Permanent Disability

A patient or injured party may have received temporary disability benefits for an extended period of time but is still unable to return to work. The award for permanent disability is dependent on the severity of the injury or illness, the age of the injured worker, and the worker's occupation at the time of the injury. The physician on record must state in a supplemental report that the patient is permanently disabled. Sometimes the BWC or the IC requests that the patient be evaluated by another physician to get an impartial opinion on disability before a final determination of permanent disability is made and compensation is paid. This independent medical evaluation (IME) is performed by a physician other than the treating physician and is often requested by nonmedical parties, sometimes attorneys.

After each case is rated for permanent disability, a settlement is made. This settlement is called a *compromise and release.* It is an agreement between the injured worker and the insurance plan or state fund, usually for a lump sum award. If the injured worker agrees with the award, the case is closed. If there is dissatisfaction with the amount of the award, the worker may appeal to the Workers' Compensation Appeals Board or the Industrial Accident Commission for additional compensation. If the injured worker is dissatisfied with that judgment, there can be further legal action. A medical practice can get involved in this process by submitting reports of medical treatment, results of treatment, and determining if there is any type of disability.

Determination of Fault

Sometimes in the case of an injury on the job, there is no question of fault and no question of cause. For example, a postal worker on delivery rounds is struck by a car while crossing the street. The postal worker was injured during the performance of his or her work, and workers' compensation is liable. However, the workers' compensation insurance carrier does have legal recourse. The carrier may encourage the postal worker to seek claims from the operator of the motor vehicle that struck him or her. This may require litigation in a court of law. If the postal worker agrees to sue, the workers' compensation insurer puts in a demand for the repayment of any paid benefits. This is known as a lien. A *lien* is a legal promise to satisfy a debt out of money received, in this case from the operator of the motor vehicle. This money is owed by the patient to the treating physician.

Sometimes a physician has rendered treatment to an injured worker but the claim is denied by the Bureau of Workers Compensation as a work-related injury. Even though the postal worker was on the job, the injury was not caused by the job. The patient may be unable to pay for the medical treatment except after legal monetary recovery resulting from a lawsuit against the operator of the motor vehicle (assuming that no-fault auto insurance is not in effect). It would be prudent for the physician to file a lien with the attorney so that when the award is made by the automobile insurer, the lawyer will be liable for the doctor's fee and will have to pay for the medical services.

CLAIMS AND REIMBURSEMENT

There are no universal methods for billing for services provided to an injured worker. Some states require a monthly statement of services; others require a statement at the termination of a nondisability claim. Some plans use an HCFA 1500, and some have their own forms. The office staff should check with the BWC to learn its policy.

The payment for the covered services represents the total amount collected by the physician. Neither the claimant nor the employer may be billed for any difference between the physician's charge and the amount allowed by the BWC, a third-party payer, or a self-insured employer. If there are questions about the reimbursement, the practice should call the plan or appeal the payment. If the service remains unpaid and overdue, send one of the letters shown in Tools 9-3 through 9-6.

There are, however, some consistent reasons for delay in claim payments, including the following:

- Lack of WC claim number
- Omission of reports, such as the employer's report not being sent
- Treatment not directly related to injury or condition
- Patient changed doctors and did not notify carrier
- Case in litigation

There are several important aspects to workers' compensation cases. A medical practice must be aware of the proper method for obtaining an identification number from the patient or employer, file claims, and report disability to the plan. If the payment received is not appropriate, the practice will appeal the payment to the insurer.

Tool 9-7 explains workers' compensation terminology.

EXERCISING KNOWLEDGE

Medicaid

Fill in the Blanks

1. Medicaid is a program for _____ .

2. Medicaid is administered by _____ .

3. The states play a _____ role in the benefits of the program by _____ .

4. Covered benefits in the program include _____ .

5. _____ and _____ are also covered by the program.

6. An important time to check eligibility on the Medicaid card is _____ .

7. Medicaid cards are issued _____ .

8. Another name for EPSDT is _____ .

9. The purpose of EPSDT is _____ .

10. Medicaid patients can be billed for _____ .

Define These Terms or Abbreviations

11. ADC

12. SSI

13. AFDC

14. MI

Applying Concepts

15. Mrs. Fox was in last week. She is in the spend-down program and must spend $125 per month before Medicaid becomes her insuring plan. Last week she had services for $50.00 with Dr. Jones and services for $80.00 with Dr. Todd. The bill in this practice was $45.00. Do I collect from Mrs. Fox, or do I bill Medicaid? (All these services occurred in the same month.)

16. Jim Smith said he forgot his Medicaid card. He was eligible last month. Can the medical office bill Medicaid for his service this month? Why?

17. The new patient this afternoon has GHO plan and Medicaid. Which insurance is primary, and which is secondary?

18. How does the practice learn if a patient is eligible for Medicaid?

19. There is another physician's name on the restricted status Medicaid card of Mrs. Smith. Will this practice be paid for the services it rendered?

20. A Medicaid patient also has CHAMPUS. Which insurance is primary? Which is secondary?

CHAMPUS and CHAMPVA

Fill in the Blanks

1. _____ , _____ , and _____ are entitled to CHAMPUS medical benefits.

2. The CHAMPUS fee schedule is updated at the beginning of the fiscal year, which starts on _____ .

3. The deductible for a retiree who receives outpatient services is _____ .

4. The copayment for a retiree who receives outpatient services is _____ .

5. The inpatient deductible for active-duty family members is _____ .

6. A nonparticipating physician may accept assignment of the claim by _____ ; a participating physician may accept assignment of the claim by _____ .

7. A nonavailability statement is _____ .

8. The patient needs a nonavailability statement for _____ .

9. There are three levels of appeal: _____ , _____ , and
   _____.

10. The first level of appeal must be requested within _____
    days of receiving the EOB.

11. The second level must be requested within _____ days of the
    notice of the reconsideration and is held at _____ .

12. The third level of appeal must be requested within _____
    days after the formal review and is held at _____ .

13. Patients can submit their own claims to CHAMPUS on Form _____.

14. Providers submit claims to CHAMPUS on Form _____ .

**Define These Terms
or Abbreviations**

15. DEERS

16. HBA

17. NAS

18. CMAC

19. USMTF

20. FI

21. TriCare

Applying Concepts

22. Mrs. Weber is in the office because she is short of breath. Her husband
    is a lieutenant colonel in the Army. Her visit and services were as
    follows:

Office visit	$40	allowed	$37
Vital capacity	$24	allowed	$23
Total	$64		$60

    Mrs. Weber has met her deductible for the year, and her doctor has
    checked yes in item 27 of HCFA 1500. How much is the check from
    CHAMPUS? _____ How much is her cost share? _____

23. Mrs. Brown came in for her annual physical. She is the wife of retired Admiral G. Brown and has not met her deductible for the year. The bill for Dr. Green's services taken on assignment is as follows:

	Cost, $	Allowed, $
New patient visit	115	105
Electrocardiogram	45	37
Laboratory (19 tests)	47	21
Urinalysis	10	7
Stool occult blood	9	6
	$226	$176

How much is the check from CHAMPUS? _____ How much does Mrs. Brown owe the doctor? _____ Does the doctor write off any amount? If so, how much?

Workers' Compensation

Fill in the Blanks

1. The first law enacted for job-related injuries covered _____ .

2. The five types of compensation for job-related injuries are _____ , _____ , _____ , _____ , and _____ .

3. The two types of disability are _____ and _____ .

4. The first thing an employee should do when injured on the job is to _____ .

5. The first thing an employer should do when an employee reports an injury is to _____ .

6. The three types of funding for workers' compensation payments are _____ , _____ , and _____ .

7. _____ pays for workers' compensation insurance.

8. The Industrial Commission is _____ .

9. The _____ determines when a worker is ready to return to work.

10. The number used in the claim form for submitting a claim to the workers' compensation carrier is called a _____ .

Define These Terms

11. Temporary disability

12. Permanent disability

13. Lien

14. Employers' report of occupational injury or illness

15. Physician on record

16. Doctor's final report

17. Injury

Applying Concepts

18. Why were workers' compensation laws put into effect?

19. Mr. Brown is in the office to have the doctor suture a wound he received while unpacking crates at the Brown Furniture Company. What are the steps the administrative assistant must follow to submit this claim?

20. Because of his injury, Mr. Brown must not work for 3 days. Is there anything the administrative assistant must do for Mr. Brown or the practice at the end of the 3 days?

21. What does the practice do if it feels that the payment for the claim for Mr. Brown was unfair?

▼ **TOOL 9-1**
CHAMPUS LETTER FOR SIGNATURE AUTHORIZATION

CHAMPUS

REPRESENTATIVE FACSIMILE SIGNATURE AUTHORIZATION FORM

Dear Provider:

It is a CHAMPUS requirement that to verify services were rendered, you or your authorized representative must sign each claim form. To fulfill this requirement, you must submit with any of the three options listed below:

1. You may elect to **personally sign** each claim.
2. You may elect to have a **representative sign** each claim.
3. You may elect to use your **facsimile signature** on each claim (i.e., rubber stamp).

To assure prompt adjudication of your claims, <u>complete the reverse side of this form as follows.</u> (If you need additional copies, you may photocopy this form.)

☐ If you elect to personally sign each claim, complete **SECTION I— PROVIDER'S ACTUAL SIGNATURE.**

☐ If you elect to have a representative sign each form, complete **SECTION II—REPRESENTATIVE SIGNATURE.** This form must then be notarized. See SECTION IV.

☐ If you elect to use a facsimile signature, complete **SECTION III—FACSIMILE SIGNATURE.** The example of the signature stamp must be indicated in the appropriate box. This form must then be notarized. See SECTION IV.

FOR GROUPS/CLINICS. This form must be completed and signed by each individual provider practicing within the group/clinic. Example: If the group/clinic elects to have a representative sign each claim for all providers with your group/clinic, each individual provider must complete and sign SECTION II of this form.

FOR COMPUTER-GENERATED CLAIMS: Please attach a sample of your computer-generated claim form. **THEN,** if you have a representative's name listed on your computer-generated claims, please complete **SECTION II—REPRESENTATIVE SIGNATURE.** If your name is listed on your computer-generated claims, complete **SECTION III—FACSIMILE SIGNATURE.** This form must then be notarized. See SECTION IV.

Once you have completed this form, mail it to the address listed below.

Thank you for your cooperation in this matter.

▼ **TOOL 9-1 (CONTINUED)**
CHAMPUS LETTER FOR SIGNATURE AUTHORIZATION

REPRESENTATIVE/FACSIMILE SIGNATURE AUTHORIZATION FORM
Please complete all applicable sections of this form

CHAMPUS Provider # _____   **Federal Tax ID #** _____

Provider Name: _____   **Specialty** _____

GROUP/CLINIC Name: _____

SECTION I—PROVIDER'S ACTUAL SIGNATURE

If you are the provider of service and you will be personally signing your name on each claim sent to us, please sign your name here: _____

(Provider's Actual Signature)

SECTION II—REPRESENTATIVE SIGNATURE AUTHORIZATION (must be notarized)

Each representative listed below is authorized to complete and sign all forms required by OCHAMPUS, on behalf of the provider named above to authorize services, care, and treatment rendered by this provider to CHAMPUS patients, and any related documentation that might be required by fiscal administrators of OCHAMPUS.

The representative's signatures and typed (printed) names, and official titles with the organizations as authorized above, are as follows:

_____   _____

(Representative's Actual Signature)   *(Representative's Printed/Typed Name and Title)*

_____   _____

(Representative's Actual Signature)   *(Representative's Printed/Typed Name and Title)*

_____   _____

(Physician's Signature OR Officer of the institutional provider, facility, OR Owner of the provider of service, such as Ambulance, Medical Supply, Pharmacy, etc.)   *(Date)*

SECTION III—FACSIMILE SIGNATURE AUTHORIZATION (must be authorized)

I hereby authorize the Fiscal Intermediary of OCHAMPUS, to accept my facsimile or stamp signature (shown below) as my true signature for all purposes under the CHAMPUS program in the same manner as if it were my actual signature (shown below). For computer-generated claims, please attach a sample copy of your claim.

_____   _____

(Provider's Actual Signature)   *(Facsimile or Stamp Signature)*

SECTION IV—NOTARY PUBLIC (please notarize if you completed SECTION II and/or III)

Subscribed and sworn to before me this _____(day) of _____ (month) 1994.

NOTARY PUBLIC in and for _____ county, state of _____

NOTARY SIGNATURE _____

Provider Certification Unit, P.O. Box 3067, Columbus, IN 47202-3067

ADSI FCN 24 Side 2 of 2 (1/94)

▼ TOOL 9-2
REQUEST FOR CHANGE OF PHYSICIAN ON RECORD

Tracy Lewis, M.D.
4915 Muirwoods Lane
Green Ash, America 45299

Claim No. _____

Claimant Name _____

Date:

Please consider this request to change the attending physician in my claim as follows:

FROM DOCTOR

_____

TO DOCTOR

_____
(Name)

_____
(Street Address)

_____
(City, State, ZIP Code)

REASON FOR CHANGE_____

_____

_____

EFFECTIVE DATE _____

_____
(Claimant's Signature)

_____
(Claimant's Address)

▼ **TOOL 9-3**
LETTER TO USE WHEN NO WORKERS' COMPENSATION PAYMENT IS RECEIVED

Tracy Lewis, M.D.
4915 Muirwoods Lane
Green Ash, America 45299

Date:

To: Carrier/State Fund

Employer _____

Insured _____

Insured's SS No. _____ - _____ - _____

To Whom It May Concern:

Our records indicate that a claim for the case referred above dated _____ remains unpaid.

Your cooperation in furnishing the present status of this claim will be greatly appreciated. A notation on the bottom of this letter will be sufficient.

Regards,

Tracy Lewis, M.D.

cc: Employer
    Insured

_____

_____ No employer's report on file
_____ No doctor's first report on file
_____ Did not receive itemized claim
_____ Payment was made—Check No. _____ Date _____
_____ Other reasons: see below

▼ TOOL 9-4
FORM LETTER FOR STATUS OF EMPLOYER'S REPORT FOR WORKERS' COMPENSATION

If the insurance company notifies the office that the employer's preliminary report of the injury has not been received, send this letter to the employer.

Tracy Lewis, M.D.
4915 Muirwoods Lane
Green Ash, America 45299

Date:

To: Employer

RE: Case No.: _____

Patient: Injured: _____

Date of Injury/Illness: _____

Dear Employer:

I have been informed by your workers' compensation insurance administrator that they have not received the employer's report in regard to the injured person referred to above.

Unless you have already done so, I would appreciate your cooperation in completing and sending this report so the case may be closed. I will contact you within the next seven days to determine the status of this report.

If you have any questions, please contact my office.

Sincerely,

Tracy Lewis, M.D.

cc: Insured
    Administrator

▼ **TOOL 9-5**

LETTER TO BUREAU OF WORKERS' COMPENSATION WHEN EMPLOYER INFORMATION HAS NOT BEEN RECEIVED

Tracy Lewis, M.D.
4915 Muirwoods Lane
Green Ash, America 45299

Date:

Department of Labor
Bureau of Workers' Compensation
State

RE: Date of Initial Claim _____

Claims Processor _____

Employer _____

Insured (Patient) _____

Patient's SS No. ____ - ____ - ____

Dear Sir or Madam:

All attempts to collect the above outstanding claim have been unsuccessful. Please initiate follow-up proceedings to determine liability and advise us of your findings.

Sincerely,

Tracy Lewis, M.D.

cc: Administrator
    Employer
    Patient

▼ **TOOL 9-6**
APPEALS LETTER FOR FEE INCREASE

Tracy Lewis, M.D.
4915 Muirwoods Lane
Green Ash, America 45299

Date:

Medical Review Board
Department of Labor
Bureau of Workers' Compensation
Your state

RE: Patient _____

Date of Service: _____

Procedure(s): _____

_____

My Fee: $_____ Amount Paid: $_____

In view of the nature and extent of services performed for the above patient, I feel that the reimbursement made is extremely low.

Attached is a copy of the medical/operative report.

After examining the report, I feel confident you will authorize additional payment.

Sincerely,

Tracy Lewis, M.D.

cc: Claims Processor

▼ **TOOL 9-7**
WORKERS' COMPENSATION TERMINOLOGY

Workers' compensation has developed a group of special terms whose meanings differ from normally accepted terminology. WC terminology refers to the employee's diminished ability to compete in the open labor market. The employee's right to indemnity benefits is determined not by the nature of the permanent impairment but by its effects on his or her ability to work.

An entire set of terms has been developed to describe the job-related effects of certain impairments. These terms should be used by the physician in communicating with the insurer.

The following guidelines, listed in ascending order of disability, may be used to describe the job-related effects of pulmonary disease, heart disease, abdominal weakness, and spinal disorders. For lower extremity disabilities, only guidelines g and h are applicable.

(a) *Disability Precluding Very Heavy Lifting.* This means that the employee has lost approximately one-quarter of his or her preinjury lifting capacity. A statement such as "unable to lift 50 pounds" is not meaningful. The total lifting effort, including weight, distance, endurance, frequency, body position, and similar factors, should be considered.

(b) *Disability Precluding Very Heavy Work.* This means that the employee has lost approximately one-quarter of his or her preinjury capacity for performing activities such as bending, pulling, and climbing or other activities involving comparable physical effort.

(c) *Disability Precluding Heavy Lifting.* This means that the employee has lost approximately half of his or her preinjury lifting capacity.

(d) *Disability Precluding Heavy Lifting, Repeated Bending and Stooping.* This means that the employee has lost approximately half his or her preinjury capacity for bending, lifting, and stooping.

(e) *Disability Precluding Heavy Work.* This means that the employee has lost approximately half of his or her preinjury activities, such as bending, stooping, lifting, pushing, pulling, and climbing or other activities involving comparable physical effort.

(f) *Disability Resulting in Limitation to Light Work.* This means that the employee can do work in a standing or walking position with a minimum of physical effort.

(g) *Disability Resulting in Limitation to Semisedentary Work.* This means that the employee can do work approximately one-half the time in a sitting position and approximately one-half the time in a standing position with a minimum of demands for physical effort whether standing, walking, or sitting.

WORKERS' COMPENSATION TERMINOLOGY

(h) *Disability Resulting in Limitation to Sedentary Work.* This means
that the employee can do work predominantly in a sitting position at a
bench, desk, or table with a minimum of demands for physical effort and
with some degree of walking and standing permitted.

Subjective symptoms also can result in permanent disability. Their effects
can best be evaluated by (1) a description of the activity which produces
the disability, (2) the duration of the disability, (3) the activities which are
precluded by and those which can be performed with the disability, and (4)
the means necessary for relief. In addition, the following definitions should
be used to describe pain:

Minimal pain constitutes an annoyance but causes no handicap in the performance of the particular employment activity.

Slight pain can be tolerated but would cause some handicap in the performance of the employment activity precipitating the pain.

Moderate pain can be tolerated but would cause a marked handicap in the
performance of the employment activity precipitating the pain.

Severe pain would preclude the employment activity precipitating the pain.

CHAPTER 10

Private Insurance Plans and Self-Insured Organizations

State of Insurance commissioners on behalf of PC

CHAPTER OVERVIEW

This chapter deals with the nation's oldest insurers for traditional medical insurance plans, Blue Cross and Blue Shield plans. The Blue Cross and Blue Shield organization is not a single company but a network of independently operated companies. Each is free to work with local doctors and hospitals to provide prepaid cost effective healthcare benefits to their subscribers. Although each company is able to operate independently, they are unified by their membership in the Blue Cross and Blue Shield Association. The association requires members to maintain certain standards in order to retain their licensed right to use the Blue Cross and Blue Shield names and symbols.

Although Blue Cross and Blue Shield plans have traditionally been associated with a UCR fee for service method of payment, these insurers are in a period of transition. The method of paying physicians' practices is changing to an RBRVS method of payment. The nonprofit philosophy of this association is also undergoing significant changes in this dynamic healthcare environment. Some Blue Cross and Blue Shield plans have corporations within their organization offering stock to raise capital to aggressively market managed care products.

Aspects of self-insured plans are also covered in this chapter. These are continuing to increase in numbers as employers look to contain healthcare costs.

After reading the material in this chapter and doing the exercises, you will be able to:

■ *Explain the important features of Blue Cross and Blue Shield plans, especially those which affect claims processing*
■ *Cite the factors that have caused Blue Cross and Blue Shield plans to move from a UCR to an RBRVS method of payment*
■ *Evaluate the information on the identification cards issued to all Blue Cross and Blue Shield subscribers*
■ *Describe the Federal Employees Program (FEP)*
■ *Use the coordination of benefits (COB) birthday rule as developed by Blue Cross and Blue Shield plans*
■ *List the services that are covered under the Blue Cross and Blue Shield reciprocity system*
■ *Define self-insured plans and explain their increasing popularity*

THE HISTORY OF BLUE CROSS
AND BLUE SHIELD

The first local "Blues" plan was created in 1929 when an employee of Baylor University in Dallas, Texas, asked a group of schoolteachers to pay $6 a year each into a fund. In return, Baylor University Hospital would provide up to 21 days of care per year for the teachers and their families. The hospital received additional income, and the teachers were assured that their families would have hospital care if the need arose.

Thus, the idea of prepaid healthcare was put into practice. Although the original intent of the plans was to provide hospitalization, the program has been expanded to include outpatient services, other institutional services, and even certain home healthcare services. Over the next several years the concept of prepaid health coverage with specified and limited benefits grew.

The Blue Cross and Blue Shield companies provide two different types of healthcare benefits: Blue Cross covers hospital services, and Blue Shield covers outpatient and physician services. Many of these plans are cooperative enterprises that cover both hospital and physician services, but some are separate entities which may have overlapping benefits.

TIMELINE FOR DEVELOPMENT

The timeline below outlines the development of Blue Cross and Blue Shield from the initial conception:

1929 Baylor University Hospital offers 21 days of prepaid care to 1300 teachers and their families for $6 per year. The hospital receives additional income, and the teachers are covered for the services.

1932 Concept of member hospitals to be used only by subscribers is developed.

1933 The symbol used by the St. Paul, Minnesota, plan is adopted as the symbol for Blue Cross.

1938 American Medical Association's House of Delegates passes a resolution endorsing voluntary health insurance and encouraging physicians to join prepaid healthcare plans.

1939 The Blue Cross symbol is adopted by American Hospital Association, the approving agency for the accreditation of new prepaid hospitalization plans.

1939 California Physicians' Service of Palo Alto, California, is formed. This is the first prepaid plan covering physicians' services.

1939 The Buffalo, New York, Blue Shield designs the logo Blue Shield uses as its trademark.

1948   The Blue Cross Association is organized to coordinate the increasing number of plans in the United States.

1948   A name and symbol are adopted by Associated Medical Care Plans, the approving agency for new plans similar to the California Physicians' Service.

1951   Associated Medical Care Plans changes its name to National Association of Blue Shield Plans.

1977   National Association of Blue Shield Plans joins the Blue Cross Association; one president is responsible for both Blue Cross and Blue Shield.

1986   The boards of directors of the Blue Cross and Blue Shield Association are combined into a separate corporation called the Blue Cross and Blue Shield Association. Local corporations also are merged into one unit. Except for Ohio, Pennsylvania, New York, Missouri, and California, only one corporation exists within state boundaries.

DISTINCTIONS OF BLUE SHIELD

Blue Cross and Blue Shield plans are different from other traditional medical insurance plans in five distinct ways:

1. Blue Cross and Blue Shield are nonprofit organizations. All the money received as premiums is paid out in benefits with the exception of the financial reserves.

2. An individual enters into a contract with a Blue Cross and Blue Shield plan. The individual is known as a *subscriber,* not a policyholder, and is issued a *certificate,* not a policy. This certificate outlines the benefits and responsibilities of the medical plan.

3. Healthcare providers sign contracts with Blue Shield companies that enable Blue Shield to assign a claim to a practice and make direct payments to it. Service benefit contracts are available when a Blue Shield plan offers contracts to physicians so that they can become participating providers. When a physician becomes a participating provider, the medical practice submits all claims for its patients and the physician accepts the approved amount on all covered services as the total payment. Sometimes the plan reimburses 80 percent of the approved amount, and the patient is responsible for the remaining 20 percent; in other cases the payment is 90 percent, and the patient is responsible for the remaining 10 percent. Sometimes the patient is responsible for a fixed amount, or copayment, and the provider is paid 100 percent of the allowed amount minus the copayment.

For example, Dr. Brown is a participating provider with Blue Shield. He submits a claim for $100 for his services. Blue Shield allows $90 and pays $81, or 90 percent. The patient is responsible for 10 percent, or $9. The amount the plan pays is not always evident on the certificate.

There are nonparticipating providers in Blue Cross and Blue Shield plans who have not signed a contract with Blue Shield. These providers can bill their entire fee to the patient. The patient is responsible for filing the claims and receives payment from the plan. In some plans, a non-participating physician can accept assignment on a case-by-case basis.

4. Blue Cross and Blue Shield plans cannot change their rate structure or benefits package without approval from state governing agencies. Other private plans are able to adjust premiums or change benefits without state approval.

5. Blue Cross and Blue Shield plans are available to individuals and small groups that are unable to get benefits elsewhere. There is also transferability of a subscriber from one local plan to another when the subscriber moves from one area into another served by a different Blue Cross and Blue Shield corporation.

BENEFIT OPTIONS

A variety of benefit packages and plan options for subscribers are offered by Blue Cross and Blue Shield companies, ranging from traditional indemnity to managed care such as HMOs and PPOs. Many of these structures require preauthorization and second opinion consultations. The rules for preauthorization and claim reporting vary with the benefit options.

Some of these plans involve subscriber liability, that is, out-of-pocket costs. These programs are also called cost-sharing programs. Patients with this type of coverage are responsible for a deductible, a copayment, or both. Usually the per family deductible is twice the amount of the per person deductible. Medical expenses incurred by individual patients covered under a family contract are applied toward the family deductible. If the contract contains both a deductible and a copayment, the copayment requirements go into effect after the deductible has been met.

Blue Shield Payment for All Services Based on Medical Necessity

The purpose of the Blue Shield medical necessity program is to discourage the use of outmoded or ineffective diagnostic or surgical procedures which add to medical costs without offering equivalent benefits to patients. Since 1991 the Blue Shield Association, along with medical experts from the

American College of Physicians and other medical associations, has reviewed procedures in the different specialties to identify procedures that were considered obsolete or of questionable value in medical practices. The guidelines used were as follows:

- New procedures of unproved value
- Established procedures of questionable usefulness
- Procedures which are redundant when performed in combination with other procedures
- Diagnostic procedures which do not provide additional information when repeatedly performed for the same condition

An initial list of procedures was compiled and is reviewed and updated continuously.

Clinical Guideline for Preventive Care

The Blue Cross and Blue Shield Association also worked with the American College of Physicians to develop clinical guidelines for preventive care for adults with certain diseases. Included in the study were strategies for breast, colon, cervical, and lung cancer; heart disease; hypertension; diabetes; thyroid disease; and osteoporosis. Member plans have also received a recommended model benefit package for pediatric preventive care. This 3-year collaboration allowed the Blue Cross and Blue Shield Association to issue a model benefit package based on these guidelines to its 69 member plans to incorporate screening and preventive medicine coverage into their packages.

CERTIFICATE

A subscriber of a Blue Cross and Blue Shield plan is issued a certificate indicating his or her benefit package and a phone number to call for eligibility, preauthorization, and other information. There are some very important things to look for when a patient presents a Blue Cross and Blue Shield identification card.

Reciprocity Plan

A double-ended arrow with the letter N may appear on the patient's certificate; numerals are printed within the arrow. Figure 10-1 shows the double arrow that may appear on the subscriber's card. The arrow indicates that patient is enrolled in a *reciprocity plan.* Coverage under this plan enables the Blue Shield plan in the state where the services are provided to pay for these covered services, making it unnecessary to file a claim with the subscriber's

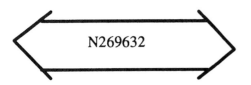

FIGURE 10-1   Certificate for a Blue Shield reciprocity plan.

out-of-state plan. Reciprocity is a cooperative payment arrangement between the various Blue Cross and Blue Shield companies. Certain services are covered only through reciprocity, including the following:

- Surgery
- Technical surgical assistance
- Anesthesia
- Inpatient medical services (medical care visit, intensive care, concurrent care, consultation)
- Days covered under reciprocity (additional days may be approved by patient's home plan)
- Emergency accident care
- Emergency medical care
- Radiation therapy and chemotherapy
- Elective abortion (as allowed by state law)

The following services are not covered by the reciprocity program:

- Maternity care and surgical services related to complications of pregnancy
- Second surgical opinion
- Services not billed on the claim form
- Newborn care, well baby care, and immunizations
- Routine physical exams
- Outpatient radiology, ultrasound, and nuclear medicine and outpatient ECG, EEG, and other electronic diagnostic services except as part of emergency treatment
- Dental, vision, and hearing services
- Dialysis
- Physical, occupational, speech, and respiratory therapy
- Mental health treatment provided in a psychiatric hospital or another special-purpose facility
- Long-term care or rehabilitative psychiatric care, day or night care for psychiatric conditions, and outpatient mental heath treatment
- Skilled nursing caretaker services

The reciprocity program generally makes payments to providers rather than to subscribers. Benefits are paid at the local payment schedule. For an out-of-state subscriber whose card does not contain the double arrow, claims must be filed with the patient's home plan.

Central Certification

Central certification is a program that covers the employees of a company that has offices, plants, and people in several states and whose employees travel a great deal or change location frequently. All personnel, payroll, and health records are maintained in a central location, usually the company headquarters. The identification number on the subscriber's card indicates this type of reciprocity. Claims are filed and paid by the local plan where the treatment was rendered. Central certification can be identified on a subscriber's card by the map of the United States which appears in the upper right-hand portion of the certificate (see Figure 10-2).

Federal Employees Program

The *Federal Employees Program (FEP)* is a governmentwide plan for providing medical insurance for federal employees. The words *Governmentwide Service Benefit Plan* appear on all subscribers' cards. The subscriber identification number begins with the letter R followed by eight digits. Also important to note on the subscriber card is the kind of coverage. FEP 101, 102, 104, 105; FEP 101 (Single); and FEP 102 (Family) are known as *high option* policies, and FEP 104 (Single) and FEP 105 (Family) are known as *low option* policies. The basic coverage is similar, but the copayment for the high option is lower than that for the low option. Figure 10-3 lists the benefits for the FEP.

Both options require that first aid emergency care be obtained within 72 hours. Also, mammograms are a payable benefit, and all prosthetic and orthotic services are subject to medical review.

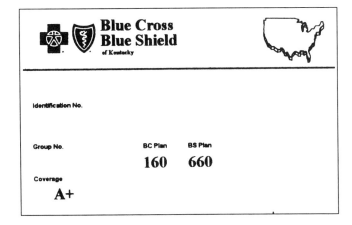

FIGURE 10-2 Blue Cross and Blue Shield certificate with central certification.

Name of Plan		Code	Deductible, $	Maximum Benefits
High option	Single	101	200	No limit except mental health
	Family (2 persons)	102	400	No limit except mental health
Low option	Single	104	250	$500,000 limit plus mental health limit
	Family (2 persons)	105	500	$500,000 limit plus mental health limit

FIGURE 10-3   Benefits of the federal employees program.

COORDINATION OF BENEFITS

Coordination of benefits (COB) is a nonduplication provision that was pioneered by Blue Cross and Blue Shield to prevent overpayment for services. With COB, the primary insurance plan is responsible for paying the full benefit amount allowed by its contract. The secondary insurance plan is responsible for any part of the benefit not covered by the primary plan provided that the benefit is covered by the secondary plan. Blue Cross and Blue Shield also refined COB for dependent children who are covered first by the plan of the parent whose birthday occurs earlier in the calendar year. This is called *the birthday rule.*

For example, Michael and Christine are the parents of Celia, and both have healthcare plans which cover Celia. Michael's birthday is August 8, and Christine's is December 24. Michael's plan is the primary plan for Celia because his birthdate occurs earlier in the year. Any deductible or copayment not covered by Michael's plan should be submitted to Christine's plan for payment.

If the birthdates of the parents are identical, the plan that has been in effect the longest becomes primary for the dependent. Although this rule was initiated by Blue Cross and Blue Shield, many other insurance plans have adopted it for coordination of benefits.

METHODS OF PHYSICIAN PAYMENT

Many Blue Cross and Blue Shield plans determine physician payment using the lowest amounts of *usual, customary, and reasonable (UCR)*. The *usual* is

TABLE 10-1

Sample Procedure Charge Distribution for UCR Calculation

Charge, $	No. Services	Accumulated Percentages (Percentiles)
250	2	2.4
300	2	4.9
325	12	19.5
350	30	56.0
360	20	80.5
370	10	92.6
395	4	97.6
425	2	100

the fee that the provider normally submits for service. The *customary* is the range of fees charged by physicians in similar specialties for the same service in the same geographic area. *Reasonable* refers to the fee the insurance company determines after analyzing the customary and usual data received on Blue Shield claims (see Table 10-1).

The ninetieth percentile of services is $370. In other words, the ninetieth percentile occurs in the $370 charge; up to 80.5 percent of the number of services fall in the range of $360. Between $360 and $370 is the ninetieth percentile. The insurance company has determined that $370 is the reasonable fee for the service.

If a physician submits a bill for $400, unless there are special circumstances, the payment will be $370. If another physician files a claim for $350, that physician will be paid $350. Remember, payment is the *lowest* of the usual, customary, and reasonable rates.

RBRVS

Many Blue Cross and Blue Shield organizations are changing to a Resource Based Relative Value Scale (RBRVS) method of payment. Several Blue Cross and Blue Shield organizations are not changing over to RBRVS immediately and completely. Too many providers would incur significantly reduced payments if a few conversion factors were incorporated as they are in the Medicare fee schedule. The transition to RBRVS began by simply taking the Blue Cross and Blue Shield UCR values for CPT codes (the dollar amounts) and dividing the dollar amounts by the RVUs of the codes as published in the *Federal Register*, thus giving the plan a conversion factor for each CPT code. Common procedures were grouped to facilitate the use of a single conversion factor for the grouping. Some BCBS plans still have as many as 38 different conversion factors. Table 10-2 illustrates the process of conversion from UCR to RBRVS. Conversion factors range from $38.36 to $88.66.

Using the RVU of a specific code and multiplying it by the conversion factor allows a plan to develop a fee for a service. Fees for targeted proce-

TABLE 10-2

Conversion from UCR to RBRVS

Procedure Code	199X UCR, $	+	RBRVS Units	=	199X CF, $
29881	1689		19.81	=	85.13
59400	1530		39.89	=	38.36
59510	1989		44.98	=	44.25
63030	2378		30.75	=	77.35
66984	2400		27.07	=	88.66

dures and those felt to be overpriced can be reduced easily by reducing the conversion factor.

CLAIMS REPORTING

There is a time limit on the reporting of Blue Cross and Blue Shield claims. Claims must be submitted within 6 months to 1 year from the date of service, depending on the contract. Many Blue Cross and Blue Shield companies require the use of their own specific claim forms, but most also accept HCFA 1500 (12/90). It is wise to check with the specific plan about its claims requirements. Universally, the most current CPT-4 and ICD-9-CM codes are used in the completion of claim forms. In addition, all BCBS plans now allow the reporting of claims electronically.

LEAVING THE TRADITIONAL INDEMNITY ROLE

Blue Cross and Blue Shield plans have been dynamic in their approach to healthcare reform. Since the national association has decided that the companies can change their nonprofit tax status under the Blue Cross and Blue Shield trademark, many of them are converting themselves into for-profit companies or establishing for-profit subsidiaries. This involves a variety of changes in managed care options such as HMOs or PPOs; in the future, these plans will no doubt consider integrated delivery systems, and so joint ventures with groups and hospitals may evolve. Blue Cross and Blue Shield companies have an HMO in every single state. HMO-USA, the coordinator of over 70 Blue Shield HMO networks, is very much like the reciprocity plan. Blue Cross and Blue Shield HMO plans can provide care for subscribers who are temporarily away from their home plans. These HMOs are easy to offer employers who have locations in several states because care can be provided to the patients in each state. There is one central HMO that subcontracts with its sister plans in the other states to provide care. All claims are processed by the central HMO, using standardized procedures and claim forms. Employers can use HMOs or other managed care products in each state with the same consistent coverage.

SELF-INSURED PLANS

A majority of the American population has medical insurance coverage and the majority of those covered have private health insurance, generally through their employers. During the 1970s large employer groups first turned to HMOs as an alternative to traditional medical insurance because their premiums were increasing dramatically. Several approaches have been taken by the employers such as cutting benefits and shifting costs to employees with higher deductibles and copayments. Utilization targets with penalties and incentives have also been attempted but this, too, met with little success.

In the early 1980s, as healthcare costs continued to increase, employers needed to find a way to contain the cost of their medical insurance premiums. A number of employers decided to self-insure or become self-funded. *Self-insurance* refers to the assumption of claims risk by an employer, a union, or another group. *Self-funded* refers to the payment of insurance claims from an established bank or trust account.

The most recent efforts have involved contracting directly with providers (doctors and hospitals) for services either on a capitated or a predetermined price basis. *Direct contracting* entails negotiating with providers for medical services on a capitated or predetermined price basis. Employers are finding that they can achieve discounts and specially designed benefits to include preventive care through such direct contracting. This method of health insurance is especially popular in small or midsize cities which are dominated by a few large employer groups.

Employers are also interested in patient care data so that they can monitor cases and make sure that the negotiations for the purchasing of services are effective. The cost effectiveness of medical care is important to the employer. Self-insured plans are exempt from state-mandated benefit laws that require insurance plans to include specific benefits. This exemption was established in the *Employee Retirement Income Security Act of 1974 (ERISA)*. An employee benefit plan is defined under ERISA as "any plan, fund, or program which is established or maintained by an employee organization for the purpose of providing for its participants or beneficiaries medical, surgical, or hospital care or benefits in the event of sickness, accident, disability, death, or unemployment."

Benefits to Employers

Self-insurance offers other advantages to employers. Self-insured plans are also exempt from most premium taxes and are allowed to retain the interest from their cash reserves. Self-insured plans also are not subject to laws governing capital and financial reserve requirements as are state regulated plans. They do not contribute to state risk pools, which finance insurance for high-risk, low-income individuals through state taxes. Employees and various trade unions also felt that these self-insured plans were beneficial to them. In contract negotiations with employers, additional medical benefits were negotiated by the workers. The workers received additional benefits, but those benefits were not taxable for the employees.

Companies with self-insured plans are also not subject to community ratings or experience ratings of their premium rates as with a contracted insurance plan. *Community rating* is a method of establishing premiums by which an insurer's premium is the same for all individuals in a specific geographic area. *Experience rating* is a system that is often used by insurers to set premiums on the basis of the insured's past loss experience with a group. For example, experience rating may be based on service utilization for the employer group. The more services that are provided to the employees, the higher the premium is for the employer. Also included in premiums of traditional plans are costs for uncompensated care, insurance company profits, and cross-subsidies for highly compensated care. Self-insured plans avoid these additional costs.

In addition to containing premium costs, employers are limiting their future liability for retirement benefits. Much cost shifting occurs as those under age 65 are more likely to have to pay premium contributions than are current workers. In the past the employer assumed all the responsibility for medical plans for its retired employees until they reached age 65 and were eligible for Medicare.

Claims Reporting to Self-Insured Employers

Self-insured plans sometimes employ an established insurance plan, HMO, PPO, or a third-party administrator (TPA) to handle the claims and benefits paperwork. The administrator is also responsible for the reports the employer wants for cost containment and quality assurance.

Denials of Claims or Coverage

A medical practice must be aware that in cases of denials of claims and/or coverage, there is some legal recourse with ERISA plans. For the practices having contracts with the self-insured plan, follow the plan's appeal process. If this is not successful, the state insurance regulatory agency may be able to offer assistance. If no contract exists, the *patient* must follow the appeal procedures outlined in the plan document. If the appeal is not successful, encourage the patient to call the state regulatory agency. Some state agencies will take the complaint and then forward it to the Federal Department of Labor. All state agencies and their phone numbers are listed in Tool 12-4. If all else fails, the practice and/or the patient may have to consult a lawyer.

EXERCISING KNOWLEDGE

Fill in the Blanks

1. _____ is the oldest insurer.

2. The first plan was created in _____ at _____ .

3. Five distinctions of Blue Cross and Blue Shield are:

   a. _____

   b. _____

   c. _____

   d. _____

   e. _____

4. Two principles in the guidelines for Blue Cross and Blue Shield medical necessity are: _____ and _____ .

5. The double arrow that sometimes appears on a subscriber's card indicates _____ .

6. Central certification is _____ .

7. Federal employees have a choice of _____ and _____ .

Define These Terms

8. Certificate

9. Birthday Rule

10. FEP

11. High option

12. Self-insured

13. Community rating

14. Experience rating

Applying Concepts

15. Mary Jones was born on June 4 and is covered by Prudential Insurance. Her husband, Michael, was born on December 17 and is insured by Blue Cross and Blue Shield of Illinois. Their daughter Ann was born on March 5. What insurance plan covers Ann?

16. Mr. Brown was seen in the office of Dr. Friedman in Illinois for a second surgical opinion. He was temporarily working in the Chicago branch of his company. Mr. Brown lives in Indiana. To which state Blue Cross and Blue Shield plan does Dr. Friedman bill this visit?

CHAPTER 11

Managed Care Plans

CHAPTER OVERVIEW

When people hear the term managed care plan, *they usually think of an HMO or PPO. However, most physician practices today hold at least one contract with a managed care organization, and it has been predicted that by the turn of the century all medical practices will receive the majority of their payments from managed care plans.*

Managed care involves the application of administrative methods to medical resource monitoring systems designed to control healthcare costs and patients' access to providers and ensure quality of care. The parties in managed care plans are the insurance payer, the provider delivery system, and the patient.

After reading the material in this chapter, doing the exercises, and using the end-of-chapter tools, you will be able to:

■ *Explain the four kinds of HMOs: staff model, group model, independent physician association, and network model*
■ *Articulate the differences between HMOs and PPOs*
■ *Define the following terms:*
 — *Exclusive provider organization (EPO)*
 — *Triple option plan (TOP)*
 — *Vertically integrated plan (VIP)*
 — *Group practice without walls (GPWW)*
 — *Point of service (POS) product*
 — *Physician hospital organization (PHO)*
■ *Evaluate the potential impact of a managed care plan on a physician practice by assessing the potential growth of the plan, the long-range goals of the practice, and the projected payment rates of the plan*
■ *Implement a step-by-step procedure for analyzing a hypothetical contract*
■ *Identify the kinds of contract clauses that are sources of potential difficulty for a practice*

HOW MANAGED CARE PLANS BECAME IMPORTANT

In the 1970s the cost of healthcare began to rise. Healthcare costs increased more rapidly than did the costs of other goods and services which consumers buy. Accordingly, premiums for medical insurance also rose. Since many employers purchase medical insurance for their employees, they became concerned. As we discussed in Chapter 10, employers began channeling their employees into HMOs. HMOs were the first alternative delivery system and the first to use capitation. HMOs provide some stabilization in premium rates for employers. They also provide equal or better benefits for employees. Once large and powerful employers began to promote an alternative delivery system, they sparked competition within the healthcare industry.

Some experts say that the traditional healthcare delivery system has been moving toward an alternative delivery system since the 1980s, when competition in healthcare began. At that time there were some creative plans, physicians, and hospitals willing to compete by accepting the price controls and cost containment demands of the employers. The government also began exploring managed care and competition to control its rising medical insurance costs. Competition has continued to increase, producing other types of managed care organizations, including PPOs, IPAs, and PHOs. Competition has produced a wide variety of organizations. As a result, the healthcare delivery system is reforming itself to meet the demands of those who fund medical insurance.

Competition has slowed the increases in healthcare costs, but major funders still want consistent and proven controls for their premium dollars. Medical insurance premiums also remain unaffordable for many consumers. Several factors have been cited as contributing to unaffordable medical insurance costs, including the following:

- *Medical inflation* (percentage of increase in the medical component of consumer prices)
- *Cost shifting* (billing of higher rates to better-paying insurance plans from money-losing patient categories, such as Medicare, Medicaid, and uncompensated care)
- *Utilization* (rate of use of medical services)

There is no doubt that any future healthcare delivery system should attempt to monitor and control all these factors. For now, the use of managed care in an alternative delivery system offers the best method of control. Managed care uses administrative methods to assure the appropriate use of healthcare dollars. The goal of managed care is to provide quality medical care at an affordable cost.

METHODS FOR CONTROLLING HEALTHCARE COSTS

Managed care plans use several methods to assure the appropriate use of healthcare dollars. A managed care plan relies on three administrative methods to control costs. There are theories about why each method works. Table 11-1 shows these methods and theories.

TABLE 11-1
Methods and Theories of Managed Care Plans

Method	Theory
1. Panels of providers (mainly physicians and hospitals) have passed a credentialing process and signed a contract to deliver care to an enrolled population. Providers accept some risk for the loss of funds.	Providers will work together to control healthcare costs.
2. Out-of-pocket costs for patients if they do not use the panel of providers.	Patients will not spend extra dollars for the same services they could receive from contracted providers.
3. Medical resource monitoring through utilization management and quality improvement programs.	The best-quality care is also the most cost-efficient care when usage reports are shared and providers are measured according to standards.

Administrative methods 1 and 3 directly control healthcare costs, and method 2 indirectly controls healthcare costs with financial incentives for patients to use providers in the panel, restricting their access to nonparticipating providers.

Definition of Managed Care

Managed care is the application of administrative methods to controlling healthcare costs and patients' access to providers. Managed care's administrative methods integrate the financing and delivery of medical care for enrollees. They combine an insurance payer with medical resource monitoring and a provider delivery system.

THE ALPHABET SOUP OF MANAGED CARE

Managed care terminology is full of abbreviations and acronyms. The managed care industry has been called an alphabet soup because there are so many abbreviations representing the various organizations. Medical office personnel who can recognize abbreviations and know what the letters mean work well with managed care plans as well as enjoying more job satisfaction.

Major abbreviations and their meaning in the alphabet soup include the following:

ADS (alternative delivery system): a managed care plan which finances and delivers cost-efficient care without compromising the quality of medical care for its enrollees.

ASO (administrative services only), also called a *TPA* (third-party administrator): an organization which contracts with self-insured employers and other insurance mechanisms to provide administrative methods such as provider contracting, utilization controls, enrollment services, and claims processing. ASO/TPAs provide utilization reports outlining the use of medical resources for their clients.

HMO (health maintenance organization): briefly described in Chapter 1, an HMO is an organization licensed by the state which is required to provide certain basic benefits and preventive medical care for a defined population for a fixed monthly payment. An HMO has an obligation to its *members* (enrollees) to provide the medical care associated with prepaid benefits. For this reason, HMOs must hire or contract with physicians to deliver this care. HMOs must also build, buy, or contract with hospitals for hospital care. HMOs call these hired or contracted physicians, hospitals, and other types of medical professionals *participating providers.* Participating providers are usually at risk for covering the financing of benefits which have been prepaid by members. Many HMOs exclude risk taking from hospital, pharmacy, and other types of providers, placing only physician providers at risk along with themselves as an insurance mechanism. They establish *withhold accounts* and risk pools during the contracting process. In *risk pools,* HMOs contribute money to the pool from which they pay claims. Pools are established with separate budgets for hospital, physician, pharmacy, and other services. At the end of a designated time period, HMOs may pay physicians some or all of the extra money left in the pools after all the medical claims for the period have been paid.

Several HMOs use incentive methods for distributing the money remaining in risk pools or withhold accounts. They perform an assessment and issue a report card. A *report card* totals a physician's compliance with certain rules of the HMO, such as the following:

—Sending specimens to designated laboratories

—Number of hours the practice is open

—Number of prescriptions written from a drug formulary

—Audit of medical records

—Efficient use of medical resources

—Patient satisfaction survey results

Some HMOs have no risk for any physician or provider but offer payment at a discounted rate. Others may employ physicians, giving them a salaried contract. There are four types of HMOs. The type of HMO is based on how the physicians are organized and paid.

Types of HMOs

The four types of HMOs differ in several ways.

1. *Staff model.* Participating physicians are salaried employees of the HMO. These salaried physicians provide all the medical care to the HMO's members.
2. *Group model.* Participating physicians are members of an independent multispecialty group practice who have contracted with the HMO to deliver services to its members. The HMO may contract to pay the group on a fee for service basis or negotiate capitation. Referrals and consultations to nonparticipating physicians are usually paid out of the capitation rate for the group unless a case has been preauthorized.
3. *Independent practice association.* Physician services for HMO members are arranged for by contracting either directly with physicians or through a formally organized physician association. These formally organized associations, which are known as independent practice associations (*IPAs*), negotiate contracts with managed care plans for member physicians. Physician members hold formal contracts with IPAs. IPAs can negotiate capitation rates with HMOs and then arrange for payment of their physicians by either fee for service or capitation. IPA-type HMOs commonly have large panels of participating physicians. Patients are attracted to these large panels because of easy access and a wider choice of physicians, which may include their current physicians.
4. *Network model.* Physician services are arranged for HMO members by contracting with two or more independent multispecialty group practices. Each group receives capitation payments from the HMO for members who designate a group as their primary source for medical care.

HMOs offer the most comprehensive benefits but have very strict cost controls. They are known for applying a lock-in. A *lock-in* is a system in which members can receive services only from participating physicians. If members receive care from a nonparticipating provider, no benefits are paid; thus, members are locked into the panel. HMOs are also known for pioneering the gatekeeper concept. A *gatekeeper* is a primary care physician (PCP) who is responsible for coordinating and authorizing the services of specialists. In this manner, the gatekeeper PCP is the case manager. A member must always go to the gatekeeper to have the gate opened to other participating providers. This is known as a referral, which was discussed in Chapter 2. Remember from that chapter the importance of noting the name of the gatekeeper PCP which appears on many HMO members' ID cards. A specialty practice should not treat a patient in nonemergency situations unless the referral has been authorized by the gatekeeper PCP.

Let us further discuss PPOs, which were introduced in Chapter 1.

A *PPO (preferred provider organization)* is an organization which forms panels of physicians, hospitals, and other healthcare providers to deliver care to an eligible population. An *eligible population* is enrolled, but it is not a defined population as with an HMO because the enrollees are not locked in to receiving care from the panel. If the eligible population of a PPO uses a PPO participating provider, maximum benefits and minimum out-of-pocket costs occur. When enrollees see nonparticipating providers, there is generally a limit for out-of-pocket costs, such as $1000 per individual or $3000 per family per calendar year. Nonparticipating providers can collect from the patient all their fees beyond the PPO allowable fee.

As competition increased in healthcare, independent HMOs and PPOs became competitors. To accommodate clients' demands, they now offer similar benefit packages and products, making it difficult to distinguish an HMO from a PPO. As PPOs grew in the 1980s, taking over more of the HMO market share, HMOs wanted to remain competitive and appeal to employer groups and patients. Thus, HMOs invented the POS product option for their members.

A *POS* is a *point of service* product. HMO members enrolled in a POS product can decide at the point of seeking a medical service to use a nonparticipating provider (a physician or hospital that is not in the panel). When an HMO member seeks the services of a nonparticipating provider, the benefits are reduced. The member must pay out-of-pocket costs that usually amount to 20 to 30 percent of the HMO's allowable fee for the service. Until the invention of the POS, HMOs always adhered to the lock-in concept.

PPOs are becoming more like HMOs in retaliation. As HMOs grew in the 1980s, PPOs wanted to appeal more to self-insured employers and other groups desiring more managed care. PPOs invented the EPO.

An *EPO* is an *exclusive provider organization*. If a PPO enrollee has chosen the EPO product option, that enrollee is locked in to using a selected panel of PPO providers. If the enrollee strays from the panel (except with an emergency or when there is preauthorization), none of the benefits are payable and the patient is liable for the entire amount.

There are some other trends in product offerings among HMOs and PPOs. In an effort to compete with indemnity insurance plans and offer one-stop shopping for large employer groups and the government, some HMOs and PPOs are offering triple option plans.

A *TOP* is a *triple option plan*. This type of organization offers at least three health insurance product options:

1. HMO (with a lock-in of members, who must seek care from participating providers or benefits will not be paid)
2. PPO (with no lock-in of enrollees, in which case patients can seek care from nonparticipating providers but only 70 to 80 percent of covered benefits are paid)
3. Indemnity benefit plan (no lock-in, but coverage is provided for illness and injury)

Most of the national plans which began as indemnity benefit plans are now TOPs, offering HMO and PPO product options. Examples of TOPs include Blue Cross and Blue Shield, Prudential, and Aetna. Since medical insurance plans are still changing, medical office personnel need to be aware that the indemnity products of a TOPs may include physician contracts. Physicians may sign contracts with a managed indemnity plan of a national insurance company. *Managed indemnity plans* are plans that have indemnity benefits but also have a contract with physicians to accept a maximum allowable fee (MAF) for any patient enrolled in any of their plans even if the doctor does not participate in the organization's HMO or PPO products. Office staff who do the posting must be aware of these umbrella contracts because the difference between the MAF and the doctor's charge should be written off the patient's account. A variety of spinoff products have been applied by many insurance and managed care plans. During contract evaluation, these variations should be learned.

By now you are probably aware of how managed care plans have changed healthcare delivery. Healthcare delivery is always in the process of being refined. Continuous change is required to offer the best possible benefit packages for consumers at an affordable cost. Some experts say that the only thing constant in working with insurance and managed care plans is change. The plans of today are changing dramatically to keep up with demands for healthcare reform.

Providers today are changing to keep up with the demands of healthcare reform and managed care plans. Physicians and hospitals are reorganizing to streamline operations and contain costs. They are reorganizing themselves and merging into larger groups to compete for contracts to deliver healthcare. Small physician practices are merging to form larger group practices. Hospitals are integrating with physicians to deliver healthcare as a group. As these changes occur, the alphabet soup list of options grows longer. There are many abbreviations associated with reorganization and mergers of providers. We shall describe major acronyms and terms below. You may find others used in your local community. If that is the case, try to relate them to one of the major abbreviations and terms listed here. Organizations and plans like to invent their own abbreviations, but their basic definitions are the same.

> *Managed competition* or *managed cooperation* This is the model for healthcare reform. It is a form of managed care which allows groups of providers alone or together with insurers to submit bids and negotiate payment, often in the form of capitation, for delivering care to a population.
>
> *PHO* (*physician hospital organization*) Physicians and hospitals form a relationship for contracting with managed care organizations. Hospitals send contracts to physicians on their staffs which must be evaluated by the individual practice. Often physicians invest in the

development of a PHO, which may offer MSO services. Forming a PHO is often the first phase in the reorganization of providers.

MSO (management services organization)   This is a turnkey operation for managing the business side of a medical practice. Business staff personnel manage the operation as one large group practice, providing claim reporting and billing, the purchase of supplies, personnel administration, the pension plan, and malpractice insurance for the physicians. If the MSO has multiple practice locations, it is known as a *group practice without walls (GPWW)*. A GPWW involves a group of physicians who have a joint venture arrangement for administering the business side of their practices. The doctors practice the clinical side of medicine (evaluate and manage patients) at their separate offices. There are usually multiple office sites for a GPWW. An important feature of a GPWW is that all the physicians share the assets and risks in the business. The formation of MSOs and GPWWs is another phase in the reorganization of providers.

VIP (vertically integrated plan)   A VIP is a legal and formally integrated group of employed providers (hospitals, physicians, nursing homes, home health agencies, pharmacies, and others) working with a common vision and goal. The providers deliver services jointly to a defined population through a seamless continuum of preventive and primary care, inpatient and outpatient hospital care, long-term care, and all the other needed services. A VIP is paid on a capitation basis by the government and/or insurance and managed care plans. Plans may be integrated with the VIP. A VIP can be initiated by plans, hospitals, physicians, or other healthcare entities. VIPs are also known as integrated service networks (ISNs). The VIP is the last phase in the reorganization of healthcare providers.

Since there are many organizations in various phases of change, reorganization, and merger, a physician practice receives many contracts. Insurance and managed care plans are deleting old contracts, decreasing the size of their panels, and recontracting. Contracts must be evaluated to determine whether it is a good business decision to sign them. Most medical practices take a team approach to contract evaluation. Key office personnel are often asked to participate in contract evaluation as they must comply with the payment schedules and other rules contained in the contract. Their opinions are needed regarding how current operations will be affected if the contract is signed. Issues include the following:

- Claim submission
- Methods and levels of payment
- Referrals and authorizations
- Use of restricted laboratory or x-ray facilities
- Preparation for on-site evaluation by a plan's staff including medical records

- Completion of contract application papers and listing of physician qualifications
- Other increased paperwork

When a medical practice contracts with a managed care organization, it will be dealing with that organization for a long time. It is much easier to reject a contract initially, not entering into a relationship, than it is to later sever a contract with a managed care plan and the patients enrolled in that plan. In the past, many physician practices were harmed financially because they entered into contractual relationships without properly reviewing the contract for payment and risk clauses. Managed care organizations have failed and can fail again, leaving a practice with unpaid claims. It is important to properly review the contract clauses and ask questions about the structure of the organization and the sponsoring entity. Plans are initiated by many organizations (see Figure 11-1).

In the figure there are national insurance companies, physicians, hospitals, employer groups, labor unions, and small business associations, to name a few. It is important to know who and what you will be working with. Questions that should be asked include the following:

What type of plan are you?
Who sponsors or owns you?
What is your target market for patients?
How much and how do you pay doctors?
How can we work together?

The competitive environment of healthcare reform has created a climate in which bad contracts and harmful relationships can occur. A medical practice cannot be too cautious in evaluating a managed care contract. Once a contract is signed, it becomes a document which is legally binding.

Many employees involved in the physician payment process report, "All new managed care contracts end up on my desk." As an employee of a medical practice, the initial review and certainly the payment process aspect of a new contract may become your responsibility. Your job may be to gather behind the scenes information to help the physician and office manager decide whether to accept or reject the contract.

MANAGED CARE CONTRACTS: AN OVERVIEW

Doctors and hospitals often think that there are only disadvantages in contracting with managed care organizations and that the managed care plan gets all the advantages. However, contracts are two-way agreements which

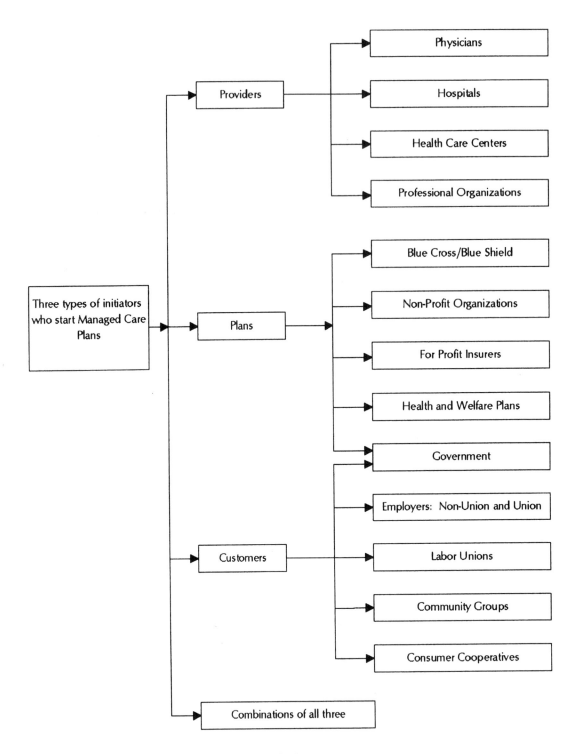

FIGURE 11-1 Typical initiators of managed care organizations.

hold advantages and disadvantages for both parties. The key is to negotiate a contract in which both parties have advantages and disadvantages which blend into an overall "win-win" situation for everyone.

Some advantages and disadvantages for all parties involved in managed care contracting are listed in Table 11-2.

TABLE 11-2

Advantages and Disadvantages of Managed Care Contracting

	Advantages	**Disadvantages**
Patient	Cost reduction	Less attention
	Better benefits	Restricted use of providers
		General confusion
Managed care plan	Fixed rates	Contract demands
	Cost reduction	Adverse member reactions
	Easy claims payment	Multiple contract rates
	Small number of providers	
Hospital	Possible volume increase	Reduced fees
	Prompt payment	Contract demands
		Complex billing
Physician	Possible volume increase	Reduced fees
	Prompt payment	Contract demands
	Maintaining current patients	Complex billing
		Upsets patient relations
		Upsets referral patterns

Negotiating contracts with managed care organizations which are advantageous for medical practices is possible if the principles of good negotiation are used. These principles include the following:

1. Maintaining a positive philosophy
2. Being prepared for negotiations
3. Developing a formal contract evaluation list of contract points to be clarified and points to be negotiated

Tool 11-1 is provided for this purpose.

Some managed care contracts have deadline dates for their return. There may be limitations on the time a practice team can spend evaluating a managed care contract. Review the cover letter accompanying the contract for any deadline dates. Log in the date when the contract was received by the practice and, if applicable, the deadline date for returning it (see Tool 11-2). Next, review all informational materials. Be prepared to call plan representatives with your questions. Some organizations send one contract for a group practice signature, while others require each physician to sign an individual contract. Ask if all physicians in the practice must join or if participation is optional. Plan representatives are very helpful in providing this type of information. It is best to gather all the information before the team spends time reviewing the contract. The team may not have to spend a lot of time evaluating the contract if information gathered before the contract review reveals that the practice and the organization are not compatible and that there will be no advantages for the practice in signing the contract.

The team begins by taking three steps before actually evaluating the wording in the contract:

1. Research the potential growth of the managed care organization and its potential impact on the practice. Tool 11-3 can be used as a guide when a plan's representatives are phoned. Try to find out about the marketing plans of the organization. Determine whether this organization will dominate the area. Ask what types of patients will enroll. Try to determine if they are a younger or older population; young families and older retired adults require many services.

2. Consider the doctors' long-range goals for the practice. How big does the practice want to be, and how many hours do the physicians want to work? Do the physicians want to use the participating hospitals associated with the plan? If the participating hospitals are not the ones the physicians frequently use, extra time will have to be allotted. Within the long-range goals of the practice, consider capacity limits. Is there room for expansion to accommodate more patients? If the practice is operating at full capacity, its goal may be to maintain its existing patients. Ask the managed care plan if the contract can specify treatment of existing patients only. An *existing patients only* provision allows a practice to keep the established patients who may join the plan. If the practice is not at full capacity, there is an opportunity to expand. The practice has the advantage of making the current staff more productive and will be able to afford to accept a reduced fee for service payment or do well under a capitation rate. Tool 11-4 can help the team determine the capacity of the practice. If everything seem favorable for entering into a relationship with this organization, the next step is to evaluate the payment rates. This is where the input of office posting and billing staff is especially important.

3. Analyze payment rates to see whether they are adequate to accommodate the needs of the practice. In Chapter 3 we discussed methods of payment. The method of payment should be outlined in every contract. If the fee for service method is offered, payment could be lower. Some contracts include maximum allowable fees (MAFs) and must include capitation rates when this method of payment is offered.

If a managed care organization offers payment under a fee for service method and does not include MAFs for the common procedures, ask the plan representative to tell you the MAFs for the top 20 CPT codes used by the practice. Since these codes usually account for 80 percent of a practice's income, this will give you some idea of whether the practice can make a profit with the offered payment amounts. Expect at least a 20 percent reduction in the fees for most CPT codes compared with the actual charges of the practice. A 20 percent reduction may not be the case in every practice, especially with fees for E&M codes. However, if a plan mandates more than a 20 percent reduction, speak to the doctor or office manager about continuing the contract review. The practice may lose money on treating these patients and may not be able to offset the losses with other types of paying patients.

Determining whether fee for service rates are profitable is a complex process that involves a determination of the total expenses for the practice of providing the 20 most frequently used CPT codes. Both fixed and variable costs (total expenses) are considered in analyzing fee for service rates. Fixed costs are costs which have to be paid regardless of the volume of patients seen in the office, such as rent, salaries, and malpractice premiums. Fixed costs do not change no matter how many patients are seen. Variable costs do change with the volume of patients. Examples of variable costs are the costs associated with purchasing supplies, extra equipment, and maintenance. Variable costs are the true costs of providing a service once the fixed expenses have been paid. The practice makes a profit only after the fixed and variable costs have been paid. If a practice is fairly certain it has enough patients of all payment types to meet its fixed costs, the true costs for treating additional patients become the variable costs. It is then a matter of determining the profits per CPT code for those top 20 income-producing procedures. Table 11-3 shows how a practice can calculate the profit margin by CPT code after deducting any withholds and variable costs. Never count on a withhold being returned or being a part of the profit margin. Withhold amounts are treated as writeoffs from the patient's account but are debited to an account in the managed care organization's name in case it returns some of that money.

Profit margin = managed care fee minus withhold minus variable costs

The differences between columns 2 and 3 are calculated and listed in column 4. Columns 5 and 6 are subtracted from column 3 to determine the profit margin for each CPT code. If there is no withhold in the contract, column 5 is not completed. If the practice has never performed a cost accounting for variable costs by CPT code, the team should estimate and work toward deve-

TABLE 11-3

Profit Margin by CPT Code after Fixed Costs Are Met

CPT Code	Our Charge	Managed Care Fee	Writeoff	Withhold	Variable Cost	Profit Margin
99205	120.00	90.00	30.00	18.00	4.00	68.00
99213	38.00	30.00	8.00	7.60	3.00	19.40
58120	500.00	420.00	80.00	84.00	0.00	336.00
Column 1	Column 2	Column 3	Column 4	Column 5	Column 6	Column 7

loping some type of variable cost accounting system for frequently used CPT codes.

Don't panic. You are not completely responsible for calculating variable costs or determining whether the practice is meeting its fixed expenses with its current payer mix. This is the job of the practice accountant, who should be on the contract evaluation team. However, you may be asked to complete columns 1 through 3 and compare the managed care fees with the fees received from other major payers.

If the managed care organization uses capitation as its method of payment, the practice needs to know how much it costs to provide the CPT codes and services included in the capitation rate per patient. Both fixed and variable costs are considered in a capitation rate analysis. Population demographics and the age and gender of the current patients in the practice are helpful in determining total expenses per patient. Tool 11-5 can be shared with the accountant, who will be primarily responsible for organizing these statistics. An actuary may be contacted at this point because a capitation rate analysis is very complex. Some of the numbers needed in the patient profile analysis may not be readily available. If the practice has a computer, there are statistics that have been entered in the computer. For example, in Tool 11-5, item 10 asks for a percentage of patients by their top 10 employer groups. The employers of patients are entered in the computer for insurance purposes. Some software packages have the capability of using the employer-patient data to generate a report giving the number of patients in each patient employer group, and this data can be used to create a top-10 list. If not, office staff may be asked to list the most frequent patient employer groups from memory. This listing is a starting point to determine whether the targeted employer groups of the managed care organization are some of the employer groups of the current patients.

Item 11 in Tool 11-5 asks for the percentage of payment by type of insurance plan. The practice should have a readily available report for these statistics. With knowledge of the major sources of payment, the practice evaluation team can strive to keep a balanced mix of payers.

While no single report or analysis will give the evaluation team and physicians enough information to accept or reject a contract, the more information a practice has in making this decision, the better the decision will be.

CONTRACT EVALUATION

Once the three steps listed above have been completed and a relationship with the managed care organization appears favorable, the actual evaluation of the contract document begins. The team then uses the contract evaluation list (Tool 11-1). This list has the headings "Give Points" in the right column and "Contract Breakers" in the left column. Under "Give Points," the team documents the issues in a contract which it does not especially like but which the practice can live with if they are explained. When give points are clarified by the plan's representative, they can be accommodated by the practice. This column is also used to record issues which were not addressed in the contract and need clarification, for example, whether this is a gatekeeper plan. Give points are the opposite of contract breakers.

The "Contract Breakers" column is used to document clauses in the contract which the practice will not accept unless they are changed. These clauses call for negotiation with the plan's representative and will break the contract evaluation process if their wording is not modified. The evaluation process will reject the contract if there is a contract breaker.

Contract Breakers

While contract breakers are different for each practice, certain common and dangerous contract clauses should be contract breakers for any practice. Physicians should never sign a provider contract which has a cross-indemnification hold harmless clause. A *cross-indemnification hold harmless clause* obligates physicians to assume full responsibility for themselves and the managed care organization if a malpractice case arises. For example, if physicians are sued by patients and suits are also filed against the managed care organization, this indemnification clause will force the physician to reimburse the managed care organization for any costs connected with those suits. The specific wording of a cross-indemnification hold harmless clause may be as follows: "Provider agrees to indemnify XYZ managed care organization from any and all liability, claim, or expense of any kind, including court costs and lawyer fees, which result from negligent acts or omissions by Provider or employees of Provider regarding the duties and obligations of Provider under this contract." Medical malpractice insurers have concerns when physicians indemnify other parties from liability in malpractice suits. When these clauses are seen, have the malpractice insurer for the practice review them. Many malpractice insurers will not cover the physicians in a suit if these types of clauses exist in an executed contract. Malpractice insurers can make suggestions for modifications of the wording which will be acceptable to them so that they can insure the practice. For example, the following clause would not be harmful: "Each party agrees that it shall not be responsible for any liability, loss, damage, or expenses caused by acts of the other party." If the malpractice insurer has a concern, put this item on the negotiation list in the "Contract Breakers" column. Most managed care organizations are willing to negotiate this clause.

Physicians should also avoid exclusivity clauses. *Exclusivity clauses* are clauses which require the physician to work exclusively for the managed care organization, treating only its patients and giving up all other current patients. These clauses also require the physician to sign a participating provider contract only with this managed care organization. The physician will not be free to sign up with any other managed care organization. These types of clauses may be against federal or state antitrust laws unless the physician is becoming an employee of the managed care organization. Unless this is the case, the team should refer this clause to a lawyer and place it in the "Contract Breakers" column.

Physicians should never sign a contract which implies that payment rates are subject to a "favored nation" clause. This clause obligates the practice to report to the managed care organization whenever the physician accepts a lesser rate from another contracting managed care plan either under fee for service or capitation payment rates. The plan with the favored nation clause has the right to lower its payment rate to match the rate paid by the lowest paying contracting plan. Whenever the team sees a clause like this one, it should place it in the "Contract Breakers" column to be negotiated out of the contract. It can be a financial and administrative burden to keep track of individual rates, especially if the physician holds multiple contracts with many different plans.

Give Points

While give points may be different for every practice, certain clauses should always be questioned. If the team does not see specific clauses referencing these subjects, they should be placed in the "Give Points" column on the contract negotiation list to possibly be added to the contract language. The plan's representative should be asked to clarify these issues and may be able to send additional policies of the organization for review so that the team knows how the organization deals with these subjects. Here are a few examples.

- The annual provision for payment negotiations. There must be a way for physicians to have payment rates increased each year by at least the normal rate of inflation. This is extremely important because it is common to see evergreen clauses in contracts. *Evergreen clauses* state that the contract is renewable each year unless it is discontinued by either party. Think about it. If there are no provisions for annual fee raises and the contracts are evergreen, the initially accepted rate in the first year of the contract, such as a reduced fee for service rate of 20 percent, becomes a 40 percent reduction after 5 years because of the normal rate of inflation. As an example, pretend 5 years has passed with an inflation rate of 4 percent each year; 4% × 5 years = 20%. Add this to the first year's 20 percent reduction, and the payment reduction has grown to 40 percent.
- A specified level of coverage for malpractice insurance which cannot be changed in the middle of the contract year. The practice wants to be able to budget malpractice premium payments and does not want them to increase in midyear.

- A significant financial penalty if a patient uses the services of a non-participating physician. A 10 percent penalty is not enough. Managed care contracts should contain at least a 20 percent benefit reduction for patients who go outside the participating panel to receive care. A significant incentive for patients must be present to keep patients in the panel and promote increased volume for physicians who have signed a contract to gain or maintain these patients.

- A written physician appeal mechanism with due process. There must be a fair process with a few levels within the managed care organization for appealing decisions in a timely and organized manner. Ask to see the appeal policy, especially the policy for MAFs.

- Termination of the contract without cause by either party. Since there are so many organizations in varying stages of development, terminating without a reason is a legal way for physicians to end bad relationships quickly. Since these clauses work for both parties, the managed care organization can immediately cancel a physician contract without cause. These clauses are used as an escape mechanism for the managed care organization to shrink its panel of providers or cancel provider contracts if it becomes financially insolvent. The organization will then have no obligation to pay any money due after the date of termination, realizing that physicians will not abandon their patients. Remember that this clause works both ways. The evaluation team should ask the plan's representative if the clause can be modified to give the practice 3 or 4 months' notice if the organization terminates the contract without cause. This will give the practice time to end relationships with patients.

A formal legal contract contains a lot of words. Each word should be read so that nobody overlooks other contract breakers and give points. Each practice is different and has a different method of operation and a different philosophy. What one practice accepts and what others reject in a contract are very different. While a practice may obtain the opinions of lawyers, consultants, and accountants, only the physicians in the practice and the members of a contract evaluation team can decide whether they are willing to work with the rules of a specific managed care organization.

As each contract is read, payment rules may be described. These rules especially concern the office staff, who must follow them in the physician payment process. Tool 11-6 ends with a list of instructions. List specific payment rules on this chart while you read the contract. The chart helps organize the rules of each managed care organization and can be used in discussions by the team. Tools 11-1 and 11-6 should be used concurrently in reading a managed care contract. They should be readily accessible to jot down specific issues. There are 30 other issues to consider when reading a managed care contract.

Thirty Administrative Issues

There are 30 administrative issues in every managed care contract which the practice evaluation team should cover when reading a contract. If an issue appears which will break the contract evaluation process, list it as a contract breaker on Tool 11-1. If any of these issues are not found in the contract, list them as give points on Tool 11-1.

We have grouped these 30 issues into technical issues, payment issues, and rules regarding medical resource monitoring. Under each issue, there is an explanation.

Technical Issues

1. All parties to the contract must be clearly identified by name.

    Explanation: It is not a legal contract between responsible parties unless those parties are named. The team fills in the name of each doctor in the practice on each individual contract or fills in the name of the practice corporation if it is permitted to sign one contract for all the physicians in the practice.

2. There should be a clause stating that the contract is subject to state law if the plan is regulated by the insurance commissioner in the state.

    Explanation: The standard language in provider contracts must be approved by the department of insurance if it is regulated by state law, either before or after the contract is signed. There are standard contract clauses the state requires in provider contracts, and these clauses vary. Examples would be clauses pertaining to patient confidentiality and patient rights.

3. Unilateral changes in terms should not be permitted without prior written notice to the physician.

    Explanation: This clause is fairly standard in any legal contract. If changes are made by either party, they must be initialed by the other party or an addendum must be signed by both parties.

4. Physician termination rights must be outlined as a separate contract clause.

    Explanation: There has to be a legal mechanism to end any relationship. Most contracts require 30 to 60 days' notice from a provider terminating a contract. Make sure the termination rights address who will notify the patients in the event of termination. Mailing notification letters to patients could be costly for the practice.

5. There should be language outlining the procedure for performing services after the contract has been terminated.

    Explanation: Some contracts specify that the physician must treat patients until they can be transferred to another physician. If a physician has a unique specialty, such as being the only oncologist in town, there may be no other qualified physician to whom to transfer patients.

6. Articles of incorporation, bylaws, physician administrative manuals, and other documents by which the physician will be bound are mentioned in the contract as being available for review.

Explanation: It is only fair to allow the other party to review all rules before signing a contract. Hidden rules which cannot be shared promote an unhealthy relationship.

7. Names of marketing materials which the organization can use the physician's name in advertising should be listed.

    Explanation: All plans want to use the physician's name on a marketing list and patient directory, but any additional use should be authorized by the practice.

8. If physicians are required to pay annual dues, initiation fees, or marketing fees, the amount should be specified in the contract.

    Explanation: The amounts and payment dates should be listed in the contract so that they cannot easily be changed upward.

9. If physicians are required to accept all patients who are referred to them, the contract should state this requirement.

    Explanation: If the contract does not state this, ask the plan's representative if a practice can close its acceptance of new patients. If so, ask how many days' notice to give and whether the practice must be closed to all new patients from other insurance plans.

10. Methods by which the practice can identify enrolled patients should be mentioned.

    Explanation: It is important not only to ask to see the plan ID card but also to ask whether the different benefit plan numbers or benefit plans can be easily distinguished. Just because a patient is a member of XYZ HMO does not mean that all members of XYZ HMO have the same benefit package.

11. If all doctors associated with the practice must join the organization, the contract should state this when it addresses patient coverage by backup physicians.

    Explanation: Plans have different rules on this issue. Ask the organization if all the doctors associated with the practice must join and how it treats new physician associates and semiretired physicians.

12. If the physicians must be available to the patients 24 hours a day, a clause should state this.

    Explanation: If a nonparticipating physician provides coverage, ask how this will be handled.

13. Arbitration procedures must be listed in the contract.

    Explanation: This clause protects both parties and assures settlement of a dispute by a fair party. When healthcare and money are mixed, emotions go out of control. Binding arbitration is best with an objective arbitrator hired by both parties as the last recourse for an appeal.

Payment Issues

14. The method or methods of payment must be specified in the contract. If the contract pays on a capitation basis, all CPT codes or a list of all

services either included or excluded in the capitation rate must be in the contract. A level of stop loss must be specified. *Stop loss* is the maximum amount of money that can be lost by the practice beyond the capitation payment per patient. Stop loss is a financial endpoint for those occasional catastrophic patients. Ideally, stop loss should be no greater than $10,000 cumulative per patient per contract year. A lesser amount may be negotiated, depending on the procedures included in the capitation rate. If the contract pays on a fee for service basis, the method of calculating the MAF should be described.

Explanation: The rationale by which the organization determines payment should be analyzed to make sure it is fair. Very detailed explanations are required in regard to capitation rates because plans can base these rates on many factors, including the age and sex of patients.

15. Withhold amounts, types of risk pools (hospital, referral, primary care, ancillary services), and financial incentives should be thoroughly explained. Details on how amounts are determined and who makes the decision to distribute any remaining funds to physicians should be present.

Explanation: Usually these decisions are made by the board of trustees and the management. The board ideally should be composed of several practicing physicians.

16. The contractual time limit for claims submission is specified as a separate clause.

Explanation: Most managed care organizations allow 30, 60, or 90 days (not 365 days) from the date of service for claims to be received by them or the claims will not be paid.

17. The contractual time limit for fee for service claims payment is specified. When a clean claim is submitted, some contracts state 30 days and some state 60 days. For capitation payments, there should be a date each month by which to expect payment.

Explanation: Practices want to know the specific number of days or the day of the month when they can expect payment. This provides a date on which to follow up if payment is not received. Before signing the contract, ask the plan representative for the plan's definition of a clean claim.

18. The specific circumstances in which the physician can bill the patient should be listed.

Explanation: This is especially important in contracts in which the ultimate payer may not be the party offering the contract because it is a third-party administrator (ASO/TPA) for a self-insured employer or another funder of medical insurance. If the funder defaults on payment, contracts state that the practice cannot bill the patient. If the contract states that the practice cannot bill the patient, this is a good time to ask about reinsurance levels. *Reinsurance* is another insurer that was retained by the funder to cover claims should it default. Reinsurance also covers claims of catastrophic patients after a certain level of expense, such as $50,000 or $100,000, is reached. Ask the organization if its self-funded clients carry any type of reinsurance for insolvency when they go out of business and ask for the level of reinsurance carried for catastrophic patients. The presence of reinsurance offers some protection for the payment of claims for the doctor's services. If there is no reinsurance, ultimately the patient will be responsible when the funder goes out of business. The number of months after which the patient can be billed should be clarified. A time limit should be specified, or the practice may be delaying payment indefinitely.

19. Major patient copayments, coinsurances, and deductibles are made known in the contract or through other materials.

    Explanation: If this information changes, ask how the practice will be notified. To collect the correct amounts at the time of service and to avoid billing patients for small amounts, it is important that the practice be informed of any change in copayments and deductibles.

20. The contract should outline noncovered benefits and specify that the patient will pay for excluded services if the physician prescribes them.

    Explanation: Traditionally, plans allow physicians to bill patients for exclusions in their benefits.

21. Coordination of benefits (COB) issues should be addressed to determine whether the benefits, fee schedule, discounts, and withholds apply if the managed care organization is the secondary insurance plan.

    Explanation: Some plans may cover any remaining balances left by the primary insurance plan, including benefits that are not normally covered. Ask the plan for a detailed description of its COB procedure.

Medical Resource Monitoring

22. Prior authorization requirements and procedures should be contained in the contract or available for review.

    Explanation: Everyone in the practice who is involved with managed care contract rules should be informed of any new tasks to prevent mistakes from occurring with actual patients.

23. If the contract limits referrals to participating providers, there should be some way to notify the practice of updates and deletions before their effective date.

    Explanation: There may be fines against a physician who refers outside the panel of providers. Make sure the organization has an adequate procedure for notifying the practice of updates and that the practice has an adequate procedure in place to comply with this rule.

24. If the contract limits referrals for laboratory, radiologic, or other diagnostic tests to certain facilities, the names of those facilities must be listed in the contract.

Explanation: Almost every managed care plan has a contractual relationship with a lab or x-ray facility. It reduces costs by referring to that facility. The higher the volume referred to the facility, the greater the reduction in costs.

25. If the contract limits referrals to participating hospitals, the names of those hospitals should be identified in the contract.

    Explanation: There may be fines against a physician who refers outside the panel of participating hospitals.

26. If the physician must maintain active privileges at a participating hospital to maintain privileges with the managed care organization, the contract should state this.

    Explanation: If this clause exists and the doctor has no active privileges with a participating hospital but still wants to join the organization, ask if there is an exception for a physician with only courtesy privileges. Maintaining active privileges to admit a rare patient is very time-consuming for a physician.

27. The retention policy for medical records should be made known either in the contract or with a separate policy.

    Explanation: Ideally, the length of time a physician must retain medical records should correspond with state law or the current policy of the practice to avoid unnecessary work for personnel in the practice. There should be one consistent policy for record retention for all patients in the practice.

28. The entity which controls quality of care must be specified.

    Explanation: All physicians want to have physician peers establish the quality of care standards by which they will be evaluated. Ideally, there should be a committee of local physician peers revising the standards to account for local practice patterns.

29. Peer review, utilization management, and quality assurance rules should be in the contract or available on request.

    Explanation: Before signing a contract, it is important to review the rules with all personnel in the practice who must comply with them.

30. If physicians are required to serve on a utilization or quality improvement committee at some time, this should be stated in the contract.

    Explanation: If a clause like this is seen, ask about the number of hours involved and the time of the meetings. The doctors' schedules may make it impossible for the doctors to serve on a committee. This clause will need negotiation. If the organization requires doctors to serve on a committee, it should purchase special malpractice insurance for decisions made by the committee. Most likely, the clinical malpractice insurer of the doctor does not cover peer review.

Before the team finalizes its contract evaluation list it must consider evaluating the rules and procedures of the party's utilization management programs. This is called assessing the utilization hassle factor. When you assess the *utilization hassle factor,* ask the managed care organization detailed questions about its utilization management programs. Next, determine what you can live with in this area or place these issues in the "Contract Breakers" column. The following questions should be asked:

1. What types of review do they perform: preauthorization review, concurrent review, or retrospective review? Are there any procedures which must be performed on an outpatient basis or in the office setting?
2. Who establishes the utilization control standards? What is the name of the medical director(s)?
3. Who will carry out the review process and make decisions? Do nurses make any review decisions?
4. Will review personnel phone or visit the practice?
5. How will the physician be informed of a utilization management decision which stops a patient's benefits while the patient is hospitalized? How long does the doctor have to appeal this decision before the patient is informed? Who informs the patient, the doctor or the plan?

Since managed care organizations can be initiated by many types of entities and combinations of entities, it is becoming important to ask detailed questions about the board of trustees in regard to its level of involvement, responsibilities, and management expertise. A board of trustees should be composed of reputable people with minimal financial motivation. After asking these questions, the practice evaluation team may feel more comfortable about a long-term relationship with this organization. The following questions should be asked:

1. How is a trustee appointed?
2. What is the composition of the board?
3. Do the articles of incorporation designate the organization as non-profit or for profit?
4. If the plan sells stock, how many shares of stock do board members own? How many shares of stock do participating physicians own? How many shares of stock does management own? Top-level management should own some shares of stock to maintain its commitment; this is referred to as "golden handcuffs."
5. Do trustees receive formal orientation when appointed?
6. For which committees does the board provide oversight?
7. Has the board developed a strategic plan?
8. Does the board have goals, objectives, and policies?
9. Does the board receive quarterly reports regarding enrollment, member satisfaction, and utilization management?
10. Did the board receive last year's audited financial report? Ask for a copy of this report so that the team can evaluate the financial status of the organization.

11. What is the organization's mission?

12. Has a long-range marketing plan been approved by the board? Ask for a copy of the marketing plan so that the evaluation team can determine whether the future markets of this plan are the markets the practice desires.

By asking these questions, a practice can determine the level of involvement of the board and the quality of the management team. Ideally, there will be physicians on the board and the practice will know these physicians and feel comfortable with their decisions.

When all the information has been gathered, it is time for the practice evaluation team to accept or reject the contract. If the team has uncovered complicated legal issues, consultation with a lawyer is advised. Some state medical associations review managed care contracts and offer free legal advice. Check with your state association. If the decision is to accept the contract, Tool 11-7 can be used so that the practice will not make mistakes when working with a managed care plan.

EXERCISING KNOWLEDGE

Fill in the Blanks

1. List the three methods managed care plans use to control healthcare costs.

   _____

   _____

   _____

2. List four services which ASOs and TPAs can offer their clients.

   _____ _____ _____ _____

3. HMOs call their enrollees _____ .

4. The four types of HMOs are _____ , _____ , _____ , and _____ .

5. Physicians and hospitals that form contractual relationships to work with managed care plans are known as _____ .

6. List the advantages to the physician in managed care contracting.

   _____ _____ _____

Spell out these acronyms.

   7. POS

   8. EPO

   9. IPA

  10. MSO

  11. GPWW

  12. PHO

Applying Concepts   *Read the entire managed care contract with XYZ managed care plan. After reading the contract, answer the questions.*

XYZ, Incorporated

PARTICIPATING PHYSICIAN AGREEMENT

This AGREEMENT is effective on _____, 19XX, between XYZ, INC ("XYZ") and _____ ("PHYSICIAN").

I.   RECITALS

    1.1   XYZ is a (STATE) nonprofit service corporation, duly licensed by the Insurance Commissioner of the State of (STATE), pursuant to Insurance Code Section 0000 to issue benefit agreements covering the provision of healthcare services and to enter into agreements with PHYSICIAN.

    1.2   PHYSICIAN is a "licensee" as that term is defined under Business and Professions Code Section 00000.

    1.3   XYZ intends by entering into this agreement to make available quality healthcare to XYZ members by contracting with PHYSICIAN. PHYSICIAN intends to provide such quality healthcare in a cost-effective manner.

II.   DEFINITIONS

    2.1   "Benefit Agreement(s)" means the written agreement entered into by XYZ and groups or individuals under which XYZ provides, indemnifies, or administers healthcare benefits.

    2.2   "Emergency" means a sudden onset of a medical condition manifesting itself by acute symptoms of sufficient severity that the absence of immediate medical attention could reasonably result in

1. Permanently placing the Member's health in jeopardy

2. Causing other serious medical consequences

3. Causing serious impairment to bodily functions

4. Causing serious and permanent dysfunction of any bodily organ or part

2.3   "Hospital Services" means those acute care inpatient and hospital out-patient services which are covered by XYZ Benefit Agreement. Hospital services do not include long-term nonacute care.

2.4   "Medically Necessary" means services or supplies which, under the provisions of this Agreement, are determined to be

1. Appropriate and necessary for the symptoms, diagnosis, or treatment of the medical condition.

2. Provided for the diagnosis or direct care and treatment of the medical condition.

3. Within standards of good medical practice within the local medical community.

4. Not primarily for the convenience of the Member and the Member's physician or another provider.

5. The most appropriate supply or level of service which can safely be provided. For hospital stays, this means that acute care as an inpatient is necessary because of the kinds of services the Member is receiving or the severity of the Member's condition and that safe and adequate care cannot be received as an outpatient or in a less intensified medical setting.

2.5   "Medical Services" means those services provided by a Participating Physician and covered by an XYZ Agreement.

2.6   "Member(s)" means enrollees or enrolled dependents covered by an XYZ Benefit Agreement.

2.7   "XYZ Benefit Agreement" means a Benefit Agreement pursuant to which Members have a financial incentive to use Participating Providers.

2.8   "Participating Hospital" means a hospital which has entered into an agreement to provide Hospital Services as a Participating Provider.

2.9   "Participating Physician" means a physician who has entered into an agreement to provide Medical Services as a Participating Provider and who is a "licensee" as that term is defined in Business and Professions Section 00000.

2.10 "Participating Provider" means a hospital, other health facility, physician, or other health professional which has entered into an agreement with XYZ to provide healthcare services for prospectively determined rates.

2.11 "Utilization Management" means a function performed by an organization or entity acting as an agent of XYZ to review and authorize whether Medical Services provided or to be provided are Medically Necessary.

III. RELATIONSHIP BETWEEN XYZ AND PHYSICIAN

3.1 XYZ and PHYSICIAN are independent entities. Nothing in this Agreement shall be construed or be deemed to create a relationship of employer and employee or any relationship other than that of independent parties contracting with each other solely for the purpose of carrying out the provisions of this Agreement.

3.2 Nothing in this agreement is intended to be construed or be deemed to create any rights or remedies in any third party, including but not limited to a Member or a Participating Provider other than a PHYSICIAN.

IV. PHYSICIAN SERVICES AND RESPONSIBILITIES

4.1 PHYSICIAN shall provide to Members Medical Services which are Medically Necessary and which are in accordance with the applicable XYZ Benefit Agreement and this Agreement.

4.2 PHYSICIAN shall accept and maintain evidence of assignment of benefits for the payment of Medical Services provided to Members by PHYSICIAN under the applicable XYZ Benefit Agreement.

4.3 PHYSICIAN agrees to admit or arrange for admission of Members only to Participating Hospitals. In case of an Emergency, as that term is defined in this Agreement, PHYSICIAN agrees to use a Participating Hospital unless the case has been authorized within forty-eight hours of admission.

4.4 PHYSICIAN agrees to refer Members to other Participating Providers unless the case has been preauthorized by the plan.

4.5 PHYSICIAN agrees to participate in the Utilization Management provided in Article VII and to abide by decisions resulting from that review subject to the rights of reconsideration and arbitration provided by Section 7.5.

4.6 PHYSICIAN has accurately completed the Participating Physician Credentialing Application which accompanies this Agreement and has been accepted by XYZ. PHYSICIAN shall promptly notify XYZ of any change in the information contained on the Application, including any change in its principal place of business, within seven (7) days of such change.

V. XYZ SERVICES AND RESPONSIBILITIES

5.1 XYZ agrees to pay PHYSICIAN compensation pursuant to the provisions of Article VI.

5.2   XYZ agrees to grant PHYSICIAN the status of "Participating Physician" with full rights and obligations.

5.3   XYZ agrees to continue listing PHYSICIAN as a Participating Physician until this Agreement terminates pursuant to this Agreement.

5.4   XYZ agrees to provide PHYSICIAN with a list of all Participating Physicians, Participating Hospitals, and other Participating Providers.

5.5   XYZ agrees to provide appropriate identification cards for Members.

VI.   COMPENSATION AND BILLING

6.1   PHYSICIAN shall seek payment only from XYZ for the provision of covered Medical Services except as provided in Section 6.2. The payment from XYZ shall be limited to the amounts referred to in Section 6.6, less co-payments and deductible amounts as provided in Section 6.5.

6.2   PHYSICIAN may also seek payment for the provision of Medical Services from other sources as provided in Section 6.3, and as available pursuant to the coordination of benefit provisions in Section 6.4.

6.3   PHYSICIAN agrees that the only charges for which a Member may be liable and be billed by PHYSICIAN shall be for Medical Services not covered by the applicable XYZ Benefit Agreement for copayments and deductible amounts.

6.4   In a case in which XYZ, under the applicable XYZ Benefit Agreement, is primary under applicable coordination of benefit rules provided in (STATE) Administrative Code Sections 000000 through 000000, XYZ shall pay the amounts due under this Agreement reduced as provided in Section 6.5. In a case in which XYZ is other than primary under the coordination of benefits rules referred to above, XYZ shall pay only those amounts which when added to amounts received by PHYSICIAN from other sources equals one hundred percent of the amounts required by this Agreement.

6.5   XYZ shall deduct any copayments and deductible amounts required by the applicable XYZ Benefit Agreement from allowed payment due PHYSICIAN from XYZ pursuant to this Agreement.

6.6   PHYSICIAN agrees to accept the fee schedule as provided in Exhibit A, attached to and made part of this Agreement or PHYSICIAN's billed charges, whichever is less, as payment in full for all Medical Services provided to Members. Such payment shall be for Medical Services provided on or after the effective date of this Agreement.

6.7   Prior to October 1 of each year, XYZ shall make fee schedule revisions which shall be effective on January 1.

6.8   PHYSICIAN shall bill XYZ on an approved form or electronic billing format acceptable to XYZ within thirty (30) days of performing the Medical Services. PHYSICIAN shall furnish, on request, all information reasonably required by XYZ to verify and substantiate the XYZ provisions of Medical Services and the charges for such services. XYZ reserves the right to review all such information submitted by PHYSICIAN when necessary and in accordance with this Agreement.

6.9   XYZ shall pay PHYSICIAN within thirty (30) days of receipt of billings which are accurate, complete, and otherwise in accordance with Section 6.8.

6.10   PHYSICIAN shall use the current year's CPT codes in reporting services and shall not unbundle charges with separate CPT codes when one code is appropriate. If XYZ bundles the CPT codes, PHYSICIAN shall not bill the member and shall accept the bundled payment as payment in full.

6.11   PHYSICIAN shall not charge Members for Medical Services denied as not being Medically Necessary under Section 7.2.

6.12   XYZ shall require PHYSICIAN to return any payment made in error and reserves the right to deduct payment made in error from future payments.

VII.   UTILIZATION MANAGEMENT

7.1   XYZ shall establish a Utilization Management program which shall seek to assure that Hospital Services and Medical Services provided to Members are Medically Necessary.

7.2   Utilization Management for inpatient Medical Services shall include

    1. "Preadmission review" to determine whether a scheduled inpatient admission is Medically Necessary

    2. "Admission review" to determine whether an unscheduled inpatient admission or an admission not subject to preadmission review is Medically Necessary

    3. "Concurrent review" to determine whether a continued inpatient hospital stay is Medically Necessary

7.3   XYZ shall conduct retrospective review to determine whether outpatient services were Medically Necessary. Any appeal of a decision under this section shall be commenced by requesting a review by XYZ. If not satisfied, PHYSICIAN may request arbitration.

7.4   There shall be no retrospective denials of any inpatient services approved under Section 7.2.

7.5   PHYSICIAN may appeal a Utilization Management decision. The appeal shall begin by requesting reconsideration by the organization or entity making the initial decision. If PHYSICIAN is not satisfied with that result, he or she may request a review by XYZ. If PHYSICIAN continues not to be satisfied, he or she may request arbitration.

VIII. RECORDS MAINTENANCE, AVAILABILITY, INSPECTION, AND AUDIT

8.1   PHYSICIAN agrees to allow review and duplication of any data free of charge and other records maintained on Members which relate to this Agreement. Medical records shall be made available as necessary for provision of Medical Services and as otherwise necessary to carry out the terms of this Agreement. Such availability, review, and duplication shall be allowed upon reasonable notice.

8.2   Ownership and access to records of Members shall be controlled by applicable law.

IX.   LIABILITY, INDEMNITY, AND INSURANCE

9.1   Neither XYZ nor PHYSICIAN nor any of their respective agents or employees shall be liable to third parties for any act or omission of the other party.

9.2   PHYSICIAN, at his or her sole expense, agrees to maintain one million dollars per occurrence and one million dollars in aggregate as insurance for professional liability and comprehensive general liability.

9.3   Upon request by XYZ, PHYSICIAN shall provide XYZ with copies of insurance policies or evidence of the ability to respond to any and all damages as provided in Section 9.2.

X.   MARKETING, ADVERTISING, AND PUBLICITY

10.1   XYZ shall use its best efforts to encourage Members to use the services of PHYSICIAN by publishing the physician's name in a provider directory without a marketing fee.

10.2   XYZ shall have the right to use the name of PHYSICIAN during marketing to prospective members.

10.3   Except as provided in Section 10.2, neither XYZ nor PHYSICIAN shall use the other party's name, trademarks, or logo in advertising or promotional materials.

XI.   DISPUTE RESOLUTION

11.1   XYZ and PHYSICIAN agree to meet in good faith to resolve any problems or disputes that may arise under this Agreement.

11.2   In the event that any problem or dispute concerning the terms of this Agreement, other than a Utilization Management decision as provided for in Article VII, is not satisfactorily resolved, XYZ and PHYSICIAN agree to arbitrate such problem or dispute. Such arbitration shall be initiated by either party making a written demand for arbitration on the other party. Within thirty (30) days of that demand, XYZ and PHYSICIAN shall each designate an arbitrator and give written notice of such designation to the other. Within thirty (30) days after these notices have been given, the two arbitrators selected by this process shall select a third neutral arbitrator and give notice of the selection to XYZ and PHYSICIAN. The arbitration shall be binding on both parties in any subsequent litigation or other dispute.

XII. TERM AND TERMINATION

12.1 When executed by both parties, this Agreement shall become effective as of the date noted on page 1 and shall continue in effect until terminated pursuant to this Agreement.

12.2 Either party may terminate this Agreement by giving at least ninety (90) days' prior written notice. Nothing contained herein shall be construed to limit either party's lawful remedies in the event of a material breach of this Agreement.

12.3 Notwithstanding termination, XYZ shall continue to have access to records for four (4) years from the date of provision of the Medical Services to which the records refer. Such records shall be available in accordance with Article VIII, to the extent permitted by law and as necessary to fulfill the terms of this Agreement.

XIII. GENERAL PROVISIONS

13.1 Assignment
No assignment of the rights, duties, or obligations of this Agreement shall be made by PHYSICIAN.

13.2 Notices
Any notice required to be given pursuant to the terms and provisions of this Agreement shall be in writing, postage prepaid, and shall be sent by certified mail, return receipt requested, to XYZ or PHYSICIAN at the addresses below. The notice shall be effective on the date indicated on the return receipt.

13.3 Severability
In the event any provision of this Agreement is rendered invalid or unenforceable by an Act of Congress or of the (STATE) Legislature, or declared null and void by any court of competent jurisdiction, the remainder of the provisions of this Agreement shall remain in effect.

13.4 Entire Agreement
This Agreement, together with exhibits, contains the entire Agreement between XYZ and PHYSICIAN relating to the rights granted and the obligations assumed by this Agreement. Any prior promises or negotiations, either oral or written, relating to the matter of this Agreement not expressly set forth in this Agreement are not in effect.

13.5 Amendment
This Agreement or any article or section of it may be amended at any time during the term of the Agreement by mutual written consent of duly authorized representatives of the parties.

FOR (XYZ)   FOR (PHYSICIAN)

_____   _____

Title: _____   Title: _____

Date: _____   Date: _____

EXHIBIT A

XYZ shall pay PHYSICIAN the lesser of billed charges or the maximum allowable fee minus a withhold amount of twenty percent (20%) as determined by the relative value units currently published in *Relative Values for Physicians* by McGraw-Hill Healthcare Management Group. Conversion factors for this contract year are

Evaluation and Management Services	$ 5.50
Anesthesiology Services	$ 34.00
Surgery Services	$100.00
Radiology	$ 17.50
Laboratory and Pathology	$ 10.84
Medicine	$ 6.50

Answer these questions about the contract by circling Y (yes) or N (no). List the contract clause where you found the answer.

13. Is XYZ subject to regulation by the insurance commissioner?   Y   N   Clause _____

14. Is XYZ's definition of *medical necessity* in the contract?   Y   N   Clause _____

15. Do members have a financial incentive to use participating providers?   Y   N   Clause _____

16. According to XYZ's definition, is a participating provider only a physician?   Y   N   Clause _____

17. Are there any cross-indemnification hold harmless clauses?   Y   N   Clause _____

18. Must the physician maintain evidence of assignment of benefits by having the patient's signature to assign benefits?   Y   N   Clause _____

19. Do referrals to nonparticipating providers require preauthorization?   Y   N   Clause _____

20. Will XYZ provide a list of participating providers?   Y   N   Clause _____

21. In cases of COB, when XYZ is the secondary insurance plan, will XYZ pay the difference up to its maximum allowable fee?   Y   N   Clause _____

22. Can the member be billed for excluded benefits, copayments, and deductibles?   Y   N   Clause _____

23. Does XYZ pay the physician by fee
    for service?   Y   N   Clause _____

24. Are conversion factors listed in Exhibit A?   Y   N   Exhibit _____

25. Must the contract be in effect to receive
    payment as a participating physician?   Y   N   Clause _____

26. Can the physician bill a member for
    services denied as not medically necessary?   Y   N   Clause _____

27. Can the physician appeal a utilization
    management decision all the way to
    arbitration?   Y   N   Clause _____

28. Can XYZ deny benefits for inpatient
    admissions after the patient is discharged?   Y   N   Clause _____

29. Can the physician advertise participation
    in the XYZ plan?   Y   N   Clause _____

30. Is there an evergreen clause in this
    contract?   Y   N   Clause _____

31. Does XYZ have access to records after
    termination?   Y   N   Clause _____

32. Are written promises which are not
    contained in the contract valid?   Y   N   Clause _____

Extra Credit   33. Use Tool 11-1 to complete your own contract evaluation list for the
                            XYZ plan.

▼ **TOOL 11-1**
CONTRACT EVALUATION LIST

Contract Breakers
(Need negotiation or no contract is signed)

Give Points
(Need inclusion in contract or clarification)

▼ TOOL 11-2
MANAGED CARE CONTRACT LOG

Managed Care Organization Name	Date Received	Deadline for Return	Date Returned

▼ **TOOL 11-3**
MANAGED CARE ORGANIZATION RESEARCH FORM

1. Name of Organization _____ Type _____

2. Names of Targeted Employer Groups or Patient Groups _____

    _____

3. Current Enrollment _____ Expected Enrollment Next Year _____

4. Current Patient Mix   % males _____   Expected Patient Mix   % males _____

                             % females _____   % females _____

    Current Average Age _____   Expected Average Age _____

5. Percent of Total Organization Budget Devoted to Marketing _____

6. Percent of Total Organization Budget Devoted to Administration _____

7. Has the organization been certified or inspected for its quality assurance program?

    Yes _____ Name of Agency _____ Date _____ No _____

8. Has the organization ever been in trouble with the insurance commissioner in any state?

    No _____ Yes _____ Date _____ Details _____

9. Has the organization had any lawsuits?

    No _____ Yes _____ Details _____

10. If the organization has a withhold amount or bonus pool, what is the track record for returning these
    funds? _____

▼ **TOOL 11-4**
PRACTICE CAPACITY DETERMINATION

	Current Level	Maximum Capacity
General Questions		

1. Number of hours physicians want to work per week on a regular basis _____ _____

2. Hours available to see patients in the office or clinic per week _____ _____

3. Number of patients who can be seen in the office or clinic per week _____ _____

4. Hours of surgery, OR, and special procedure time available per week _____ _____

5. Number of surgeries and OR procedures that can be performed per week _____ _____

6. Number of hours per week of physician services delegated to other healthcare professionals _____ _____

7. Hours available per week for other healthcare professionals to provide services _____ _____

▼ **TOOL 11-5**
PATIENT PROFILE ANALYSIS

1. Active number of patients in the practice _____

2. Average age of patients in the practice _____

3. Gender of patients in the practice _____ % female _____ % male

4. Average revenue collected per patient per year _____

5. Average expenses per patient per year _____

6. Average cost of lab and x-ray per patient per year _____

7. Average variable cost per procedure _____
    (calculate variable costs for the codes and average them)

8. Average number of referrals to specialists per year _____

9. Average cost of referrals to specialists _____

10. Patient breakdown by top 10 employer groups:

    _____ _____ % _____ _____ % _____ _____ %
    _____ _____ % _____ _____ % _____ _____ %
    _____ _____ % _____ _____ % _____ _____ %
    _____ _____ %

11. Revenue breakdown by type of insurance:

    Medicare _____ %

    Medicaid _____ %

    HMO _____ %

    PPO _____ %

    Integrated network via capitation _____ %

    Workers' compensation _____ %

    Indemnity (traditional) insurance _____ %

    Self-pay _____ %

    Others (specify each) _____ %

    TOTAL 100%

▼ **TOOL 11-6**

CHART OF RULES FOR A MANAGED CARE ORGANIZATION

1	2	3	4	5	6	7	8	9
Organization Name and Sponsor	Hospitals on Panel	Lab/Other Diagnostic Facilities on Panel	Office Referral Authorization Needed, Y/N	Mandatory 2d Opinion on Procedure, Y/N	Authorization (PAC) Needed and Phone No., Y/N	PAC Outpatient and Other Services	Continued Stay Review Program, Y/N	Drug Formulary Used, Y/N

Cut and paste next to the form above

10	11	12	13	14	15	16	17	18	19
Claim-Filing Address	Method of Payment: FFS, Capitation, Withhold	Appeal Contact Address and Phone No.	No. Days to File an Appeal	Annual Deductible per Patient/ Family	Co-payment Amounts	Co-insurance Amounts	Benefits with Maximum Dollar Limits	Preventive Services Covered, Y/N	Major Benefits Excluded

▼ TOOL 11-6 (CONTINUED)
CHART OF RULES FOR A MANAGED CARE ORGANIZATION

Instructions for using this tool:

Grid the rules of each plan in the rows provided. If any plan changes a rule, update the tool. Write yes or no in the columns when Y or N appears. If you write no, be happy there is no rule for this column. Use it when reviewing a contract or to grid all of the contracts the practice has in place. This tool can be entered in a computer program which is specially designed.

Column 1. List the name of the organization and any sponsors. Sponsors are the organizations that operate the plan.

Column 2. List the hospitals which the managed care organization will let you use for its enrollees. As the list changes, update it.

Column 3. List the laboratory or x-ray facilities you can use.

Column 4. Write yes if there is a referral required before your doctor can examine the patient. Note whether the referral authorization comes on paper, comes from a PCP, or is the phone number for a phone authorization procedure. You may want to write in how long a referral lasts, e.g., three visits, per illness, per pregnancy.

Column 5. Write yes if there is a second opinion program. You may also write in the names of the specific procedures as they affect your doctor's specialty.

Column 6. Write yes if you must call before your doctor hospitalizes a patient on an elective basis. Write no if you need to authorize emergency or maternity admissions and how long you have to do this. List phone number. If you do not want to call, note if authorizations may be faxed or mailed. List the fax number or mailing address.

Column 7. List other procedures which require authorization if they affect procedures being performed by any of your doctors.

Column 8. List if someone will be reviewing hospitalized patients' charts during inpatient care. Make sure the doctors in the practice know so that they are sure to respond to any special notes from reviewers which may be on patients' charts.

Column 9. Write yes if the doctors in the practice must prescribe medications from a formulary adopted by the plan. Often it is the participating pharmacies which must comply with the rules on formularies. Sometimes a plan may profile physicians in regard to the degree to which they comply with the formulary. Write in any special rules like this here.

Column 10. This is an optional column. Not all plans have the same filing address, and it may be best to obtain this address from the enrollee ID card.

Column 11. List the method of payment: (1) fee for service FFS (note how payment is determined: UCR, McGraw-Hill, RBRVS, other), (2) capitation, (3) FFS and capitation. List if there is a withhold on the fee for service and/or capitation payments.

Column 12. List the person's name in charge of appeals, the department which handles appeals, its address and phone number.

Column 13. List the number of days you have to file an appeal from either the date of service or the date of payment. You can note any special materials a particular plan may require to be included before an appeal is considered.

▼ **TOOL 11-6 (CONTINUED)**
CHART OF RULES FOR A MANAGED CARE ORGANIZATION

Column 14. List any deductible requirements per individual or per family.

Column 15. List copayment amounts for each plan's major benefit options. Example: Benefit code 1 requires a $5 copayment, but benefit code 2 requires a $10 co-payment.

Column 16. List coinsurance amounts which are percentages.

Column 17. List benefits with maximum dollar limits if they affect any of the services your physicians are providing.

Column 18. Write yes if the plan covers preventive care or if your physicians provide preventive care. Ignore the column if your doctors provide no preventive care. Make special notes on the plan's policy for when these services are covered. It may be a law in your state to cover preventive benefits for children. Preventive benefits can be covered periodically, depending on the patient's age.

Column 19. List excluded benefits by category if they affect any of the services your physicians are providing.

Create a column 20 for special notes. Managed care organizations are changing rapidly, and nobody knows what rules will be created next.

▼ **TOOL 11-7**
DOS AND DON'TS WHEN WORKING WITH MANAGED CARE

DO

1. Label each patient's chart with the name of the patient's managed care organization.

2. Bill each organization within 1 day of providing service if possible. If this is not possible, bill at least twice a month.

3. Monitor the number of days it takes to be paid under a fee for service method. Document a pattern of lateness if capitation checks are overdue. Promptly call your provider relations representative with documented trends in late payment.

4. Appeal inconsistent fee for service payments for the same CPT code or unreasonable payments inconsistent with the contracted fee schedule.

5. Appeal unsound utilization decisions directly to the medical director of each organization. During appeals, be prepared to provide either oral or written clinical symptoms of the patient and results of diagnostic testing or procedures performed.

6. Request financial reports each year and have the doctors review them before recontracting time.

7. Request board of trustee names and committee chairs' names. Have your doctor phone them frequently to offer input.

8. Network with other practices involved with the managed care organization and make appeals as a group to the medical director when the group as a whole is dissatisfied.

9. Make copies of each plan's participating physicians, hospitals, pharmacies, and other providers. Keep them handy in patient treatment rooms and offices to minimize confusion when referring to the other participating providers. Involve the patients in the selection process if possible. Patients have a responsibility in this process.

10. Read the rules of each organization and attempt to write global office procedures which accommodate all managed care organizations.

DON'T

1. Bill a patient who is a member of a managed care organization unless it is for a deductible, copayment, or excluded benefit.

2. Let your doctors accept the decision of a nurse reviewer if you feel the patient's care would be compromised. Have your doctor always speak to a medical director when services have been denied. The doctor and patient are entitled to due process. Don't let the doctors discharge a patient or cancel a test which they feel is medically necessary when benefits have been denied. Encourage the doctors to work with the plan to resolve the problem.

3. Discuss the managed care organization negatively with your patients who are members of the organization. Patients are generally not prepared to understand the workings of a managed care organization. Ventilate your complaints to the doctors and have them call the medical director.

4. Discriminate against managed care organization patients by not giving them timely appointments.

Quality Improvement Controls in a Medical Practice

CHAPTER OVERVIEW

Quality improvement (QI)—the precept that continuous improvement in the day-to-day operations of a company is both desirable and possible—was implemented over two decades ago in manufacturing and is now applied by every business that provides a product or service to customers. Quality improvement efforts, which are usually performed by a team, are a powerful tool in this age of accountability and have been adopted by medical practices across the country. To remain a player in healthcare, a practice must streamline its operations to achieve the highest degree of efficiency at the lowest possible cost.

In recent years several external factors have led medical practices to formalize procedures designed to monitor QI. Examples are managed care rules and inspections; regulations promulgated by the Occupational Safety and Health Administration (OSHA), Medicare, and the Clinical Laboratory Improvement Act (CLIA); and the advent of capitation.

After reading the material in this chapter, doing the exercises, and using the end-of-chapter tools, you will be able to:

■ *Articulate the rationale for developing a QI approach that includes all the levels of personnel in a medical practice*
■ *List ways to use QI techniques to monitor payment, especially methods of determining whether capitation payments are covering a practice's expenses*
■ *Use formal methods of tracking delays in payment*
■ *Recognize when to resubmit rather than appeal a denied claim*
■ *Use QI in making quantitative assessments of changes that have been made to improve the quality of care*
■ *Apply the concept of continuous quality improvement (CQI) programs to a medical practice*

QUALITY IMPROVEMENT CONTROLS IN A MEDICAL PRACTICE

Most medical practices are already doing a lot to assure customer satisfaction. However, the office personnel may be doing their jobs independently to satisfy the customer, with no organized program to systematically study operations and improve problem areas. Every practice has problems with changes. Since all the personnel in a medical office are dependent on one another for smooth operations, sometimes the only way to improve operations is through a team approach, enlisting the help of everyone involved. A quality improvement plan offers a starting point for coordinating everyone's efforts. To start your office's plan, follow these steps:

1. Identify a key person who will be responsible for QI. A physician should be in charge of the QI plan, and all the physicians in the practice should be involved.
2. Survey all staff members to identify problem areas.
3. Meet to identify and prioritize problem areas.
4. Write a QI plan (see Tool 12-1).
5. Pick one problem area to study and create an action plan. List the expected outcome and the desired results of an action plan. This could be a policy outlining the steps which the staff should take for any office task.
6. Start a QI plan notebook and record the first action plan.
7. Implement the action plan by announcing it to the staff members and physicians.
8. Set a trial period after announcing the action plan. Let the plan take effect.
9. Measure the results of the action plan after the trial period. Record the results in the QI notebook.
10. If the action was successful, tackle the next problem. If the action was not successful, adjust the action plan, implement it, and measure it again.

A QI program gets better with time and practice. The longer you keep it up, the more everyone will want to be involved.

QUALITY IMPROVEMENT IN THE MONITORING OF PAYMENT

You are probably doing a lot already in the area of monitoring claims before and after they are reported. Quality improvement is in place but is not routinely evaluated through a formal process. Most practices follow a calendar of routine tasks like clockwork each month. Figure 12-1 shows a posting and billing calendar policy which could be a topic for a QI study. Are posting and billing occurring in accordance with the policy of the practice?

In addition to the posting and billing calendar policy, certain time periods are used for monitoring claims that were reported to insurance plans but were not processed. Regardless of the method of payment, claims must be

Posting and Billing Calendar Policy

Effective Date:	9/10/XX
Policy:	Posting and Billing Calendar
Purpose:	To maintain a steady cash flow
Procedure:	Personnel involved with posting and billing will perform these tasks during the time periods listed below

Tasks with Plans	Time Period (within)
Post charges, payments, and writeoffs	Daily
Report insurance claims	1 day from initially posted charge and within 7 days of date of service.
Run monthly reports (e.g., accounts receivable, outstanding claims for all payers, outstanding claim listings by individual plan)	Second working day of each month
Resubmit claims not received by plans	Within 30–60 days of original claim
Post payments from EOBs	Daily
Check plan payments and reasons for denial	Daily, correct and resubmit simple errors; submit a formal appeal on denials due to medical necessity and any disallowances above $50 (see appeal policy)

Tasks with Patients	Time Period (within)
Statement mailed to patients for outstanding out-of-pocket costs and patients seen outside the office*	Weekly billing on a cycle
Statements mailed to patients for outstanding out-of-pocket costs	60–90 days, second statement with second dunning request
Balances greater than $100, phone call in addition to third letter	90–120 days, third statement with third dunning request
Outstanding patient accounts reviewed by doctor monthly to decide about pursuit of payment	5 working days after doctor's determination
Doctor to decide on pursuit of payment (options: send fourth statement, send to collector, write off)	5 working days after receipt of list

*Patients seen in hospital, emergency room, nursing home, or other place of service.

FIGURE 12-1 Posting and billing calendar policy.

followed at specific intervals to check their status until EOBs are received by the practice. This includes receipt and processing of claims. Because they deal with so much paper, plans can lose paper claims. Electronic billers do not track the status of claims in regard to receipt by a plan. However, not all claims are sent electronically, and so after 30 days, medical office personnel must check to see if the paper claims are in the computer systems of the insurance plans or were lost somewhere in the process. Even after 30 days with fee for service payers, electronic billers should check to see if their claims have been caught in edits. Corrections and additional information can then be given quickly to free these claims from edits.

Outstanding claims should be monitored for their status at regular 30 day intervals. Practices which are not computerized for billing must use tickler files at 30-, 60-, 90-, and 120-day intervals to monitor claims until they are adjudicated. Computerized practices use aging reports at 30-, 60-, 90-, and 120-day intervals to monitor outstanding claims at several levels of detail. Figure 12-2 shows a report that is run every 30 days to capture outstanding claims by major payer types. The practice determines which plans make up the payer types. Figure 12-2 is the starting point for monitoring outstanding claims. Begin with the payer who has the most money outstanding. When a practice receives the accounts receivable report, a careful review should be made of fee for service payers with outstanding balances. A practice must monitor these payers to maintain a steady cash flow. Capitation payers must also be monitored, but not as closely, to assure that reported claims have been processed. Start with column 6 to learn the percentage of outstanding money in claims owed by the individual payer. Start investigating the payer with the largest percentage of money outstanding in accounts receivable. For simplification, the figure groups all payers into seven types. With all the plans today, it is more realistic to have 30 types or more. In Fig-

Accounts Receivable by All Payers

Date of Run: 01-02-9X

1	2	3	4	5	6
Payer type	Charges, $	Writeoffs, $	Payments, $	Receivable, $	%
Self-pay	2,664.75	513.84	699.17	21,080.90	12.4
Private plan	3,840.18	601.67	2,923.60	14,907.00	8.8
Medicare	15,270.00	4,999.80	12,347.90	24,345.80	14.4
Medicaid	967.10	47.80	1,045.90	10,187.00	6.0
XYZ plan	34,333.00	12,525.00	18,764.00	56,126.90	33.2
Managed care	60,345.00	36,710.00	24,289.00	37,128.00	21.9
Workers' compensation	1,237.90	384.50	451.29	5,483.00	3.2
Totals	118,657.93	55,782.61	60,520.86	169,258.60	

Column 1 = payer type
Column 2 = charges for services reported
Column 3 = writeoffs incurred during posting of payments for monthly period
Column 4 = payments received during monthly period
Column 5 = total amount of money owed to practice by each payer
Column 6 = percentage of total money owed by individual payer

FIGURE 12-2   Accounts receivable by all payers.

Outstanding Claims by Individual Payer

Date of Run: 01-02-9X

XYZ Plan		31–60	61–90	91–120	121+	Credits
		$54.00	0.00	0.00	0.00	0.00

Stanley Smith	Home Phone 368-1245		Last payment 09-23-9X
10869 Dallas Rd	Work Phone 864-9876		
King, PA 19209			
Patient No. 4320	XYZ	Benefit No.	ID No. 28843986

Date	Procedure	Amount	Remaining	Diagnosis	Report 1 Plan	Report 2 Plan
11-08-9X	80005	9.00	9.00	250.00	11-08-9X	
11-08-9X	99214	45.00	45.00	250.00	11-08-9X	
1	2	3	4	5	6	7

Column 1 = date of service
Column 2 = CPT code
Column 3 = charge amount for the service
Column 4 = amount remaining unpaid for the report period
Column 5 = diagnosis reported on same line with procedure
Column 6 = date posted or date reported to primary insurance plan
Column 7 = date posted or reported to secondary insurance plan (a date would appear in this column
        if XYZ were the secondary insurance plan)

FIGURE 12-3   Outstanding claims by individual payer.

ure 2-2, XYZ plan represents 33.2 percent of the outstanding money. Let's assume XYZ is a fee for service plan. Begin monitoring a fee for service payer by ordering a more detailed report on all outstanding claims of the XYZ plan according to the cycle outlined in the posting and billing calendar. Identify claims which are 31 to 60 days old, 61 to 90 days old, and 91 to 120 days old. Figure 12-3 shows an excerpt of a single claim in this report. This claim is 31 to 60 days old. Here's how to monitor this claim to determine its receipt and/or status in the claims process of an insurance or managed care plan.

Stanley Smith's claim was reported to XYZ plan on 11/08/9X. Because of the cycle or the process of running this report to sort claims 31 to 60 days old, the claim is 55 days old. It's time to call the XYZ plan to determine the claim status. Tool 3-3, Claim Reporting Rules By Plan, should contain the claim status phone number for XYZ plan. Some plans are developing automatic phone access to their computer systems to speed up the checking of a claim's status. If a phone call reveals that the plan cannot locate the claim, promptly report another claim. If lost claims continue to be a problem with XYZ plan, document the fact that XYZ plan loses claims. Tool 12-2 contains a column for this purpose. Until a pattern of lost claims is well documented, investigate other ways of working with XYZ plan, such as electronic claim submission and sending all claims by special mail, e.g., "return receipt requested" or special courier. If a pattern of documented problems continues, have the doctor write a letter to the chief executive officer of XYZ plan and include a copy of the tracking sheet, Tool 12-2. If the situation persists, perhaps the QI team can study the problem. This may not be easy to resolve because XYZ plan provides one-third of the practice's income (see Figure 12-2).

Next let's assume that XYZ is a capitation payer. The status of reported claims is monitored after 90 days, but not by phone. Phoning to check claims status takes a great deal of time when the capitation payment has already arrived and all that is outstanding is claims processing or services not included in the capitation rate. Figure 12-3, which lists all patient claims for the payer, can be copied and mailed with a cover letter to each capitation payer to request the status of these claims. Tool 12-3 is an example of a cover letter for Figure 12-3 which can be used for this purpose. Some capitation payers may never send the practice an EOB for capitated services. When this is the case, Tool 12-3 and Figure 12-3 can be used at monthly cycles to determine the status of outstanding claims.

Once the monitoring process determines that claims have been received and/or timely adjudication is occuring, QI control in the monitoring of EOBs begins. Capitation and fee for service payers must be separated to monitor EOBs and payment. Capitation payment occurs before the EOB, and so the monitoring procedures must be different. Procedures used to track fee for service payers will be addressed first.

Studying Slow Fee for Service Payers

Aging reports by payer for delayed periods of time (e.g., 61 to 90 days and 91 to 120 days or more) enlighten a practice about slow fee for service payers. What can be done to further study these problems? When chronically slow payers are identified, this is a problem that can be studied by the QI team. You provide the documentation and let the team resolve it. If the payer has a contract with the practice, there should be a contractual time limit within which a claim must be paid. A 30-day limit is standard in most contracts. Check the contract to see if the plan may be in breach of contract with the practice. Have the office manager send a letter and the documentation to the plan's provider relations department. Follow the steps in the plan's provider grievance procedure. Pull out the contract and research arbitration procedures after the grievance procedure is exhausted. If the problem is not resolved, perhaps the contract should be terminated. This will be a QI team decision.

If the practice does not have a contract with the plan and documentation with letters has not improved a slow payment situation, check with the insurance commissioner in your state to determine if there is a *prompt pay law* which may offer you some help in breaking the pattern of delayed payment. Maybe your state has a law that mandates that interest is due on outstanding claims. Begin by calling your state insurance regulation department, which is headed by an insurance commissioner (see Tool 12-4 for a list of insurance commissioner phone numbers by state). Insurance regulation departments have names that vary by state, but all state insurance commissioners are responsible for overseeing private medical insurance plans to protect the consumer. When calling the insurance commissioner, ask for the consumer complaint department. This department can tell you whether there is a prompt pay law to help physician practices get paid when no contract is in effect as well as procedures to follow with their assistance. If there is a prompt pay law which applies to this slow payer, create a stamp "Prompt pay law XXX.000 in this state requires that this claim be paid within XX days" and stamp each claim. Electronic billers can place this message in their free form fields.

In addition to learning about the presence of a prompt pay law, ask the insurance regulation department if there is a special form to complete to register a formal complaint for slow payers. Ask about other types of complaints which the insurance commissioner will investigate, such as unfair benefit denials. Ask who should complete a complaint form. Do not be surprised if the consumer (patient) instead of the practice must register benefit denial complaints. If this is the case, obtain a copy of the consumer complaint form and involve the patient in registering a formal complaint against the payer. There is no harm in involving patients, as they have generally paid all or some of the premium and expect timely payment of their doctors. Tool 12-5 can be used if your insurance commissioner does not have a form for this purpose.

Sometimes federal laws preempt state insurance laws. Self-insured plans which are regulated by ERISA (Employee Retirement Income Security Act of 1974, 29 U.S.C. 1001-1461) are a good example. ERISA preempts state laws in regard to claim processing or improper benefit denials by self-insured employers. At present there is little legal recourse for a physician practice that has not received prompt payment from a self-insured plan. Healthcare reform may include revision of ERISA. Insurance commissioners also cannot help with slow payments and unfair benefit denials by government plans. A practice must read the manuals provided by government plans and follow their procedures to get claims paid on time and must follow the appeals process of these plans when a low payment is received.

Studying Low Fee for Service Payers

Sometimes slow fee for service payers are also low payers. What can be done to identify fee for service payers which chronically delay payment and pay unacceptable fees? If your computer cannot break down maximum allowable fees (MAFs) by CPT code and by payer, you may want to keep a tracking sheet for claim payments when there are large differences between the charges billed by the practice and the fees paid. Start by tracking commonly billed procedures and use the same sheet (Tool 12-2) on which payment delays are tracked. Slow and low payers are also good candidates for the QI team to study. Your state medical association may also provide some advice, because if your practice is having problems with a plan, other practices probably are having problems too. If your practice is the only one having trouble with a plan, the QI team should study the office's claims procedures.

SENDING ANOTHER CLAIM BECAUSE OF SIMPLE ERRORS

When the EOB is received, a practice can tell if the claim has been adjudicated correctly. EOBs give instant feedback. If a claim has been denied, pull the claim to see if you have made a simple error. Since the claim was denied, you have to start all over again (see Table 12-1).

All these problems can be resolved by submitting a new claim. Since you will be submitting new information which was not on the original claim, the plan's computer should recognize this as a new claim. After all, the original claim has already been denied and adjudicated, and this information should be in the plan's computer system.

If you find a pattern of claim denials for simple errors, this is another problem for the QI team to investigate. Have someone else in the office check claims before they are sent. Computer software packages can also offer assistance. They can prevent simple errors because certain boxes on the claim, such as date of service and assignment of benefits items, can be programmed as required fields for the requirements of each plan.

REGISTERING A FORMAL APPEAL

There are times during the posting of the EOB when a decision has to be made to register a formal appeal. This is very different from submitting a new claim since there is extra time and paperwork involved. Detailed clinical information must be given which may involve the physician. The first step is to know and follow the appeals policy of the payer. Most practices learn about the appeals policies of the major plans they work with by referring to physician administrative manuals, contracts, and newsletters. Plan representatives may also be phoned to learn specific policies. Be timely in registering an appeal, as there is often a cutoff date for registering a formal appeal. Some plans allow only 60 days from the date of the EOB to register

TABLE 12-1

Simple Errors and Reasons for Denials

Simple Error	Reason for Denial
Incorrect patient identification number	Plans pay benefits only for a valid ID number.
Incomplete date of service	Month, date, and year are required.
Incorrect or missing place of service	Plans accept two digits or two letters; you must know the plan's preference.
Incomplete and unrecognizable code numbers generated by the plan's computer	Plans install and delete code numbers at their own pace; you must know which year's version of the codes the plan accepts as well as the modifiers it uses.
Incorrect provider number	Some plans issue their own provider numbers, which may not be the SS or tax ID numbers of the physician or practice.
Assignment box left blank	Some plans use this box to determine where the check is sent.
Missing name and address of facility where services were rendered	Plans require this for medical resource monitoring.
Missing plan code or group number	Some private plans require a plan code or group number.

an appeal. Be aware that some plans are instituting paperless review procedures which will decrease the time spent gathering and documenting detailed information.

The next step is to consistently identify claim denials of total charges and disallowances to be formally appealed. *Disallowances* are not denials of total charges but represent certain charges that are not paid because they are above the maximum allowable fee. Every practice should have a policy for determining when to appeal a disallowance. Some practices set a dollar amount limit, such as $50 or $200, depending on the specialty. Some practices set a percentage, such as 20 percent of the billed charge, beyond which an appeal will be registered with the plan. When there is a specific policy, the staff does not have to check with a supervisor before registering an appeal. Appeals are automatic and consistent. Standard form letters are used to appeal disallowances in working with a plan which does not accept verbal requests (see Tool 12-6). When you appeal disallowances resulting from low MAFs, include the data you have collected on Tool 12-2 regarding what other plans pay for the same CPT code if the plan you are appealing to is a much lower payer than others for this code. Use phrases like "Medicare allows $1636, Medicaid allows $1233, XYZ plan allows $2100, and your MAF is

$1088." Plans do not like to be told that they are very different from other payers. Tool 12-2 is very handy, and it works.

Unfortunately, there are many other reasons why a practice may want to appeal a claim, and some of these reasons are not easy to identify and file. This is especially true when claims are denied because of no medical necessity and possible exclusions in the patient's policy. Table 12-2 shows a listing of reason codes. Reasons marked with an asterisk require a formal appeal to

TABLE 12-2
Reason Codes Which Require a Formal Appeal

1 CODE	2 REASON
100	Services payable at 100%
19	Dependent over age 19
1YR	*Limited to one per year
21	Dependent over age 21
2ND	COB secondary payment
3YR	*Allowed once in 3 years
6MO	*Allowed once in 6 months
80%	Service(s) payable at 80%
ADD	Need additional info
ADM	*Administrative adjustment
AOP	Approved out-of-plan
AVE	*Authorized number of visits exceeded
BE	*Billing error
BOI	Bill other insurance
CAP	*Capitated service
CMC	*Contracted maximum charge
COB	Possible COB involved
COS	*Cosmetic service not covered
DNC	*Dental services not covered
DUP	*Duplicate (previously processed)
ELIG	Pending eligibility
ERR	Claim processing error or adjustment
EXP	*Experimental service not covered
FUD	*Included in surgical package
INFO	Pending additional information
MAX	Maximum benefits paid
MED	*Not medically necessary
N/C	*Noncovered services
NER	*Noncovered emergency services
NOA	No answer to inquiry
NOD	No ordering doctor listed
NPD	Nonparticipating doctor
NPP	Nonparticipating provider
NREF	*No referral or unauthorized
PCI	*Patient convenience item not covered
PRE	Prior to effective date
TNR	*Not related to diagnosis
UA	*No authorization number; do not bill patient

be initiated by the practice whenever it suspects the claim was not adjudicated properly by the insurance plan.

There are many reasons in addition to those listed in the table which require special explanations when you register a formal appeal. Regardless of the specific reason, a standard opening for an appeal letter can be developed. All that is left to do is insert the special explanations and attach the clinical information (e.g., operative reports or progress notes). Figure 12-4 shows an EOB with a denial of the total charges for Sylvia Jones as explained by reason code NREF (no referral or unauthorized). Specialty practices may see reason codes of this type when in fact the referral was authorized by the patient's primary care physician.

Tool 12-7 shows how a standard appeal cover letter can be created with templates covering most of the special explanations.

Templates can be created for the many different reason codes. Table 12-2 can be used to start your list of reason code templates. Template titles to insert in a standard appeal letter are established to specify the type of template desired by the user. It is important to include a statement that the practice will follow the formal appeal until the claim is resolved. Duplicate appeal letters can be placed in tickler files or recalled in your computer every 30 days.

When the first level of reconsideration is unsuccessful, proceed to the next level. Watch the time limits for registering a second-level appeal. Some practices send a copy of all second-appeal letters to the benefits leader at the patient's employer, if applicable. This shows the employer group that has offered the plan that there may be an administrative problem with that plan.

Patient Name					Member ID No.		Group No.		Account No.	
Date of Service	Procedure Code	No. Services	Service Code	Total Billed	Copay	Plan Benefit	Deductions			Amount Payable
							Other	Code	Withhold	
Explanation:										
122189	Jones Sylvia					289368476	AF26	00260	2042	
09/27/XX	99213	1	MD	29.00	.00	.00	.00	NREF	.00	.00
				29.00	.00	.00	.00		.00	.00*
122243	Roses Edith					402182107	AF20	01278	87	
10/09/XX	80019	1	MD	22.00	.00	22.00	.00		.00	22.00
10/09/XX	99213	1	MD	28.00	9.00	19.00	.00		.00	10.00
10/09/XX	80061	1	MD	35.00	.00	35.00	.00		.00	35.00
10/09/XX	36415	1	MD	5.00	.00	3.00	.00	CMC	.00	3.00
				90.00	9.00	79.00	.00		.00	70.00*
TOTAL** total for patient*				119.00	9.00	79.00	.00		.00	70.00**

FIGURE 12-4 Statement of benefits.

This may cause the plan to resolve the problem sooner because employer groups are the plan's customers.

In the case of Sylvia Jones (Fig. 12-4), her doctor, a specialist, has a contract with XYZ plan. However, because of the NREF (no referral authorized), he will not be paid and cannot bill Ms. Jones. Since the contract is between the doctor and the plan, he must appeal. When all levels of appeal have been exhausted within XYZ plan, a participating practice must next use arbitration if arbitration procedures exist in the contract. The contract must be reviewed to determine whether the arbitration procedures are worth considering. Arbitration is a consideration if Dr. Smith notes a pattern of many denials and losses of large amounts of money as a result of errors in claims processing by XYZ plan.

When patients who are enrollees of private plans must pay for medical costs resulting from unfair denials that are said to be exclusions in their policies, remember the insurance commissioner. When all levels of appeal have been exhausted within the plan's administrative levels, the research you did in learning how to get help for unfair benefit denials should pay off. Involve and encourage the patient to register a complaint with the state insurance department.

COLLECTION RATES

Everyone likes to know how he or she is doing compared with others in their field. When it comes to reporting and collecting physician payments, it is no different. Within the healthcare delivery system there have always been standards for claim collection rates. However, old standards are affected by all the changes going on in healthcare today. There are more contracts holding physicians to MAFs, more capitation contracts not only for primary care physicians but also for specialists, more denials as a result of advanced insurance computer edits, increasing practice overhead, and more mergers. All these factors have made it difficult for physicians to determine how a practice is doing and whether the employees are doing the best they can. Two collection ratios are still valuable in determining how efficiently a practice is collecting payments for services. They cannot be evaluated monthly but should be reviewed quarterly and annually.

Gross Collection Ratio

The gross collection ratio includes the total payments received by a practice for a specific period without any writeoffs. The *gross collection ratio* is the total payments for the period divided by the total charges without writeoffs. For example, $400,000 (payments) divided by $800,000 (charges) equals a gross collection rate of 50 percent. This means that for every dollar charged, the practice is collecting 50 cents. This is not a good ratio, but it may be the best the office staff can do if the doctor is a specialist and has a payer mix consisting of managed care contracts, Medicaid, and Medicare.

Net Collection Ratio

The net collection ratio, also known as the adjusted collection ratio, excludes writeoffs from the total payments received by a practice in a specific period. The *net collection ratio* is the total payments for the period divided by the total charges after the writeoffs have been deducted. For example, $400,000 (payments) divided by $450,000 (charges minus writeoffs) equals a net collection rate of 88 percent.

Different types of writeoffs can be identified by types, for example, contractual, bad debt, professional courtesy discounts, and others. All services are posted at the doctor's regular fee schedule amounts. Professional courtesy discounts and other discounts are credited using special codes created by a practice. Each code is specific for each type of writeoff. This allows a practice to track the categories in which most of the writeoffs have occurred.

Collection rates should be between 90 and 100 percent after writeoffs are taken. If net collection rates are low, this may be a problem for the QI team.

Posting Withholds and Extra Fees

Posting payments from a fee for service payer which does not have a contract with the practice is relatively simple. However, check the dates of service, the CPT codes, the amount billed, and the amount paid. These items on the EOB should agree with the services billed to the plan. If there is a credit balance after posting because the patient has paid in advance, the patient is entitled to a refund. If there is a balance due from the patient, a statement is sent in the next billing cycle.

When a practice has a contract with a managed care plan, posting is somewhat more complicated. There are payments, writeoffs, and possibly withhold amounts, bonuses, and primary care physician (PCP) management fees to debit and credit. *PCP management fees* are paid to primary care physicians by managed care plans to compensate for the extra work required of a primary care physician. All money amounts must be identified as separate entries. Separate entries are necessary to keep track of the practice's financial dealings with the plan. Figure 12-5 shows total withhold amounts per patient.

On the EOB for Sam Brown, there is a total withhold of $7.77 from claim 22853447. Marvin Morris, the patient listed above Sam Brown, has a total withhold of $18.55. Both claim withhold amounts must be treated as separate entries; $7.77 must be credited to Sam Brown's account as though it were a payment. Sam Brown's account for this claim is considered closed.

Name I.D. No. Claim No.	Patient's Name Acct. No.	Date(s) of Service	CPT Code or Service	Total Expenses	Expenses Excluded	Reason Codes	Copay or Deduc- tible	Withhold	Benefit Paid
MORRIS	Marvin	7/24/9X	99223	150.00	45.00	160a		7.35	97.65
24919409	79	7/25/9X	99233	75.00	27.00	160a		3.36	44.64
4090832-0		7/26/9X	99232	55.00	27.00	160a		1.96	26.04
		7/27/9X	99232	55.00	27.00	160a		1.96	26.04
		7/28/9X	99232	55.00	27.00	160a		1.96	26.04
		7/29/9X	99232	55.00	27.00	160a		1.96	26.04
			TOTALS	445.00	180.00			18.55	246.45
BROWN	Sam	3/14/9X	99204	80.00	16.00	160a	15.00	4.48	44.52
15539654	576	3/14/9X	93000	45.00	5.00	160a		2.80	37.20
22853447		3/14/9X	81000	10.00	3.00	160a		0.49	6.51
			TOTALS	135.00	24.00			7.77	88.23

FIGURE 12-5   EOB with withhold totals.

An account is opened for XYZ managed care plan. The withhold amounts are treated as debits owed by the plan. Figure 12-6 shows a managed care organization's account with a practice.

As of 5/26/9x, XYZ plan owes this practice $247.77. Total disallowances have been $324.00. Figure 12-6 is valuable in determining financial gains and losses with managed care plans at any point in time. If any or all of the withhold amounts are repaid, the money is returned in one large payment which can be credited to XYZ plan's statement. There is no crediting to individual patient accounts. If withhold amounts are not returned, XYZ's statement must be closed at the end of the practice's fiscal year, with the amounts not returned identified as discounts. The practice will have to evaluate its participation in XYZ plan while keeping the discounted fees in mind should any withhold money be returned.

Date	Patient	Service	Charge	Disallow	Withhold
3/14/9x	Brown	99204	80.00	16.00	4.48
3/14/9x	Brown	93000	45.00	5.00	2.80
3/14/9x	Brown	81000	10.00	3.00	.49
5/26/9x	White	93501	1500.00	300.00	240.00
			Total	324.00	247.77

FIGURE 12-6   XYZ plan statement.

Monitoring the Capitation Rate

Capitation payments per patient per month involve a different procedure for posting payments. The financial survival of a practice depends on the profit or loss resulting from the capitation rate. There is still a great deal of experimentation with prices for capitation rates. When a patient receives services included in a capitation rate, that patient's account is debited. This is done to assure that all practice expenses are captured in the capitation rate evaluation process. At least every month and quarter and at the end of the contract year, the capitation rate should be evaluated. Practice expenses for total services provided must be compared with the total amount of capitation payments received from the plan and patient cost sharing payments, e.g., co-payments.

If the practice is computerized, the monitoring of *capitation rates* is easier. Depending on the sophistication of the software, there are several ways to monitor the profits and losses resulting from a capitation rate.

Method 1

Maintain separate accounts for each capitation patient. Each time a capitation check is received from a managed care plan, a listing of patients' names is attached. This list is then used to credit each patient's account. A central account must be credited for the managed care plan in case your computer system cannot tie all patient credits together to come up with a grand total of capitation payments. Figure 12-7 shows a list of patients' names received with a capitation check. Our list contains only eight patient names to keep the example simple. A standard list would contain 200 names or more. It is

---

Report No.
Cap 150R2

Tracy Lewis, M.D.

Enrollee No.	I.D. No.	Birthdate	Sex	Capitation Rate
Glauser, Dan	X1476890	4/11/94	M	20.00
Loch, Robin	X5932560	5/14/74	F	20.00
Lofgren, Bill	X3926702	7/1/53	M	20.00
Russell, Tim	X1474920	1/9/35	M	20.00
Stevens, Jean	X3742985	6/13/56	F	20.00
Warren, Jim	X5837772	9/1/56	M	20.00
Weber, Ed	X5292419	12/31/40	M	20.00
Witte, R.C.	X6945964	5/4/33	M	20.00
				160.00

FIGURE 12-7 Capitation payment listing.

wise not to accept a capitation rate unless the plan can guarantee a large group of patients. This minimizes the risk for the practice. Some plans pay fee for service until a threshold of 200 patients, for example, has been assigned to the practice.

Keeping a separate account for each patient takes a tremendous amount of work. Some of those patients may never receive services, yet they are entered on ledger cards or stored by name in the computer. Some capitation rates, especially for specialists, are so low (e.g., $.40, $.25) that it may not be worth the staff's time to post them. The only cost efficient way to record a low rate is to have a computer download capitation payments to each patient's account. This technology is just being developed. Imagine having to credit 5000 patients' accounts each month with a capitation rate of 25 cents. It is not cost-efficient to post these accounts by hand. The check for $160 is posted in an account with the plan's name. At the month's end a total of the services provided to capitation patients is compared with the amount of money received by the practice from the plan and the patient payments from cost sharing.

At the end of the month or quarter and certainly before capitation renegotiation time, the practice must determine the profitability of remaining in certain capitation arrangements. A report identifying the services provided and the income for the period must be compiled. Reconciliation can be accomplished by using a computer. Figure 12-8 shows gains (profits) and losses for each member of the plan for 1 month. The patient listing is abbreviated to simplify the example; a true listing would include several hundred names.

The gain (loss) in column 8 reflects the individual patient account gain or loss. For example, Ed Weber had a service for $42.00. Deduct the capitation payment of $20.00 and the net loss for his account is ($22.00). The reconciliation report reflects a grand total at the bottom for the gains and losses for all XYZ members.

Figure 12-8 shows that all services for capitation patients from 1/1/9X to 1/31/9X totaled $374.00 and that payment was $20.00 per member per month with $10.00 under FFS code 90703. All these services were included in the capitation rate with the exception of 90703. The total capitation payment is $160 plus $10.00 fee for service (90703) for a total of $170.00, and the practice lost $204.00 by being a participant in XYZ plan. XYZ has no co-payments, deductibles, coinsurance, or withholds. If there was patient cost sharing and/or withhold amounts, the reconciliation report would treat those direct payments as additional payments made on behalf of XYZ plan to the practice.

Method 2

Use one account in the name of the capitation plan. All patients under this plan are debited to this account when they receive a service. The total capitation payment is credited to this account each month. Any cost sharing,

For the Period 01/1/9X through 01/31/9X

XYZ Plan

1	2	3	4	5	6	7	8
Acct. No.	Member Name	DOS	CPT	FFS Charge	No. Pts/Service	Payment	Gain (Loss)
X147	Russell, Tim				0	20.00	20.00
X593	Loch, Robin				0	20.00	20.00
X694	Witte, R.C.	2/1/9X	99214	65.00	1		
		2/1/9X	93000	45.00	1		
		2/1/9X	90703	*10.00	0	*10.00	
						20.00	(90.00)
X529	Weber, Ed	2/10/9X	99213	42.00	1	20.00	(22.00)
X583	Warren, Jim				0	20.00	20.00
X3742	Stevens, Jean	2/25/9X	99211	20.00	1	20.00	0.00
X392	Lofgren, Bill	2/18/9X	99215	150.00	1	20.00	(130.00)
X482	Glauser, Dan	2/18/9X	99213	42.00	1	20.00	(22.00)
	Total Members	8	Totals	374.00	6	170.00	(204.00)
	*FFS						

Column 1 = member number
Column 2 = name of member
Column 3 = service date
Column 4 = procedure or service
Column 5 = fee for service charge
Column 6 = number of service units or visits. Zero denotes no service or FFS payment
Column 7 = capitation rate for monthly period
Column 8 = individual patient account gain or loss for the period with a total gain or loss for the members of XYZ plan
Note: The asterisk and FFS notation indicate that this was not a capitated service, but was paid under fee for service (FFS).

FIGURE 12-8 Reconciliation report for a capitation plan.

such as deductibles, copayments, and coinsurance, is posted as credits. There may be some services that are *carved out* (excluded from the capitation rate). Carved out services are posted to the same account because this is money owed by the plan. At any point in time, the balance of the account of the plan can be determined. Figure 12-9 shows method 2 and all the activities in the plan's account for the month of March. Coming into the month, there was a loss of $1250. Payment at $20 *per member per month (pmpm)* for 200 patients was $4000, which brought the account to a gain of $2506.00. There will be seasonal losses under capitation payment. It is best to evaluate them quarterly, but look at the gains and losses each month.

Since capitation payments are needed on a timely basis each month to enable the practice to meet its expenses, someone needs to monitor capitation payments to see that they are received on time. If they are not received on time, they should be tracked (see Tool 12-8). This tool can also be used to document errors in payment such as codes paid under the capitation rate which are carved out.

Date	Patient	I.D. No.	CPT	ICD	Charge	Payment	Balance
							(1250.00)
3/2/9X	Mary Jones	XYZ 1	99214	250.00	65.00		(1315.00)
			93000	414.00	45.00		(1360.00)
3/3/9X	Jackie Davis	XYZ 5	99201	427.00	50.00		(1410.00)
3/3/9X	Jim Connors	XYZ 26	99213	719.07	42.00		(1452.00)
3/20/9X	Carl Schmidt	XYZ 24	99213	250.01	42.00		(1494.00)
3/31/9X	Payment					4000.00	2506.00
3/31/9X	Mary Wolf	XYZ52	99214	V42.0	65.00		2441.00
			81000	V42.0	10.00		2431.00

FIGURE 12-9 Capitation plan account.

THE QUALITY IMPROVEMENT CONNECTION

There is a definite connection between capitation payments and quality improvement in a physician practice. If a practice is willing to accept risk in the form of a capitation method of payment, it must be willing to streamline all its current operations, even in the area of patient care. The adoption of a QI program which studies patient care is vital for a practice to survive under a capitation system. A QI program is also important for a practice that wants to be part of an IPA or GPWW, or use direct contracting with employer groups. For the first time, the medical resources used by a practice in the provision of care for common diagnoses and procedures need to be thoroughly studied under formal protocols. Care which is not efficient or effective has to be eliminated. Perhaps a patient does not need a visit and a phone call will suffice. Perhaps not all of the work needs to be provided by the doctor because physician assistants, nurses, and medical assistants can handle the situation. Experts believe that quality medical care is also the most cost-efficient form of care in regard to the long-term outcome of patients' conditions.

Defining and Measuring Clinical Quality with Guidelines

Quality medical care must be defined before it can be measured, and some managed care organizations are defining and measuring it by using standards of care or clinical guidelines (see Chapter 3). The American Medical Association (AMA) refers to these standards as practice parameters, but most physicians feel comfortable calling them *practice guidelines*. Regardless of the name, managed care is sparking the development of over a thousand guidelines for diagnoses, procedures, and preventive services. These guidelines contain criteria which tell an auditor what should be done and when it should be done for any diagnosis, procedure, or condition. There are criteria for the treatment of asthma, diabetes, hypertension, coronary artery bypass, prostatectomy, cataract extraction, hysterectomy, and tonsillectomies, to name a few. In the area of preventive care, there are defined intervals and age ranges at which physicians should perform Pap smears, mammography, and pediatric immunizations. Each day the list grows longer. When a practice works with managed care, it will soon be connected with QI, standards of care, and audits to determine physician performance.

Physician performance can now be measured against a standard of care established by a managed care plan. Once the standard has been established, *quality* can be defined as the degree of conformance to a standard. The plan sets the degree of conformance as a percentage; this percentage is called the *audit compliance rate.* Suppose the manged care organization defines an audit compliance rate of 80 percent. This means that if 80 percent of all the patient charts audited reveal that the physician has met the criteria for the standard of care, the physician will have an acceptable compliance rate and the plan will consider the doctor to be practicing quality medical care. If the plan finds that only 70 percent of the charts have met the standard of care, the results will be unacceptable: there is a need for quality improvement, and the plan must take corrective action. *Corrective action* is a formal process of outlining the actions the plan will take to improve the quality of care. Examples of corrective actions are feedback of the results to all the physicians audited, educational programs about acceptable treatment, meetings with physicians with unacceptable audit compliance rates, and the termination of some physician contracts. After corrective action, there is always a reaudit.

The Reaudit

A reaudit is necessary to determine if a plan's corrective action has improved care. Quality improvement is an ongoing program designed to objectively and systematically monitor and evaluate the quality of patient care, pursue opportunities to improve patient care, and resolve problems. QI programs must be continuous so that they can incorporate better ways of treating patients and are often referred to as continuous quality improvement (CQI) programs. These programs have three parts:

1. Structure
2. Process
3. Outcome

Much of their *structure* is rooted in the credentialing procedure and organization of the physician panel and the conducting of ongoing patient surveys. Patients' complaints are tallied regarding how long patients had to wait to get an appointment, how long they waited once they arrived, and how difficult it was to reach physicians. The *process* involves the standards of care audits used in measuring the quality of physician care. The *outcome* involves monitoring the effects of patient treatment at specific points in time, for example, at 6 months, 1 year, and every year up to 10 years. Outcome measures determine whether the current methods of treatment result in the best long-term cure, symptom control, or prevention of illness. If the outcome of patient treatment is not effective, the plan starts over by evaluating its structure and process.

Adopting a Clinical CQI Program

Most physician practices are either thinking about or have already adopted their own CQI programs to improve office operations. However, CQI programs to monitor the treatment of patients within the office are in their infancy.

Some practices work with managed care plans in the development of standards of care. The managed care plan allows these practices to conduct their own studies while it monitors the process. In this manner, the managed care organization introduces clinical CQI to the practice. Other practices do not have this arrangement with managed care plans but prefer to adopt their own standards of care and conduct their own studies in addition to complying with studies conducted by managed care plan employees. If your practice takes its own CQI approach in clinical care studies, follow these steps:

1. Form a CQI committee chaired by a physician who can appoint other physicians, supervisors, receptionists, billers, nurses, and medical assistants to the committee.
2. Have the committee identify diagnoses, procedures, and preventive services which are of interest to the practice by referring to frequently used ICD-9-CM and CPT-4 codes. Try to pick conditions and services in which you will have a large number of patient charts to study (at least 30 charts per physician) to extract statistically significant results.
3. Obtain copies of standards of care which have already been written. One resource is the *Directory of Practice Parameters* published by the AMA. It is a listing of over a thousand guidelines developed by national medical specialty societies and other physician organizations. The listing contains the title of the parameter (the AMA's word), the sponsoring organization, the source (journal or publication), and the contact person's name and phone number. This person can be phoned to obtain a copy of the listing. Some of the standards are available on CD-ROM. Call the AMA's customer service number, 1-800-621-8335. If you

have questions, ask customer service to connect you to the practice parameters department.

The federal government, through the Agency for Health Care Policy and Research (AHCPR), has developed what it calls *clinical practice guidelines,* which are available free of charge by calling the AHCPR Publications Clearinghouse at 1-800-358-9295 or by writing to AHCPR Publications Clearinghouse, P.O. Box 8547, Silver Spring, MD 20907. There are guidelines for benign prostatic hyperplasia, early HIV infection, sickle cell disease, low back pain, cataracts in adults, pressure ulcers in adults, urinary incontinence in adults, acute pain management, and unstable angina. The list is still growing.

4. Review the copies and select three to study in the first year. Make modifications to the standards by requesting the input of all the physicians involved in the practice. Once the standards are agreed on by the physicians, adopt them. Tool 12-9 is an example of a standards of care audit tool. It lists 20 criteria which should be recorded in each audited chart and asks if information is documented in the chart, calling for a yes or no response from the auditor. The auditor gives points for yes and no answers in regard to whether information is documented. Table 12-3 shows how this is done.

   The first column in the table lists 20 criteria. The committee will have to determine the relative weight of each criterion in terms of its importance to the other criteria that must be met. It is best to keep this simple; in our example, all the criteria are of equal importance so that they can be scored with the same weight.

5. Draft a timetable for implementation. Define an audit compliance rate. Try to keep the audit compliance rate achievable for the first year. Set a goal of 80 percent or less of the criteria to be met.

6. Appoint an auditor (a member of the committee) to carry out the process.

7. Create a method to identify the charts of the patients involved in the study. Computer software can be modified with the help of a software consultant to select patient names with the ICD-9-CM or CPT codes to be studied within specific dates of service. If you have reported a claim, the ICD-9-CM or CPT-4 code exists in your computer and can be called up. Charts can also be tagged with a special identifier as patients are treated, but this method takes longer to compile a representative sample to study.

8. For the first audit, select at least 30 charts for each physician providing treatment during a period of 1 year or more.

9. Have the auditor review the charts and record the findings on a separate form for each chart.

10. Have the QI committee review the results and take corrective action in either structure or process. Criteria with a score of 0 percent are discussed, and the tool may be modified if there is a problem with its structure. The process is continuous.

TABLE 12-3

Sample Audit Tool Scoring

Criteria		Yes	No	Score, %
1.	Duration of symptoms is addressed in chart	____	0	0
2.	Risk factors for hypertension are recorded	1	____	100
3.	Past medical, family, and social histories are recorded	1	____	100
At least annually, physician exam includes:				
4.	Height	____	0	0
5.	Weight	1	____	100
6.	Description of fundi	1	____	100
7.	Description of heart findings	1	____	100
8.	Description of carotid pulse	1	____	100
9.	Description of femoral pulse	1	____	100
At least annually, lab tests include:				
10.	UA	1	____	100
11.	BUN or creatinine	1	____	100
12.	Serum cholesterol	1	____	100
13.	Fasting serum glucose	____	0	0
14.	Serum potasssium	1	____	100
15.	ECG	1	____	100
16.	Chest x-ray	____	0	0
17.	BP greater than 150/95 on two separate visits prior to diagnosis	1	____	100
Management includes:				
18.	Low-sodium diet prescribed	1	____	100
19.	Hypertension management education	1	____	100
20.	At least one visit within 12 months	1	____	100
Total Score (5 percent per point)		16	____	80%

THE FUTURE OF PRACTICE GUIDELINES

The steps listed above presuppose that the practice has identified diagnoses and/or procedures as CQI audit topics. Many other topics are possible. Tool 12-10 is a form which can be used to list study topics. Candidates for CQI topics include:

- Patient satisfaction (see Tool 12-11)
- Implementation of master problem sheet (Tool 7-1)
- Implementation of master medication sheet (Tool 7-2)
- Utilization of preventive medicine record (Tool 7-3)

There are two trends driving the use of practice guidelines by physicians today. One is the movement away from the fee for service method of payment and into capitation. The other is the use of computers in a medical practice. To fully implement practice guidelines into the daily operations of a medical practice, the guidelines must be computer-driven and on-line. The guidelines must be linked to computerized patient medical records so that physicians and others in the practice can verify and treat according to the guidelines. It is hoped that someday the computer will do quality of care studies. All it takes is software to tell the computer what to do. The future of practice guidelines is directly linked to totally automated computer systems for patient care. Paper will be eliminated, and the doctor will carry a hand-held computer.

When practice guidelines are fully developed, it is predicted that payers will move away from strict medical resource monitoring on a case-by-case basis. Payers will look at broad spectra of care to determine compliance with guidelines. Preauthorization will be eliminated, and the practice will be free of extra paperwork and phone calls. This will allow additional time to study patient care. The practice will become the cost center and will work together with insurance and managed care plans.

EXERCISING KNOWLEDGE

Fill in the Blanks

1. The six areas for QI study in a medical practice are _____ , _____ , _____ , _____ , _____ , and _____ .

2. After _____ days, the status of a claim should be checked.

3. After receiving the accounts receivable report for all payers, one begins checking claims status with the plan which has the _____ outstanding balance.

4. When claims are denied for simple errors, a _____ claim is submitted correctly.

5. In a formal appeal, _____ must be provided to the plan.

6. Two other names for stardards of care are _____ and _____ .

7. The three parts of CQI are _____ , _____ , and _____ .

Define These Terms

8. Prompt pay law

9. Disallowance

10. Outcome

11. Net collection rate

12. Gross collection rate

13. Quality improvement

Applying Concepts

Use Table 12-2 for reason codes. Use the summary of statement of benefits on the next page to answer questions 14–20.

14. Is this statement of benefits an EOB?

15. Why was 99396 excluded (denied) for payment for Kathy Decker on 2/19/XX?

16. What is the MAF for 93000?

17. List the CPT code which has been excluded for payment because it was medically unnecessary?

18. What services are included in the capitation for William Wilmer? What is the total benefit payment for the noncapitated services?

19. What is the total withhold on this statement of benefits?

20. This plan allows $_____ for 99213, $ _____ for 80061, and $ _____ for 84436.

SUMMARY OF STATEMENT OF BENEFITS

PROVIDER NAME: James Smith, MD INC.
PROVIDER I.D. No.:   000000000
DATE OF STATEMENT: NOV 10, 19XX
GROUP No.   0000000

COMPREHENSIVE MEDICAL BENEFITS

Employee Name I.D. No. Claim No.	Patient Name Patient Acct No. Provider if Assoc or Drg No.	Date(s) of Service	CPT Code or Service	Total Expenses	Expenses Excluded	Notes (see over)	Copay Amount	Benefit Paid
DECKER 055328442	KATHY 1600	03/06/XX	99213	29.00			*10.00	
91102070266 79			TOTALS	29.00	**5.80†		10.00	13.20
DECKER 055328442	KATHY 1600	02/19/XX	99396	29.00	29.00	3YR		
91102080266 89			TOTALS	29.00	29.00			.00
WILMER 271205508	WILLIAM 994	03/26/XX	36415	5.00	5.00	CAP		
910107034 89		03/26/XX	84436	11.00	2.20	CMC		8.80
		03/26/XX	85025	15.00	15.00	CAP		
		03/26/XX	80019	22.00	22.00	CAP		
		03/26/XX	93000	38.00				38.00
		03/26/XX	99205	100.00	100.00	CAP	*10.00	
		03/26/XX	82270	5.00				5.00
		03/26/XX	81000	8.00	8.00	CAP		
		03/26/XX	86999	22.00	22.00	MED		
		03/26/XX	80061	35.00	10.00	CMC		25.00
					**15.36†			
			TOTALS	261.00	$199.56		10.00	61.44
						Page Total		74.64
						Grand Total		74.64

*Payment amount is reduced by deductible coinsurance amounts, other insurance benefits, Medicare benefits, and/or benefits paid to employee.
†Withhold this amount = 20% on noncapitated services.
PLEASE DO NOT RETURN THIS BULK PAYMENT CHECK. SEE REVERSE SIDE FOR INSTRUCTIONS AND NOTES

▼ **TOOL 12-1**
QUALITY IMPROVEMENT PLAN

I. Purpose
To promote excellence in patient care within our practice at the lowest possible cost.

II. Scope
Our quality improvement plan includes both the clinical and administrative areas of medical practice. These areas are

   A. Medical care delivery
      1. Patient satisfaction with our services
      2. Timely patient access to services with timely receipt of care
      3. Effective and efficient medical care with long-term cures or symptom reduction in cases of chronic illness
      4. Periodic preventive care at specified intervals
      5. Health education and the need for patient compliance
      6. Comprehensive medical records with the recording of all information required to support continuity of care
   B. Billing and payment systems
      1. Accurate and timely reporting and follow-up on claims to achieve medically necessary benefits for patients
      2. Consistent approaches to monitoring claims after reporting
      3. Appropriate operations to comply with rules of third-party payers and contractual relationships
      4. Effective reporting systems to evaluate and monitor billing and payment processes
      5. Consistent collection policies
      6. Retention of a well-trained staff with proven skills
   C. Compliance with federal and state laws
      1. Policies and procedures, revised as necessary, to comply with federal regulations
      2. Policies and procedures, revised as necessary, to comply with state regulations
   D. Facility and equipment
      1. Accessible, pleasant, and safe patient care locations
      2. Purchase of equipment and supplies at the lowest cost
      3. Continuous evaluation of the latest computer technology
   E. Productivity of personnel
      1. Time studies to determine how personnel can be most efficient
      2. Elimination of identified obstacles to productivity
      3. Studies of the processes involved in patient care
   F. Communication
      1. External communication, written and oral, to patients, other physicians, and third-party payers which is clear and professional
      2. Open communication among all levels of staff; physician-to-staff directives that are clear and accurately carried out

▼ **TOOL 12-1 (CONTINUED)**
QUALITY IMPROVEMENT PLAN

   G. Medical records
        1. Confidential medical records with adequate policies to cover all requests for review
        2. Procedures for medical record management for access and content
        3. Adequate documentation

III. Plan
The quality improvement plan will prioritize topics of study. Our efforts will be ongoing and will include all physicians and personnel in the practice. We shall use survey tools and verbal communication at regular meetings to evaluate topics for study.

IV. Responsibility
The physicians and the manager of the practice will be responsible for the QI plan. They will appoint a person to initiate, monitor, and report the results of QI activities.

V. QI records
Quality improvement activities will be maintained in a permanent central binder.

VI. Evaluation
Each topic of study will be evaluated on a predetermined schedule. Studies will be continuous and will undergo revisions until the desired outcomes occur.

▼ TOOL 12-2
TRACKING FEE FOR SERVICE PAYER DELAYS AND PAYMENTS

Organization where claim was sent _____

Contact person _____ Phone number _____

1	2	3	4	5	6	7	8
Claim No./ Acct. No.	Date Claim Reported	Date Claim Paid	Number of Days until Paid	Charge Amount	Amount Paid	Difference in Charge vs. Paid Gain (Loss)	Comments (e.g., lost claims)

Instructions for using this internal form: To calculate delays, subtract column 2 from column 3. To calculate the difference between paid amounts and charges, subtract column 6 from column 5 and place the difference in column 7.

▼ **TOOL 12-3**
LETTER TO CHECK THE STATUS OF REPORTED CAPITATION CLAIMS

Date:

ATTN: Claims Supervisor
XYZ Plan
P.O. Box 0000
Columbus, America 43216

Re: Status of outstanding claims which are not processed but have been prepaid under our capitation rate

Dear Claims Supervisor:

I am writing to check the status of some reported claims. The attached report includes the names of patients whose claims have not been processed. Some are over 90 days old. Please advise our office if you have received them and give the status of adjudication.

I am concerned that the data necessary to evaluate the success of this benefit plan may be compromised if the services are not processed in a timely manner.

If we can answer any further questions or if any claim requires additional information, please let our office know.

Sincerely,

Tracy Lewis, M.D.
TL/jd
enclosures

▼ TOOL 12-4
STATE INSURANCE REGULATORY AGENCY PHONE NUMBERS

State	Telephone No.	Fax No.	Toll-Free No.
Alabama	205-269-3550	205-240-3194	
Alaska	907-349-1230	907-349-1280	
American Samoa	011-684-633-4116	011-684-633-2260	
Arizona	602-912-8400	602-255-5316	
Arkansas	501-686-2900	501-686-2913	800-852-5494
California	916-445-5544 (except area codes 213 & 310, dial 213-897-8921)	916-445-5280	800-927-4357 in state only
Colorado	303-894-7499	303-894-7455	
Connecticut	203-297-3802	203-566-7410	
Delaware	302-739-4251	302-739-5280	800-282-8611
District of Columbia	202-727-8000	202-727-7940 202-727-8055	
Florida	904-922-3100	904-488-3334	800-342-2762
Georgia	404-656-2056	404-657-7493	
Guam	011-671-477-5106	011-671-477-2643	
Hawaii	808-586-2790	808-586-2806	
Idaho	208-334-4250	208-334-4398	800-721-3272
Illinois	217-782-4515	217-782-5020	
Indiana	317-232-2385	317-232-5251	800-622-4461 in state only
Iowa	515-281-5705	515-281-3059	
Kansas	913-296-3071	913-296-2283	800-432-2484
Kentucky	502-564-6027	502-564-6090	
Louisana	504-342-5900	504-342-3078	
Maine	207-582-8707	207-582-8716	800-300-5000 in state only
Maryland	410-333-2521	410-333-6650	800-492-6116
Massachusetts	617-521-7777	617-521-7770	
Michigan	517-373-9273	517-335-4978	
Minnesota	612-296-6848	612-296-4328	
Mississippi	601-359-3569	601-359-2474	800-562-2957
Missouri	314-751-4126	314-526-6075	800-726-7390 in state only
Montana	406-444-2040	406-444-3497	800-332-6148
Nebraska	402-471-2201	402-471-4610	
Nevada	702-687-4270	702-687-3937	800-992-0900 in state only
New Hampshire	603-271-2261	603-271-1406	
New Jersey	609-292-5363	609-292-0896	
New Mexico	505-827-4601	505-827-4734	800-947-4722
New York	212-602-0429	212-602-0437	800-342-3736
North Carolina	919-733-7349	919-733-6495	800-662-7777 in state only
North Dakota	701-224-2440	701-224-4880	800-247-0560 in state only
Ohio	614-644-2658	614-644-3743	800-686-1526
Oklahoma	405-521-2828	405-521-6635	800-522-0071
Oregon	503-378-4271	503-378-4351	
Pennsylvania	717-783-0442	717-783-1059	
Puerto Rico	809-722-8686	809-722-4400	
Rhode Island	401-277-2223	401-751-4887	
South Carolina	803-737-6160		800-768-3467
South Dakota	605-773-3563	605-773-5369	
Tennessee	615-741-2241	615-741-4000	800-342-4029
Texas	512-463-6169	512-475-2005	800-252-3439 in state only
Utah	801-538-3800	801-538-3829	800-439-3805 in state only
Vermont	802-828-3301	802-828-3306	
Virgin Islands	809-774-2991	809-774-9458	
Virginia	804-371-9694	804-371-9873	800-552-7945 in state only
Washington	206-753-7300	206-586-3535	800-562-6900
West Virginia	304-558-3386	304-558-1610	800-642-9004 in state only
Wisconsin	608-266-3585	608-266-9935	800-536-8517 in state only
Wyoming	307-777-7401	307-777-5895	800-438-5768

▼ **TOOL 12-5**
INSURANCE COMPLAINT FORM

Date:

To: State Insurance Commissioner
     Address
     City, State, ZIP Code

Re: Complaint and request for investigation of: _____
                                                         (Plan name)

On behalf of _____
                          (Patient's name and insured's name)

ID Number _____ Group Number _____

Summary of Complaint _____
_____
_____
_____
_____
_____

Name of official contacted at plan _____ Date _____

Official's response _____
_____
_____
_____

_____ Date _____
(Signature of patient)

_____ Date _____
Verified by (Signature of a member of physician staff)

Other correspondence is attached.

▼ **TOOL 12-6**
APPEAL LETTER FOR DISALLOWANCES

Date:

ATTN: Review Board
XYZ Plan
P.O. Box 0000
Columbus, America 43216

Re: Jerry Henderson
ID No.7853248211
Benefit Code 078
Transaction No. 135967

Dear Administrator:

I am requesting special reconsideration of the disallowance for the patient referenced. A copy of the EOB is circled for your convenience when reviewing this matter. I am also enclosing our research into what other plans are allowing for this CPT code. Your maximum allowable fees are below what comparable plans are allowing.

We feel certain our fees are cost-efficient and use Relative Value Units per McGraw-Hill's *Relative Values for Physicians*. Our conversion factor has been stable for the last two years.

I would appreciate your calling or writing my office with a decision. We will contact you after thirty days if we have not heard from you.

Best regards,

Tracy Lewis, M.D.
TL/jd
Enclosures

▼ **TOOL 12-7**
STANDARD APPEAL LETTER WITH A TEMPLATE

Date:

ATTN: Review Board
XYZ plan
P.O. Box 0000
Columbus, America 43216

Re: Sylvia Jones—your insured
ID No. 289368476
Group No. AF2600260
Transaction No. 122189

Dear Administrator:

I am requesting a special review of the claim recently processed for the patient referenced. A copy of the EOB is circled for your convenience in this review. I have information to convey cause for reconsideration.

Template: A copy of the referral form is provided which will indicate that I did have authorization to treat this patient from the primary care physician.

Thank you for your reconsideration. If you need further information, please do not hesitate to contact our office. We will contact you in 30 days if the matter has not been corrected on a future EOB.

Sincerely,

James Smith, MD
JS/jd
Enclosures

▼ **TOOL 12-8**
TRACKING CAPITATION DELAYS AND PAYMENT ERRORS

Organization where claim was sent _____

Contact person(s) _____ Phone number _____

1	2	3	4	5	6	7	8
Cap Date Due	Cap Date Paid	Number of Days Until Paid (2-1)	Total Cap Payment	Error Type	CPT Code	(MAF) FFS Payment Amount	Difference in Patient Cap Rate vs. FFS Payment for Error Type Gain (Loss)

Instructions for using this internal form: Document capitation payment delays and claim processing errors for capitation plans. Error types are recorded from EOBs and are appealed with a separate cover letter or phone call to the plan.

Error types for column 5   NCC = not a capitated code but paid under capitation rate = loss (MAF for the code)

CC = capitated code but paid under fee for service = gain (MAF for the code)

▼ TOOL 12-9
BENIGN ESSENTIAL HYPERTENSION: ADULT CARE

Patient name _____ Date of audit _____

	Criteria	Yes	No	Score
1.	Duration of symptoms is addressed in chart	____	____	____
2.	Risk factors for hypertension are recorded	____	____	____
3.	Past medical, family, and social histories are recorded	____	____	____
At least annually, physician exam includes:				
4.	Height	____	____	____
5.	Weight	____	____	____
6.	Description of fundi	____	____	____
7.	Description of heart findings	____	____	____
8.	Description of carotid pulse	____	____	____
9.	Description of femoral pulse	____	____	____
At least annually, lab tests include:				
10.	UA	____	____	____
11.	BUN or creatinine	____	____	____
12.	Serum cholesterol	____	____	____
13.	Fasting serum glucose	____	____	____
14.	Serum potassium	____	____	____
15.	ECG	____	____	____
16.	Chest x-ray	____	____	____
17.	BP greater than 150/95 on two separate visits prior to diagnosis	____	____	____
Management includes:				
18.	Low-sodium diet prescribed	____	____	____
19.	Hypertension management education	____	____	____
20.	At least one visit within 12 months	____	____	____
Total score (5 percent per point)				____

▼ **TOOL 12-9 (CONTINUED)**
BENIGN ESSENTIAL HYPERTENSION: ADULT CARE

HOW TO SCORE: Each of the 20 criteria is worth one point. Each yes answer is recorded as 1 point in the yes column. Each no answer is recorded as 0 in the no column. A score of 1 point in each row is scored as 100 percent for the criterion row. A score of 0 in each row is scored as 0 percent for the criterion row. This is done to see how the practice scored on each criterion and to identify areas which need improvement. Each criterion row of 100 percent needs no improvement.

The goal is to obtain 20 yes answers for a perfect score of 20 points, worth 5 percent each point: 20 × 5 percent = a total of 100 percent compliance. In our example, we want to meet a compliance rate of 80 percent. One audit tool is used for each patient chart. If 30 charts are audited for each physician in the practice, add the total point score percentages for the 30 charts and divide by 30 to obtain a total average percentage compliance rate per doctor. Then add all the doctors' total average percentage scores and divide this by the number of doctors audited for a total average percentage compliance rate for the practice.

The next chart contains outcome measurements to be recorded each year and can be used up to 10 years or more to record the long-term outcomes of treatment for each patient. Patients can be surveyed when they return for office visits, directly by phone, or in a survey letter. You may want to add questions about the patient's lifestyle as a result of management and treatment. While it is the patient, as the consumer, who must ultimately be satisfied with care and while a practice is certainly concerned about what its patients think, patients' responses are subjective. It is best to develop your own audit tools to record objective clinical findings if you want to impress managed care organizations and self-insured employer groups.

BENIGN ESSENTIAL HYPERTENSION OUTCOME MEASUREMENTS

Patient name _____   Date of audit _____

Audit outcomes once a year

Criterion			Yes	No	Score
1.	After 6 months of treatment	BP 150/100 or less	_____	_____	_____
2.	History of	Myocardial infarction	_____	_____	_____
3.	History of	Stroke	_____	_____	_____
4.	History of	Peripheral arterial disease	_____	_____	_____
5.	History of	Other organ failure	_____	_____	_____
Total					_____

Instructions: Record patient's name. Yes answers are worth 0 points if a positive history is found. No answers are worth 1 point when no history is found. The goal is to find no history of any organ disease. Each no point is scored at 100 percent in the score column. Since there are five criteria and all are equally weighted, subtract 20 percent from 100 percent for each yes answer. Average total percentage scores by physician. Then combine the average of all physicians' scores to calculate the total score for the practice.

▼ **TOOL 12-10**
QI STUDY TOPICS

Topic	Date of Service Range	Start Date	Complete Date	Practice Compliance Rate

List topics studied on this central form. It can then be presented to managed care organizations as needed. Suggestions for other study topics: Patient satisfaction (see survey, Tool 12-11). Also use as audit tools the master problem, medication, and preventive medicine sheets in Chapter 7. (See Tools 7-1, 7-2, and 7-3)

▼ **TOOL 12-11**
PATIENT SURVEY

I. DEMOGRAPHIC DATA

Your age _____

Male/female   S   M   D   W

Address _____
_____

1. Is our practice currently the main
source of healthcare for your family?   Yes   No

II. SPECIALTY INFORMATION
2. Do you feel that you understand the
medical specialty and the services that
this practice offers?   Yes   No

III. PHYSICAL SURROUNDINGS
3. Is the location of this office convenient
for you?   Yes   No

4. Do you find our reception area
comfortable?   Yes   No

5. Are our parking areas adequate?   Yes   No

IV. FRONT OFFICE PERSONNEL
6. Do you find our office personnel
(business manager, receptionist)
friendly and courteous?   Yes   No

7. Are your phone calls handled in a
prompt, courteous manner?   Yes   No

8. Have our payment and billing policies
been explained to your satisfaction?   Yes   No

V. NURSING PERSONNEL
9. Do our nurses give you enough
information about your health status,
such as telling you your weight and
blood pressure?   Yes   No

VI. DOCTOR
10. Does the doctor tell you enough
about your illness?   Yes   No

11. Does the doctor spend enough
time with you?   Yes   No

VII. TIME SPENT WAITING
12. Do you have to wait too long in the
reception area before you are called to
see the doctor?   Yes   No

13. Do you have to wait too long in the
examination room before the doctor
comes in to see you?   Yes   No

VIII. AFTER HOURS AND WEEKEND CARE
14. Do you have difficulty reaching the
doctor after hours?   Yes   No

15. Is our answering service prompt and
courteous?   Yes   No

16. Is the doctor prompt in returning
your calls?   Yes   No

IX. PHONE CALLS
17. Are your phone calls to the doctor
during the work day returned promptly?   Yes   No

X. ANCILLARY SERVICES
18. Do you find it inconvenient to go
someplace else for certain x-rays or
lab tests?   Yes   No

19. Is the emergency room we use
convenient for you?   Yes   No

20. Are you satisfied with the hospital
this practice uses?   Yes   No

XI. COST OF OUR SERVICE
21. Are you familiar with our credit and
billing policies.   Yes   No

22. If not, would you like to receive a
brochure explaining these policies?   Yes   No

23. Have you used other health services
(like an urgent care center) in the past
because you felt it would be less
expensive?   Yes   No

XII. SCHEDULING
24. Do you have trouble scheduling an
appointment?   Yes   No

25. Are our office hours convenient
for you?   Yes   No

XIII. EDUCATIONAL INFORMATION
26. Is the doctor providing you with
enough information?   Yes   No

27. Would you be interested in receiving
a health newsletter from this office?   Yes   No

XIV. SERVICES OFFERED
28. Are you satisfied with the range of
services offered by this practice?   Yes   No

29. Are there any specific services that you would like
to see our practice provide? If so, what are they? _____
_____
_____

Information Sources

Newsletters

American Medical News. Free to doctors with AMA membership.

CPT Assistant. Authoritative coding information from the American Medical Association. Call 1-(800) 621-8335 to order.

Part B News. Published by the United Communications Group, this newsletter has the latest Medicare information. Call (301) 816-8950.

Other Print information

Doctor's Resource Service. American Medical Association, P.O. Box 109050, Chicago, IL 60610-9613. Call 1-(800) AMA-1066 to order a series of tapes and publications about managed care and health care reform.

Source Book of Health Insurance Data. Published annually by Health Insurance Industry of America (HIAA), P.O. Box 41455, Washington, D.C. 20018. To order, call (202) 223-7780 or 7539.

The State of Health Care in America. Published annually by Business and Health Special Reports, Five Paragon Drive, Montvale, NJ 07645-1742. Call 1-(800) 223-0581 or (201) 358-2289 for ordering information.

National Associations

American Academy of Procedural Coders (AAPC)
2144 South Highland Drive, Suite 100
Salt Lake City, UT 84106
Call 1-(800) 626-CODE for an information packet, including information on how to take a certification examination. Also ask if there is a local chapter in your area.

American Association of Medical Assistants, Inc. (AAMA)
20 North Wacker Drive
Chicago, IL 60606
Call 1-(800) 228-2262 for information.

American Health Information Management Association (AHIMA)
Society for Clinical Coding
919 North Michigan Avenue, Suite 1400
Chicago, IL 60611
Call 1-(800) 621-6828 for information.

Glossary

abuse   an incident or practice of a provider which, although not considered fraudulent, is inconsistent with recognized standards of care.

ADC related   refers to Medicaid recipients who meet ADC eligibility requirements but do not receive ADC financial assistance. Generally, these recipients are pregnant women and children covered under Healthy Start.

adjudication   the operational process carried out by a plan from the receipt of a claim through the completion of an explanation of benefits.

adjusted historical payment basis   the payment for a service in 1991; the basis of charges for the initial phase-in period of the Medicare fee schedule.

administrative law judge   a lawyer who works for the Social Security Administration and is involved in the claims appeals process.

administrative services only (ASO)   an organization which contracts with self-insured employers and other insuring mechanisms to provide administrative services, such as provider contracting, utilization controls, enrollment services, and claims processing.

AFDC (Aid to Families with Dependent Children)   a Medicaid program for those whose incomes and resources are insufficient to meet the cost of medical care.

allowed amount   an individual determination made by a Medicare carrier for a covered Part B medical service or supply. It is the appropriate reimbursement based on the Medicare fee schedule for a CPT code.

allowed fee   the allowed amount for a benefit according to the maximum allowable fee.

Alphabetic Index   an index of patient conditions; found in Volume 2 of ICD-9-CM.

alternative delivery system (ADS)   a managed care plan which finances and delivers cost-efficient care without compromising the quality of medical care for its enrollees.

annual limit   a limitation of benefits set for certain services. After the limit is met, further services are excluded. Examples include 20 outpatient mental health visits or 30 physical therapy sessions per calendar year.

ANSI 837   American National Standards Institute format for electronic claims transmission approved by leaders in the medical insurance industry.

appeal   the submission of additional clinical and other pertinent information to a plan to overturn a denied claim.

assessment   the portion of the SOAP format that documents an evaluation of a condition and the doctor's impression or diagnosis.

assignment   an agreement by which a provider must accept Medicare's allowed amount. The check for reimbursement is then sent to the provider.

audit compliance rate   percentage of conformance to a standard of care or other established criteria.

authorization number   a number or notation assigned by a plan and given to the person requesting preauthorization when the plan's preauthorization agent validates the medical necessity of a service.

benefit   the amount payable by a plan, as covered in the policy, toward the cost of a medical service.

benefit codes   notations identifying the set of benefits for which an enrollee is eligible; also known as plan or group numbers, and can be identification numbers. They may be found on an ID card. The notations used are assigned by the plan.

benefit period   a specified period up to 90 days during which a deductible is applicable for Medicare Part A.

billed amount   the charge of a physician or other provider.

birthday rule   coordination of benefits for dependent children who are covered first by the insurance plan of the parent whose birthday occurs earlier in the calendar year.

bundling   the adjudication of two or more procedures under one allowed fee because the plan believes that the services are part of one procedure code.

Bureau of Workers' Compensation (BWC)   the administrative branch of the workers' compensation system.

capitation   a method used by managed care plans to pay physicians. Physicians are prepaid a certain amount per patient assigned to the practice per time period. The amount is paid for a group of services regardless of how many services are provided to these patients. The risk for controlling resource use is shifted to the doctor.

capitation rate   the fixed prepaid amount of payment under capitation. Also known as cap rate.

carrier   an organization contracted by the federal government to implement the Medicare program and handle claims from physicians, other providers, and beneficiaries.

case management   a process in which a plan's case manager intervenes in catastrophic patient cases by arranging alternative benefits and places for care.

categorically needy   refers to a Medicaid recipient who is eligible for assistance under Title IV Aid to Dependent Children or Title XVI Supplemental Security Income (SSI).

central certification   a Blue Cross/Blue Shield program that covers the employees of a company with offices, plants, and people in several states. All records are maintained in a central location, but claims can be reported where the service was provided.

certificate   Blue Cross/Blue Shield's terminology for a policy.

CHAMPUS (Civilian Health and Medical Program of the Uniformed Services)   a cost-sharing program for military families, retirees and their families, some former spouses, and survivors of deceased military personnel.

CHAMPVA (Civilian Health and Medical Program for the Veterans Administration)   a health benefits program for families of veterans with 100 percent service-connected disability and the surviving spouses and children of veterans who died from a service-connected disability.

claim   a request to an insurer on behalf of the insured to adjudicate benefits under the policy. It can be submitted electronically or in paper form. Identifies services provided by the doctor for insurance and managed care plans.

clean claim   information submitted on a claim which is complete and correct according to the insurance or managed care plan's rules.

CMAC (CHAMPUS maximum allowable charge)   the maximum allowable fee paid to providers under the CHAMPUS program.

code fragmenting   unbundling (see the definition of unbundling).

coding conventions   directions for using a coding system.

coinsurance   dollar amounts which the enrollee must pay for covered services based on a percentage or a ratio of allowed services. Some plans have deductibles, after which coinsurance applies.

combination code   one ICD-9-CM code which describes two conditions.

community rating   a method of establishing premiums by which an insurer's premium is the same for all individuals in a specific geographic area.

compromise and release   a settlement between an injured worker and an insurance plan or state fund for a permanent disability.

concurrent care   care occurring mainly in the hospital when two physicians report the same diagnosis code with subsequent hospital care codes.

conditional coverage   services that are covered on the basis of the condition or diagnosis of the patient.

confirmatory consultation   a type of consultation requested by a patient or plan to confirm the medical necessity or appropriateness of a treatment that was previously recommended by another physician.

consent form for medical treatment   a form stating that a patient has been informed of the possible risks of a certain procedure and that consent has been given for the treatment.

consultation   the rendering of an opinion or advice by a physician regarding the evaluation and/or management of a specific problem at the request of another physician.

contributory factors   criteria which do not have to be provided with every patient encounter.

controlling factor for time   time becomes a controlling factor in selecting the level of E&M code according to the time listed in its description, and when over 50 percent of the total time of the visit is spent by the physician either counseling or coordinating care with the patient face to face.

conversion factors   dollar multipliers which represent the payment per relative value unit. Used by plans to determine MAFs.

coordination of benefits (COB)   the coordination of operations between two or more plans to assure that neither plan issues payment for benefits in excess of 100 percent of a provider's services.

copayments   dollar amounts which an enrollee must pay toward certain covered services, such as office visits, mental health visits, and hospitalizations.

corrective action   the formal process for outlining the actions a plan has taken to improve identified problems in the quality of care.

cost sharing   an arrangement between the insured and the insurer, as outlined in the policy, which allows patients to share the cost of medical services with the insurer.

cost shifting   the billing of higher rates to better paying insurance plans by providers to cover money-losing patient categories, such as Medicare, Medicaid, and uncompensated care.

critical care   constant physician attendance during the course of 1 day because of the critical nature of the patient's condition.

cross-indemnification hold harmless clause   a contract clause which obligates physicians to assume full responsibility for themselves and the managed care organization if a malpractice case arises.

Current Procedural Terminology, 4th Edition (CPT-4)   a book maintained and published annually by the American Medical Association which lists numbers for the procedures performed by physicians.

cutoff date   a period of time, beginning with the actual date of service, after which a claim will not be adjudicated.

day sheet   the daily summation of all the financial activities of a practice.

deductible   a fixed dollar amount which an enrollee must pay for covered services each year before medical benefits begin.

DEERS (Department of Defense Enrollment Eligibility Reporting System) a worldwide database of military families used to confirm benefits under CHAMPUS.

denial a message from a plan notifying a practice or patient that a claim or service will not be adjudicated.

dependent a spouse, child, or person other than the policyholder who is eligible to be covered under the benefit package.

diagnosis related groups fixed, flat reimbursement rates for hospital admissions up to certain lengths of hospital confinement.

diagnostic statements ICD-9-CM codes representing medical terms describing patient diagnoses and/or conditions.

direct contracting negotiation with providers by employers and other groups for heathcare services on a capitated or predetermined price basis.

disallowances denials of charges above the maximum allowable fee.

discharge planning the early planning and arranging of needed patient services from a higher-cost place (usually the hospital) to a lower-cost place (usually the patient's home or a nursing home).

documentation the chronological recording of pertinent facts about and observations of a patient's health status in a logical sequence.

double coding the practice of reporting two diagnoses in the diagnostic statement by using the ICD-9-CM coding conventions to more accurately describe the patient's condition.

down coding the changing of a CPT code by a plan producing less payment than the original code because the plan believes the greater service was not justified by the diagnosis reported on the claim.

dunning request a message on a statement; generally used for outstanding patient account statements to convey the degree of delinquency.

durable medical equipment regional carriers (DMERCs) regional Medicare carriers responsible for processing durable medical equipment, prosthetics, orthotics, and supplies.

effective date the date medical benefits begin for enrollees carried by a plan.

electronic funds transfer (EFT) electronic transfer of money to the bank of a practice for the payment of claims by Medicare.

eligible population a term which applies to PPO enrollees who can seek elective services from nonpanel providers of the PPO at the cost of a reduction in benefits.

emergency room a hospital-based facility, open 24 hours a day, for treating patients who need immediate medical attention.

Employee Retirement Income Security Act of 1974 (ERISA) a federal law which regulates self-insured employers.

encounter   the physical contact of a patient with a provider of medical services, either the doctor or other medical personnel employed by the practice.

encounter form   the form on which the services provided to and the diagnosis of a patient are noted.

end-stage renal disease (ESRD)   the condition of individuals with chronic kidney disease who require dialysis or kidney transplantation; a criterion for Medicare coverage.

enrollee   any individual covered under a benefit package for whom benefits are still in effect.

enrollment period   the period of time during which a beneficiary meets eligibility requirements for Medicare. There are three enrollment periods: initial, special, and general.

episode of care   one payment per spell of illness for all treatment.

evergreen clause   a clause which makes a contract renewable each year unless it is terminated by either party.

exclusion   the amount which is not payable by the plan toward the cost of a medical service because the service is not a benefit outlined in the policy.

exclusive provider organization (EPO)   a benefit package option offered by a PPO. If an enrollee has chosen the EPO product option, the enrollee is locked into using a selected panel of PPO providers. If the enrollee goes outside the panel (unless it was an emergency or was preauthorized), none of the benefits are payable and the patient is liable for the entire amount.

exclusivity clause   a contract clause which requires a physician to work exclusively for the managed care organization, treating only its patients and giving up all other current patients.

existing patients only   an arrangement with a managed care organization to care for only existing patients enrolled in that organization with no obligation to accept any new patients of that organization.

experience rating   a method used by insurers to base new premiums on the insured's past medical costs paid by the insurer.

explanation of benefits (EOB)   a remittance which explains how benefits were adjudicated by the plan.

face-to-face time   the time a physician spends face to face with a patient and/or patient's family.

fair hearing   the second level of Medicare claims appeal.

family coverage   medical insurance for an individual and that individual's dependents.

Federal Employees Program (FEP)   a governmentwide plan that provides medical insurance for federal employees.

Federal Register   published by the U.S. Government Printing Office to document the acts and actions of Congress.

fee for service   the traditional method by which physicians are paid a fee for each service when submitting a claim after a service has been provided.

financial policy   an outline of the credit policy of a practice; describes when and how payment is expected from the patient.

fiscal intermediary   an organization contracted by the government that handles claims under Part A of the Medicare program.

follow-up days   a specific number of days after a procedure in which physician payment includes routine follow-up encounters (visits) with the doctor. Can include preoperative and intraoperative services as well as postoperative work, depending on the plan.

fraud   intentional deception or misrepresentation which an individual makes, knowing it to be false; the deception could result in an unauthorized benefit to the provider or another person.

freedom of information privilege   the ability to obtain information about government operations under the Freedom of Information Act.

gatekeeper   a primary care physician who is responsible for coordinating and authorizing the services of specialists and other providers for the enrollees assigned to his or her care. Primary care physicians can be family practitioners, internists, pediatricians, or obstetricians and gynecologists, depending on the managed care plan's rules.

geographical practice cost index (GPCI)   an index developed by Medicare to compare the resource costs of different geographic areas with the national average in regard to the relative value units of physician work, overhead, and malpractice liability.

global period   the number of days considered as a package for payment in the RBRVS method of payment in which 000 means the day of the procedure, 010 means 10 days, and 090 means 90 days; includes payment for preoperative, intraoperative, and postoperative care. For procedures with 90 days, the preoperative global period begins the calendar date before the procedure.

gross collection ratio   total payments divided by total charges without writeoffs.

group practice without walls (GPWW)   a group of physicians who have a joint venture arrangement for administering the business side of their practices and managed care contracting.

HBA (health benefits adviser)   an adviser at uniformed services hospitals and clinics who assists individuals in understanding their CHAMPUS benefits.

HCFA 1500   a paper form which provides a standard format for capturing all the information and data needed by most plans to process a claim.

HCFA (Health Care Financing Administration)   an agency within the Department of Health and Human Services that administers the Medicare program.

Health Care Financing Administration Common Procedural Coding System (HCPCS)   a listing maintained by HCFA which uses alphanumeric descriptions for the services of providers. It is used by government plans and is accepted by some private plans. It consists of CPT, Level II or national codes, and Level III or local codes.

health insurance claim number (HICN)   a number that identifies beneficiaries as being enrolled in Medicare.

health maintenance organization (HMO)   a deliverer of healthcare and medical insurance for individuals which is subject to state regulation, covers preventive care, monitors care and contracts with physicans and other providers.

health professional shortage areas (HPSAs)   designated areas by Medicare where there is a shortage of doctors and other medical practitioners. Use of HCPCS modifiers on claims brings bonus payments to these providers from Medicare.

highest degree of specificity   the use of all of the required number of digits listed in ICD-9-CM categories.

hospital discharge management   care by the doctor who discharges a patient on the last day of a multiple-day hospital stay.

hospital observation E&M   services provided to patients who are designated as being admitted to observation status in a hospital, not as inpatients.

identification card   a small card which is issued by an insurance or managed care plan after enrollment. It is valid as long as the patient or the person who enrolled on behalf of the patient maintains eligibility or pays the applicable premiums.

independent practice association (IPA)   a formally organized physicians' association which can negotiate contracts with insurers.

Industrial Commission (IC)   a government agency that determines levels of disability, resolves disputed claims, and establishes workers' compensation policy.

inpatient care   services provided to a patient who is admitted to a hospital with the status of an inpatient.

insured   an individual who is eligible to enroll on behalf of himself or herself and any dependents.

insurer   an insurance or managed care plan which has agreed to accept the risk of underwriting the cost of medical benefits for an individual or group of individuals.

intermediaries   insurance plans under contract to the Health Care Financing Administration to administer Part A of the Medicare program.

International Classification of Diseases-Clinical Modification, 9th Revision (ICD-9-CM)   a book maintained by the U.S. Department of Health and Human Services that lists alphanumeric and numeric descriptions for diagnoses, symptoms, and conditions.

key components criteria which must be met and documented in the medical record when reporting evaluation and management CPT codes.

laboratory summary sheet a sheet that visually identifies values for laboratory tests done in the office.

ledger card a chronologically itemized paper record of a patient's services and payments.

letter of termination a letter sent to a patient, by certified mail, informing the patient of the termination of the patient-doctor relationship.

level of service criteria for the key components defined in an evaluation and management CPT code number.

listed surgical procedures a guideline in CPT which recommends the surgical code number as having a standard number of follow-up days to pay for uncomplicated services as a package.

lock-in a status which occurs when the enrollees of a managed care plan must seek nonemergency services from the provider panel to receive medical benefits. If the enrollee seeks the services of a nonpanel provider, no services are covered.

main term a boldface word in the Alphabetic Index of ICD-9-CM and CPT.

managed care the application of administrative methods to control healthcare costs and patient access to providers; the administrative methods integrate the financing and delivery of medical care for enrollees.

managed care organization a legal entity which uses managed care methods to control healthcare costs.

managed care plans insurance mechanisms and healthcare delivery systems operated by private companies which contract with providers and strictly monitor medical resource utilization. They also monitor provider practice patterns and the quality of medical care.

managed competition a form of managed care which allows groups of providers or groups of providers and insurers to submit bids and negotiate payment, often in the form of capitation, to secure a contract to deliver care to a population.

managed indemnity plan an insurer with indemnity benefits (covers only illness or injury) who contracts with physicians and monitors medical resources.

management services organization (MSO) a turnkey operation for managing the business side of a medical practice. The business staff manages the operation as one large group practice providing management services such as claim reporting and billing, purchasing of supplies, personnel administration, the pension plan, malpractice insurance for physicians, and managed care contracting.

mandated Medigap transfer or crossover a claim for which a Medicare beneficiary elects to assign benefits under a Medigap policy to a participating physician or supplier.

mandatory assignment   a Medicare regulation which requires physicians to accept the Medicare allowed amount as payment in full, such as laboratory services done in the office.

manual system   a handwritten system of billing and reporting the claims.

master medication sheet   a summary list of the drugs prescribed, the dosage, the number dispensed, the dates started, and the dates stopped.

master problem sheet   a summary list of past or current patient medical conditions which may affect current care.

maximum allowable fee (MAF)   the payment amount allowed by a plan for each CPT code. When a claim is adjudicated, payment for the CPT code is equal to either the billed charge or the MAF, whichever is lower.

Medicaid   a state and federally funded entitlement program, operated by the states, for medical, rehabilitation, and other health-related services furnished to families with dependent children, the aged, the blind, and the disabled whose income and resources are insufficient to pay for medical care.

medical director   a physician who is responsible for monitoring the clinical care provided by participating physicians to the enrollees of a plan.

medical inflation   the percentage of increase in the medical component of consumer prices.

medical necessity   describes a service which is (1) appropriate for the diagnosis being reported, (2) provided in the appropriate location, (3) not provided for the patient's convenience or the convenience of the patient's family, and (4) not custodial care (custodial care does not have to be provided by a trained medical professional).

medical release   a document allowing medical records to be sent to insurance plans, lawyers, and others for a specific purpose.

medically indigent   a Medicaid phrase for individuals who, because of previous medical expenses, have inadequate resources to cover current medical expenses.

Medicare   a federally funded entitlement program for medical insurance for patients over age 65, certain disabled individuals, and those with end-stage renal disease.

Medicare economic index (MEI)   an index used by Medicare to update physician fee levels in relation to changes in inflation, productivity, and specific health sector practice expense factors, including malpractice, personnel costs, and rent.

Medicare transaction system   a transaction system developed and implemented by Medicare to consolidate automated claims processing.

Medigap   an insurance policy designed for Medicare beneficiaries that covers the deductible and copayment amounts not covered under the Medicare policy.

Medpard   a directory developed by Medicare carriers which includes all participating providers of Part B services; compiled by county and physician specialty.

members   enrollees of a health maintenance organization.

National Electronic Information Corporation (NEIC) founded by several major insurance plans; a clearinghouse for electronic claims submission.

net collection ratio also known as adjusted collection ratio; the total payments divided by the total charges after writeoffs have been deducted.

nonavailability statements CHAMPUS verifications given to enrollees within the ZIP Code zone of a military hospital to use nonemergency care outside the zone. INASs are inpatient nonavailability statements, and ONASs are outpatient nonavailability statements. These statements are needed for specific services.

noncovered services services excluded from coverage.

nonparticipating physician a physician who does not have a formal contract with a plan.

not reasonable and necessary A Medicare phrase which refers to services that are not reasonable and necessary for the diagnosis and treatment of an illness or injury or to improve the diagnosis or treatment of a malformed body part.

objective the part of the SOAP format that documents the physical examination of the patient.

Office of the Inspector General (OIG) an office established at the Department of Health and Human Services by Congress in 1976 to identify and eliminate fraud, abuse, and waste in government programs.

one-time payment authorization the application of wordage specified by Medicare in having the beneficiary sign once to permit the practice to assign benefits and release medical information to Medicare and Medigap plans.

open enrollment a specified period during which an individual can select and submit an application to enroll in an insurance or managed care plan.

optical character recognition devices scanning devices that transfer data from printed or typed claim forms to the computer data systems of plans for adjudication.

ordering physician a physician who orders nonphysician services for a patient, such as diagnostic laboratory tests, clinical laboratory tests, pharmaceutical services, and durable medical equipment.

outcome the effects of patient treatment at specific points in time.

out-of-pocket costs: any payments made by the enrollee directly to the provider of services under cost-sharing arrangements with a medical insurance plan.

Part A Medicare's hospital insurance program; provides insurance against the cost of hospital and related posthospital services for elderly and disabled beneficiaries.

Part B Medicare's supplementary medical insurance program; provides insurance benefits for medically necessary physician services, hospital outpatient services, and various other limited ambulatory services and supplies. It is a voluntary program and requires beneficiaries to pay a monthly premium, deductible, and coinsurance.

participating physician   a physician who has a formal contract with a medical plan.

PCP management fee   compensation for the supervision and administrative paper work of patient care by a primary care physician.

peer review   a process in which physicians review the care provided by other physicians to identify abnormal practice patterns.

pegboard system   a manual system for entering charges, payments, and adjustments in a practice. The entry is written once but entered on multiple documents such as the ledger card and superbill.

permanent disability   an illness or injury that prohibits an individual from performing his or her regular job.

physician hospital organization (PHO)   an entity in which physicians and hospitals form a relationship for contracting with managed care organizations. Some PHOs also provide management services functions.

physician on record   the initial treating physician of an injured worker in a workers' compensation case.

physician peer review profiling   reports from claim data created by plans for the analysis of physician services provided to enrollees.

plan   the portion of the SOAP format that includes the recording of recommended treatments, tests ordered, other tests contemplated, new medications or adjustments in medications, therapies, and planned surgical procedures.

plan identification card   a small card which is issued by an insurance or managed care plan after enrollment. It is valid as long as the patient or the person who enrolled on behalf of the patient maintains eligibility or pays the applicable premiums.

pmpm   per member per month; usually the capitation rate is set per member per month.

point of service (POS)   a benefit package option for HMO members who can decide at the point of seeking medical service to use a nonparticipating provider (a physician or hospital not in the panel). When an HMO member seeks the services of a nonparticipating provider, the benefits are reduced. The member must pay out-of-pocket costs of generally 20 to 30 percent of the HMO's allowable fee for the service.

policy   a document that outlines covered and noncovered benefits and any requirements of the insured and dependents for obtaining care; a contract between a patient and a medical insurance mechanism.

policyholder   another name for an insured.

practice brochure booklet   printed materials that acquaint patients with a practice and its policies. The booklet describes the staff, the training of the physicians, and their medical specialties.

practice guidelines   a term synonymous with *standards of care* and practice parameters.

preauthorization a requirement to notify a plan of certain services before they are provided; enables the plan to determine the medical necessity of a service. Does not guarantee benefits or payment if the patient is not a valid enrollee at the time of service.

preexisting condition (PEC) a medical condition which has been diagnosed and treated before the effective date of a policy. A plan will not cover preexisting conditions until the enrollee waits a period of time, such as 60 or 90 days, during which no treatment was given for the condition.

preferred provider organization (PPO) a panel of providers under contract and connected with a medical insurance mechanism which pays the panel a reduced fee for service rate, not holding the provider at risk. Consumers have financial incentives to use the panel of preferred providers.

premium the cost of funding a medical benefit package. Premiums are usually paid by the insured in full or in part to keep benefits effective. Some employers pay the whole premium for their employees. In some government plans, such as Medicaid, no premium is paid by the enrollee; the cost for the benefit package is funded by the government.

preventive maintenance sheet a summary sheet for the medical record that lists when and what preventive services are due, such as mammograms, prostate screenings, sigmoidoscopies.

primary diagnosis the chief condition assessed during an encounter with the physician that justifies the medical services provided; the condition for which the primary procedure is performed.

primary insurer the plan which is responsible for processing or paying its portion of benefits first for patients enrolled in multiple plans before any other plan pays its portion.

primary procedure the chief procedure provided during an encounter; usually the most expensive and extensive procedure.

professional component the reporting of physician professional services with CPT modifier –26 when the physician interprets test results and there is no code number describing the service.

prolonged services the services of a physician who provides care involving face-to-face patient contact that is beyond the time specified in an E&M CPT code.

prompt pay law state legislation outlining the time in which third-party payers have to pay clean claims submitted by providers.

prorating procedures a percentage reduction of the allowed amounts for the second, third, fourth, fifth procedures performed within the same operative session or on the same date.

provider identification number a number or an alphanumeric which is assigned to a physician to identify the physician to a plan.

purging the reduction of inactive documents within the office medical record.

qualitative a descriptive term used in the laboratory section of CPT meaning confirmation of the presence of a substance.

quality the degree of conformance to a standard.

quality improvement (QI) the application of continual improvement in the day-to-day operations and management of an organization; usually overseen by a team of employees.

quantitative a descriptive term used in the laboratory section of CPT meaning confirmation of the total amount of a substance.

reason codes notations on the explanation of benefits representing the actions taken by a plan in adjudicating a claim.

recall the notification of a patient that it is time to schedule an appointment or procedure.

reciprocity plan a cooperative payment arrangement between the various Blue Cross and Blue Shield companies; allows a practice to bill the Blues in the state where the patient received services, not the patient's home state.

reconsideration the first level of appeal for CHAMPUS. A letter is sent to the contractor within 90 days of the date on the EOB.

referral an authorization from a patient's primary care physician. It can be a paper form or an authorization number.

referring physician a physician who requests a service.

registration the process of collecting information about a patient and orienting the patient to the policies of a medical practice.

registration form a document for collecting information needed by the practice to set up patient accounts; requests patients' addresses, phone numbers, responsible parties, and names of insurance plans.

reinsurance an insurer that has been retained by an insurance or managed care plan or group practice to cover claims when a funder defaults or to cover claims of catastrophic patients after a certain level of expense, such as $50,000 or $100,000.

relative value unit (RVU) part of a physician payment method which assigns a single number according to relative weights for each CPT code. The numbers are called units of physician services and make each code mathematically related to all the other codes in accordance with the skill, time, work of the physician, and other factors.

report card a report developed by a managed care organization to capture physician performance in specific areas, such as degree of patient satisfaction, audit of medical records, referral, and utilization of resources.

residual subcategories subcategories in the ICD-9-CM coding system in which the coder lacks specific information from the physician or the book does not provide adequate information for the coder to classify the condition into a more descriptive subcategory.

Resource Based Relative Value Scale (RBRVS) a method of physician payment implemented by the Health Care Financing Administration which determines the unit value for a CPT code by assigning three separate unit values: (1) physician work, (2) practice expense, and (3) malpractice expenses. Also known as the Medicare fee schedule (MFS).

restricted status a Medicaid status in which, because of prior abuse of privileges, a patient is limited in the choice of physician and pharmacy.

review of systems (ROS) documented information in the medical record about illnesses of the various systems in a patient's body.

risk a chance for loss of funds.

risk pools accounts into which HMOs contribute money to pay claims. Pools are established with separate budgets for hospital, physician, pharmacy, and other services. At the end of a designated time period, HMOs may pay physicians some or all of the extra money left in the pools after all medical claims for the period have been paid.

rule of nines the method used in calculating the extent of body surface covered in a burn victim.

second opinion a requirement that a patient must obtain the opinion of an impartial physician regarding the necessity of a planned procedure before the procedure is performed.

secondary insurer the plan which is responsible for processing or paying its portion of benefits second for a patient enrolled in multiple plans.

self-funded refers to the payment of medical insurance claims from a bank or trust account established by an employer or group.

self-insured plan a plan in which an employer or other group assumes the full risk for the payment of employee medical services by taking the premium it would have paid to an insurance plan and establishing a fund to cover benefits.

separate procedure guideline a procedure that is ordinarily done as a part of a larger procedure; if it is performed alone for a specific purpose, it is considered a separate procedure that is reported by itself.

signature on file an authorization validating either the release of information or the assignment of benefits.

site of service A Medicare phrase which refers to a reduction of payment for the doctor because of the place the service was provided. For example: a visit occurred in a hospital outpatient department, rather than the office.

smart card a card that allows access to a patient's medical record and benefit eligibility via a computer network.

SOAP a medical record format that documents the patient's treatment in an organized and consistent manner listing subjective, objective, assessment, and plan.

spend-down a deductible or amount of money that must be paid for services before a patient is eligible for Medicaid benefits.

sponsor   a military person whose relationship to a patient makes the patient eligible for CHAMPUS.

staged procedure   surgery planned in stages.

standards of care   the minimum sets of services which should be provided for a patient's condition.

starred procedure   used when CPT does not recommend a code as having a standard number of follow-up days so that it can be paid as a package.

stop loss   the maximum amount of money that can be lost by a physician beyond what capitation has paid per patient.

subjective   the part of the SOAP format that documents the chief complaint and the reason for the medical visit; includes the chief complaint and history of the present illness. This is the information the patient tells the doctor.

subrogation   a process coordinated between insurance companies for the payment of medical claims resulting from accidents or illnesses when the plan which first receives a claim believes that the claim may be the liability of another insurance company, such as automobile or homeowner's insurance.

subscriber   an enrollee of a Blue Cross and Blue Shield plan.

subterm words   words that are indented under the main term in the Alphabetic Index of ICD-9-CM. They are individual line entries which describe essential differences in etiology or clinical type.

superbill   an encounter form.

surgical disclosure letter   notification to a Medicare beneficiary when assignment is not taken and the nonemergency procedure charge is over $500.

surrogate UPIN   a temporary UPIN that is issued by Medicare if the ordering or referring physician has not been assigned a permanent UPIN.

Tabular List   contains the numbers or alphanumerics of ICD-9-CM; in Volume 1.

temporary disability   the recovery period after a job-related illness or injury in a workers' compensation case.

third-party administrator (TPA)   an organization which contracts with self-insured employers and other groups to provide administrative methods, such as provider contracting, utilization controls, enrollment services, and claims processing.

third-party payers   insurance mechanisms which pay the doctor. Insurance and managed care plans underwrite and accept the financial risk for the healthcare of the consumers enrolled.

time   a component of E&M CPT coding; can be used as a guideline for average length of time of an encounter between a physician and a patient or it can be used as a controlling factor.

traditional indemnity benefits   benefits which are paid only when a patient is ill or injured. A diagnosis which implies that the patient has a pathologic condition or symptom must be reported on the claim for payment to be received under these policies.

TriCare a new program of managed care that is available to CHAMPUS beneficiaries.

triple product option (TOP) an organization which offers at least three health insurance product options, usually an HMO, a PPO, and an indemnity benefit plan.

truth-in-lending statement a form documenting a formal agreement between a patient and the practice if the patient owes an amount of money which will take more than four installments to repay.

unbundling the reporting of two or more procedure codes when the plan believes they are part of another procedure also reported on the same claim.

Unique Provider Number (UPIN) an HCFA assigned provider number for individual physicians; identifies physicians to Medicare on a nationwide basis and is used in physician profiling.

universal claim form the standardized insurance claim form, the HCFA 1500, used to report claims to most plans.

upcoding the reporting of a more complex procedure not justified by the diagnosis(es).

unspecified a subcategory in the Tabular List of ICD-9-CM, usually ending in 9 or 0, which is selected because the physician and/or other medical personnel have not documented or specified enough information to select a more specific subcategory.

usual, customary, and reasonable (UCR) a method of determining physician payment which looks at historical fees billed by physicians and sets payment for a procedure on the basis of what other physicians have charged. The UCR method can base the maximum allowable fee on a percentile of historical billings, such as the fiftieth to eightieth percentile.

utilization the rate of use of medical service resources.

utilization hassle factor the degree of disruptions and extra work a managed care organization causes a practice.

utilization management the monitoring of care to assure that only medically necessary benefits are paid.

vertically integrated plan (VIP) a legal and formally integrated entity of employed providers (hospitals, physicians, nursing homes, home health agencies, pharmacies, and others) working with a common vision and goal. The providers deliver services jointly to a defined population through a seamless continuum of preventive and primary care, inpatient and outpatient hospital care, long-term care, and all other services in between. The VIP is paid capitation by the government and/or insurance and managed care plans. Plans may be integrated with the VIP. A VIP can be initiated by plans, hospitals, physicians, or other healthcare entities. Also known as ISNs (integrated service networks). The VIP is the last phase in the reorganization of providers in healthcare reform.

volume performance standard a medical resource monitoring mechanism set by Congress for the Medicare program to slow the rate of increase in expenditures for physician services.

waiting period a length of time a policyholder and/or his or her dependents must wait until they are eligible to enroll, including the application processing period.

waiver of liability letter notification to a Medicare beneficiary by a medical practice that the services performed may not be covered under the Medicare program.

welcome packet a mailable collection of information for patients, including a practice brochure booklet, financial policy, and registration form.

withhold account a system in which a certain portion of the payment due to the physician is held by the HMO (e.g., 10 to 40 percent) for a defined period, until the HMO has had time to pay all the claims for that period. If an HMO exceeds its budget for the payment of claims for the period, the withheld money will not be paid to the doctor. If the HMO stays within its budget, return of the withhold amount can be determined by the plan.

workers' compensation a requirement of the federal government for employers of patients who are injured or become sick on the job. It is operated by various plans chosen by the employer or can be operated by the state government.

Workgroup for Electronic Data Interchange (WEDI) an advisory body formed to standardize electronic billing formats of insurance and managed care plans.

writeoffs charges for services which are credited to the patient's account.

Answers to Exercises

Chapter 1

1. Patient, doctor, plan
2. Government plans and private plans
3. Medicare, Medicaid, Champus, workers' compensation
4. Health maintenance organization and preferred provider organization
5. (a) Understand and comply with the rules and regulations of each plan, (b) know whether there are contractual relationships between the practice and each payer, (c) assist the physician and other employees in understanding what needs to be done to comply, (d) assist in the design of forms for reporting services and/or purchase computer software in order to submit data quickly and consistently, (e) assure that the practice is receiving the optimum entitled payments, and (f) assist patients in understanding their benefits and what they need to do to receive maximum benefits
6. A plan in which an employer or another group is the payer. The employer's funds are at risk for healthcare benefits provided to employees or members of the group.
7. Contacting the plan before hospitalizing a patient or performing an operation or an expensive test to explain the clinical reasons why the service is necessary for the patient's treatment
8. The historical method by which physicians are paid a fee by submitting a claim after the service is provided
9. A method used by managed care plans to pay physicians. Physicians and other providers are prepaid a certain amount per patient assigned to the practice per time period, generally per month.
10. Summer
11. Fall
12. As soon as Congress acts. Congress does not act upon this the same date each year.
13. By writing to the government program
14. Regulations
15. State

Chapter 2

1. Registration, medical encounter, exit, billing, and posting
2. Primary insurance plan
3. When the patient enters the office
4. Once

5. Plan ID card
6. Diagnoses
7. The HCFA 1500
8. The physical contact of a patient with a provider of medical services
9. The form used to document the condition of a patient and the services provided; used in communicating this information to the billing personnel
10. Identifies services provided by a doctor for an insurance or managed care plan
11. A document that explains the benefits being paid, denied, or pending for the plan's payment period
12. An authorization from the patient's primary care physician
13. Financial policy and registration form. A practice brochure booklet is included if the practice has one.
14. Assignment of benefits to the physician and authorization of the release of medical information to pay a claim
15. As a reference source in case there is a problem in the processing of a claim
16. Because of a contractual agreement between the doctor and the plan / The difference between the billed charges and the allowed amount are written off.
17. Yes
18. Yes
19. 99202
20. 99212
21. 90702
22. 93000
23. 81000
24. 382.00
25. 786.50
26. 782.3
27. 784.0
28. 380.6
29. 45300
30. 47000
31. 99238
32. 32020
33. 44155
34. All charges are due and payable within 30 days of the first billing. / For services not covered by your insurance plan, payment in advance is necessary. / If other circumstances warrant an extended payment plan, our credit counselor will assist you in these special circumstances.

Chapter 3

1. Premium
2. Plan identification card (ID card)
3. Benefit
4. Out-of-pocket costs
5. Copayments
6. Deductibles
7. Coinsurance
8. Primary insurer

9. Coordination of benefits (COB)
10. Participating physician
11. No, above it by $4
12. No, below it
13. 20.0
14. $3,000 (20 units × $150 = $3,000)
15. 6
16. 120
17. 90
18. 36.52
19. No
20. No / The RVU and RBRVS systems contain different unit value amounts and different dollar conversion factors.
21. XYZ's preadmission certification assures the medical necessity of services provided in the most cost-efficient setting. All hospital admissions must be precertified except for emergency admissions, not including psychiatric admissions and maternity admissions. Outpatient hospital surgery, MRIs, and physical therapy must be certified. Physical therapy does not need certification until 10 sessions are done. An 800 number is called at least 5 days before the admission. If approved, an authorization number is given to be placed in item 23 of the HCFA 1500.
22. No
23. Yes

Chapter 4

1. Arthritis associated with Henoch-Schonlein purpura or serum sickness (713.6)
2. Yes / 011.64
3. To code and report the underlying diseases, such as Hunter's disease or mucopolysaccharidosis
4. The modified terms on the right and left of the brace must be present in the patient's condition to select this code
5. One or more terms to the right of the colon must be present in the patient's condition to select this code
6. An explanatory note to identify a synonym for thromboangitis obliterans / Buerger's disease is an eponym
7. An explanatory note to define enthesopathies
8. The code was added to ICD-9-CM when it was created
9. No / The doctor should be asked for more clinical details.
10. Yes / The patient must have one condition or more present to select this code.
11. Cold 460
12. Pneumonia 487.0
13. Vaginitis 099.53; index this word by the condition
14. Foreign body 930.1; there is no way to designate the right eye
15. Cholelithiasis 574.20; no mention of cholecystitis or cholelithiasis
16. Otitis 381.3
17. Varicose vein-esophagus-bleeding 456.0; indent to three levels / There was no mention of cirrhosis or portal hypertension.
18. Acne 706.1; ask the doctor to be more specific about the type of acne

19. Cataract-senile-nuclear 366.16; when the fourth digit is selected, the fifth-digit selections appear

20. Charcot-Marie-Tooth 356.1

	Index Word	Code	Hint
21.	Photophobia	368.13	Always code symptoms first
	Status (post) cataract extraction	V45.6	
22.	Vaccination tetanus	V03.7	The reason for the encounter is to receive a vaccination.
	Wound forearm complicated	881.10	
23.	Infection urinary	599.0	When a disease is found during a routine visit, code it first.
	Infection E. Coli	041.4	
	Attention to urethrostomy	V55.6	
24.	Status (post) cardiac pacemaker	V45.01	The reason for the encounter is due to status post pacemaker.
	Arteriosclerotic cardiovascular	429.2	The disease is still present but under control by the pacemaker.
25.	Anxiety acute stress reaction	308.0	Mrs. Johnson has an illness to code first.
	Conflict parent-child	V61.20	
26.	Cough	786.2	
	Exam radiologic NEC	V72.5	
27.	Contraception	V25.2	The diagnosis is the outcome desired.
28.	Delivery twins	V31.00	The twins have the same diagnosis, submitted on two separate claims.
29.	Infarct myocardium posterior	410.61	5th digit of 1 is used because the episode is initial treatment.
30.	Infarct myocardium healed	412	

31.	Hypertension cardiorenal	404.00	4th digit specifies malignant. 5th digit of 0 is used because heart and renal failure were not mentioned.
32.	Pain chest-wall	786.52	(Anterior) has no meaning.
33.	Buerger's	443.1	(thromboangitis obliterans)
34.	Arteriosclerosis cardiac	414.0	Two codes are needed because there is no combination code.
	Arteriosclerosis cardiovascular	429.2	
35.	Neoplasm spleen—flexure	153.7	
36.	Neoplasm lung—lower lobe	197.0	The lung is the secondary site.
	Neoplasm breast	174.9	The breast is the primary site.
37.	Neoplasm esophagus contiguous site	150.8	The esophagus is the primary site.
	Neoplasm stomach	197.8	The stomach is the secondary site.
38.	Neoplasm cervix	233.1	
39.	Fracture malleolus medial open	824.1	
40.	Fracture humerus (closed) anatomical neck	812.02	
41.	Fracture femur shaft	821.01	
42.	Wound, open foot	892.1	
43.	Wound, open thigh	890.0	
44.	Wound, open hand complicated	882.1	

45. Injury   910.2
       superficial
          nose

46. Injury   864.01
       internal
          liver
             contusion

47. Hematoma   432.1
       subdural
          nontraumatic

    Late   326
       effect(s) of
          meningitis

48. Dislocation   837.0
       fibula
          distal end

    Late   905.4
       effect(s) of
          fracture
             extremity
                lower

49. Complications   996.2
       mechanical
          device
             nervous system

50. Complications   996.85
       graft
          bone marrow

Chapter 5

1. Evaluation and Management, Anesthesiology, Surgery, Radiology, Pathology and Laboratory, and Medicine.
2. Vertebral corpectomy (vertebral body resection), partial or complete, for excision of intraspinal lesion, single segment
3. Parent
4. Revised words in the description with this printing
5. A new code number and description with this printing
6. −57
7. −32
8. No / The description in CPT already includes the professional component.
9. A result planned in stages or a staged procedure / more extensive than the original procedure / for therapy after a diagnostic surgical procedure
10. −78 is attached to a related procedure. −79 is attached to an unrelated procedure.
11. 99202 / Three lower required components were met. The level chosen must be

coded to the two components which were met. The criteria for a low complexity of decision making are exceeded. CPT says that the criteria must be met or exceeded to select a level of service.

12. 99213 / Two criteria were met for the established patient. The selected code is from one level lower for low complexity decision making.
13. 99214 / Yes
14. No
15. 99212, 99354
16. Preventive medicine
17. 30 per day
18. Calendar date or day
19. 99238
20. Can
21. Yes
22. Yes
23. Yes
24. 15
25. No
26. 99238
27. Cardiopulmonary resuscitation 92950
28. Intermittent positive pressure breathing-initial 94650, subsequent 94651
29. Allergy tests—intradermal—allergen extract 95024 × 20 units
30. Immunization—passive tetanus 90703, office and other outpatient visits 99211
31. Electrocardiogram—tracing 93005
32. Catheterization—injection 93526, 93543, 93555, 93556 (no radiologist involved)
33. Physical medicine—hydrotherapy 97036 × 3 units
34. Psychotherapy—individual 90843
35. Injection—intramuscular—antibiotic (Rocephin 250 mg) 90788
36. Special services—unusual travel 99082
37. Emergency department visits 99282
38. X-ray—calcaneous 73650 minimum of two views
39. Ultrasound—pregnant uterus 76815
40. X-ray with contrast—bile duct—guide stone removal 74327
41. Magnetic resonance imaging—knee 73721
42. Mammography—screening 76092
43. Angiography—brachial artery 75658
44. Thyroid—nuclear medicine—uptake 78001
45. Urinalysis 81000
46. Thyroid—panel 80092
47. Blood—in feces 82270
48. Culture—bacteria—urine 87086
49. Candida—skin test 86485
50. 12 or more automated chemistries, hemogram, automated, and manual differential WBC count, or hemogram and platelet count, automated, and automated complete differential WBC count, and thyroid stimulating hormone
51. Alanine aminotransferase, albumin, aspartate aminotransferase, bilirubin, direct, bilirubin, total, calcium, carbon dioxide content, chloride, cholesterol, creatinine, glucose, lactate dehydrogenase, phosphatase, alkaline, phosphorus (inorganic phosphate), potassium, protein (total), sodium, urea nitrogen, uric acid

52. Chemical peel 15789-52 use modifier 52 as only the forehead was peeled.
53. Shaving—skin lesion 11312
54. Excision—skin lesion—benign 11401
55. Prosthesis—breast—insertion 19340
56. Excision—skin lesion—malignant 11644
57. Wound repair—skin and tissues 13132, plus 11644
58. Whitman procedure—see acetabulum reconstruction 27122
59. Velpeau cast 29058
60. Fracture—nose—without manipulation 21310
61. Arthroscopy—surgical—knee 29881
62. Femur—repair—with graft 27170
63. Atherectomy—percutaneous—aorta 35491
64. Pacemaker—conversion 33214
65. Aorta—repair—suture 33320
66. Colon—endoscopy—removal of polyp 45384
    Colon—endoscope—biopsy 45380
    (do not use –51 unless told otherwise by a specific plan)
67. Cholecystectomy—laparoscopic 56341
68. Repair—hernia—incisional 49566
    Implantation—mesh—hernia repair 49568
69. Gastrostomy tube—insertion 43750; the note under 43750 refers to the S&I code 74350
70. Hysteroscopy—endometrial ablation 56356
71. Prostate—excision—transurethral 52601
72. Cesarean section 59510
73. A and J
74. L, M, G, Q, V
75. Always used in place of CPT and HCPCS Level II codes if there is a better code description of the service
76. Level III, then Level II, then Level I.
77. When the plan accepts these codes and if they provide a more specific description than CPT codes
78. A and J
79. G0001
80. Q0114

Chapter 6

1. Other
2. Birthdate and sex
3. Item 10b
4. 6
5. 11a
6. 13
7. 18
8. 21
9. 20
10. 24D
11. 27

12. 24G
13. 29
14. 32
15. 33
16. Electronic claims submission: a paperless method of sending claims information
17. Optical character recognition / A scanner transfers information from the claim form into the data banks of the plan's computer during claims processing.
18. Medicare Transaction System / A system to consolidate Medicare claims processing
19. American National Standards Institute / A national standard for the transmission of electronic claims.
20. National Electronic Information Corporation / A clearinghouse which accepts data in a single format and edits, sorts, and distributes the information into formats acceptable by the various plans.
21. Workgroup for Electronic Data Interchange / A group formed to standardize automatic claims filing and payments between hospitals, physicians, employers, and insurers.
22.

HEALTH INSURANCE CLAIM FORM

1. MEDICARE MEDICAID CHAMPUS CHAMPVA GROUP HLTH PLAN FECA OTHER ☒ ☐ ☐ ☐ ☐ ☐ ☐	1a. INSUREDS ID NUMBER 281-46-6000T

2. PATIENT'S NAME SAMPLE, RONALD	3. PATIENT'S BIRTHDATE SEX 08 MM 04 DD 21 YY M ☒ F ☐	4. INSURED'S NAME SAMPLE, RONADL

5. PATIENT'S ADDRESS (No., Street) 26 MAPLE STREET	6. PATIENT RELATIONSHIP TO INSURED self ☐ spouse ☐ child ☐ other ☐	7. INSURED'S ADDRESS (No.,Street) 26 MAPLE STREET

CITY GREEN ASH	STATE AM	8. PATIENT STATUS single ☐ married ☐ other ☒ employed full-time part-time ☐ student ☐ student ☐	CITY GREEN ASH	STATE AM.

ZIP CODE 45299	TELEPHONE (513-666-4444)		ZIP CODE 45299	TELEPHONE (593) 666-4444

9. OTHER INSURED NAME SAMPLE, RONALD	10. IS PATIENT CONDITION RELATED TO: a. employment? ☐ Yes ☒ No b. auto accident? ☐ Yes ☒ No c. other accident? ☐ Yes ☒ No	11. INSURED'S POLICY GRP OR FECA # NONE

a. OTHER INSURED'S POLICY OR GROUP # 281-45-6000		a. INSURED'S DATE OF BIRTH SEX 08 MM 03 DD 21 YY M ☒ F ☐
b. OTHER INSURED'S DATE OF BIRTH 08 MM 04 DD 21 YY		b. EMPLOYER'S NAME OR SCHOOL NAME RETIRED
c. EMPLOYER'S NAME OR SCHOOL NAME RETIRED		c. INSURANCE PLAN NAME MEDICARE- NATIONWIDE

d. INSURANCE PLAN NAME AARP	10d. RESERVED FOR LOCAL USE	d. IS THERE ANOTHER HEALTH PLAN?

12. PATIENT'S OR AUTHORIZED PERSON'S SIGNATURE SIGNED SIGNATURE ON FILE DATE 08-19-94	13. INSURED'S OR AUTHORIZED PERSON'S SIGNATURE signed SIGNATURE ON FILE

23.

HEALTH INSURANCE CLAIM FORM

1. MEDICARE MEDICAID CHAMPUS CHAMPVA GROUP HLTH PLAN FECA OTHER ☐ ☐ ☐ ☐ ☐ ☐ ☒		1a. INSUREDS ID NUMBER ABC 19064	
2. PATIENT'S NAME LANES, MARY	3. PATIENT'S BIRTHDATE SEX 01 MM 30 DD 44 YY M ☐ F ☒	4. INSURED'S NAME RAYMOND LANES	
5. PATIENT'S ADDRESS (No., Street) 1123 APPLE LANE	6. PATIENT RELATIONSHIP TO INSURED self ☐ spouse ☐ child ☐ other ☐	7. INSURED'S ADDRESS (No.,Street) 1123 APPLE LANE	

CITY GREEN ASH	STATE AM	8. PATIENT STATUS single ☐ married ☒ other ☐ employed full-time part-time ☐ student ☐ student ☐	CITY GREEN ASH	STATE OHIO
ZIP CODE 45299	TELEPHONE (583) 333-4444		ZIP CODE TELEPHONE 45299 (583) 333-4444	

9. OTHER INSURED NAME	10. IS PATIENT CONDITION RELATED TO:
	
	a. employment?
	  ☐ Yes ☒ No
	b. auto accident?
	  ☐ Yes ☒ No
	c. other accident?
	  ☐ Yes ☒ No
		11. INSURED'S POLICY GRP OR FECA #
		NONE

a. OTHER INSURED'S POLICY OR GROUP #		a. INSURED'S DATE OF BIRTH SEX 01 MM 30 DD 44 YY M ☒ F ☐
b. OTHER INSURED'S DATE OF BIRTH MM DD YY		b. EMPLOYER'S NAME OR SCHOOL NAME ABC CEMENT
c. EMPLOYER'S NAME OR SCHOOL NAME		c. INSURANCE PLAN NAME BLUE CROSS, BLUE SHIELD FLORIDA
d. INSURANCE PLAN NAME	10d. RESERVED FOR LOCAL USE	d. IS THERE ANOTHER HEALTH PLAN? NO
12. PATIENT'S OR AUTHORIZED PERSON'S SIGNATURE SIGNED_SIGNATUR ON FILE_____ DATE_08-19-94_		13. INSURED'S OR AUTHORIZED PERSON'S SIGNATURE SIGNATURE ON FILE

24. Ruth Brown

14. DATE OF CURRENT: ◄ ILLNESS (First symptom) OR INJURY (Accident) OR PREGNANCY(LMP) MM DD YY					15. IF PATIENT HAS HAD SAME OR SIMILAR ILLNESS. GIVE FIRST DATE MM DD YY				16. DATES PATIENT UNABLE TO WORK IN CURRENT OCCUPATION MM DD YY MM DD YY FROM TO					
17. NAME OF REFERRING PHYSICIAN OR OTHER SOURCE					17a. I.D. NUMBER OF REFERRING PHYSICIAN				18. HOSPITALIZATION DATES RELATED TO CURRENT SERVICES MM DD YY MM DD YY FROM TO					
19. RESERVED FOR LOCAL USE									20. OUTSIDE LAB? $ CHARGES ☐ YES ☐ NO					
21. DIAGNOSIS OR NATURE OF ILLNESS OR INJURY. (RELATE ITEMS 1,2,3 OR 4 TO ITEM 24E BY LINE) ──┐ ▼ 1. L 715.9 3. L ___.___ 2. L 244.9 4. L ___.___									22. MEDICAID RESUBMISSION CODE ORIGINAL REF. NO. 23. PRIOR AUTHORIZATION NUMBER					

24. A						B	C	D	E	F	G	H	I	J	K
From DATE(S) OF SERVICE To						Place of Service	Type of Service	PROCEDURES, SERVICES, OR SUPPLIES (Explain Unusual Circumstances) CPT/HCPCS MODIFIER	DIAGNOSIS CODE	$ CHARGES	DAYS OR UNITS	EPSDT Family Plan	EMG	COB	RESERVED FOR LOCAL USE
MM	DD	YY	MM	DD	YY										
4	25	9X	4	25	9X	11	1	99212	1	25 00					

25. FEDERAL TAX I.D. NUMBER SSN EIN	26. PATIENT'S ACCOUNT NO.	27. ACCEPT ASSIGNMENT? (For govt. claims, see back)	28. TOTAL CHARGE	29. AMOUNT PAID	30. BALANCE DUE
31-0000978 ☒	1379	☐ YES ☒ NO	$	$	$
31. SIGNATURE OF PHYSICIAN OR SUPPLIER INCLUDING DEGREES OR CREDENTIALS (I certify that the statements on the reverse apply to this bill and are made a part thereof.) *Tracy Lewis* 4/29/9X SIGNED DATE	32. NAME AND ADDRESS OF FACILITY WHERE SERVICES WERE RENDERED (If other than home or office)		33. PHYSICIAN'S, SUPPLIER'S BILLING NAME, ADDRESS, ZIP CODE & PHONE # Tracy Lewis, M.D. 4915 Muirwoods Court Green Ash, Am 45299 (593) 000-1230 PIN# GRP#		

(APPROVED BY AMA COUNCIL ON MEDICAL SERVICE 8/88)   *PLEASE PRINT OR TYPE*   FORM HCFA-1500 (U2) (12-90) FORM OWCP-1500   FORM RRB-1500

PHYSICIAN OR SUPPLIER INFORMATION

25. Marvin Friedman

14. DATE OF CURRENT: ILLNESS (First symptom) OR INJURY (Accident) OR PREGNANCY(LMP)		15. IF PATIENT HAS HAD SAME OR SIMILAR ILLNESS. GIVE FIRST DATE		16. DATES PATIENT UNABLE TO WORK IN CURRENT OCCUPATION

17. NAME OF REFERRING PHYSICIAN OR OTHER SOURCE | **17a. I.D. NUMBER OF REFERRING PHYSICIAN** | **18. HOSPITALIZATION DATES RELATED TO CURRENT SERVICES**

19. RESERVED FOR LOCAL USE | **20. OUTSIDE LAB?** YES / NO | $ CHARGES

21. DIAGNOSIS OR NATURE OF ILLNESS OR INJURY. (RELATE ITEMS 1,2,3 OR 4 TO ITEM 24E BY LINE)

1. 562.10
3.

22. MEDICAID RESUBMISSION CODE ORIGINAL REF. NO.

23. PRIOR AUTHORIZATION NUMBER

24. A DATE(S) OF SERVICE	B Place	C Type	D PROCEDURES, SERVICES, OR SUPPLIES CPT/HCPCS MODIFIER	E DIAGNOSIS CODE	F $ CHARGES	G DAYS OR UNITS	H EPSDT	I EMG	J COB	K RESERVED FOR LOCAL USE
1 19 XX 1 9 XX	11	1	45330	1						

25. FEDERAL TAX I.D. NUMBER 31-000098 SSN EIN X

26. PATIENT'S ACCOUNT NO.

27. ACCEPT ASSIGNMENT? YES / NO

28. TOTAL CHARGE $ | **29. AMOUNT PAID** $ | **30. BALANCE DUE** $

31. SIGNATURE OF PHYSICIAN OR SUPPLIER SIGNED 01-29-XX DATE

32. NAME AND ADDRESS OF FACILITY

33. PHYSICIAN'S, SUPPLIER'S BILLING NAME, ADDRESS, ZIP CODE & PHONE #
Tracy Lewis,M.D.
4915 Muirwoods Court
Green Ash, AM 45299 (593)000-1230

(APPROVED BY AMA COUNCIL ON MEDICAL SERVICE 8/88) PLEASE PRINT OR TYPE

FORM HCFA-1500 (U2) (12-90)
FORM OWCP-1500 FORM RRB-1500

26. Tim Levy

14. DATE OF CURRENT: ILLNESS (First symptom) OR INJURY (Accident) OR PREGNANCY(LMP)	15. IF PATIENT HAS HAD SAME OR SIMILAR ILLNESS. GIVE FIRST DATE MM DD YY	16. DATES PATIENT UNABLE TO WORK IN CURRENT OCCUPATION FROM MM DD YY TO MM DD YY
17. NAME OF REFERRING PHYSICIAN OR OTHER SOURCE	17a. I.D. NUMBER OF REFERRING PHYSICIAN	18. HOSPITALIZATION DATES RELATED TO CURRENT SERVICES FROM MM DD YY TO MM DD YY

19. RESERVED FOR LOCAL USE | 20. OUTSIDE LAB? YES NO $ CHARGES

21. DIAGNOSIS OR NATURE OF ILLNESS OR INJURY. (RELATE ITEMS 1,2,3 OR 4 TO ITEM 24E BY LINE)
1. L707.1   3. L428.9
   250.01
2. L___.__   4. L414.8

22. MEDICAID RESUBMISSION CODE   ORIGINAL REF. NO.
23. PRIOR AUTHORIZATION NUMBER

24. A DATE(S) OF SERVICE From To MM DD YY MM DD YY	B Place of Service	C Type of Service	D PROCEDURES, SERVICES, OR SUPPLIES CPT/HCPCS MODIFIER	E DIAGNOSIS CODE	F $ CHARGES	G DAYS OR UNITS	H EPSDT Family Plan	I EMG	J COB	K RESERVED FOR LOCAL USE
07 02 9X 07 02 9X	11	1	99214	1,2						TR40976

25. FEDERAL TAX I.D. NUMBER SSN EIN | 26. PATIENT'S ACCOUNT NO. | 27. ACCEPT ASSIGNMENT? YES NO | 28. TOTAL CHARGE $ | 29. AMOUNT PAID $ | 30. BALANCE DUE $

31. SIGNATURE OF PHYSICIAN OR SUPPLIER... SIGNED DATE | 32. NAME AND ADDRESS OF FACILITY WHERE SERVICES WERE RENDERED | 33. PHYSICIAN'S, SUPPLIER'S BILLING NAME, ADDRESS, ZIP CODE & PHONE #
Tracy Lewis, M.D.
4915 Muirwoods Court
Green Ash,AM(593)-000-1230
PIN# GL09090909 GRP#

(APPROVED BY AMA COUNCIL ON MEDICAL SERVICE 8/88) PLEASE PRINT OR TYPE
FORM HCFA-1500 (U2) (12-90) FORM OWCP-1500 FORM RRB-1500

Chapter 7

1. The chronological recording of pertinent facts and observations by healthcare professionals regarding a patient's health and treatment in a logical sequence

2. Provides a historical prospective on the medical treatment of the patient, substantiates payment, and documents the reasonableness and medical necessity of the services

3. The SOAP format

4. Patient's name on each page; date; reason for the encounter; diagnosis or impression; notations of tests and therapies ordered; and recommendations or instructions to the patient

5. A separate chart

6. To provide a summary of the problems affecting a patient at a particular time which may affect the patient's current treatment

7. To enable the doctor to see the medication history of the patient quickly and review the last renewal and amount of medication, its effectiveness, and its relationship to the health of the patient

8. Sending a letter to the patient as proof of the termination and relating the nature of the unfinished treatments

9. Legible, in permanent ink, and signed by the caregiver

10. Sign an authorization to release medical information

11. Subjective, objective, assessment, plan / An organized format of documentation

12. Minimum sets of services which should be provided for a patient's condition

13. A summary of the problems affecting a patient at a particular time which may affect current care

14. A listing of the immunizations and other tests for preventive healthcare

15. The medical history of the patient, including the chief complaint, the reason for the visit, and the history of the present illness

16. The physical examination of a patient by the healthcare professional

17. The evaluation of a condition and the doctor's impression or diagnosis

18. The recommended treatment, the tests or other workup ordered, new medications and adjustments in medications, therapies, and planned surgical procedures

19. In the chart of Mary Jones:
    7/7: telephone call P.M.
    T 100°, throat not as sore, ears still ringing
    Ann Friend, CMA

20. In the chart of Mary Jones:
    7/8: telephone call
    Appointment canceled for 7/10
    Ann Friend, CMA

Chapter 8

1. Part A (hospital) and Part B (physician services, outpatient services)

2. Initial, special, general

3. Taxes paid by employees and self-employed persons with matching contributions from employers

4. Enrollees / 25% of the expense of the Part B program

5. Begins with the first day of illness on which the Medicare patient receives in-patient services and ends when the patient has been out of a hospital or skilled nursing facility for 60 consecutive days

6. Surgery, consultations, home, office, and institutional services

7. Routine physical checkups / excluded

8. Conditional coverage

9. Mammography; flu, pneumococcal, and hepatitis B vaccines; therapeutic shoes for diabetics

10. Railroad retirees

11. One-time authorization

12. Participating / nonparticipating

13. Participating providers

14. Nonparticipating providers

15. Limiting charge

16. 16 percent of the intraoperative surgical procedures

17. RVU for procedure codes, GPCIs, conversion factors

18. 5 years

19. Review, fair hearing, administrative law judge, and appeals council

20. Fraud / abuse

21. Employer group health plans are offered by employers for employees.

22. Care of the terminally ill patient and substitute care for caregivers of home care patients

23. Health insurance claim number identifying a beneficiary as an enrollee in the Medicare program

24. Notification to a beneficiary when assignment is not taken and the charge for the nonemergency surgery is over $500

25. Site of service results in a reduction of payment dependent upon the site or place service is provided

26. XYZ plan

27. $14.40 / $100 deductible + $28.60, or total of $ 128.60 / $82

28. No / Claims must be filed within 1 year of date of service

29. a. True, b. false, c. false, d. false, e. false, f. false, g. false, h. false, i. false, j. false, k. true

30. Yes / insurance allowed $600, paid $400. Medicare pays $200 as the MAF of the primary insurer is $600.00.

Chapter 9

Medicaid

1. Families with dependent children, the blind, the aged, the disabled, and the medically indigent whose resources are not sufficient to meet the costs of medical care

2. HCFA and the states

3. Operational / determining eligibility

4. Inpatient hospital, outpatient hospital, physicians' services, laboratory, x-ray, skilled nursing, and home health care for those over 21 years of age; EPSDT, rural health, and family planning

5. Nurse midwife services / immunizations

6. At the time of service

7. Monthly, every 2 months, or every 6 months at the discretion of the states

8. Early and periodic screening, diagnosis, and treatment.

9. To cover screening and diagnostic services or to treat physical or mental defects in recipients under age 21

10. Noncovered services and amounts up to their spend-down, if applicable

11. Aid to Dependent Children / families and children whose income is insufficient to cover medical costs.

12. Supplemental Security Income / financial assistance for a Medicaid recipient

13. Aid to Families with Dependent Children / families and children whose income is insufficient to cover medical expenses

14. Medically indigent, referring to individuals who are in need of financial assistance and/or whose income and resources do not allow them to pay for the costs of medical treatment

15. Bill Medicaid because the spend-down amount was with the services of Dr. Jones and Dr. Todd

16. If the staff checks with the welfare department and the department confirms that the patient is eligible for Medicaid, the practice can then bill Medicaid. This is not a good situation; make patients aware they must bring the card before receiving service.

17. GHO is primary, and Medicaid is secondary.

18. By looking at the eligibility date on the Medicaid card

19. No

20. CHAMPUS is primary, and Medicaid is secondary.

CHAMPUS

1. Families of active-duty personnel, retired service personnel and their dependents, and dependents of service personnel who die on active duty

2. October 1

3. $150 per person or $300 per family per fiscal year

4. 25% of allowed charges

5. Small daily fee or $25 per admission whichever is more

6. Checking YES in BOX 27 of HCFA 1500

7. A statement from the uniformed service hospital that states that it cannot provide the care needed by a patient who lives within the ZIP Code area of the hospital.

8. Certain inpatient and outpatient services

9. Reconsideration, formal review, and independent hearing

10. 90 days

11. 60 days, CHAMPUS headquarters

12. 60 days, a location convenient to both parties

13. DD2642

14. HCFA 1500

15. DEERS is the Defense Enrollment Eligibility Reporting System. It is a comput-

erized data bank which lists all active and retired military members and should list their dependents.

16. HBA is the health benefits advisor, an individual at military hospitals or clinics to assist beneficiaries with questions about the CHAMPUS program.

17. A nonavailability statement is a certification from the uniformed service hospital that indicates it cannot provide the care a patient needs.

18. Champus maximum allowable charge is the highest amount CHAMPUS allows for covered care. This is the fee that cost sharing is calculated on.

19. Uniformed service medical treatment facilities are hospitals and clinics throughout the world where CHAMPUS beneficiaries can receive treatment without cost sharing.

20. The fiscal intermediary or contractor that processes the claims for CHAMPUS and CHAMPVA received within a particular area of the United States.

21. TriCare is a managed care benefit option offered to CHAMPUS service families.

22. CHAMPUS pays $48.00. Mrs. Weber pays $12.

23. CHAMPUS pays $19.50. $176.00 − 150.00 (deductible) = $26.00 × 75% = $19.50 Deductible of $150.00 + $26.00 − $19.50 = $156.50. Yes, $226.00 − 176.00 = $50.00

Workers' Compensation

1. To provide for job-related injuries to Federal Employees

2. Medical treatment, loss of wages, permanent disability, medical or vocational rehabilitation, compensation to families for an employee who is fatally ill, and death benefits

3. Permanent / temporary

4. Report to the employer the nature of the work-related injury

5. Send a report of occupational illness or injury to BWC or the Industrial Commission

6. Employer self-funded plan, state fund, and independent plan.

7. Employers

8. The adjudicatory branch of the workers' compensation system, determining levels of disability, resolving disputes, and establishing workers' compensation policy

9. Physician on record

10. Claim or identification number

11. The recovery period after a job-related injury after which an employee is able to resume normal job activities

12. An illness or injury that prohibits a person from performing his or her regular job

13. A legal promise to satisfy a debt out of moneys received

14. A report sent to the BWC or Industrial Commission, telling them of the nature of the illness or injury and details about when, where, and how it happened

15. The initial physician an employee sees for treatment of a work-related injury

16. A statement indicating that care has been completed and patient is able to return to work

17. An illness or disease arising out of or in the course of employment

18. To protect employees against medical expense losses due to industrial accidents

19. Schedule the appointment. Be certain the patient brings the identification or claim number with him and that this practice is the physician on record. After the service has been rendered, file the claim to the workers' compensation plan of the Brown Furniture Company.

20. No. In the state where the injury occurred, temporary disability does not begin until the employee has missed 7 days of work

21. The practice must appeal to the workers' compensation plan of the Brown Furniture Company, including information that will document the need for additional reimbursement.

Chapter 10

1. Blue Cross/Blue Shield
2. 1929 / Baylor University in Dallas, Texas
3. a. Nonprofit organizations b. Individual enters into a contract with the plan c. Healthcare providers sign contracts with the plans d. Blue Cross/Blue Shield plans cannot change their rate structure or their benefits without state government approval e. These plans offer transferability to a plan in another state
4. To evaluate established procedures of questionable usefulness / To evaluate new procedures of unproven value
5. That the patient is enrolled in a reciprocity plan
6. A reciprocity program in which claims are filed locally
7. High option and low option
8. Similar to a policy outlining the benefits
9. Coordination of benefits when dependent children are covered by the policy of the parent whose birthdate occurs earliest in the year
10. Federal Employees Program, a governmentwide plan for providing medical insurance for federal employees
11. A range of benefits selected by federal employees
12. Assumption of claims risks by an employer, a union, or another group
13. A method of establishing premiums by which an insurer's premium is the same for all individuals within a group in a specific geographic area
14. Premiums are set by insurers on the basis of the insured's past medical claim loss experience
15. Mary Jones' plan
16. Indiana / A second opinion is not covered by the reciprocity plan

Chapter 11

1. Panels of providers, out-of-pocket costs or financial incentives for patients to use the panel, and medical resource monitoring
2. Provider contracting, utilization controls, enrollment services, and claims processing
3. Members
4. Staff model, group model, independent practice association, and network model
5. Physician hospital organizations
6. Possible increase in volume of patients, prompt payment, and maintenance of current patients

7. Point of service
8. Exclusive provider organization
9. Independent practice association
10. Management services organization
11. Group practice without walls
12. Physician hospital organization
13. Yes, 1.1
14. Yes, 2.4
15. Yes, 2.7
16. No, 2.10
17. No, 3.1 and 9.1
18. Yes, 4.2
19. Yes, 4.4
20. Yes, 5.4
21. Yes, 6.4
22. Yes, 6.3
23. Yes, 6.6
24. Yes, Exhibit A
25. Yes, 6.6
26. No, 6.10
27. Yes, 7.3
28. No, 7.4
29. No, 10.3
30. Yes, 12.1
31. Yes, 12.3
32. No, 13.4

33.

Contract Breakers	**Give Points**
1. Which hospitals participate?	1. Patient financial incentive not specific. What is the patient's penalty for using nonparticipating physicians?
2. Names of any participating labs, x-ray, or diagnostic facilities	2. Need patient copayment amounts and deductibles for all benefit options.
	3. Will you change malpractice coverage amounts before notifying me?
	4. Please send more information regarding the definition of a clean claim, claim-filing address, and copies of ID cards for all benefit packages.
	5. This contract contains no clauses regarding termination without cause. What is the procedure to follow if the contract is breached by either party?
	6. Must I accept all patients referred to me?

7. Who carries out the review process and makes decisions?

8. Is this a gatekeeper plan? If so, what are the referral procedures?

9. If information changes on my credential application, do we notify XYZ in 7 calendar days or 7 working days?

10. How often do I get a list of providers if there are changes?

11. Is there a phone number to verify the eligibility of members? What are the hours of operation?

12. Can I have a list of XYZ's bundling rules?

13. Who informs patients if I am terminated from XYZ?

Chapter 12

1. Payment and claim reporting; compliance with rules and laws; patient satisfaction; documentation and study of clinical care; use of supplies, computers, and other resources; productivity of personnel
2. 30
3. Highest
4. New
5. Special explanations
6. Practice parameters / practice guidelines
7. Structure, process, and outcome
8. Legislation outlining the time limit private third-party payers have for paying claims
9. Denial of charges above the MAF
10. Monitoring of the effects of patient treatment at specific points in time
11. Also known as the adjusted collection ratio; the total payments divided by the total charges after the writeoffs have been deducted
12. Total payments divided by total charges without writeoffs
13. Application of continual improvement in the day-to-day operations and management of an organization; usually a team effort
14. Yes
15. Code 99396 is allowed once every 3 years (she must have had a preventive medicine visit in the last 3 years)
16. At least $38.00
17. 86999
18. 36415, 85025, 80019, 99205, 81000 / $76.80
19. $21.16 ($15.36 plus $5.80)
20. $29 / $25 / $8.80

Index

A

Adjudication:
  claims processing, 41
  diagnosis coding (ICD-9-CM) and, 65
Administrative law judge, Medicare claim
  rules, 253
Administrative services only (ASO):
  defined, 326
  managed care plans, 342
Aged, Medicaid eligibility, 275
Aid to Families with Dependent Children
  (ADC), Medicaid eligibility, 275
Allowed condition, workers'
  compensation, 292
Alternative delivery system (ADS),
  defined, 326
American Medical Association (AMA),
  102–103, 139, 196, 202, 210, 382, 384
American National Standards Institute
  (ANSI), 182
Ancillary professional services payment,
  Medicare, 239
Anesthesia assistant, Medicare payment,
  239
Annual limits, claims processing, 42
Appeals:
  CHAMPUS, 288–289
  Medicare, 251–253, 270
  quality improvement, 372–376, 396, 397
Appeals council, Medicare claim rule, 253
Assessment, SOAP format documentation,
  207–208
Audits:
  clinical quality, 383–384, 386
  documentation methods, 212
  site review checklist, 222–223
Authorization number, preauthorization,
  44
Automobile injury, Medicare claim rules,
  251

B

Benefit codes, described, 40
Benign essential hypertension, 399–400
Billing. *See* Posting and billing
Blind, Medicaid eligibility, 275
Blue Cross and Blue Shield. *See also*
  Private plans
  Association, 312–313

benefit options, 312–313
benefits coordination, 316
certificate, 313–316
  central certification, 315
  Federal Employees Program, 315–316
  reciprocity plan, 313–315
claims reporting, 318
distinctions of, 311–312
history of, 310–311
payment methods, 316–318
preventive care guidelines, 313
role changes in, 318–319
Brace }, diagnosis coding (ICD-9-CM)
  conventions, 78
Burns, diagnosis coding (ICD-9-CM),
  90–91

C

Cancer, diagnosis coding (ICD-9-CM),
  85–87
Capitation:
  described, 6, 51
  health maintenance organization
    (HMO), 324
  managed care plan contract evaluation,
    341–342
  monitoring of, 368, 370, 379–382, 393,
    398
Cardiovascular services, CPT, 130–131, 155
Carrier fair hearing, Medicare claim rules,
  appeals, 252–253
Case management, described, 51, 53
Central certification, Blue Cross and Blue
  Shield certificate, 315
Certified registered nurse anesthetist,
  Medicare payment, 239
CHAMPUS (Civilian Health and Medical
  Program of the Uniformed Services),
  280–289. *See also* Universal claim
  form (HCFA 1500)
  appeals, 288–289
  benefits, 282, 283
  catastrophic out-of-pocket limit, 285
  claims reporting, 286–288
  cost sharing (deductibles and
    coinsurance), 282
  DEERS, 281–282
  overview, 2, 280
  differences in, 282–284

eligibility, 280
identification card, 281
payment, 286
secondary coverage, 285
signature authorization letter, 300–301
TriCare program, 285–286
CHAMPVA (Civilian Health and Medical
  Program for Veterans
  Administration), 289–290
  benefits, 290
  eligibility, 289
  overview, 289
  payment and claims reporting, 290
Childbirth, diagnosis coding (ICD-9-CM),
  87–88
Circulatory system disorders, diagnosis
  coding (ICD-9-CM), 83–84
Civilian Health and Medical Program for
  Veterans Administration (CHAMPVA).
  See CHAMPVA
Civilian Health and Medical Program of
  the Uniformed Services (CHAMPUS).
  See CHAMPUS
Claim denial. *See* Denial of claim
Claims process. *See* Insurance claims
  process
Clean claim, claims processing, 41
Clinical quality, definition and
  measurement of, 382–384. *See also*
  Quality improvement
Closed fracture, diagnosis coding
  (ICD-9-CM), 89
Codes, encounter form, 20–23, 24. *See also*
  entries under specific coding systems
Coinsurance:
  CHAMPUS, 282
  claims processing, 42
Collection rates, 376–382
  capitation rate monitoring, 379–382
  generally, 376
  gross collection ratio, 376–377
  net collection ratio, 377
  posting withholds and extra fees,
    377–378
Colon :, diagnosis coding (ICD-9-CM)
  conventions, 77
Combination code, diagnosis coding
  (ICD-9-CM), 65–67
Community rating, self-insured plans, 320

Complications:
diagnosis coding (ICD-9-CM), 91–92
SOAP format documentation, 208
Computerized systems, 177–182
checks, examples of, 46–47
electronic claims, 178–182
optical character recognition (OCR), 177
smart card, documentation methods, 212
Confidentiality:
facsimile (fax) records, 210–211
medical release form, 210, 219
Confirmatory consultation, CPT subcategory, 124
Consent form:
documentation methods, 212
sample of, 221
Consultation, CPT subcategory, 123–124
Contracts, physician requirements, Medicaid, 274. *See also* Managed care plans
Contributory factors, CPT component, 118–119
Conventions, diagnosis coding (ICD-9-CM), 76–81
Conversion factor, Medicare fee schedule, 242–244
Coordination of benefits (COB):
Blue Cross and Blue Shield, 316
claims processing, 42–43
managed care plans, 343
Copayments, claims processing, 42
Cost sharing:
CHAMPUS, 282
claims processing, 41–42
Counseling, documentation methods, 209
CPT (*Current Procedural Terminology*, AMA), 10, 12, 101–138
coding principles, 115
computerized checks, 46–47
documentation with modifiers, 152
encounter form codes, 20–23
evaluation and management, 116–128
components of, 116–120
excluded services, 126–128
generally, 116
subcategories overviewed, 121–126
HCPCS and, 142
ICD-9-CM codes and, 81
integumentary system, 137–138, 153
managed care plans, 334–336
maximum allowable fee, 47, 48
Medicare, fee schedule, relative value unit procedure codes, 241
medicine, 128–131
cardiovascular services, 130–131, 155
generally, 128–129
immunizations, 129
injections, therapeutic and diagnostic, 129–130
special services and reports, 131
musculoskeletal system, 138, 154
overview of, 102–103

pathology and laboratory, 132–134
radiology, 131–132
structure of, 103–114
format, 104–105
guidelines in, 106
index, 104
modifiers, 108–114
notes in, 105–106
revised codes, 106–107
subcategories and ranges, 104
unlisted procedures, 107–108
wording in, 105
surgery, 134–137
uses of, 103
Critical care, CPT subcategory, 125
Critical pathway. *See* Insurance claims process
Cross-indemnification hold harmless clause, managed care plan contract evaluation, 337
Current Procedural Terminology (CPT, AMA). *See* CPT (*Current Procedural Terminology*, AMA)
Custodial care, defined, 45
Cutoff date, claims processing, 41

D

Deductibles:
CHAMPUS, 282
claims processing, 42
DEERS (Defense Enrollment Eligibility Reporting System), CHAMPUS and, 281–282
Deficit Reduction Act, 236
Denial of claim:
Medicare, not reasonable and necessary denial, 230–231, 260
prevention of, diagnosis coding (ICD-9-CM), 64–65
quality improvement, claim resubmission, 372–373
self-insured plans, 320–321
Dependent, defined, 40
Diagnosis coding. *See* ICD-9-CM (*International Classification of Diseases—Clinical Modification*, DHHS)
Diagnosis related group (DRG), defined, 62
Diagnostic injections, CPT, 129–130
Diagnostic statement, diagnosis coding (ICD-9-CM), 69
Diagnostic tests. *See* Laboratory/diagnostic tests; Radiology
Disability, workers' compensation, 293
Disabled, Medicaid eligibility, 275
Disallowance, quality improvement, appeals, 373, 396, 397
Discharge planning, case management, 53
Documentation, 195–223
importance of, 195–196
inadequate, fines for, 196–197
preventive care, 216

principles of, 197–201
quality of care and utilization of resources, 196
Documentation methods, 201–212
audits, 212
consent form, 212, 221
counseling, 209
face-to-face physician/caregiver encounter, 201–202
facsimile (fax) records, 210–211
medical release form, 210, 219
smart card, 212
SOAP format, 202–209
telephone calls, 209
template use, 209–210
termination of physician-patient relationship, 211
time period of retention of records, 211
Durable medical equipment, prosthetics, orthotics, and supplies (DMEPOS):
carriers of, 269
regionalization, 251

E

Effective date, defined, 40
Electronic claims, described, 178–182. *See also* Computerized systems
Emergency room, CPT subcategory, 124–125
Employee Retirement Income Security Act of 1974 (ERISA), 3
payment monitoring, quality improvement, 371
self-insured plans, 319
Encounter form, 20–23
CPT/ICD-9-CM code matching, 24
example of, 37
Enrollee, defined, 40
Enrollment. *See also* Identification card
components, 39–41
Medicare, 225–227
Episode of care method, described, 6
Eponyms, diagnosis coding (ICD-9-CM) conventions, 80–81
ERISA. *See* Employee Retirement Income Security Act of 1974 (ERISA)
Essential hypertension, 399–400
Ethics, medical release form, 210
Evergreen clause, managed care plan contract evaluation, 338
Examination, CPT component, 117
Exclusion:
CPT, 126–128
defined, 40–41
diagnosis coding (ICD-9-CM) conventions, 76
Exclusive provider organization (EPO), described, 328
Exclusivity clause, managed care plan contract evaluation, 337–338
Exit, insurance claims process, 23, 25
Experience rating, self-insured plans, 320

Explanation of benefits (EOB):
claims processing, 25, 27–28, 41, 43
quality improvement:
appeals, 372–373, 375
claim errors, 372
payment monitoring, 370
External cause codes, diagnosis coding
(ICD-9-CM), 92–94

F

Face-to-face physician/caregiver
encounter, documentation methods,
201–202
Fair hearing. *See* Hearings
Family coverage, defined, 40
Fault determination, workers'
compensation, 293–294
Favored nation clause, managed care plan
contract evaluation, 337–338
Federal Employees Program, Blue Cross
and Blue Shield certificate,
315–316
Federal law, private plans, 3
Fee for service:
described, 6
payment monitoring, quality
improvement, 370–372, 392
Fees, posting of, collection rates, 377–378
Formal appeal. *See* Appeals
Fracture, diagnosis coding (ICD-9-CM),
89
Fraud and abuse, Medicare, 254–255
Freedom of Information Act of 1966, 2,
271

G

Gap filler, Medicare, 234
Gastrointestinal system, 156
Geographic practice cost indices, Medicare
fee schedule, 242
Government plans, described, 2-3. *See also
entries under names of specific plans*
Gross collection ratio, quality
improvement, 376–377
Group practice without walls (GPWW),
described, 330

H

HCPCS (*Health Care Financing
Administration Common Procedural
Coding System*), 10, 12, 115, 134,
138–144, 196, 202. *See also* Health
Care Financing Administration
(HCFA)
CHAMPUS, 287
CHAMPVA, 290
claims processing, 41
coding levels in, 139
encounter form codes, 20–23
examples, 142
Medicaid, 138–139, 274, 279–280
Medicare, 227–228
modifiers, 143–144

overview, 138–139
posting and billing, 25, 26
steps for using:
for government plans, 139
level II categories, 140–141
for nongovernment plans, 140
temporary codes, 142
Health Care Financing Administration
(HCFA), 2. *See also* HCPCS (*Health
Care Financing Administration
Common Procedural Coding System*)
Medicaid, 274
Medicare, 227–228
regional offices of, listed, 259
Health insurance claim number (HICN),
Medicare identification card, 233
Health maintenance organization (HMO).
See also Managed care plans
Blue Cross and Blue Shield, 318–319
described, 4, 5, 326
managed care plans and, 324
types of, 327–331
Health Professional Shortage Areas,
Medicare, 240
Hearings:
CHAMPUS, 289
Medicare claim rules, appeals,
252–253
History:
CPT component, 117
SOAP format documentation,
203–206
Hospital charges, insurance claims
process, 28–29
Hospital inpatient, CPT subcategory,
123
Hospital observation, CPT subcategory,
123
Hypertension, 83–84, 399–400

I

ICD-9-CM (*International Classification of
Diseases—Clinical Modification*,
DHHS), 10, 12, 61–99
circulatory system disorders, 83–84
combination codes, 67
complications, 91–92
conventions in, 76–81
denial of claim, prevention of, 64–65
encounter form codes, 20–23
external cause codes, 92–94
history of, 61–62
ICD-10 and, 94
injury, 89–91
Medicare and, 65
neoplasms, 85–87
newborns, 89
organization of diseases:
alphabetic index, 68–76
tabular list, 67–68, 69, 72
overview, 62
pregnancy, childbirth, and puerperium,
87–88

sequencing, 65–67
use of, 62–64
V codes, 81–83
Identification card. *See also* Enrollment
Blue Cross and Blue Shield certificate,
313–314
CHAMPUS, 281
CHAMPVA, 289, 290
described, 40
insurance claims process, 16, 18–20
Medicaid, 275–277
Medicare, 232–233
Immunizations, CPT, 129
Inadequate documentation, fines for,
196–197. *See also* Documentation
Inclusions, diagnosis coding (ICD-9-CM)
conventions, 76
Index:
CPT, 104
diagnosis coding (ICD-9-CM),
68–76
Inflation, Medicare fee schedule, 248
Injections, therapeutic and diagnostic,
CPT, 129–130
Injury, diagnosis coding (ICD-9-CM),
89–91
Inpatient nonavailability statement
(INAS), CHAMPUS, 283–284, 288
Insurance claims process, 13–37. *See also*
Third-party payers
Blue Cross and Blue Shield, 318
CHAMPUS, 286–288
CHAMPVA, 290
critical pathway, 13–14, 15
described, 41–43
encounter form, 20–23, 24
exit, 23, 25
hospital charges, 28–29
Medicaid, 279–280
medical practice and, 6–10
monitoring, 25, 27–28
posting and billing, 25
quality improvement, claim
resubmission, 372
registration, 14–20
self-insured plans, 320
workers' compensation, 294–295
Insurance industry. *See* Third-party payers
Insured, defined, 40
Integrated service network (ISN),
described, 330
Integumentary system, CPT, 137–138,
153
Internal injury, diagnosis coding
(ICD-9-CM), 90
*International Classification of Diseases—
Clinical Modification* (ICD-9-CM,
DHHS). *See* ICD-9-CM
(*International Classification of
Diseases—Clinical Modification*,
DHHS)
Italic type, diagnosis coding (ICD-9-CM)
conventions, 80

L

Laboratory/diagnostic tests. *See also*
        Radiology
    CPT, 132–134
    managed care plans, 343–344
    Medicare, 238–239
    plan identification card, 18
    summary sheet, sample of, 217
Late effects, diagnosis coding
        (ICD-9-CM), 91
Level of service. *See* Service level
Lozenge, diagnosis coding (ICD-9-CM)
        conventions, 78

M

Malpractice insurance, managed care plan
        contract evaluation, 338
Managed care, defined, 325
Managed care plans, 323–364. *See also*
        Health maintenance organization
        (HMO)
    Blue Cross and Blue Shield, 318–319
    capitation, 6. *See also* Capitation
    contract advantages and disadvantages,
        331–336
    contract evaluation, 336–346
        administrative issues, 340–341
        contract breakers, 337–338
        give points, 338–339
        medical resource monitoring, 343–346
        payment issues, 341–343
        trustees, 345–346
    contract log form, 357
    cost control methods, 324–325
    diagnosis related group (DRG), 62
    evolution of, 323–324
    health maintenance organization
        (HMO) types, 327–331
    organization research form, 358
    overview of, 4–5, 323
    patient profile analysis, 360
    practice capacity determination, 359
    rules for:
        listed, 364
        summary chart, 361–363
    terminology of, 325–326
Managed indemnity plan, described, 329
Management service organization (MSO),
        described, 330
Master medication sheet, sample of, 215
Master problem sheet, sample of, 214
Maximum allowable fee (MAF):
    described, 47–50
    health maintenance organization
        (HMO), 329
    managed care plan contracts, 334, 342
    quality improvement:
        appeals, 373–374
        payment monitoring, 371–372
Medicaid, 273–280
    administration of, 274–275
    claim reporting, 279–280
    diagnosis related group (DRG), 62

eligibility, 275–277
HCPCS, 138–139, 279–280
overview of, 2, 273–274
payment, 279
physician contract requirements, 274
restricted benefits, 277, 278
spend-down, 277–279
Medical decision making, CPT
        component, 117–118
Medical director, 51, 53
Medical history. *See* History
Medically necessary:
    Blue Shield and, 312–313
    criteria for, 44–45
Medical practice, third-party payers and,
        6–10
Medical record. *See* Documentation
Medical release form:
    documentation methods, 210
    Medicare, one-time authorization,
        235
    sample of, 219
Medical resource monitoring, 43–54
    capitation, 51
    computerized checks, 46–47
    physician cost monitoring, 47–50
    physician-plan contracts, 45–46
    preauthorization, 44–45
    utilization management, 51–54
Medicare, 225–271
    claim rules, 249–253
        administrative law judge, 253
        appeals, 251–253
        appeals council, 253
        automobile liability and work-related
            injury, 251
        generally, 249
        regionalization, 251
    as secondary payer, 249–251,
        264–268
    described, 2
    diagnosis coding (ICD-9-CM) and, 65
    diagnosis related group (DRG), 62
    enrollment, 225–227
    fee schedule (Resource Based Relative
        Value Scale, RBRVS), 240–249
        conversion factor, 242–244
        formula computation, 244–246
        geographic practice cost indices,
            242
        phase-in-period, 246–247
        relative value unit procedure codes,
            241
        volume performance standard,
            247–249
    fraud and abuse, 254–255
    HCPCS and, 138–139
    ID card, 232–233
    management and responsibility of,
        227–232
        benefits, 228–230
        conditional coverage, 231–232
        exclusions, 228

not reasonable and necessary denial,
            230–231, 260
        prepayment screens, 232
        preventive medicine benefits, 232
    medical release form, one-time
        authorization, 235
    Medigap coverage, 234
    out-of-pocket costs, 233–234
    rule changes in, 236–240
        ancillary professional services
            payment, 239
        assistants at surgery, 240
        Health Professional Shortage Areas,
            240
        laboratory/diagnostic tests, 238–239
        Medicare Participation Program, 236
        nonparticipating physicians, 236–238
        Site of Service differential, 240
        surgical financial disclosure, 238, 263
    trust funds for, 227
    universal claim form (HCFA 1500), 160
Medicare Catastrophic Coverage Act of
        1988, 65
Medicare Participation Program,
        described, 236
Medicare Transaction System (MTS),
        182
Medicine (CPT, AMA), 128–131
    cardiovascular services, 130–131, 155
    immunizations, 129
    injections, therapeutic and diagnostic,
        129–130
Medigap coverage, Medicare, 234
Monitoring, insurance claims process, 25,
        27–28. *See also* Medical resource
        monitoring
Morbidity/mortality, SOAP format
        documentation, 208
Musculoskeletal system, CPT, 138, 154

N

National Electronic Information
        Corporation (NEIC), 182
NEC (not elsewhere classified), diagnosis
        coding (ICD-9-CM) conventions, 80
Neoplasms, diagnosis coding (ICD-9-CM),
        85–87
Net collection ratio, quality improvement,
        377
Newborns, diagnosis coding (ICD-9-CM),
        89
Nonparticipating physicians, Medicare,
        236–238
NOS (not otherwise specified), diagnosis
        coding (ICD-9-CM) conventions, 80
Not elsewhere classified (NEC), diagnosis
        coding (ICD-9-CM) conventions, 80
Not otherwise specified (NOS), diagnosis
        coding (ICD-9-CM) conventions, 80
Not reasonable and necessary denial,
        Medicare, 230–231, 260
Nursing facility service, CPT subcategory,
        126

O

Obstetrics/gynecology, diagnosis coding (ICD-9-CM), 87–88
Office progress note, sample of, 218
Omnibus Reconciliation Act, 236, 247
One-time authorization, medical release form, Medicare, 235
Open enrollment. *See* Enrollment
Open fracture, diagnosis coding (ICD-9-CM), 89
Open wounds, diagnosis coding (ICD-9-CM), 90
Optical character recognition (OCR), described, 177
Out-of-pocket costs:
  CHAMPUS, 285
  claims processing, 42
  Medicare, 233–234
Outpatient code editor (OCE), diagnosis coding (ICD-9-CM) and, 65

P

Parentheses, diagnosis coding (ICD-9-CM) conventions, 79–80
Pathology. *See* Laboratory/diagnostic tests
Patient history. *See* History
Patient profile analysis, managed care plans, 360
Payment methods, described, 6. *See also* Insurance claims process
Payment monitoring, quality improvement, 366–372, 392
Peer review, defined, 53. *See also* Physician peer review profile
Permanent disability, workers' compensation, 293
Physician assistant, ancillary professional services payment, Medicare, 239
Physician cost monitoring, described, 47–50
Physician hospital organization (PHO), described, 329–330
Physician on record, workers' compensation, 292, 302
Physician payment process. *See* Insurance claims process
Physician peer review profile, described, 51, 52
Physician-plan contracts, described, 45–46
Physicians. *See* Medical practice
Plan, SOAP format documentation, 209
Plan identification card. *See* Identification card
Point of service (POS) product, health maintenance organization (HMO), 328, 329
Poisoning, diagnosis coding (ICD-9-CM), 92–94
Policy, defined, 40
Policyholder, defined, 40
Posting and billing:
  collection rates, 376–382. *See also* Collection rates

insurance claims process, 25
options in, universal claim form, 157–159
payment monitoring, quality improvement, 366–372
Preadmission certification, described, 56
Preauthorization:
  defined, 6–7
  described, 44–45
  sample form, 59
Preauthorization number, 45
Precertification:
  defined, 6–7
  plan identification card, 19
Preexisting condition, defined, 41
Preferred provider organization (PPO):
  Blue Cross and Blue Shield, 318–319
  described, 4–5, 327–328
Pregnancy, diagnosis coding (ICD-9-CM), 87–88
Premiums, enrollment, 39–40
Prepayment screens, Medicare, 232, 261
Preventive care:
  Blue Cross and Blue Shield, 313
  documentation, 216
  Medicare, 232
Primary diagnosis, sequencing, diagnosis coding (ICD-9-CM), 65–67
Primary insurer, claims processing, 42, 43
Private plans, 3–5, 309–322
  Blue Cross and Blue Shield, 309–319. *See also* Blue Cross and Blue Shield
  overview of, 309
  self-insured plans, 3, 319–321
Procedure coding. *See* CPT (*Current Procedural Terminology*, AMA)
Prolonged service, CPT subcategory, 126
Puerperium, diagnosis coding (ICD-9-CM), 87–88

Q

Quality improvement, 365–402
  appeal, formal, 372–376
  claim resubmission, 372
  clinical quality:
    benign essential hypertension example, 399–400
    definition and measurement of, 382–384
    program for, 384–385, 390–391
  collection rates, 376–382
    capitation rate monitoring, 379–382, 393, 398
    gross collection ratio, 376–377
    net collection ratio, 377
    posting withholds and extra fees, 377–378
  future trends, 387
  overview of, 53–54, 365
  patient survey, sample form, 402
  payment monitoring, 366–372, 392
  team approach to, 365–366

R

Radiology. *See also* Laboratory/diagnostic tests
  CPT, 131–132
  Medicare, 239
RBRVS (Resource Based Relative Value Scale). *See also* Medicare: fee schedule
  Blue Cross and Blue Shield, 317–318
  defined, 49–50
Reason codes, monitoring, insurance claims process, 27
Reciprocity plan, Blue Cross and Blue Shield certificate, 313–315
Referral:
  insurance claims process, 14
  managed care plans, 343
Regionalization, Medicare claim rules, 251
Registration, insurance claims process, 14–20
Registration form, insurance claims process, 16, 17
Reinsurance, managed care plan contract evaluation, 342–343
Relative value unit (RVU), defined, 48–49
Release form:
  documentation methods, 210
  sample of, 219
Resource monitoring. *See* Medical resource monitoring
Retention of records, documentation methods, 211
Risk, third-party payers, 1
Rule of nines, burns, diagnosis coding (ICD-9-CM), 90–91

S

Secondary diagnosis, sequencing, diagnosis coding (ICD-9-CM), 65–67
Secondary insurer:
  CHAMPUS, 285
  claims processing, 42
  Medicare claim rules, 249–251, 264–268
Second opinion:
  CPT subcategory, 124
  preauthorization, 44
Section symbol, diagnosis coding (ICD-9-CM) conventions, 78
Self-insured plans, 319–321
  claims reporting, 320
  denial of claims or coverage, 320–321
  described, 3
  employer benefits, 320
  overview of, 319
  payment monitoring, quality improvement, 371
Sequencing, diagnosis coding (ICD-9-CM), 65–67, 87
Service level, CPT component, 119–120
Site of Service differential, Medicare, 240
Site review, checklist for, 222–223
Smart card, documentation methods, 212

SOAP (subjective, objective, assessment, plan) format, documentation methods, 202–209
Special services and reports, CPT, 131
Square bracket [], diagnosis coding (ICD-9-CM) conventions, 77
Standards of care, documentation, 195–196
State law:
    private plans and, 3
    regulatory agencies, listing of, 394
Statute of limitations, documentation methods, 211
Subjective, objective, assessment, plan (SOAP) format, documentation methods, 202–209
Subrogation, claims processing, 43
Superficial injury, diagnosis coding (ICD-9-CM), 90
Supplementary Security Income (SSI), Medicaid, 275
Surgery:
    CPT, 134–137
    Medicare:
        assistants at, 240
        surgical financial disclosure, 238, 263
Symbols, diagnosis coding (ICD-9-CM) conventions, 77–78

T

Telephone calls, documentation methods, 209
Templates, documentation methods, 209–210
Temporary disability, workers' compensation, 293
Termination (of physician-patient relationship):
    documentation methods, 211
    sample letter, 220
Therapeutic injections, CPT, 129–130
Third-party administrator (TPA):
    defined, 326
    managed care plans, 342

Third-party payers. *See also* Insurance claims process
    claims processing, 41–43
    defined, 1–2
    enrollment, 39–41
    government plans, 2–3
    managed care plans, 4–5
    medical practice and, 6–10
    medical resource monitoring, 43–54.
        See also Medical resource monitoring
    payment methods, 6
    private plans, 3–5
Time, CPT component, 119
Time period, for retention of records, 211
Traditional indemnity benefits, private plans, 3
TriCare program, CHAMPUS, 285–286
Triple option plan (TOP), health maintenance organization (HMO), 328–329
Trustees, managed care plan contract evaluation, 345–346
Trust funds, Medicare, 227
Truth-in-lending form:
    example of, 36
    insurance claims process, 25

U

Underlying condition, diagnosis coding (ICD-9-CM) conventions, 79
Uniformed Services Medical Treatment Facility (USMTF), CHAMPUS, 283
Universal claim form (HCFA 1500), 157–193
    billing options, 157–159
    computerized systems, 177–182
    overview, 159–160
    patient and insured information requirements, 160–168
    physician or supplier information requirements, 168–176
Usual, customary, and reasonable:
    Blue Cross and Blue Shield, 316–317
    defined, 48

Utilization hassle factor, managed care plan contract evaluation, 344–345
Utilization management, described, 51–54

V

V codes:
    CHAMPUS and, 287–288
    diagnosis coding (ICD-9-CM), 81–83
Vertically integrated plan (VIP), described, 330
Veterans, CHAMPVA, 289–290
Volume performance standard, Medicare fee schedule, 247–249

W

Welcome packet:
    example of, 32–33
    registration, insurance claims process, 14, 16
Withholds, posting of, collection rates, 377–378
Workers' compensation, 290–295
    benefits, 291
    claims and reimbursement, 294–295
    compensation for employees, 291–292
    employer information not received letter, 305
    fault determination, 293–294
    fee increase appeals letter, 306
    forms, 292–293
    overview of, 3, 290
    payment for coverage, 291
    physician on record, 292, 302
    status of employer's report letter, 304
    terminology in, 307–308
    unpaid claims letter, 303
Workgroup for Electronic Data Interchange (WEDI), 181
Work-related injury, Medicare claim rules, 251
World Health Organization (WHO), 61
Wounds:
    CPT, 137–138
    diagnosis coding (ICD-9-CM), 90